SCHEMES OF ARRANGEMENT

SECOND EDITION

Schemes of arrangement are an important and flexible mechanism that can be used to reorganise a company's capital. Schemes have undergone a renaissance over the last twenty years, particularly as a debt restructuring device in the aftermath of the 2008 financial crisis when companies and their advisors needed to develop effective tools for dealing with financial distress. The Covid-19 pandemic has provided a further incentive for jurisdictions to ensure that they have an effective debt restructuring mechanism in place. Schemes have also become the mechanism of choice for recommended takeovers. This book performs a critical, contextual and comparative analysis of schemes and their uses, examines recent developments in this area, including the Corporate Insolvency and Governance Act 2020, and considers whether further reform is needed to ensure that schemes continue to develop as an indispensable tool for companies for the future.

JENNIFER PAYNE is the Linklaters Professor of Corporate Finance Law at the University of Oxford. She writes widely in the fields of company law, corporate finance law, financial regulation and corporate insolvency. She is a contributor to *Palmer's Company Law* and a founder editor of both the *Journal of Corporate Law Studies* and the *Oxford Business Law Blog*. She is currently a member of the Expert Advisory Panel to the Law Commission on its Intermediated Securities project.

SCHEMES OF ARRANGEMENT

Theory, Structure and Operation

SECOND EDITION

JENNIFER PAYNE
University of Oxford

CAMBRIDGE
UNIVERSITY PRESS

CAMBRIDGE
UNIVERSITY PRESS

University Printing House, Cambridge CB2 8BS, United Kingdom

One Liberty Plaza, 20th Floor, New York, NY 10006, USA

477 Williamstown Road, Port Melbourne, VIC 3207, Australia

314–321, 3rd Floor, Plot 3, Splendor Forum, Jasola District Centre, New Delhi – 110025, India

103 Penang Road, #05–06/07, Visioncrest Commercial, Singapore 238467

Cambridge University Press is part of the University of Cambridge.

It furthers the University's mission by disseminating knowledge in the pursuit of education, learning, and research at the highest international levels of excellence.

www.cambridge.org
Information on this title: www.cambridge.org/9781108835329
DOI: 10.1017/9781108883672

First published 2014
Second edition 2021

A catalogue record for this publication is available from the British Library.

Library of Congress Cataloging-in-Publication Data
Names: Payne, Jennifer, 1970– author.
Title: Schemes of arrangement : theory, structure, and operation / Jennifer Payne, University of Oxford.
Description: Second edition. | Cambridge, United Kingdom ; New York, NY : Cambridge University Press, 2021. | Includes index.
Identifiers: LCCN 2021032841 | ISBN 9781108835329 (hardback) | ISBN 9781108792912 (paperback) | ISBN 9781108883672 (ebook)
Subjects: LCSH: Assignments for benefit of creditors – Great Britain. | Debtor and creditor – Great Britain. | Corporate reorganizations – Great Britain. | Bankruptcy – Great Britain. | BISAC: LAW / Corporate
Classification: LCC KD2139 .P39 2021 | DDC 346.4107/8–dc23
LC record available at https://lccn.loc.gov/2021032841

ISBN 978-1-108-83532-9 Hardback

CONTENTS

FOREWORD TO THE FIRST EDITION

There has long been perceived to be a gap in the market for a monograph of this kind. A number of texts deal with schemes as part of company law or restructuring and insolvency law. However, there did not seem to be one place in which the many years of learning in respect of schemes of arrangement could be found.

The statutory text is so brief, and so much of the law consists of case law, that no real idea of the subject can be gained without either knowing or finding the cases set out and explained in this work.

Professor Jenny Payne has done an excellent job of researching, collating and explaining all conceivable aspects of schemes. The English scheme as it now exists is a witness to the genius of English law in using a brief statutory provision originating in the nineteenth century to handle shareholder and creditor reorganisations, restructurings and takeovers in cases involving large sums and considerable complexity.

The success of English law schemes has been such that they have been exported to other English-law-based jurisdictions throughout the British Commonwealth and, more recently, have influenced the development of Continental legal systems.

Recent developments are particularly noticeable in what the European Commission calls 'pre-insolvency' situations, in which debt needs to be restructured to prevent insolvency and the threat of insolvency proceedings. Our EU partners have statutory compromises and compositions in the context of insolvency proceedings, but in the past have not generally had the equivalent of English schemes for pre-insolvency situations. In particular, they lacked (and in most cases still lack) the tremendous flexibility of the English scheme. Nor do they have the long and detailed experience together with the expertise developed in English practice. This has led to some 'good' forum shopping by companies from other EU Member States seeking to restructure through schemes here and to some recent attempts in Continental jurisdictions to adopt a scheme-like mechanism.

Another relatively recent development has been the ability of the scheme in England or in an English-law-based jurisdiction to act parallel to a US Chapter 11 reorganisation, sometimes assisted by an administration or provisional liquidation in the English-law-based jurisdiction.

The legislation in England has somehow resisted any significant amendment. The utility of pre-insolvency schemes could be improved by enabling the court to protect assets by staying attacks by creditors, as in Singapore. But even without a stay, the scheme continues to work well in most cases.

The very comprehensive statement of the law in this work is a 'must have' for anyone dealing with this field.

Gabriel Moss QC
South Square
Visiting Professor in Corporate Insolvency Law at the University of Oxford

FOREWORD TO THE SECOND EDITION

In the foreword to the first edition of Professor Jennifer Payne's book in 2013, Gabriel Moss QC (now very sadly deceased) described how the English scheme of arrangement had come to play a major role in takeovers and creditor restructurings involving large sums and considerable complexity. He also rightly identified that the scheme had become the 'pre-insolvency' restructuring tool of choice for many companies based in other jurisdictions, especially from the EU, whose domestic laws did not contain a process that would enable their debts to be restructured without entering a formal insolvency proceeding.

The success of the creditor scheme in international restructuring was due to a number of factors: the continuing popularity of English law as the governing law of choice for international debt instruments; the inherent flexibility of the statutory provisions that allowed scheme techniques to be adapted with great speed to changing market conditions; the considerable ingenuity and expertise of English lawyers and insolvency practitioners; and a supportive and commercially experienced judiciary in the Chancery Division.

Launched into this area, the first edition of Professor Payne's book was genuinely ground-breaking. It contained a penetrating analysis of the conceptual framework of the scheme, and a comprehensive guide to practice and procedure. It was, both in its timing and in its content, first in its class.

The second edition has been eagerly awaited and arrives at a particularly important time for the future of the English scheme of arrangement.

At home, the popularity of the scheme for both takeovers and creditor restructurings has steadily increased. Moreover, the Covid-19 pandemic proved to be the catalyst for the introduction in 2020 of an additional new Part 26A 'super-scheme' for companies in financial difficulty, based on the long-established Part 26 creditors' scheme but without any numerosity requirement and with a discretionary power for the court to sanction the scheme against the opposition of a dissenting class.

Abroad, other jurisdictions have been actively promoting their own restructuring offerings as an alternative to the English scheme. Some in the common law world have sought to downplay the importance of the governing law of the debt as a basis for the assumption of jurisdiction to restructure a debtor company; and, in the civil law world, the EU has promulgated its own directive on preventative (pre-insolvency) restructuring. Brexit also leaves unanswered questions as to how UK schemes will be recognised in those EU Member States that have not yet adopted the UNCITRAL Model Law on cross-border insolvency.

A traveller in this new and developing landscape – whether practitioner or judge, and whether from home or abroad – needs a comprehensive and reliable guide. Building on the established reputation of the first edition, Professor Payne's second edition explains and analyses the existing law and practice clearly and concisely, and provides invaluable insight into the principles that will form the basis for future developments. It is an essential resource for anyone operating in this most important area.

The Hon Mr Justice Snowden
High Court of Justice, England & Wales

PREFACE AND ACKNOWLEDGEMENTS

In the seven years since the first edition of this book was published there have been an enormous number of developments in scheme jurisdiction as a result of legislative changes but also owing to the large number of scheme cases that have occurred. This period has also seen huge political and economic changes which could not have been anticipated seven years ago, including Brexit, the Covid-19 pandemic and the economic and regulatory consequences of these phenomena. Both Brexit and the pandemic have played a part in shaping the use and development of schemes, as discussed in this book. Brexit has implications for the use and recognition of foreign schemes of arrangement while Covid-19 and the financial distress it has caused have driven a growth in schemes and prompted the government to introduce wide-ranging reforms to the UK debt restructuring regime via the Corporate Insolvency and Governance Act 2020, which includes a new 'super scheme' in the form of the Part 26A restructuring plan. At the same time, judges have been developing the scheme jurisdiction, responding in part to these large-scale changes but also to the increasingly innovative and boundary-testing uses of schemes by companies and their advisors. In the preface to the first edition of this book, I noted that the development of my interest in schemes had coincided with a renaissance in the use of schemes and that it was a good time to be thinking and writing about this topic. Nothing in the last seven years has changed that. If anything, this period has intensified the importance of schemes, particularly as a debt restructuring tool, not only in the UK but globally, with debt restructuring reforms elsewhere in the world, including the 2019 EU Restructuring Directive, using the UK scheme as inspiration.

The second edition of this book follows the pattern of the first edition, covering both member and creditor schemes. However, in a change to the first edition, the material in Chapter 8 of that edition, which considered schemes in other parts of the world, has been redistributed to the relevant chapters of the second edition and discussed there in order to maximise the value of this comparative material. As a result, there is no longer a stand-alone chapter on this topic, though all of the material is retained, updated and used to reflect on the content and substance of the UK provisions and policy debates and choices more generally. Chapter 9 of the first edition, which set out the necessary reforms to schemes, has therefore become Chapter 8 in this edition. Some of those reforms have been implemented since the first edition, most notably the introduction of a cross-class cramdown via the new Part 26A restructuring plan and the introduction of a restructuring moratorium, but a number of reforms are outstanding and fresh challenges have emerged which must be addressed.

This edition, like the last, owes a great deal to the many people who have assisted me along the way. This includes conversations with colleagues on the topic of schemes in particular and debt restructuring in general at numerous conferences, workshops, meetings, seminars and post-conference dinners. I have benefitted enormously from discussions in the Corporate Finance Law and Corporate Insolvency Law graduate classes that I teach in Oxford, so special thanks go to the students in those classes over the last seven years and to the colleagues with whom I have taught those classes: Louise Gullifer, Roy Goode, Kristin van Zweiten, Chris Hale, Gabriel Moss, Horst Eidenmueller, Richard Salter, Ed Greene, Nick Segal and Felicity Toube. Colleagues in the wider restructuring community, especially at the International Insolvency Institute, have also been invaluable, including Reinhard Bork, Janis Sarra, Stephan Madaus, Ted Janger, Jay Westbrook, Ignacio Tirado, Riz Mokal, Irit Merovach, Sarah Paterson and Jennifer Marshall. Over this period, Louise Gullifer, Kristin van Zweiten and I organised a number of Insolvency Law conferences in Oxford under the auspices of the Commercial Law Centre at Harris Manchester and thanks go to the participants at these events, particularly the conference in January 2015 dedicated to schemes of arrangement, for the vigorous and stimulating conversations on these topics. I would also like to acknowledge the general support and encouragement I received from other colleagues, in particular Niamh Moloney and Eilis Ferran.

Special thanks go to Richard Snowden who has kindly agreed to write the foreword for this edition. I would also like to note the very sad loss of Gabriel Moss (1949–2019) who wrote the foreword for the first edition and was an inspiration to me and to many others. He is much missed.

Many thanks to my excellent research assistant Rabin Kok. I would also like to thank Cambridge University Press, particularly Marianne

Nield, for guiding this book through its various stages of production with such care and skill.

Last, but not least, I'd like to thank my husband, Nick, and my three children, Tom, Emily and Oliver, for their support and encouragement. This book is dedicated to them.

This book aims to state the law as at 1 January 2021. This is a rapidly developing field and there have been exciting changes to schemes and restructuring plans since that date, not least the development of cross-class cramdowns, the issue of the interaction between these mechanisms and the Cape Town Convention, and the question of whether restructuring plans are insolvency proceedings. There is no doubt more to come in this area, which will need to wait until the next edition for discussion.

Jennifer Payne
Oxford

TABLE OF CASES

United Kingdom – England

United Kingdom – Scotland

European Court of Justice

Australia

Bermuda

British Virgin Islands (BVI)

Canada

Cayman Islands

Channel Islands

Germany

Hong Kong

India

Ireland

Malaysia

New Zealand

Singapore

South Africa

United States

TABLE OF LEGISLATION

United Kingdom

Statutes

Statutory Instruments

European Union

Directives

Regulations

International

Australia

Australian Companies Act 1936 12n
Australian Corporations Act 2001
s.411 12n, 19n, 49n, 56n, 229n
s.411(1) 171n
s.411(4)(a) 171n
s.411(4)(a)(ii)(A) 74n
s.411(4)(b) 171n
s.411(10) 171n
s.411(17) 12n, 162-63, 173n
s.413 186n
s.415D 242n, 248n, 295n, 296n, 326n, 385n
s.434J 248n, 295n
s.451E 248n, 295n
Part 5.3A 56n, 229n
New South Wales Act 1899 12n
Treasury Laws Amendment (2017 Enterprise Incentives No. 2) Act 2017 242n, 248n, 295n

Bermuda

Bermuda Companies Act 1981
s.99 13n, 19n, 35n, 162n
s.99(2) 73n

British Virgin Islands (BVI)

Business Companies Act 2004
s.179A 13n, 19n, 73n, 153n, 162n
Part IX 193n

Canada

Canadian Bankruptcy and Insolvency Act 1985 295n
Canadian Business Corporations Act 1985
s.190 53n
s.192 13n, 49n, 73n, 84n
s.192(3) 164n
Canadian Companies' Creditors Arrangement Act 1985 295n

Cayman Islands

Companies Law (as revised) 13n, 19n, 73n, 162n

Germany

German Corporate Stabilization and Restructuring Act (Unternehmensstabilisierungs- und –restrukturierungsgesetz) 307n

Hong Kong

Companies Ordinance, Cap 622 19n, 49n, 73n, 75n, 164n, 166n
  Companies Ordinance, Cap 32 149n

India

Indian Companies Act 2013 13n, 240n
  s.230 73n
  s.230(4) 87n
  s.230(7)(a) 199n
  s.230(9) 40n
  s.230 (11)–(12) 162n
Indian Companies Act 1956 13n, 240n

Ireland

Irish Companies Act 2014, 14n
Irish Companies (Amendment) (No. 2) Act 1999 4n
Irish Companies (Amendment) Act 1990 4n

Malaysia

Malaysian Companies Act 2016
  s.366 13n
  s.366(2) 73n
  s.368(2) 241n
Malaysian Companies Act 1965
  s.176 13n
  s.176(10) 241n

New Zealand

New Zealand Companies Act 1993
  s.236 13n, 49n, 73n, 170n
  s.236(2)(b) 170n
  s.236(2)(c) 170n
  s.236A 73n, 163n
  s.236B 163n

ABBREVIATIONS

AIM	Alternative Investment Market of the London Stock Exchange
ASIC	Australian Securities and Investments Commission
BGH	Bundesgerichtshof (Germany's Federal Supreme Court)
BVI	British Virgin Islands
CAMAC	(Australian) Corporations and Markets Advisory Committee
CBCA	Canada Business Corporations Act 1985
CCAA	(Canadian) Companies' Creditors Arrangement Act 1985
CLR	Company Law Review
COMI	centre of main interest
CVA	company voluntary arrangement
DTI	Department of Trade and Industry
ECJ	European Court of Justice
EEA	European Economic Area
FCA	Financial Conduct Authority
IBNR	incurred but not yet reported obligations
LLP	limited liability partnership
RIS	Regulatory Information Service
SEBI	Securities and Exchange Board of India
UKLA	UK Listing Authority
UNCITRAL	United Nations Commission on International Trade Law

1

Introduction

Schemes of arrangement, or 'schemes', are a valuable and flexible tool for reorganising a company's capital. They have been around for over a century.[1] The current provisions are found in Part 26 of the Companies Act 2006. Section 895(1) defines a scheme of arrangement as 'a compromise or arrangement between a company and its creditors, or any class of them, or its members, or any class of them'. A scheme of arrangement is therefore a statutory mechanism for the implementation of a wide range of corporate transactions. However, the statutory provisions provide relatively few details regarding the operation and utilisation of schemes, and consequently much of the law in this area has been developed by the courts.

This chapter will provide an introduction to schemes, and also to this book, introducing some of the themes and ideas that will be developed in detail in later chapters. In section 1.1 a general overview of schemes is provided, including a consideration of some of the main uses to which schemes are put, and also the main advantages and disadvantages of this mechanism. In section 1.2 the historical development of schemes will be examined, in order to provide some context for the current statutory provisions. In section 1.3 the purpose and scope of this book will be discussed, including a summary of the contents and function of each of the chapters that follow, and an introduction to the main arguments and ideas that will be pursued therein.

1.1 An overview of schemes

The statutory provisions in the Companies Act 2006 do not prescribe the subject matter of a scheme and, in theory, a scheme could be a compromise or arrangement between a company and its creditors or members about anything that they can properly agree amongst

[1] See section 1.2.

themselves. As a result, companies can use schemes for a wide variety of internal reorganisations of debt and/or equity capital, as long as the necessary approvals have been obtained.[2] Schemes of arrangement have not always been valued. As recently as 2000, it was common for them to be regarded as a complex, cumbersome and costly procedure of little practical value to companies, particularly as a debt restructuring tool.[3] However, in recent years schemes have enjoyed something of a renaissance. They have become popular as a mechanism to effect a takeover of a target company by a bidder. They are also used regularly as a mechanism for restructuring financially distressed companies. Indeed, the value of the English scheme of arrangement for rehabilitating financially distressed companies is such that it has become common for companies incorporated outside the UK to seek to make use of this mechanism.[4] Although these are the most common forms of scheme, there are many other corporate restructurings or reorganisations that can be (and are) effected via schemes. This renaissance owes much to the development of the scheme jurisdiction by the English courts, and in particular to the pragmatic and commercially sensible line that the courts have tended to adopt regarding schemes of arrangement.

Schemes have many advantages that help companies to reorganise their debt and/or equity capital effectively. One of these benefits is their flexibility. At the core of the scheme is the idea that it can be used by companies, creditors and members to agree a very wide range of reorganisations or alterations in relation to the company's capital, provided that the agreement is subsequently sanctioned by the court. This enables schemes to be used either as an alternative to or alongside more

[2] See e.g. *Scottish Lion Insurance Co Ltd* v. *Goodrich Corp* [2010] CSIH 6; 2010 SC 349, in which the Lord President confirmed that there was nothing in the legislation to suggest that a solvent scheme of arrangement should be treated differently from an insolvent one; cf. the view of Lord Glennie at first instance in *Scottish Lion Insurance Co Ltd* v. *Goodrich Corp* [2009] CSOH 127; 2010 SLT 100. One question that has arisen recently is whether the Aircraft Protocol to the Cape Town Convention, 16 November 2001, imposes any restrictions on the court's power to sanction a scheme of arrangement; for discussion see *Re MAB Leasing Ltd* [2021] EWHC 379 (Ch).

[3] See *Report of the Joint DTI/Treasury Review of Company Rescue and Business Reconstruction Mechanisms* (2000) at para. 43. For a slightly earlier but similar opinion see Report of the Insolvency Law Review Committee (Cork Committee), *Insolvency Law and Practice* (Cmnd 8558, 1982) ch. 7. Similar comments were made about creditor schemes in Australia, leading to the introduction of deed of company arrangements in 1993: Australian Law Reform Commission, 'General Insolvency Inquiry', Report No. 45, 1988 Vol 1 at 25–6 and 31.

[4] See Chapter 7.

traditional mechanisms for reorganising a company's capital. As we shall see, schemes can provide some advantages over the more traditional methods. For example, Chapter 3 explores why schemes are often the mechanism of choice for recommended takeovers, rather than the more traditional takeover offer. Schemes can also be used to effect reorganisations of the company, or its debt or equity capital, that could not be achieved easily by other means alone. So, for example, it is possible to use a scheme to redomicile a corporate group, something for which there is no mechanism under the Companies Act 2006.[5]

A second advantage of schemes is the finality and certainty that a completed scheme can provide to the parties. Once a scheme has been approved by members and creditors and sanctioned by the court, it will be set aside subsequently only in very limited circumstances. In general this will be only if the consent of the members and/or creditors was obtained by fraud.[6] This stands in contrast to some of the alternative mechanisms discussed in this book, under which the transaction may remain open to challenge for some considerable period after it is complete, providing an ongoing risk for the company.[7]

A third, significant, advantage of a scheme is the fact that it allows a majority of the members or creditors to bind the minority. If a 'majority in number representing 75% in value'[8] of the creditors or members (or class of them) vote in favour of the scheme, and the scheme is subsequently sanctioned by the court, then it will bind all of the company's members or creditors in the relevant classes and the company itself.[9] This ability of the majority to bind the minority can be very useful. In debt reorganisations, for example, it is generally the case that creditor rights cannot be varied without the creditors' consent. A single dissenting creditor can therefore prevent the reorganisation. As a result, the minority have potential hold-up opportunities, which can be bypassed through the use of a scheme. This ability of the majority to bind the minority might appear less useful for member schemes, since there are other mechanisms in company law that allow the majority to bind the minority.[10] However,

5 See section 4.2.1.1.

6 See section 2.5.

7 See e.g. company voluntary arrangements (CVAs), discussed in section 5.6.

8 Companies Act 2006, s. 899(1).

9 If the company is in the course of being wound up it will also bind the liquidator and contributories of the company: ibid., s. 899(3). The scheme becomes effective once a copy of the order sanctioning the scheme is delivered to the Registrar of Companies: s. 899(4).

10 E.g. Companies Act 2006, s. 21, which allows the articles of the company to be amended by a special resolution.

even here, schemes can be useful, for example where there are a number of untraceable shareholders who must be bound by the scheme.[11] The fact that the 'majority in number representing 75% in value' can bind the minority also means that bidders contemplating a takeover can acquire 100 per cent of the target shares more easily than is possible under a traditional takeover offer, which is a significant reason for the attractiveness in practice of schemes in this context.[12]

The ability of the majority to bind the minority in a scheme is sometimes described as a 'cramdown'. However, it is important to use this term with care. In particular, the form of majority decision achievable in an English scheme is distinct from the form of cramdown available in other jurisdictions. In Chapter 11 proceedings in the USA, for example, it is possible for a whole class of creditors to be crammed down, that is, to have their rights adjusted without their consent. A similar form of cramdown is also possible in other jurisdictions, for example in Irish examinership proceedings,[13] and in the Part 26A restructuring plans introduced in the UK by the Corporate Insolvency and Governance Act 2020.[14] By contrast, the English scheme allows only the minority creditors or shareholders *within* a class to have their rights varied without their consent. Every class of members and creditors with a vote on the scheme must consent to it before the scheme will be sanctioned by the court. This is, therefore, a more limited form of cramdown, namely a cramdown of the minority within a class rather than a cramdown of a whole class. Nevertheless, this ability of the majority of a class to bind the minority can be extremely important and is one of the reasons for the popularity of the English scheme.

The majority decision-making that schemes facilitate inevitably gives rise to issues of minority protection. In order to provide that protection, and to prevent oppression, there is close court supervision of the scheme process. Two court hearings are involved.[15] The first sets up the requisite meetings of creditors or members (or classes thereof), with the meetings themselves conducted under the auspices of the court, and in accordance

11 See e.g. *Re BAT Industries plc*, unreported, 3 September 1998, discussed in section 4.4.

12 Under a traditional offer the bidder would have to acquire 90 per cent of the target shares before it can make use of the squeeze-out rule and be sure of obtaining 100 per cent of the target shares: see section 3.3.2.2.

13 See Irish Companies (Amendment) Act 1990 as amended by Irish Companies (Amendment) (No. 2) Act 1999, Part II.

14 For discussion see section 5.8.

15 More court hearings may be required in some circumstances; for example, where the scheme involves a reduction of capital an additional court hearing may be required to approve the reduction.

with directions given by the court, and considers certain jurisdictional issues.[16] The second meeting considers whether the scheme should be sanctioned. This is not a mere rubber-stamping exercise. The court has discretion to sanction a scheme of arrangement; it is certainly not obliged to do so, and there is no entitlement to have a scheme sanctioned.[17] As a result, the court can refuse to sanction a scheme even where the relevant classes have approved it. The ability of the majority to bind the minority to agree to a compromise or arrangement of the minority's existing rights is both the great benefit of schemes (to the majority) and their potential danger (to the minority). Properly balancing the interests of the majority and the minority is perhaps the central task for the courts in this area.[18] The fact that the courts are so heavily involved in them provides schemes with a dual nature: they are at once agreements between the parties (the company and its members and/or creditors) and court-sanctioned arrangements.

As regards disadvantages, schemes are sometimes perceived to be 'complex, cumbersome and expensive' in nature.[19] This is largely a consequence of the significant court supervision of schemes. The fact that two court hearings are involved has implications for the time required for a scheme (the minimum time required to effect a scheme is generally six to eight weeks) and for its costs. In a complex scheme, these disadvantages might be overstated. One of the other significant contributors to the view of schemes as complex and cumbersome is the requirement to separate groups of members and creditors into classes to consider and vote on the scheme. This requirement creates logistical and categorisation difficulties for schemes, and is undoubtedly one of the trickier issues facing a company wishing to make use of this mechanism. This is an issue that is discussed extensively in this book.[20] However, the courts have recently taken a more flexible approach towards the issue of classes in schemes,[21] and it may be that the impact of this requirement

[16] See section 2.2.3.

[17] *Scottish Lion Insurance Co Ltd* v. *Goodrich Corp* [2010] CSIH 6; 2010 SC 349 at [36] *per* Lord Hamilton, the Lord President. For discussion of the exercise of the court's sanctioning role see section 2.4.3.

[18] See e.g. J. Payne, 'The role of the court in debt restructuring' (2018) Cambridge Law Journal 124.

[19] See *Report of the Joint DTI/Treasury Review*, note [3] above, at para. 43.

[20] See section 2.3.2 for a general discussion of this issue, section 3.5.2 for a discussion of this issue in the context of member schemes and section 5.3 for a discussion of this issue in the context of creditor schemes.

[21] See e.g. David Richards J in *Re Telewest Communications plc (No. 1)* [2004] EWHC 924 (Ch). This is discussed further in section 2.3.2.

has lessened somewhat. Instead, the courts now tend to leave much of the discussion of minority protection issues until the sanctioning hearing, at which the courts have discretion whether to allow or refuse a scheme. This, of itself, can raise concerns, since the court's exercise of its discretion can provide a level of uncertainty, and risk, for the parties.

The renaissance of schemes of arrangement over the last twenty years or so has not been uncontroversial. Concerns have been raised about the use of schemes to effect takeovers, the suggestion being that the use of schemes in this context allows bidders to bypass takeover regulation or other measures put in place to protect minorities in a takeover, or that target shareholders are otherwise being disadvantaged by the bidder's use of a scheme, rather than an offer, to effect the change of control.[22] The use of schemes to restructure financially distressed companies in a way that effectively disenfranchises junior creditors has been criticised by those who consider that such schemes treat the junior creditors unfairly.[23] Another difficult issue that has arisen concerns the ability of companies incorporated outside the UK to make use of the English scheme jurisdiction. These issues will be debated in the following chapters.

This is a dynamic area of the law. Both in the UK and in other jurisdictions that make use of schemes there has been a wealth of case law and legislative developments in recent years, in some instances responding to concerns about the use to which schemes have been put, in others responding to more general concerns. Most recently in the UK, the Corporate Insolvency and Governance Act 2020 has introduced significant changes to the UK debt restructuring regime in order to respond to the economic effects of the Covid-19 pandemic.

1.2 The historical development of schemes

The origins of the scheme of arrangement lie in the Companies Act 1862. Section 136 of that Act provided for an arrangement entered into between a company and its creditors, but only where the company was about to be, or was in the course of being, wound up voluntarily. Such an arrangement would be binding on the company if sanctioned by an extraordinary resolution (75 per cent of all members), and on its

[22] See section 3.7 for discussion of this issue.
[23] See section 5.6 for a discussion of this issue.

creditors if acceded to by 75 per cent of their number and value.[24] There was no requirement for court approval of this arrangement. However, section 137 gave any creditor or contributory of a company that had already entered into such an arrangement three weeks to appeal against it to the court, and the court then had power to amend, vary or confirm the arrangement. Where a company was being wound up compulsorily, or subject to supervision, section 159 of the Companies Act 1862 empowered a liquidator, with the sanction of the court, to enter into compromises with creditors and contributories. Where the company was being wound up voluntarily, section 160 empowered a liquidator to make such compromises with the sanction of an extraordinary resolution of the company. These later sections provided the court with no jurisdiction to bind dissenting creditors.

Section 2 of the Joint Stock Companies Arrangement Act 1870 was introduced to tackle some of these issues. It was a rudimentary ancestor of sections 895–9 of the Companies Act 2006. However, its scope was still limited to compromises or arrangements proposed between a company that was in the course of being wound up, voluntarily, compulsorily or under supervision, and its creditors or any class of them:

> Where any compromise or arrangement shall be proposed between a company which is, at the time of the passing of this Act or afterwards, in the course of being wound up, either voluntarily or by or under the supervision of the Court, under the Companies Acts 1862 and 1867, or either of them, and the creditors or such company, or any class of such creditors, it shall be lawful for the Court, in addition to any other of its powers, on the application in a summary way of any creditor or the liquidator, to order that a meeting of such creditors or class of creditors shall be summoned in such manner as the Court shall direct, and if a majority in number, representing three-fourths in value, of such creditors or class of creditors present either in person or by proxy at such meeting shall agree to any arrangement or compromise, such arrangement or compromise shall, if sanctioned by an order of the Court, be binding on all such creditors or class of creditors, as the case may be, and also on the liquidator and contributories of the said company.

[24] The approval requirement was for 75 per cent of all members and creditors, not just 75 per cent of those members present and voting as is the case today (Companies Act 2006, s. 899(1)).

Accordingly, the compromise or arrangement had to be approved by a 75 per cent majority in value, and a simple majority in number, of the creditors present either in person or by proxy, and then sanctioned by the court. The fact that this provision allowed for the minority creditors to be bound by a majority decision of the relevant class was a crucial innovation of this section. It was understood that companies dealing with classes of debenture holders had faced a significant difficulty before the 1870 Act:

> before the legislation of 1870, any particular individual could hold out against a scheme, however meritorious and however beneficial it might be, in order that he might get, generally speaking, some special advantage for himself, or because he was a person who did not even take a fair view of the advantages to be gained. It was for the purpose of preventing that obstruction that the legislature passed the Joint Stock Companies Arrangement Act 1870.[25]

That remained the position until 1900, when section 24 of the Companies Act 1900 applied the provisions of section 2 of the 1870 Act '. . . not only as between the company and the creditors, or any class thereof, but as between the company and the members, or any class thereof'. Under these provisions it was still necessary at that time that the company should be in the course of being wound up, but a report of the Loreburn Law Amendment Committee submitted that it was inconvenient that a winding-up should be a condition precedent to the court approving an arrangement and this led to a change in the law.[26] Section 38 of the Companies Act 1907 provided that the Act of 1870 should also apply to a company that was not in the course of being wound up. Section 39 of the 1907 Act gave a company power by special resolution, confirmed by an order of the court, to modify its memorandum of association so as to reorganise its capital '. . . whether by the consolidation of shares of different classes, or by the division of its shares into shares of different classes . . .'.[27]

In the following year the Companies (Consolidation) Act 1908 was passed and in section 120 there appeared for the first time a readily recognisable predecessor of section 899(1) of the Companies Act 2006, requiring 'a majority in number representing three-fourths in value of the

[25] *In re Dominion of Canada Freehold Estate and Timber Co Ltd* (1886) 55 LT 347 at 351 *per* Chitty J.

[26] Loreburn Committee, Report 1906 Cd. 3052 (London: HMSO, 1906).

[27] See e.g. *Re Palace Hotel Ltd* [1912] 2 Ch 438.

creditors or class of creditors, or members or class of members, as the case may be, present either in person or by proxy at the meeting' to agree to the compromise or arrangement.[28] The only difference was that at that stage the words 'and voting' did not appear after the word 'present'. As a result, under that Act an abstention was still effectively a vote against the scheme.[29]

However, that and other amendments were made by section 53 of the Companies Act 1928. As a result, the member and creditor approval requirement was changed so that it would operate by reference to those members and creditors 'present *and voting* either in person or by proxy'.[30] Consequently, an abstention at the meeting was no longer treated as a vote against the arrangement, effectively lowering the approval threshold. In particular, section 45 of the Companies (Consolidation) Act 1908, which had re-enacted section 39 of the Companies Act 1907, ceased to have effect. It was, in effect, replaced by the extension of the definition of 'arrangement' that is now found in section 895(2) of the Companies Act 2006, that is, that the term 'arrangement' includes a reorganisation of share capital by consolidation of shares of different classes or the division of shares into shares of different classes.[31] This was then followed by sections 153–4 of the Companies Act 1929, another consolidating act.

These sections were repeated in almost identical terms in the Companies Act 1948[32] and the Companies Act 1985.[33] However, in 1947, following a recommendation of the Cohen Committee,[34] a new section added a requirement for an explanatory statement to be provided.[35] This section was re-enacted in the Companies Act 1948,[36] the Companies Act 1985[37] and the Companies Act 2006.[38] Prior to this, common law disclosure obligations had applied. This statutory enactment required that any disclosures be fair, that material interests of directors and the trustees of debenture stock be disclosed, and that where an explanatory

28 Companies (Consolidation) Act 1908, s. 120(2).
29 *Re Savoy Hotel Ltd* [1981] Ch 351 at 359 *per* Nourse J.
30 Companies Act 1928, s. 53(3) (emphasis added). The words in italics are those added by this section.
31 See now Companies Act 2006, s. 895(2).
32 Companies Act 1948, ss. 206–8.
33 Companies Act 1985, ss. 425–7.
34 The Report of the Committee on Company Law Amendment (Cmnd 6659, 1945) (Cohen Report).
35 Companies Act 1947, s. 40.
36 Companies Act 1948, s. 207.
37 Companies Act 1985, s. 426.
38 Companies Act 2006, s. 897.

statement was provided it should contain all of the information reasonably necessary to enable the recipients to determine how to vote.[39]

The provisions dealing with schemes of arrangement are now found in Part 26 of the Companies Act 2006. The Company Law Review that preceded this Act considered reforms to the statutory provisions relating to schemes alongside its more general consideration of company law reforms. It recommended that a number of changes be made, including giving the court the power to make a binding determination on the composition of classes at the first court hearing; giving the court discretion to sanction a scheme of arrangement notwithstanding a technical defect in compliance with the statutory procedure, provided this had no substantive effect on the outcome; providing a definition of 'class' within the legislation; giving the court the power to direct the manner in which scheme meetings are called, held and conducted; and abolishing the majority-in-number requirement for member or creditor sanction of a scheme.[40] Despite initial indications that these 'generally technical changes' would be introduced into the legislation,[41] in the end none of these important recommendations were included in the legislative provisions.[42] However, a Practice Statement in 2002 at least dealt with the Company Law Review's concern regarding the need for the court to consider at the first rather than the second court hearing whether class meetings have been correctly constituted.[43]

There is no public explanation of why the government did not proceed with these proposed reforms. The concern seems to have been the potentially adverse impact on minority rights. Three of the proposed reforms (the ability of the court to determine classes at the first meeting, the discretion to approve a scheme even where the classes were not formally constituted, and abolishing the headcount test) were debated by the House of Lords' Grand Committee, when considering the Companies Bill. In that Committee the Attorney General stated that these amendments would weaken safeguards for individual members and creditors that existed in the law, and that 'while I can see that they

[39] E.g. *Kaye* v. *Croydon Tramways Co* [1898] 1 Ch 358; *Re Dorman Long and Co Ltd* [1934] Ch 635.

[40] CLR, *Final Report*, URN 01/942, July 2001 paras. 13.5–13.11.

[41] DTI, *Company Law Reform – White Paper*, March 2005, para. 4.14.

[42] For discussion of these issues see sections 2.2.3, 2.3.3.2 and 2.4.2.

[43] Practice Statement [2002] 3 All ER 96, which has subsequently been replaced by Practice Statement (Companies: Schemes of Arrangement under Part 26 and Part 26A of the Companies Act 2006) [2020] 1 WLR 4493; for discussion see section 2.2.3.

would facilitate schemes for companies and large creditors and members, [they] would do that at the expense of the interests of small members and creditors'.[44] As a result, the Committee dropped the proposed changes.

Part 26 of the 2006 Act restates, with minor amendments, sections 425–7 of the Companies Act 1985. However, the sections were reordered, with the intention of providing a more logical progression through the three stages of a scheme, that is, the initial application, the meetings and the court sanction. So, section 895 sets out the scope of Part 26 and provides some definitions. Section 896 details the power of the court to summon appropriate creditor and member meetings, and sections 897–8 deal with the information that needs to be provided in advance of those meetings. Section 899 deals with the court's sanction of the scheme. Section 900 provides some additional powers to the court at the sanctioning stage where the scheme involves the transfer of the assets and liabilities of one company to another and a reconstruction or amalgamation is envisaged. Section 901 imposes an obligation on the company to file with the Registrar of Companies any amended articles of association, if these are amended pursuant to the scheme. Some small changes were made to the schemes provisions in Part 26 of the Companies Act 2006. For example, section 899 clarifies that an application for court sanction to a scheme may be made by any creditor or member, a point that had previously been assumed.[45] However, these changes relate to relatively minor matters.

The statutory scheme in the 2006 Act remains in place and unaltered, although there have been subsequent legislative changes that impact on the use of schemes.[46] One example of this is the Companies Act 2006 (Amendment of Part 17) Regulations 2015.[47] The purpose of these Regulations was to close a specific tax loophole in relation to the use of a reduction of capital in a cancellation takeover scheme so as to avoid the payment of stamp duty on a transfer of shares to the bidder.[48] Consequently, these Regulations amend section 641 of the Companies Act 2006 in order to end the use of cancellation schemes as a means of effecting

[44] *Hansard*, HL, cols GC324–6 (28 March 2006).

[45] Companies Act 2006, s. 899(2)(b).

[46] For example, the scheme jurisdiction was subsequently extended to limited liability partnerships (LLPs), so that LLPs can now also make use of Part 26: The Limited Liability Partnerships (Application of the Companies Act 2006) Regulations 2009 (SI 1804/2009), reg. 45.

[47] SI 472/2015.

[48] See BIS, *Explanatory Memorandum to The Companies Act 2006 (Amendment of Part 17) Regulations 2015 No 472*, paras. 7.3–7.4.

a change of control,[49] although cancellation schemes can still be used for other purposes, so that, for example, reductions of capital can be used in conjunction with holdco schemes.[50] The differentiation between allowed and not-allowed cancellation schemes has not been straightforward for the courts applying these provisions.[51] Another example is the Corporate Insolvency and Governance Act 2020. This Act introduces a stand-alone restructuring moratorium that can be used alongside a number of restructuring mechanisms, including a scheme of arrangement.[52] It also introduces a new mechanism in Part 26A of the Companies Act 2006, namely a restructuring plan, sometimes referred to as a 'super scheme', which is procedurally close to the scheme of arrangement but includes some additional elements, most notably the potential for a cross-class cramdown.[53]

These legislative changes to the scheme jurisdiction tell only part of the story, however. Many of the most important developments in relation to schemes in the past century have occurred not as a result of statutory changes but as a result of the judicial development of schemes of arrangement.

Before leaving this section it is worth noting that since their introduction, English schemes of arrangement have been exported to a number of other jurisdictions around the world. Many Commonwealth countries originally built their own corporate legislative structure around that of England. As a result, Australia,[54] New Zealand,[55]

[49] For discussion see 3.3.1.1.

[50] See sections 4.2.1 and 4.2.2.2.

[51] For discussion see section 4.2.2.2.

[52] See section 5.4.4.2.

[53] See section 5.8.

[54] Creditor schemes were introduced into Australia in 1899, when s. 2 of the Joint Stock Companies Arrangement Act 1870 was effectively transposed into Australian legislation: New South Wales Act 1899, s. 160. It was not until 1936 that a statutory provision for the court to sanction a compromise or arrangement between a company and its members was introduced: Australian Companies Act 1936, s. 133. For discussion of the historical development of the Australian provisions see *Re Theatre Freeholds Ltd* (1996) 20 ACSR 729 at 733–4 *per* Young J. The current Australian provisions are found in s. 411 of the Australian Corporations Act 2001 (as amended). The Australian scheme of arrangement is largely similar to the English scheme (see T. Damian and A. Rich, *Schemes, Takeovers and Himalayan Peaks: The use of schemes of arrangement to effect change of control transactions*, 3rd ed. (Sydney: Centre of Commercial, Corporate and Taxation Law, University of Sydney, 2013)) although some differences of detail are observable (e.g. s. 411(17) of the Australian Corporations Act 2001, discussed in section 3.7).

[55] New Zealand legislation has provided for schemes of arrangement for some considerable period. New Zealand schemes were initially modelled on the English scheme of arrangement (see e.g. New Zealand Companies Act 1933, s. 159) although various reforms since that period, most recently the New Zealand Companies Amendment Act 2014, have

Canada,[56] Hong Kong,[57] Singapore,[58] Malaysia,[59] India,[60] South Africa,[61] the British Virgin Islands (BVI),[62] Bermuda[63] and the Cayman Islands[64] all employ provisions akin to Part 26 of the

moved New Zealand schemes away from their English origins to some extent. The current law is contained in the New Zealand Companies Act 1993, s. 236 (as amended).

56 The scheme of arrangement was introduced into Canada in the Business Corporations Act 1978. The rules relating to court-supervised schemes of arrangement, referred to in Canada as plans of arrangement, are set out in s. 192 of the Canadian Business Corporations Act 1985. The statutory scheme provisions in Canada are much shorter and more economical than the English legislative provisions. In fact there are just two operative provisions: ss. 192(3) and 192(4). For discussion see S. B. Scott, T. O. Buckley and A. Harrison, 'The Arrangement Procedure under Section 192 of the Canada Business Corporations Act and the Reorganization of Dome Petroleum' (1990) 16 *Canadian Business Law Journal* 296; V. Torrie, *Reinventing Bankruptcy Law: A History of the Companies' Creditors Arrangement Act* (Toronto: University of Toronto Press, 2020).

57 The current scheme provisions are found in Hong Kong Companies Ordinance, Cap. 622, ss. 670–4. Although as initially introduced the Hong Kong scheme provisions were effectively the same as those in the UK, such that scheme decisions of the English courts 'are, therefore, of great weight in considering the application of the Ordinance in Hong Kong' (*Re UDL Holdings Ltd* [2002] 1 HKC 172, at [7] *per* Lord Millett), changes introduced in recent years have created some divergence between the English and the Hong Kong scheme provisions, particularly regarding takeover schemes (for discussion see section 3.7).

58 The current scheme provisions in Singapore are found in Singapore Companies Act, s. 210 and Singapore Insolvency, Restructuring and Dissolution Act 2018, Part 5. Initially schemes in Singapore were very similar to English schemes, but changes introduced in 2017 mean that creditor schemes in Singapore now diverge from their English counterparts. For discussion of the changes see Meng Seng Wee, 'The Singapore story of injecting US Chapter 11 into the Commonwealth scheme' (2018) *European Company and Financial Law Review* 553, and see sections 5.4.4 and 5.8.2.

59 The current scheme provisions are found in the Malaysian Companies Act 2016, s. 366. This Act introduced minor amendments to the previous scheme of arrangement provisions (see Malaysian Companies Act 1965, s. 176 as amended) but also introduced a new CVA mechanism and a judicial management mechanism (which is based on the UK administration provisions).

60 The current scheme provisions are found in the Indian Companies Act 2013, ss. 230–40, which introduced numerous changes to the pre-existing scheme provisions (see Indian Companies Act 1956, ss. 391–4 as amended).

61 Schemes of arrangement have been available in South Africa for some time. Until 2011, schemes were governed by s. 311 of the Companies Act No. 61 of 1973, but important changes were introduced by the South African Companies Act No. 71 of 2008, which became effective in 2011. The current scheme provisions are found in ch. 5 of the 2008 Act (for member schemes) and in ch. 6 (for creditor schemes).

62 Until 2004 the BVI had no scheme of arrangement provisions in place. However, the BVI Business Companies Act 2004, s. 179A introduced a scheme of arrangement that in all material respects replicates the UK provisions.

63 The core schemes provisions are contained in s. 99 of the Bermuda Companies Act 1981. The substance of this provision is virtually identical to the English scheme of arrangement.

64 See Cayman Islands Companies Law, as revised, s. 86, which is very similar to the English scheme.

Companies Act 2006. The value of schemes is recognised in these jurisdictions, and extensive use is generally made of these provisions. Given the common origins of the scheme of arrangement provisions in these various jurisdictions, it is not surprising that they remain close to the English model and, as a result, much of the law detailed in this book is equally applicable in these other jurisdictions. However, over time most of these jurisdictions have made changes, some small, others larger, to their scheme provisions. These are discussed, where relevant, in this volume. Other jurisdictions have also borrowed the English scheme procedure either in full[65] or in part.[66]

1.3 The scope of this book

The purpose of this book is threefold. First, it considers how schemes of arrangement are currently being utilised, in terms of their operation and the uses to which schemes are put. The latter analysis also involves a consideration of the alternatives to schemes that are available, and why schemes prove more attractive than the alternatives on many occasions. Schemes are sometimes also used in combination with these alternatives, such as in the case of schemes combined with pre-pack administrations, in order to attempt to get the best of both mechanisms,[67] and the use of schemes in combination with other mechanisms is therefore also discussed and explored. Second, some of the criticisms facing schemes are tackled, and an analysis of whether these are justified is undertaken.[68] Third, this book considers some of the challenges facing schemes, and suggests a number of areas in which schemes should be reformed.[69]

Although, as stated, schemes can be used for a wide variety of purposes, nevertheless they can be grouped into two broad categories: member-focused schemes and creditor-focused schemes. That is not to

[65] See e.g. the Irish scheme of arrangement provisions in Part 9 of the Irish Companies Act 2014. Irish schemes of arrangement are based on similar legislation to English schemes of arrangement and the Irish court follows English legal precedent.

[66] See e.g. the EU Restructuring Directive (EU) 2019/1023 which borrows concepts from both the UK scheme of arrangement and US Chapter 11.

[67] See section 5.4.3.

[68] See e.g. section 3.7 in relation to the use of schemes as an alternative to a takeover offer and section 7.5 in relation to the use of English schemes by foreign companies and whether this gives rise to concerns about forum shopping.

[69] See e.g. section 2.3.3.2 regarding the use of the headcount test for schemes.

say that schemes cannot involve both creditors and members. Clearly they can, and do. However, it is possible for the purposes of exposition to regard schemes as either member schemes or creditor schemes. This book will therefore consider schemes in these two broad categories.

Before considering member schemes and creditor schemes, however, Chapter 2 examines the mechanics of *all* schemes of arrangement, that is, the procedural issues and considerations that apply to all schemes. Broadly, there are three main steps involved in implementing a scheme of arrangement, whether a member scheme or a creditor scheme is contemplated. First, a compromise or arrangement is proposed between the company and its members or creditors. An application is made to the court for an order that a meeting or meetings be summoned.[70] Second, meetings of the members and/or creditors are held to seek approval of the scheme by the requisite majorities. Third, the scheme must be sanctioned by the court, and the order becomes effective on delivery of a copy to the Registrar of Companies.[71] Chapter 2 examines each of these stages in detail, as well as a number of issues of general importance to schemes, such as the definitions of 'compromise and arrangement' and 'company' for this purpose. The chapter also considers some of the issues and trends that have been evident in schemes in recent years, such as the fact that the court's focus on minority protection has shifted from the class meetings stage to the final court approval stage of the process. This chapter addresses the question of whether this trend should be welcomed, and considers the evolving role of the court in schemes of arrangement more generally. It also considers whether reform of the mechanics of schemes is needed, concluding that although the courts have been able to deal with many of the difficult procedural issues that have arisen, there remain a number of outstanding defects in the procedure that require statutory reform.

Chapters 3–6 then examine a number of examples of schemes in practice. The purpose of these chapters is to give a sense of the wide variety of uses to which schemes can be put. Chapters 3 and 4 examine member schemes, while Chapters 5 and 6 analyse creditor schemes. In both cases particular attention is given to the most common forms of such schemes in practice: for member schemes this is schemes used to effect a change of control of a target company as an alternative to a takeover offer (Chapter 3), and for creditor schemes this is schemes

70 Companies Act 2006, s. 896.

71 Ibid., s. 899.

used to restructure the debt of a financially distressed company (Chapter 5).

Chapter 3 examines some general issues regarding member schemes, such as the definition of 'member' for the purposes of a scheme, and considers in detail the most common use of member-focused schemes by far, namely to effect a change of control of a target company. This use of schemes is well established, and schemes have become a very common mechanism for effecting a takeover of widely held companies. Structurally, a takeover effected by a scheme is quite distinct from a traditional takeover offer. Whereas a scheme involves an arrangement proposed between a company and its members, the proposal generally coming from the board, in an offer the bidder deals not with the target company but, first and foremost, with the target shareholders. The relationship is fundamentally one of contract between the bidder and the target shareholders, albeit the relationship is then overlaid with a significant amount of regulation.

Chapter 3 then discusses the advantages and disadvantages of using a scheme rather than an offer to effect a takeover, and considers when and why a company might choose to make use of a scheme in this context. The procedural aspects of a takeover effected by a scheme are considered. In particular, it is significant that where schemes are used to effect takeovers of companies within the jurisdiction of the Takeover Panel, the City Code on Takeovers and Mergers will apply. The implications of this for schemes are discussed. One of the most difficult issues arising in any scheme is the need to separate the members and/or creditors into different classes. This issue is considered carefully in the context of takeover schemes since complex questions can arise, for example regarding whether the shares of members who have shares in the bidder, or the shares of those who have given irrevocable undertakings, should be treated as comprising separate classes. More problematic is how the bidder's shares in the target, or the shares of the bidder's subsidiaries in the target, should be treated. This raises the more general issue of minority protection for members in a takeover effected by way of a scheme. Chapter 3 examines this issue, comparing the minority protection available in a scheme with that available in a traditional takeover offer. Finally, this chapter considers whether takeovers should be able to be effected by way of a scheme of arrangement, and evaluates the criticisms of schemes used in this context. It is argued that where the parties decide to utilise a scheme rather than a takeover offer, there is no reason to be sceptical about such use of a scheme or to require additional safeguards beyond those that the law currently provides.

Chapter 4 examines some of the other examples of member schemes. There are a wide variety of uses to which member schemes can be put. One of the most common is to reorganise a corporate group by creating a new holding company for the group (a holdco scheme). There are various reasons why this might be done, but two of the most usual are to redomicile the group to a new jurisdiction, and to create additional distributable reserves for the group. Schemes can also be used to merge or demerge companies, although this is a less common use of schemes, as explained in this chapter. Some of the alternatives to schemes, such as reconstructions under section 110 of the Insolvency Act 1986, are discussed. However, the inherent flexibility of schemes means that they can also be used for a wide range of other purposes, including, for example, altering class rights or removing minority shareholders from a company. For some of these purposes good alternatives exist, and indeed for that reason schemes will be relatively rarely used to achieve these particular goals. For example, the Companies Act 2006 provides good mechanisms by which class rights may be altered,[72] and schemes generally add little benefit and are rarely used in this context. However, for other purposes company law offers no good alternative and therefore schemes are a particularly valuable tool.

Chapter 5 examines some issues of general relevance to all creditor schemes, such as the definition of 'creditor' for the purpose of a scheme of arrangement and the division of creditors into classes for the purposes of creditor schemes. The focus of this chapter, however, is one of the most common uses of creditor schemes, namely restructuring the debt of financially distressed companies. Debt restructuring allows a company facing cash flow problems to renegotiate and reduce its debts in order to improve liquidity, with a view to rescuing the company, or at least its business. Over the last two decades schemes have been used more and more for this purpose. The value of using schemes in this context is considered, and part of this analysis is to assess the other main restructuring tools available to a company in this scenario, namely the use of a workout (whereby the company enters into contractual arrangements with its creditors), of a company voluntary arrangement (CVA), of administration and, following the Corporate Insolvency and

[72] Ibid., ss. 630–5.

Governance Act 2020, of restructuring plans in Part 26A of the Companies Act 2006.

Chapter 6 examines a number of other uses for creditor schemes, and seeks to demonstrate the variety of ways in which schemes can be used to effect arrangements between a company and its creditors. Schemes are often used when a company is insolvent or practically insolvent. As discussed in Chapter 5, a scheme may be used to bring about a compromise designed to avoid an insolvent liquidation. However, a scheme may also be used where a company is wound up, either instead of or alongside liquidation. Creditor schemes may also be used where the company is solvent where, for example, an insurance company wants to vary the rights of its policyholders.[73]

Chapter 7 addresses a number of cross-border issues that arise in relation to schemes. In recent years there has been a growth of cases involving foreign companies wishing to make use of the English scheme jurisdiction. This chapter considers whether the English courts have jurisdiction to sanction a scheme involving a foreign company. Broadly, the court will wish to see that there is a sufficient connection between the scheme and England and also that the scheme will be internationally effective. Both issues are examined in the chapter together with the impact that certain EU Regulations had in this area prior to 31 December 2020 when the transition period following the UK's exit from the EU came to an end. Chapter 7 also considers the question of whether the English scheme jurisdiction *should* be available to these companies.

Finally, Chapter 8[74] provides some concluding remarks regarding schemes, and summarises the ideas and arguments that have been raised in this book. In particular this chapter examines the recent changes made in the context of schemes, many of which were recommended by the first edition of this book,[75] and considers what further reform is needed in order to strengthen schemes as a corporate tool for the future.

[73] E.g. *Re Equitable Life Assurance Society* [2002] EWHC 140 (Ch).

[74] In the first edition of this book, ch. 8 contained material relating to the use of schemes of arrangement elsewhere in the world. This material has been retained and updated but has been redistributed to the relevant sections within this book, so as to enrich the discussion and analysis.

[75] See first edition of this book, ch. 9.

2

The mechanics of a scheme of arrangement

2.1 Introduction

Before engaging in an analysis of different types of member and creditor schemes, in Chapters 3–6, it is important to consider the procedural and other issues that are of general relevance. This chapter will therefore assess the mechanics of a scheme of arrangement that are relevant to all of the schemes discussed in later chapters.

There are three main steps involved in implementing a scheme of arrangement.[1] First, a 'compromise or arrangement'[2] is proposed between the company and its members[3] or creditors.[4] A scheme will often be proposed by the board on behalf of the company.[5] An application to court must then be made under section 896 of the Companies Act 2006 for an order that a meeting or meetings be summoned. Second, meetings of the members or creditors will be held to seek approval of the scheme by the appropriate majorities. Third, the scheme must be

[1] A similar structure is adopted in schemes elsewhere, see e.g. Singapore Companies Act, s. 210; Hong Kong Companies Ordinance, Cap 622, ss. 670–4; Australian Corporations Act 2001, s. 411; BVI Business Companies Act 2004, s. 179A; Bermuda Companies Act 1981, s. 99; Cayman Islands Companies Law, as revised, s. 86.

[2] For discussion of the terms 'compromise' and 'arrangement' see section 2.1.1.

[3] In the case of a company registered under the Companies Acts, the members are the subscribers and other persons who agree to become members and whose names are on the company's register of members: Companies Act 2006, s. 112.

[4] Companies Act 2006, s. 895(1). The definition of 'creditor' for the purposes of a scheme is dealt with in section 5.2.

[5] However, an application for an order giving directions for meetings to approve a scheme can be made by any creditor or member, or by a liquidator or administrator: Companies Act 2006, s. 896(2). See section 2.2.1.

sanctioned by the court, and the order sanctioning the scheme is then delivered to the Registrar of Companies.[6]

As Chadwick LJ said in *Re Hawk Insurance Co Ltd*:

> It can be seen that each of those stages serves a distinct purpose. At the first stage the court directs how the meeting or meetings are to be summoned. It is concerned, at that stage, to ensure that those who are to be affected by the compromise or arrangement proposed have a proper opportunity of being present (in person or by proxy) at the meeting or meetings at which the proposals are to be considered and voted upon. The second stage ensures that the proposals are acceptable to at least a majority in number, representing three-fourths in value, of those who take the opportunity of being present (in person or by proxy) at the meeting or meetings. At the third stage the court is concerned (i) to ensure that the meeting or meetings have been summoned and held in accordance with its previous order, (ii) to ensure that the proposals have been approved by the requisite majority of those present at the meeting or meetings and (iii) to ensure that the views and interests of those who have not approved the proposals at the meeting or meetings (either because they were not present or, being present, did not vote in favour of the proposals) receive impartial consideration.[7]

This chapter will consider each of these stages in detail. However, before getting into the details of the procedure, two definitional issues will be addressed: (i) the meaning of the terms 'arrangement' and 'compromise', and (ii) the meaning of the term 'company' for the purpose of schemes of arrangement.

Thereafter the chapter proceeds as follows: the application to the court for meetings to be summoned is discussed in section 2.2; the meetings of the members and/or creditors (including the issue of the division of members/creditors into classes) is analysed in section 2.3; the sanction of the court is dealt with in section 2.4; and the delivery of the order to the Registrar of Companies is considered in section 2.5. Particular aspects of the process will be discussed in later chapters, where relevant.[8]

One of the significant points about schemes is the fact that, although they have a statutory basis, the statutory provisions themselves are rather brief regarding much of the detail of schemes. As a consequence, the role

[6] Companies Act 2006, s. 899(1) and (4).

[7] [2001] EWCA Civ 241; [2002] BCC 300 at [12].

[8] E.g. the issue of class meetings will be considered in more detail in the context of member schemes and creditor schemes in the relevant chapters: see section 3.5.2 for a discussion of classes in takeover schemes, and for creditor schemes see section 5.3. The general discussion of classes in schemes is contained in this chapter in section 2.3.2.

of the court has been particularly significant in developing their ambit, jurisdiction and procedural rules. The courts have developed a set of commercially practical provisions to deal with the mechanics of schemes. This can be seen throughout this chapter, including, inter alia, the interpretation of 'compromise' and 'arrangement' in section 2.1.1, the role of the court at the convening hearing in section 2.2.3, the application of the concept of 'class' for scheme purposes in section 2.3.2 and the role of the court at the sanctioning stage in section 2.4. Although the involvement of the court adds to the time and expense involved in a scheme, this pragmatic approach has meant that, on the whole, the mechanics of schemes of arrangement work well.

Nevertheless, criticisms are sometimes levelled at the scheme procedure. This chapter will assess these criticisms, and will also consider, more generally, whether the present scheme procedure is appropriate or is in need of reform. Broadly, the view taken here is that many of these criticisms are unjustified, but that some changes to the present procedure would be beneficial. Perhaps the most significant change would be the removal of the 'majority-in-number' requirement for majority voting in class meetings,[9] but a number of other suggested reforms are also proposed in this chapter.

2.1.1 *The meaning of 'compromise' and 'arrangement'*

The terms 'compromise' and 'arrangement' have no precise legal meaning and should therefore be given their ordinary commercial meaning.[10] These terms have been construed widely by the courts. In *Premier Oil*, for example, the Scottish courts reaffirmed the broad scope of the term 'compromise or arrangement', holding that the novel use of a creditor scheme in that case, to implement an acquisition, did not create a jurisdictional bar and that the creditor challenge to the scheme related rather to the commercial merits of the scheme, which was not for the court to determine.[11]

[9] See section 2.3.3.2.

[10] An 'arrangement' is partially defined as including a reorganisation of a company's share capital. This is further defined as (i) consolidating different classes of shares or (ii) dividing shares into different classes (s. 895(2)) or both. However, this definition is clearly incomplete and schemes of arrangement encompass a far wider range of circumstances than these facts. In *Re Lehman Brothers International (Europe) (in administration)* [2009] EWCA Civ 1161; [2010] 1 BCLC 496 at [29], *per* Lord Neuberger, the Court of Appeal confirmed that this is only a partial definition.

[11] *Re Premier Oil plc* [2020] CSOH 39.

The word 'compromise' offers few difficulties of interpretation. Applying the ordinary commercial meaning of this term (the settlement of a dispute) means that, for scheme purposes, all that is required is some difficulty or dispute that the scheme seeks to resolve.[12] By contrast, the concept of 'arrangement' is wider than that of 'compromise' and is not limited to something analogous to a compromise.[13] The elements of a dispute, and an accommodation of that dispute, need not be present.[14]

For both 'compromises' and 'arrangements' the courts have required that the scheme involve some element of give and take, and not simply amount to a surrender or confiscation.[15] Therefore, in a scheme between a company and its members, under which the members are simply giving up their rights or their rights are being expropriated without any sort of compensating advantage for the members, there would be no 'arrangement' or 'compromise' between the company and its members for this purpose.[16] In assessing this issue the court will take account of the surrounding circumstances, so that, in creditor schemes, for example, the court will take account of the broader restructuring of the company or group of which the scheme in front of the court is an integral part in determining whether there has been a sufficient compromise.[17] The requirement for 'give and take' does not mean that the members/creditors cannot suffer any disadvantage. In *Re Uniq plc*,[18] for example, a solvent multinational was restructured in such a way as to release the company from its burdensome obligations under a pension scheme that was in deficit. As part of this intended restructuring, the proceeds of a sale of shares would be used to provide a cash injection to the pension fund.

12 *Sneath* v. *Valley Gold Ltd* [1893] 1 Ch 477; *Re NFU Development Trust Ltd* [1972] 1 WLR 1548.

13 No element of compromise needs to be shown in order for an arrangement to fall within s. 895: *Re National Bank Ltd* [1966] 1 WLR 819 at 829 *per* Plowman J; *Re T & N Ltd (No. 3)* [2006] EWHC 1447 (Ch) at [46]–[50] *per* David Richards J.

14 *Re Guardian Assurance Company* [1917] 1 Ch 431.

15 *Re Savoy Hotel Ltd* [1981] Ch 351 at 359–61 *per* Nourse J. Earlier cases had taken a more restrictive approach (e.g. *Re General Motor Cab Co Ltd* [1913] 1 Ch 377 (CA), but see *Guardian Assurance*, ibid.). The preferable view is that adopted in the later cases, i.e. that 'arrangement' is not synonymous with 'compromise' and should be construed more broadly.

16 *Re NFU Development Trust Ltd* [1972] 1 WLR 1548. This requirement does not, however, mean that there can be no disadvantage to creditors: *Re Osiris Insurance Ltd* [1999] 1 BCLC 182.

17 See *Re Uniq plc* [2011] EWHC 749 (Ch); *Re Stripes US Holdings Inc* [2018] EWHC 2912 (Ch).

18 [2011] EWHC 749 (Ch).

Responsibility for the pensions would then be transferred from the company to a third party. As a consequence, the shareholders would find their equity stake in the company substantially reduced. David Richards J held that there was nevertheless some benefit accruing to the shareholders and creditors as a result of the wider aspects of the proposed scheme; specifically, this was the only realistic way for the company to free itself of its pensions liability, and thereby remain viable. It therefore fell within the concept of 'compromise or arrangement' for scheme purposes.

A further limitation is that the company must be a party to the arrangement: Part 26 of the 2006 Act does not apply to arrangements or compromises between the creditors or members not involving the company.

However, subject to these limitations, the courts have deliberately avoided giving the terms a narrow meaning.[19] In particular, the courts have construed the term 'arrangement' very broadly. This issue was considered in *Re Jelf Group plc*[20] in which the entire shareholding of Jelf Group plc was to be transferred to another company in a straightforward transfer scheme arrangement.[21] Despite transfer schemes being a common occurrence, Mann J had concerns about how they satisfied this element of the scheme procedure:

> There is no question of compromise involved in this case. So if the scheme is to be sanctioned by the court, it must be 'an arrangement between a company and its members'. The relevant word for present purposes is 'arrangement'. As I read the scheme I struggled to find what it was that made this scheme an arrangement between the company and its members. What has happened in this case is that the members have been made an offer and have accepted it. It is proposed that, pursuant to the scheme, all the members should sell all their shares to the purchaser. The company

[19] The breadth of the court's interpretation of the term 'arrangement' was endorsed by the Court of Appeal in *Re Lehman Brothers International (Europe) (in administration)* [2009] EWCA Civ 1161; [2010] 1 BCLC 496 at [74]. See also Lowe ACJ in the Australian case *Re International Harvester Co of Australia Pty Ltd* [1953] VR 669 who said that 'arrangement' should be construed as liberally as possible and would include virtually any arrangement that concerns the rights and obligations of the company, its members or creditors, provided that it is otherwise legal, not ultra vires the company, and does not seek a result for which another statutory procedure is required. In *Re BIS Finance Pty Ltd* [2017] NSWSC 1713 Black J accepted that schemes could be used to implement an agreed moratorium and that such schemes constituted an 'arrangement' for scheme purposes.

[20] [2015] EWHC 3857 (Ch).

[21] For further discussion see section 3.3.1.1.

> seems to have little to do with that. Looking at the terms of the scheme itself, the company seems hardly to participate in the scheme.[22]

The basis for the requisite 'give and take' on the part of the company in the past has been the company's role in registering the transfer of shares and thereby terminating the existing members' status as members. Ultimately, Mann J was satisfied to classify the transfer scheme in *Re Jelf Group* as an 'arrangement' given the existence of authority and the reliance on that authority for decades,[23] even though 'it might be thought to be a stretching'[24] of that term.

As a further example of how broadly this phrase has been interpreted, the English court has been prepared to include schemes which are being used to vary or release liabilities arising between members/creditors and one or more third parties.[25] A good example of such a situation is found in *Re T & N Ltd (No. 3)*.[26] In that case the rights held by creditors against the company's employers' liability insurers were varied as part of an arrangement between the creditors and the company. Although the scheme had no effect on the rights of the creditors against the company, it was held that the creditors' rights against the insurer were sufficiently

[22] [2015] EWHC 3857 (Ch) at [4].

[23] See also *Re SABMiller plc* [2016] EWHC 2153 (Ch).

[24] [2015] EWHC 3857 (Ch) at [10]. It is notable that Mann J stated that 'if I were considering this jurisdiction entirely afresh and without the weight of history and authority, I might well have not reached the decision that this was an "arrangement between the company and its members"' (at [7]).

[25] *Re Lehman Brothers (Europe) International (in administration)* [2009] EWCA Civ 1161; [2010] 1 BCLC 496; *Re Noble Group Limited* [2018] EWHC 3092 (Ch). The same approach has been adopted in relation to Part 26A restructuring plans: *Re Pizzaexpress Financing 2 Plc* [2020] EWHC 2873 (Ch). Other jurisdictions have also adopted this approach. The provisions in the Canadian Companies' Creditors Arrangement Act (CCAA) have been interpreted to permit releases of rights against third parties: *Re Metcalfe and Mansfield Alternative Investments II Corp*, 2008 ONCA 587 (Ontario Court of Appeal). A similar approach was adopted by Chief Justice Smellie in *Re The Sphinx Group of Companies*, Grand Court of the Cayman Islands, unreported, 5 May 2010, in which he confirmed that the law of the Cayman Islands corresponds to the law of England on this point. In Australia the courts have accepted that the release of third-party claims can properly be regarded as being an arrangement between the company and its members/creditors in certain circumstances (*Re Opes Prime Stockbroking Limited (No. 1)* (2009) 73 ACSR 385) although a less flexible approach has been adopted towards third-party releases in relation to deed of company arrangements (*City of Swan* v. *Lehman Brothers Australia Ltd* (2009) 74 ACSR 191). See also *Pathfinder Strategic Credit LP* v. *Empire Capital Resources Pte Ltd* [2019] SGCA 29 as regards the position in Singapore. By contrast, courts in the USA either disallow third-party releases or permit them only in very limited circumstances.

[26] [2006] EWHC 1447 (Ch).

closely connected to their rights against the company for this scheme to be regarded as being between the company and its creditors. This was because, to the extent that a creditor established a claim under the distribution procedures put in place by the scheme, and received payment, this claim would diminish the amount that the company would otherwise be required to pay in respect of the scheme.

This issue was considered by the Court of Appeal in *Re Lehman Brothers (Europe) International*. In that case Patten LJ stated (obiter):

> It seems to me entirely logical to regard the court's jurisdiction as extending to approving a scheme which varies or releases creditors' claims against the company on terms that require them to bring into account and release rights of action against third parties designed to recover the same loss. The release of such third party claims is merely ancillary to the arrangement between the company and its own creditors.[27]

On this view a scheme can be used to effect releases by members/creditors of claims against third parties where the relevant third-party claims are 'closely connected with their rights against the company as creditors'.[28] One of the common uses of the court's jurisdiction to sanction a scheme which includes releases involves guarantees provided by third parties.[29] The court's jurisdiction is not limited to guarantees, however. For example, a release of claims against persons involved in the preparation, negotiation or implementation of a scheme and their legal advisors also appears to be within the scope of Part 26 of the Companies Act 2006.[30]

27 *Re Lehman Brothers (Europe) International (in administration)* [2009] EWCA Civ 1161; [2010] 1 BCLC 496 at [65].

28 Ibid. at [83] *per* Longmore LJ. This was described in the following terms in *Re Opes Prime Stockbroking Ltd* [2009] FCA 813 by Finkelstein J: '[P]rovided there is a sufficient nexus between a release and the relationship between the creditor and the scheme company, the scheme can validly incorporate the release' (at [55]). This 'sufficient nexus' test was approved in *Pathfinder Strategic Credit LP* v. *Empire Capital Resources Pte Ltd* [2019] SGCA 29 at [79].

29 *Re La Seda de Barcelona SA* [2010] EWHC 1364 (Ch); [2011] 1 BCLC 555; *Re Noble Group Limited* [2018] EWHC 3092 (Ch); *Re Syncreon Group BV* [2019] EWHC 2412 (Ch). Although a scheme can properly include a compromise between creditors or members and third parties, it is clear that there is no inherent power of the court under Part 26 of the Companies Act 2006 to bind third parties to a scheme. To the extent that a scheme relates to any third party that is not a member of the relevant class of shareholders or creditors, that person must agree to be bound to the scheme before the court may assert jurisdiction over them. The third party can do this either contractually or by way of an undertaking to the court.

30 *Far East Capital SA* [2017] EWHC 2878 (Ch); *Re Noble Group Limited* [2018] EWHC 3092 (Ch).

This approach to third-party releases can be justified by a need to prevent scheme creditors undermining the terms of the scheme itself. There are, however, limits on the jurisdictional definition of 'arrangement' for this purpose.[31] These releases have the potential to be rather tangential to the relationship between the members/creditors and the scheme company. What amounts to a sufficient connection cannot be laid down with any definitiveness, but a wholly unconnected debt would certainly fail. Care is needed to determine which are sufficiently closely connected to be brought within the scheme.[32]

A related question that arises is whether the concept of a 'compromise or arrangement' is broad enough to include the imposition of financial obligations. In *Re Apcoa Parking Holdings GmbH*,[33] dissenting creditors argued that a new guarantee facility to be entered into pursuant to the terms of the schemes imposed upon the creditors a new obligation to indemnify the issuing bank.[34] Hildyard J inclined to the view that the scheme jurisdiction does not enable new and additional financial obligations to be imposed on creditors, such as requiring them to provide new guarantees and indemnities to third parties: 'I am not persuaded that obligations may be imposed under a scheme of arrangement under Part 26: in a creditors' scheme, it appears to me likely that the jurisdiction exists for the purpose of varying the rights of creditors in their capacity as such, and not imposing on such creditors new obligations.'[35] Hildyard J declined to express a concluded view on this point, but this approach has received the support of Snowden J in *Re Noble Group Ltd*[36] and Zacaroli J in *Re Instant Cash Loans Ltd.*[37] This is in keeping with the idea that while schemes allow existing obligations to be altered or extinguished by a majority (of each class), the imposition of new obligations

[31] See e.g. Lord Neuberger in *Re Lehman Brothers (Europe) International (in administration)* [2009] EWCA Civ 1161 who stated at [83] that 'the decision in *T & N Ltd (No. 3)* . . . on this point [is] near the outer limits of the scope of s. 895'.

[32] In *Re Noble Group Ltd* [2018] EWHC 3092 (Ch) the example was given of a claim by a scheme creditor in negligence against an independent financial advisor who had not cautioned against him buying the investment in the first place, aimed at recouping the difference between the original amount paid for the investment and the consideration provided under the scheme.

[33] [2014] EWHC 3849 (Ch) at [133]–[167].

[34] A similar issue arose in relation to CVAs in *Discovery (Northampton) Ltd* v. *Debenhams Retail Ltd* [2019] EWHC 2441 (Ch), discussed at section 5.6.1.

[35] [2014] EWHC 3849 (Ch) at [164].

[36] [2018] EWHC 2911 (Ch) at [103].

[37] [2019] EWHC 2795 (Ch) at [9].

requires unanimity.[38] It is reasonable for those entering a relationship with a company, as either a creditor or a shareholder, to want to understand the extent of the obligations to which they may become subject. The existence of the scheme jurisdiction means that investors should be aware that their obligations may be varied, potentially without their consent if all of the requirements of the scheme are met. The ability of the scheme to be used to impose new obligations without the consent of the individual investor would be more problematic and could undermine investors' willingness to invest in the first place. The imposition of a new obligation towards a third party should therefore be distinguished from the release of an existing obligation to third parties for this purpose. The courts will need to be alert to this issue as the distinction between varying rights and imposing new obligations may not always be clear.

The English courts have been supportive of the applicability and effectiveness of schemes, seeing them as a means of allowing a company, with the support of the requisite majorities, to force upon dissenting or non-voting creditors/members any arrangement to which they could themselves have unanimously agreed.[39] This even extends to sanctioning schemes affecting third-party rights where these are incidental to, and critical for protecting the value of, the main arrangement. The wide interpretation of 'compromise or arrangement' adopted by the courts is a benefit to those that seek to make use of the scheme jurisdiction; there are some limits imposed on this term, but they are narrowly drawn.

2.1.2 The meaning of 'company'

The statute provides two meanings for the word 'company' under Part 26 of the Companies Act 2006.[40] Where an order is sought under section 900 of the Companies Act 2006[41] (i.e. a scheme is proposed for the

[38] Although the cases to date have considered this issue in the context of creditor schemes, the same reasoning can be applied in shareholder schemes and is in keeping with the fact that under Companies Act 2006, s. 25(1), the general meeting cannot oblige shareholders to commit more capital.

[39] See e.g. *Re Guardian Assurance* [1917] 1 Ch 431; *Anglo Continental Supply Company Ltd* [1922] 2 Ch 723; *Re Norfolk Island and Byron Bay Whaling Co Ltd* (1969) 90 WN (NSW) 351.

[40] LLPs can also make use of Part 26 of the Companies Act 2006 as a result of the Limited Liability Partnerships (Application of the Companies Act 2006) Regulations 2009 (SI 1804/2009), reg. 45.

[41] Companies Act 2006, s. 895(2)(a).

reconstruction of any company or companies, or for the amalgamation of two or more companies)[42] then the word 'company' means a company within the meaning of the Companies Act 2006. Broadly, this means a company formed and registered under that Act.[43] For all other purposes the word 'company' means 'any company liable to be wound up under the Insolvency Act 1986'.[44]

The Insolvency Act 1986 confers powers upon the court to wind up both registered and unregistered companies. For this purpose, 'unregistered companies' are defined broadly: 'the expression . . . includes . . . any association and any company' with the exception of a company registered under the Companies Act 2006 in any part of the United Kingdom.[45]

Two issues have arisen in relation to the boundaries of this seemingly very broad provision. The first relates to whether unincorporated associations can be included. The second concerns whether foreign companies can be brought within this definition.

2.1.2.1 Unincorporated associations

A question has arisen whether the term 'unregistered company' can include an unincorporated association, so that the court has jurisdiction to sanction a scheme proposed by such an association. Although the definition of 'unregistered company' for this purpose includes the phrase '*any* association',[46] it has been recognised that this phrase cannot be given its literal meaning.[47] Some unincorporated associations are not the kinds of organisation that are liable to be wound up, being more in the nature of clubs.[48] The question for the court is whether Parliament reasonably intended that an unincorporated association of the sort before the court should be subject to the statutory winding-up procedure.[49]

In considering this question the court will need to examine the constitution of the association as provided for in its rules, to determine whether it should be regarded as a mere club, and therefore not an association

42 See section 4.2.3.1.
43 The definition is found in Companies Act 2006, s. 1.
44 Ibid., s. 895(2)(b). The formula in s. 895(2)(b) 'has stood substantially unchanged for over a century': *Re Rodenstock GmbH* [2011] EWHC 1104 (Ch); [2012] BCC 459 at [18] *per* Briggs J.
45 Insolvency Act 1986, s. 220(1). For the meaning of the phrase 'winding up of unregistered companies' see s. 221.
46 Ibid., emphasis added.
47 *Re Witney Town Football and Social Club* [1994] 2 BCLC 487.
48 Ibid. at 490–1.
49 *Re International Tin Council* [1989] Ch 309 at 330.

liable to be wound up. In *Re St James's Club* the Lord Chancellor considered the nature and constitution of 'clubs' for this purpose:[50]

> [T]hey are, generally speaking ... all formed on this principle: the candidate must be elected, he must then pay an entrance fee, and also an annual sum or subscription. In this club there was a rule under which, if the person elected did not pay the entrance fee and annual subscription, he ceased to be a member; there was also an express rule, that if a member's conduct was objectionable out of the house, he might be dismissed from being a member. What, then, were the interests and liabilities of a member? He had an interest in the general assets as long as he remained a member, and if the club was broken up while he was a member, he might file a bill to have its assets administered in this Court, and he would be entitled to share in the furniture and effects of the club; but he had no transmissible interest, he had not an interest, in the ordinary sense of the term capital in partnership transactions; it was a simple right of admission to, and enjoyment of, the club while it continued.

As a result, the sorts of factor that the court will consider when determining this issue will be whether the members incurred any liability as members, other than for their subscriptions, and whether there is anything else about the association that makes it unlike the club described by the Lord Chancellor in *Re St James's Club*.[51] Where the constitution of the association renders it analogous to the club described by the Lord Chancellor, it is unlikely to be considered an 'unregistered company' for scheme purposes.

In *Re Witney Town Football and Social Club*,[52] for example, creditors petitioned for the compulsory winding-up of the club, but their petition was dismissed. The club's rules were similar to those of many other social and sporting clubs. Morritt J held that the members did not constitute a partnership, nor, under the club rules, did they incur any liability as members except for their subscriptions. There was nothing in the rules meaning that 'the club has legal attributes other than those referred to by the Lord Chancellor, [which] renders it not a club within "the ordinary acceptation" of the term'.[53] This association was properly understood as a club and therefore not subject to being wound up under section 220 of the Insolvency Act 1986.

[50] (1852) 2 De GM & G 383 at 387.

[51] For discussion of the factors which may be relevant see *Re Witney Town Football and Social Club* [1994] 2 BCLC 487 at 491.

[52] Ibid.

[53] Ibid. at 491.

2.1.2.2 Foreign companies

Second, it may be asked whether foreign companies fall within the scope of these provisions. Does the English court have jurisdiction to sanction a scheme of arrangement relating to a company that is incorporated outside England, say in Germany, Singapore or the Cayman Islands, which has no establishment in England? This issue has arisen for discussion in the context of financially distressed companies situated outside the UK wishing to make use of the English scheme jurisdiction.[54]

The facts of *Re Rodenstock GmbH* illustrate the situation. In this case a German company, Rodenstock GmbH, was solvent but heading rapidly towards insolvency. The company was part of the Rodenstock group, Europe's fourth-largest manufacturer and distributor of spectacle lenses and frames. Its headquarters were in Munich, and its main distribution facilities were in Europe and Thailand. It wanted to restructure its debt and, in particular, to bind the senior lenders to a variation of their rights, in order to allow the company to implement a restructuring. This was intended to enable it to avoid going into a German insolvency process. The court was asked to consider whether this German-registered company could make use of the English scheme of arrangement procedure and, more particularly, whether the English court had jurisdiction to sanction such a scheme.

The first question to be considered is whether a foreign company is a 'company' for the purposes of a scheme. The starting point is the definition of 'company' in section 895(2)(b) of the Companies Act 2006, namely 'any company liable to be wound up under the Insolvency Act 1986'. The Insolvency Act 1986 enables the court to wind up foreign companies, such as Rodenstock GmbH, since they are regarded as unregistered companies under the Act and subsequent case law.[55] Furthermore, it is apparent from the Insolvency Act 1986 that it confers jurisdiction to wind up both insolvent and solvent companies, with no express jurisdictional restriction referable to the company's place of incorporation, centre of main interest (COMI) or establishment.[56] On

[54] The cross-border issues arising in relation to schemes are addressed further in Chapter 7. For the position in relation to Scottish companies see Insolvency Act 1986, ss. 117 and 120 which allocate jurisdiction to the High Court to wind up any company registered in England, and to the Scottish Court of Session to wind up a Scottish company. As it does not have jurisdiction to wind up a Scottish company, the English High Court appears unable to sanction a scheme in relation to such a company.

[55] See e.g. *Banque des Marchands de Moscou (Koupetschesky)* v. *Kindersley* [1951] Ch 112.

[56] Insolvency Act 1986, ss. 220 and 221. For discussion see section 7.2.1.

the face of the Insolvency Act 1986, a foreign company is liable to be wound up under the Act, and therefore is a 'company' for scheme purposes.

However, the English court will not wind up a foreign company unless a number of additional conditions are satisfied.[57] In the context of schemes this means that the court will regard itself as having jurisdiction to sanction the scheme only if the foreign company has a sufficient connection with England and the court is satisfied that there is a reasonable prospect of the scheme being effective having regard, in particular, to its prospects for recognition in other relevant jurisdictions. In *Rodenstock*, the company was incorporated in Germany and had its COMI there. It had neither an establishment in England nor any assets in England likely to be affected by the scheme. In fact, the only real connection was the senior lenders' choice of English law and English jurisdiction to govern their lending relationship with the company. Nevertheless, Briggs J held that this was a sufficient connection, and exercised his discretion to sanction this scheme. This issue is discussed in detail in Chapter 7.

2.2 Application to the court for meetings to be summoned

The first stage in the scheme process is the application to the court for meetings of the members/creditors, or classes thereof, to be summoned. This section will consider who may apply for an order, including the issue of whether hostile schemes are possible, that is, schemes initiated by a shareholder or creditor in circumstances where the company does not approve of the scheme. It will also consider the need for an explanatory statement regarding the scheme to be produced, and the role of the court at this convening hearing.

2.2.1 Who may apply for an order?

Once the proposed scheme has been formulated, an application must then be made to the court to order meetings of the creditors or members, or classes thereof, to be summoned.[58] The application for the order giving directions for the meetings to approve a scheme can be made by

[57] See sections 7.2.2 and 7.3.

[58] Companies Act 2006, s. 896(1). Applications are governed by CPR Pt 49 and para. 15 of Practice Direction 49A which requires that the claim form be supported by written evidence, including the statutory information about the company and the terms of the proposed compromise or arrangement. The claim form must seek (i)

the company, by any creditor or member of the company, or by the company's liquidator or administrator.[59] It is usual for the application to be made by the company, either via its board or via a liquidator or administrator. However, it is possible for an application to be made by a creditor or member, a point made explicit by the terms of the Companies Act 2006.[60] The question then arises as to whether a shareholder or creditor can initiate a scheme in circumstances where the company does not approve of it, that is, whether a hostile scheme is possible.

This point arose for discussion in *Re Savoy Hotel Ltd* in which a shareholder, Trust House Forte Ltd, sought to acquire control of the company, Savoy Hotel Ltd, using a scheme of arrangement.[61] The shareholder sought an order of the court to convene shareholder meetings to consider the scheme, but this application was opposed by the company, which did not support the scheme. There was little authority on this point, since schemes are generally initiated by the company, but previous cases had tended to suggest that the court has no jurisdiction to sanction a scheme in such circumstances.[62] Nourse J concluded that this was the correct approach. Ever since schemes were introduced, in the Joint Stock Companies Arrangement Act 1870, the legislation has provided for a scheme to be a compromise or arrangement proposed *between* a company and its creditors or members.[63] Nourse J stated:

directions for the convening of the meetings of members/creditors; (ii) the sanction of the court to the compromise or arrangement, if it is approved at the meeting(s) and a direction for a further hearing for that purpose; and (iii) a direction that the claimant file a copy of a report to the court by the chairman of the meeting, or of each meeting. Applications under s. 896 of the 2006 Act (to convene a meeting or meetings of creditors or members) may be listed before either an Insolvency and Companies Court Judge or a High Court Judge, but applications in respect of a scheme which gives rise to any issues regarding, for example, jurisdiction or class constitution should be listed before a High Court Judge. Applications under s. 899 of the 2006 Act (to sanction a Part 26 scheme) will be listed before a High Court Judge. Where a High Court Judge hears an application under s. 896 the same judge should, if possible, hear the application to sanction the scheme. See Practice Statement (Companies: Schemes of Arrangement under Part 26 and Part 26A of the Companies Act 2006) [2020] 1 WLR 4493.

59 Companies Act 2006, s. 896(2).

60 Ibid., s. 896(2)(b).

61 [1981] Ch 351.

62 See e.g. *In re Oceanic Steam Navigation Co Ltd* [1939] Ch 41 at 46 *per* Simonds J.

63 See Joint Stock Companies Arrangement Act 1870, s. 2 and see now Companies Act 2006, s. 895(1).

> If you were to find an Act of Parliament which referred to an arrangement 'proposed between' a person who was adult and *sui juris* and his creditors, you would assume, first, that that person would have to be a party to the arrangement and secondly, that he would have to consent to it.[64]

The company is a separate legal person and its rights cannot be overridden in the absence of an express or implied provision to that effect. The Act of 1870, in Nourse J's opinion, did not operate to override the company's rights in this way. As a result, the court does not have jurisdiction to sanction a scheme that does not have the approval of the company, either through the board or by means of a simple majority of the members in general meeting, or through the liquidator or administrator.[65] In consequence, the court will not convene meetings on the application of a member or creditor if it is clear that the scheme will not secure the approval of the company.[66] This seems correct both as a matter of statutory interpretation and as a matter of general principle. A scheme must be between a company and its members/creditors, and both sides of the compromise or arrangement need to consent to the alteration of rights that will flow from the scheme once implemented.

Nourse J was then asked to determine a second issue, namely whether, in circumstances such as those in *Re Savoy Hotel Ltd* where a shareholder seeks to make use of a scheme that is not approved by the company, the court can direct at the convening hearing that meetings be held. Nourse J held that even though it does not have jurisdiction to sanction the scheme at the sanctioning hearing, in the absence of the company's approval, nevertheless the court has the power at the convening hearing to direct that meetings be held on the application of a member or creditor.[67] Further, he stated that members or creditors of one class can apply to convene a meeting of another class.[68] However, there is an important restriction on this power: the court will not order such meetings where it is clear that the company's approval will not be obtained, since in those circumstances the court will be unable to sanction the scheme.[69]

64 [1981] Ch 351 at 365.

65 Ibid. at 365–6 *per* Nourse J.

66 In *Re Savoy Hotel* (ibid.), for example, the court refused a request from a shareholder that was opposed by the board and by other shareholders with voting control of the company.

67 Ibid. at 366.

68 Ibid.

69 Ibid.

As a result, hostile schemes are not impossible, but they are difficult to achieve in practice, owing to the need to demonstrate to the court that the consent of the company is likely to be forthcoming before the court will order meetings of the members/creditors to be held. A further practical difficulty that arises where a hostile scheme is launched is the lack of information in the hands of the hostile member/creditor. Take the example of a scheme being used to effect a takeover. The scheme process is usually run by the company, which must make information available to satisfy the relevant disclosure obligations, such as the effect of the scheme, any material interests of the directors and the effect of those interests on the scheme.[70] Ensuring that these disclosure obligations are satisfied will be much harder, if not impossible, where the scheme does not have the support of the target company's board.

2.2.1.1 Hostile member schemes

Following the reasoning in *Re Savoy Hotel Ltd*, it may be possible for a hostile bidder to acquire shares in the target and to obtain a court order convening a meeting, or meetings, as long as it remains possible at that time that the company's approval will be obtained. Whether the company's consent to a scheme is obtained via its board or its members in general meeting will be a matter for the constitution of the company in question. Most articles will vest the power of management in the board, subject to the direction of the shareholders by special resolution.[71] In such circumstances, the court will generally exercise its discretion not to order the meetings, where the board is opposed to the scheme and the directors are unlikely to change their minds. This is what occurred in *Re Savoy Hotel Ltd*. However, in circumstances where the company's articles allow for the decision to be taken by the members in general meeting, it is possible for the requisite consent of the company to be obtained, and therefore for the scheme to go ahead, and for the court to order the meetings to be held, even without the approval of the board. What is more, the possibility of a hostile scheme of arrangement is recognised in the City Code on Takeovers and Mergers, which requires that the Takeover Panel be consulted before a hostile scheme is announced.[72]

[70] Companies Act 2006, s. 897.

[71] See e.g. Model Articles for Private Companies Limited by Shares, Arts. 3 and 4; Model Articles for Public Companies, Arts. 3 and 4: The Companies (Model Articles) Regulations 2008 (SI 3229/2008), Schs. 1 and 3.

[72] City Code on Takeovers and Mergers, App. 7, s. 13.

An example of an attempted hostile scheme of arrangement arose in the UK in 2009, when Goldshield Group was the subject of such a scheme. The scheme was proposed by an entity backed by the private equity fund, HgCapital, and certain members of Goldshield's management team, who collectively held 11.36 per cent of the shares in Goldshield. In other jurisdictions, 'bear hug'-style announcements are common, whereby a potential bidder announces a proposed scheme of arrangement conditional on the support of target directors. However, the proposed hostile scheme involving Goldshield went beyond a 'bear hug' announcement, and contained a statement from the bidder that it would apply to the court for orders convening the scheme meetings. The management team planned to requisition a general meeting to approve the scheme and, meanwhile, to obtain a direction from the court permitting the bidder to circulate a scheme document. Unfortunately for the purposes of resolving this issue, HgCapital's proposal was ultimately recommended by the independent directors of Goldshield and the transaction proceeded by way of a recommended scheme of arrangement.

Another example occurred in Bermuda. Bermudan law in relation to schemes is very similar to that of the UK.[73] Validus Holdings announced a hostile scheme to acquire IPC Holdings. Validus acquired 100 shares in IPC and applied to the court for orders convening a meeting to vote on the proposed scheme. The court noted that embarking on a scheme opposed by the target board remained an unprecedented course and that there were 'severe practical difficulties in piloting such a scheme'.[74] Despite this, the court stressed it did have the power to order the convening of the meeting. However, the court ultimately decided that it was not appropriate to convene the meeting in this particular case as there was no real indication of independent shareholder support sufficient to show that the hostile scheme had some reasonable hope of success.

2.2.1.2 Hostile creditor schemes

A creditor wishing to propose a scheme also needs to demonstrate to the court that the company will approve the scheme.[75] If the company is in

[73] See Bermuda Companies Act 1981, s. 99.

[74] *Validus Holdings Ltd v. IPC Holdings Ltd and Max Capital Group Ltd* [2009] SC (Supreme Court of Bermuda) 25 Civ (13 May 2009), Ground CJ.

[75] Cf. the position in the proposed Dutch scheme (Act on the Confirmation of Private Plans, *Wet homologatie onderhands akkoord*) which is specifically set up to allow stakeholders (other than the debtor) to initiate the procedure, including creditors, shareholders and employee representatives.

liquidation or administration then generally the company's approval will be demonstrated by the approval and support of the liquidator or administrator. Generally, where the liquidator or administrator opposes the creditor's application under the scheme jurisdiction, the court will not sanction the scheme.[76]

2.2.2 *The explanatory statement*

Every notice sent out summoning the meetings must be accompanied by a statement that explains the effect of the compromise or arrangement.[77] The scheme company has a duty to place before members or creditors sufficient information for them to make a reasonable judgement as to whether the scheme is in their interests or not, and hence how to vote.[78] The extent of the information required to be supplied will depend upon the facts of the particular case. Additional guidance on the content of the explanatory statement is provided by the 2020 Practice Statement, which also states that the court at the convening hearing stage must consider the 'adequacy' of the explanatory statement.[79]

It is not enough simply to send the creditors or members a copy of the scheme: the statement must be separate from the scheme and explained in clear language.[80] The court cannot waive the requirement for an explanatory statement. Without an explanatory statement, the court will reject a scheme for non-compliance and require fresh meetings to be convened.[81] It is not the function of

[76] *In re International Contract Co (Hankey's Case)* (1872) 26 LT 358.

[77] Companies Act 2006, s. 897.

[78] *Re Dorman Long & Co Ltd* [1934] Ch 635, 657; *Re Heron International NV* [1994] 1 BCLC 667, 672.

[79] Practice Statement (Companies: Schemes of Arrangement under Part 26 and Part 26A of the Companies Act 2006) [2020] 1 WLR 4493. These include the fact and purpose of the scheme, details of the meetings to be convened and composition of classes for voting, the matters for evidence, and details of the convening hearing from which it should be clear that affected persons are entitled to attend. In *Re ColourOz Investment 2 LLC* [2020] EWHC 1864 (Ch) Snowden J made clear that the reference to the court 'considering the adequacy' of the explanatory statement is not intended to suggest that the court will generally do anything other than to ascertain that the essential elements which it would expect to see in an explanatory statement are present. In particular, the court is not expected to, and cannot, approve the contents or accuracy of the explanatory statement.

[80] *Rankin & Blackmore Ltd* [1950] SC 218 at 223.

[81] Ibid. at 224 (Lord Mackay) and 228 (Lord Patrick); *Peter Scott & Co Ltd* [1950] SLT 310 cf. *Re Clydesdale Bank Ltd* [1950] SLT 123.

the court, however, to approve the contents of the explanatory statement.[82]

In considering the adequacy of disclosure, the court will have regard to compliance by the company with other disclosure obligations applying to the circular,[83] for example under the Companies Act 2006,[84] and any requirements within the company's articles. These will be particularly relevant to communications with members. Where the company has listed securities, it will be subject to various additional disclosure requirements with which it will also need to comply.[85] The fact that the company has listed securities may also mean that there are other, additional, procedural requirements for the company, such as the need to obtain shareholder consent.[86]

The Companies Act 2006 requires, in particular, that the explanatory statement must disclose any material interests of the directors, and the effect of those interests on the scheme.[87] The directors are under a duty to give notice to the company of any information relevant to the explanatory statement.[88] 'Interest' for this purpose extends beyond an interest in the shares of the company to include any material interest in general.[89] Directors' interests as executives or option holders should therefore be disclosed, where the scheme has any bearing on those interests. Presumably a situation where the director is indebted to the company

[82] If, however, the court becomes aware of manifest deficiencies in the explanatory statement, it is entitled to decline to convene the scheme meetings unless and until those deficiencies are corrected: *Re Indah Kiat International Finance Company BV* [2016] EWHC 246 (Ch).

[83] *Re BTR plc* [1999] 2 BCLC 675; *Residues Treatment & Trading Co Ltd* v. *Southern Resources Ltd* (1988) 14 ACLR 375.

[84] Such as Companies Act 2006, s. 1144 and Sch. 5.

[85] For example, the requirement to disclose inside information as soon as possible: Regulation (EU) No 596/2014 of the European Parliament and of the Council of 16 April 2014 on market abuse (repealing Directive 2003/6/EC of the European Parliament and of the Council and Commission Directives 2003/124/EC, 2003/125/EC and 2004/72/EC), Art. 17. For discussion see L. Gullifer and J. Payne, *Corporate Finance Law: Principles and Policy* (3rd ed., Hart, 2020), ch. 11.

[86] E.g. for a company whose shares are listed on the premium section of the Main Market: Listing Rule 10, Listing Rule 11.

[87] Companies Act 2006, s. 897(2) and (3). Where the scheme affects the rights of debenture holders, the statement must give a similar explanation regarding the interests of any trustees for the debenture holders: s. 897(3).

[88] Ibid., s. 898. Failure to do so is a criminal offence. Similar obligations are placed on any relevant trustee for the debenture holders.

[89] It has been suggested that material interests do not include a nominal holding of shares for the purposes of a director's qualification in a company with a substantial issued capital: *City Property Investment Trust Corp Ltd* [1951] SLT 371.

may also need to be disclosed. Also, any alteration to the material interests of directors that might affect the attitude and voting decision of the shareholders or creditors who become aware of it must be communicated to those to whom the circular was sent.[90]

The requirement for an explanatory statement was only introduced into statute in 1947,[91] but even before this innovation the courts were developing common law obligations, requiring disclosure of material interests of directors and, where relevant, trustees of debenture stock, and ensuring that any explanatory statements that were issued provided all of the information necessary to enable the recipients to determine how to vote.[92] The courts have stated that the basic principles for determining adequacy of information contained in the statutory disclosure obligation are the same as those set out in the cases establishing the common law duty of disclosure.[93]

The information provided must be clear and sufficient to enable scheme members and creditors to determine what is proposed, the potential effect upon them, and whether to attend the convening hearing.[94] For creditor schemes it will be important to set out the alternatives if the scheme does not go ahead.[95] The courts expect scheme proponents to be candid about these issues; where, for example, schemes are proposed as having a more advantageous outcome for creditors than formal insolvency proceedings, sufficient detail as to the possible alternatives to the proposed scheme and the basis for the predicted outcomes will need to be provided both in the explanatory statement and as evidence in court.[96] The approach of the courts is summed up by the following statement:

> The essence of the duty is the requirement of reasonableness or fairness in all the circumstances, having regard to the interests of the company as a whole. A surfeit of information may well obscure the purpose of the resolution. A lack of information may constitute misrepresentation by

[90] *Re Jessel Trust Ltd* [1985] BCLC 119. In most cases the courts will assume that the relevant change is one that might influence shareholders/creditors and therefore will require a further circular.

[91] Companies Act 1947, s. 40. This followed a recommendation of the Cohen Committee: Cohen Committee's Report on Company Law Amendment (Cmnd 6659, 1945).

[92] *Re Dorman Long & Co Ltd* [1934] Ch 635 at 657 *per* Maugham J.

[93] *Re RAC Motoring Services Ltd* [2000] 1 BCLC 307 at 326–7 *per* Neuberger J.

[94] Ibid. For an example of a case in which the material in the explanatory statement was felt to be inadequate see *Re Indah Kiat International Finance Company BV* [2016] EWHC 246 (Ch). A similar approach has been adopted in Singapore: *Pathfinder Strategic Credit LP* v. *Empire Capital Resources Pte Ltd* [2019] SGCA 29.

[95] For discussion of this issue see *Re Indah Kiat*, ibid. at [70]–[80].

[96] *Re Van Gansewinkel Groep BV & Ors* [2015] EWHC 2151 (Ch) at [24] *per* Snowden J.

> omission. It is a matter of sensible judgment by the directors in each case and ultimately by the court if complaint is made to it.[97]

Therefore, in general, the courts have applied strict standards of disclosure to this circular: '[I]n dealing with disclosure or nondisclosure of material interests of directors in the context of [schemes of arrangement], the court must for obvious reasons of public policy approach the matter strictly and can only tolerate nondisclosure in a case where it is satisfied that it is essentially of a *de minimis* nature.'[98] Where the explanatory statement is misleading and has not been corrected, the courts may order that the member/creditor meetings be reconvened, after a revised explanatory statement has been provided.[99] If, however, the members or creditors have been provided with materially inaccurate, incomplete or otherwise inadequate information, and this has not been revised, the court will most likely not be able to place any reliance upon, or give effect to, an affirmative vote at the class meeting when it comes to the sanctioning stage.[100]

However, the courts have been prepared to apply a more relaxed standard where they believe that no reasonable member or creditor would have changed their decision on the scheme had the information been disclosed.[101] Moreover, even where there are imperfections in the explanatory material, if no member or creditor suggests that it has been misled, the courts may nevertheless be satisfied with the disclosures:

> [T]he question is not whether the circular might not have been differently framed, but whether there is any reasonable ground for supposing that such imperfections as may be found in the circular have had, with or without other circumstances, the result that the majority (who have approved the proposal placed before them) have done so under some serious misapprehension of the position.[102]

[97] *Residues Treatment & Trading Co Ltd* v. *Southern Resources Ltd* [1988] 14 ACLR 375 at 378 *per* White J, quoted with approval by Neuberger J in *Re RAC Motoring Services Ltd* [2000] 1 BCLC 307 at 326–7.

[98] *Re Jessel Trust Ltd* [1985] BCLC 119 at 127 *per* Slade J. In that case the information was correct when sent but altered subsequently. Slade J refused to sanction the scheme despite the fact that there were substantial majorities in favour and no one appeared in court to oppose the petition.

[99] *Re Dorman Long & Co Ltd* [1934] Ch 635.

[100] The court is, however, alert to the fact that in some instances claims about the inadequacy of information in an explanatory statement may be a tactic used by those who seek to disrupt a scheme without legitimate cause, see e.g. *Re Stronghold Insurance Company Limited* [2018] EWHC 2909 (Ch); *Re Ophir Energy plc* [2019] EWHC 1278 (Ch).

[101] *Re Minster Assets plc* [1985] BCLC 200.

[102] *Re Imperial Chemical Industries Ltd* [1936] 2 Ch 587 at 618 *per* Clauson J.

The court is also prepared to take into account the level of sophistication of the recipients in determining whether the information provided is adequate. For example, where a scheme is being proposed as an alternative to liquidation, and all of the known creditors are sophisticated institutions, the fact that the scheme documents do not spell out every instance in which the scheme differs from the outcome in liquidation will not of itself prevent the scheme from being sanctioned.[103]

The court will generally require that the notice of class meetings convened under Part 26 of the Companies Act 2006 be advertised. Any advertisement must include either the text of the explanatory statement or notification as to how those entitled to attend and vote at the meeting can obtain a copy. This form of notification is important since that may be the only way to notify some members/creditors.[104]

2.2.3 The court's role at the convening hearing

The court is 'emphatically not'[105] concerned with the merits or fairness of the scheme at this stage.[106] Instead, the court is concerned with a number of practical issues. The approach of the court is to exercise jurisdiction in a flexible and purposive manner, bearing in mind that the purpose of the regime is to facilitate compromises and arrangements between companies and their members or creditors.[107]

One of the key issues at this hearing is deciding whether the members or creditors should be split into separate classes for the purpose of voting on the scheme.[108] In addition the court will consider a number of practical issues regarding the holding of these class meetings, and otherwise will consider any other essential issue which, if decided against the

103 *Re Telewest Communications plc (No. 1)* [2004] EWHC 924 (Ch).

104 Companies Act 2006, ss. 897(1)(b), 897(4). Breach of any of the obligations in s. 897 is a criminal offence by the company and any officer in default (s. 897(5)–(8)).

105 *Re Indah Kiat International Finance Company BV* [2016] EWHC 246 (Ch) at [39] *per* Snowden J.

106 *Re Telewest Communications plc (No. 1)* [2004] EWHC 924 (Ch) at [14].

107 See e.g. *Re SABMiller plc* [2016] EWHC 2153 (Ch).

108 The substantive issues regarding different classes of creditors and members are discussed in section 2.3.2. Some jurisdictions allow class meetings to be dispensed with in some circumstances; see e.g. Indian Companies Act 2013, s. 230(9) which gives the National Company Law Tribunal (NCLT) power to dispense with the meeting of creditors or classes of them where at least 90 per cent of creditors by value swear that they agree to the scheme by way of affidavit (while on its face this provision does not apply to meetings of members; see *Re DLF Phase IV Commercial Developers Ltd* (NCLAT, 19 August 2019)).

scheme company, would mean that the court simply has no jurisdiction or would unquestionably refuse to sanction the scheme.[109]

In general, the courts have a vital part to play in scheme cases, ensuring that the requisite processes are followed and that minorities are protected from potential abuse,[110] and although this protective role is more obvious at the sanctioning stage, the courts also play an important part at the convening hearing. A key aspect of minority protection in schemes arises from the fact that the members and creditors meet and vote on the scheme in classes, and determining the correct composition of those classes is therefore central to that minority protection. Furthermore, there is no doubt that providing full and accurate disclosure to creditors and members is crucial to enable them to spot abuse and to decide how to respond to the proposed scheme.[111] As Snowden J stated in *Re Indah Kiat International Finance Company BV*,

> the court is not bound to accept at face value bare assertions in the evidence in relation to class composition or any other matter. At the convening hearing, the applicant company has the burden of adducing evidence of sufficient quality and credibility to persuade the court to act. Further, and importantly, whether or not there is any opposition, the company proposing a scheme of arrangement has a duty to make full and frank disclosure to the court of all material facts and matters which may be relevant to any decision that the court is asked to make. The scheme jurisdiction can only work properly and command respect internationally if parties invoking the jurisdiction exhibit the utmost candour with the court.[112]

By considering jurisdictional issues at the convening hearing, the courts can also address potential problems at an early stage. Recent case law has demonstrated a willingness on the part of the court to be active in fulfilling these roles at the convening hearing.

Two notes of caution have been sounded by the courts, however. First, there is a balance to be struck between those promoting the scheme and those opposing it, and while many of the issues discussed in this section seek to ensure that the courts will properly scrutinise the behaviour of the first group, the legitimacy of the actions of the latter group may also

[109] The 2020 Practice Statement states that, if possible, applications should be listed before the same judge at both the convening hearing and the sanctioning hearing: Practice Statement (Companies: Schemes of Arrangement under Part 26 and Part 26A of the Companies Act 2006) [2020] 1 WLR 4493.

[110] See J. Payne, 'The role of the court in debt restructuring' (2018) 77 *Cambridge Law Journal* 124.

[111] See e.g. *Re Van Gansewinkel Groep BV & Ors* [2015] EWHC 2151 (Ch).

[112] [2016] EWHC 246 (Ch) at [40].

require attention. Hildyard J in *Re Stronghold Insurance Company Limited* commented that he had

> experienced a growing tendency for [opposing] creditors to purport to reserve their position by floating or trailing generic points without proper explanation, elaboration or evidential base, often with the expressed expectation of returning to their points (or some of them) in the future (usually the Sanction stage) . . . This developing tendency places a growing burden, not only on the Company (which has an obligation to do its best to address and deal candidly with points of substance going to the court's jurisdiction or likely to affect its proper exercise), but also on the court, which is obliged to sift through disparate and sometimes undeveloped points without proper assistance.[113]

Second, there are limits to what the courts can achieve at this stage. The move towards addressing issues such as class composition at the convening hearing rather than at the sanctioning decision is sensible and has proved a popular change from previous practice. However, this should not be taken to mean that all issues regarding the court's jurisdiction can and should be addressed at this early stage.[114] As discussed below, there are good reasons for leaving some jurisdictional issues to be determined at the sanctioning hearing. Furthermore, the courts have emphasised that the convening stage is not an appropriate occasion to consider the fairness of the proposed scheme, which is a matter dealt with at the sanction hearing.[115]

2.2.3.1 The determination of classes

Until 2001, the court would offer no guidance to the company on the issue of class meetings at this stage.[116] Instead it would consider the issue at the sanctioning stage, when the only option for the court, if the wrong class meetings had been held, was to refuse to sanction the scheme. This practice was criticised by the Company Law Review (CLR)[117] and,

113 [2018] EWHC 2909 (Ch) at [142]–[143]. See also *Re Ophir Energy plc* [2019] EWHC 1278 (Ch).

114 See e.g. *Re Stronghold Insurance Company Limited* [2018] EWHC 2909 (Ch).

115 Ibid. at [34].

116 See e.g. *Re Hellenic & General Trust Ltd* [1976] 1 WLR 123.

117 Company Law Review, *Modern Company Law for a Competitive Economy: Completing the Structure*, URN 00/1335, November 2000 (CLR, *Completing the Structure*) at 207. The Company Law Review also proposed other changes to the procedure at this stage (see CLR, *Modern Company Law for a Competitive Economy: Final Report*, URN 01/942, July 2001, (CLR, *Final Report*), paras. 13.6–7) which have not been implemented. In particular the CLR suggested that the court should have the discretion to sanction the scheme even if appropriate class meetings had not been held, provided the court felt that the composition of the meetings had not had a substantive effect on the outcome.

subsequently, by Chadwick LJ in *Re Hawk Insurance Co Ltd*,[118] since it involved a considerable amount of wasted time and expense.

In 2002 a Practice Statement was issued, designed to produce substantive consideration of classes of creditors at the convening hearing.[119] This was replaced by an updated Practice Statement in 2020,[120] which expands on the original statement and encompasses Part 26A restructuring plans[121] as well as schemes of arrangement. The Practice Statement provides that the onus is on the applicant company to identify the correct classes, but it must draw the court's attention to any potential problems at the initial application. The Practice Statement requires all relevant members and creditors to be notified of the scheme unless there are very good reasons for not doing so. If they only object at the later sanctioning hearing, the court will expect them to show good reason why the issue was not raised at the earlier stage.[122] Whilst the court's decision on these matters at the convening stage is not final, the courts have asserted that the applicant has a legitimate expectation that, unless circumstances materially alter or fresh considerations are put before it which the court accepts should be addressed, the court will not of its own motion change its mind.[123]

Although the position in relation to classes of members was not dealt with in the 2002 Practice Statement, the criticisms made by the CLR and the court in *Hawk Insurance* apply equally to that situation,[124] and where difficult issues arise regarding the composition of classes of members, there is no reason why these same principles should not apply to those classes. This point has been clarified in the 2020 Practice Statement, which explicitly includes classes of members within its ambit.

It may be asked whether the court's role at the convening hearing should be even more definitive. In other words, should the court have the power to make binding determinations on class composition at this stage?[125] The

118 [2001] EWCA Civ 241; [2002] BCC 300.

119 *Practice Statement (Ch D: Schemes of Arrangement with Creditors)* [2002] 1 WLR 1345, which replaced *Practice Note* [1934] WN 142.

120 Practice Statement (Companies: Schemes of Arrangement under Part 26 and Part 26A of the Companies Act 2006) [2020] 1 WLR 4493.

121 See section 5.8.

122 See e.g. *DX Holdings Ltd* [2010] EWHC 1513 (Ch) at [9].

123 See e.g. *Re Hawk Insurance* [2001] EWCA Civ 241; [2001] 2 BCLC 480 at [21]; *Re Global Garden Products Italy SpA* [2016] EWHC 1884 (Ch) at [43]; *Re Lehman Bros International (Europe) Ltd* [2018] EWHC 1980 (Ch) at [72].

124 This was acknowledged in *Re SABMiller plc* [2016] EWHC 2153 (Ch) at [20], and see *Smith & Williamson Holdings Ltd* [2019] EWHC 3021 (Ch) [15]–[18].

125 This issue has arisen for discussion in Australia: see e.g. Corporations and Markets Advisory Committee (CAMAC), *Members' Schemes of Arrangement*, Discussion Paper,

CLR recommended that the court should be able to make binding determinations of this kind at the convening hearing, at the request of those proposing the scheme.[126] Although the CLR's suggestion received some initial support from the Department of Trade and Industry,[127] it did not find its way into the 2006 Act.[128] There are some practical benefits to this suggestion, but there are also potential concerns. In particular, such an approach could lead to an increase in the costs of the convening hearing and in delay. More problematically, some issues may only come to light after this hearing, such as the fact that some shareholders have links to a bidder that is attempting to take control of the company via a scheme of arrangement. Contrary to the CLR's proposal, it is preferable for the court to retain the flexibility to determine at the sanctioning hearing that classes were inappropriately constituted.[129]

2.2.3.2 The determination of other issues

2.2.3.2.1 Jurisdictional issues The 2020 Practice Statement requires scheme proponents to bring to the court's attention at the convening hearing any issues as to the existence of the court's jurisdiction to sanction the scheme, and any other issue not going to the merits or fairness of the scheme but which might lead the court to refuse to sanction the scheme.[130] Where proponents of a scheme do intend to raise jurisdictional issues of these kinds at the convening hearing (i.e. matters other than class composition), those issues will need to be indicated in the letter notifying creditors/members of the convening hearing.[131]

June 2008, para. 4.1.2 and *Members' Schemes of Arrangement*, Report, December 2009, para. 5.1.2.

126 CLR, *Final Report*, note 117 above, paras. 13.5–6.

127 DTI, *Company Law Reform – White Paper*, March 2005, para. 4.14, in which it was stated that the 'generally technical changes' suggested by the Company Law Review regarding schemes would be included in the Bill.

128 No explanation for this change appears in the explanatory statement accompanying the Act. However, when this provision was debated by the House of Lords' Grand Committee, the view seems to have been taken that the Practice Statement would largely deal with this issue, and that any further amendment to the legislative provisions would unduly threaten minority rights: House of Lords, official report, 28 March 2006, cols GC 324–6 (Lord Goldsmith).

129 CAMAC did not ultimately recommend that this reform be introduced: CAMAC, *Members' Schemes of Arrangement*, Report, December 2009, at 91.

130 Practice Statement (Companies: Schemes of Arrangement under Part 26 and Part 26A of the Companies Act 2006) [2020] 1 WLR 4493, [6].

131 *Re Van Gansewinkel Groep BV & Ors* [2015] EWHC 2151 (Ch) at [55] and [56].

One example of a jurisdictional issue which the court has been asked to determine at the convening stage arises in member schemes as a result of a change in the law in 2015. This involved an amendment of section 641 of the Companies Act 2006 and prohibits a company from reducing its share capital as part of a scheme of arrangement where the purpose of the scheme is to acquire all the shares of the company, except where the acquisition amounts to a restructuring that inserts a new holding company into the group structure.[132] In some cases companies involved in a restructuring of a company have sought guidance from the court at the convening hearing that the scheme in question is not prohibited by this amendment.[133]

Another example of such an issue is whether the court has jurisdiction to sanction a scheme relating to a foreign company.[134] In brief, the English court will have such jurisdiction where the scheme company is a company 'that is liable to be wound up under the Insolvency Act 1986'[135] and there is a sufficient connection with England to justify the exercise of the court's scheme jurisdiction in relation to a foreign company. This is closely related to the question of whether the scheme, if approved, would be recognised and thus have a substantial effect abroad.[136] As a result of the rising popularity of schemes of arrangement by overseas companies, it is increasingly the case that jurisdictional issues are raised at the convening hearing, and the 2020 Practice Statement underlines this requirement.

In consequence there is a basic requirement for a foreign scheme company to adduce at the convening hearing some evidence of a connection with England and of the prospects that the scheme will be recognised and given effect in relevant jurisdictions where there are assets (or creditors) abroad, so as at least to satisfy the court that there is a realistic prospect of the court ultimately sanctioning the scheme.

Whilst courts can potentially consider such jurisdictional issues at the convening hearing, the court is 'likely to be cautious'[137] in this context. This is for a number of reasons. The court at the convening stage will not

[132] The Companies Act 2006 (Amendment of Part 17) Regulations 2015 (SI 472/2015).

[133] See e.g. *Re Home Retail Group plc* [2016] EWHC 2072 (Ch); *Re Old Mutual plc* [2018] EWHC 873 (Ch); *Re Galliford Try plc* [2019] EWHC 3252 (Ch) discussed in section 4.2.2.

[134] See e.g. *Re Noble Group Ltd* [2018] EWHC 2911 (Ch).

[135] Companies Act 2006, s. 895(2).

[136] See e.g. *Re Magyar Telecom* BV [2013] EWHC 3800 (Ch) at [21] *per* David Richards J. For detailed discussion see Chapter 7.

[137] *Re Stronghold Insurance Company Limited* [2018] EWHC 2909 (Ch) at [32] *per* Hildyard J.

want to bind the hands of the court at the sanctioning hearing and will not want its determination of a jurisdictional issue to be used 'as a basis for persuading the judge at the sanction hearing not to revisit the question'[138] unless this is made very clear to the convening hearing judge and the judgment is given on that basis. Even then, the sanctioning court will not be bound by the decision taken at the convening hearing, though the court is unlikely to depart from a reasoned conclusion given at an earlier stage without a change of circumstance having occurred or some other very good reason. Furthermore, given the focus of the court at the convening hearing on those matters which, if decided against the scheme company, would mean that the court simply has no jurisdiction or would unquestionably refuse to sanction the scheme, the court is unlikely to wish to deal with issues involving a discretionary element or value judgement.[139] As Snowden J acknowledged in *Re Indah Kiat International Finance Company BV*, it will usually be the case that these kinds of issues 'will most appropriately be determined after a full review of the evidence and together with the other discretionary factors that fall for consideration at the sanction stage'.[140]

The courts have therefore sought to find a meaningful compromise in relation to this issue. While there is no merit in pursuing a scheme which is unlikely to be sanctioned owing to lack of jurisdiction, questions such as whether the company has a sufficient connection and whether the scheme will achieve a substantial effect do not have a simple yes/no answer. Indeed, some of the relevant considerations may not be known before the sanction stage, such as how many overseas creditors with what value of claim voted in the scheme. The compromise solution suggested by Snowden J in *Re Noble* is that the company can legitimately ask at the convening stage whether it is obvious that the court has no jurisdiction to sanction the scheme, or whether there are other factors which would unquestionably lead the court to refuse to exercise its discretion to sanction the scheme.[141] This appears to be a slight drawing back of the court's role in determining these issues at the convening hearing.

[138] *Re Van Gansewinkel Groep BV & Ors* [2015] EWHC 2151 (Ch) at [56] *per* Snowden J.

[139] *Re Stronghold Insurance Company Limited* [2018] EWHC 2909 (Ch).

[140] [2016] EWHC 246 (Ch) at [88]. Although Snowden J did not rule out the possibility that an opposing creditor might succeed in demonstrating at a convening hearing that the scheme company's evidence in relation to connection and recognition manifestly failed to pass even this low initial hurdle, 'that would, I think, be an unusual case' (at [89]).

[141] *Re Noble Group Limited* [2018] EWHC 2911 (Ch) at [76]; *Re ColourOz Investment 2 LLC* [2020] EWHC 1864 (Ch).

It is clearly correct that not all issues affecting the jurisdiction of the court will be dealt with at the convening hearing, and the courts have taken pains to emphasise that no inference can be drawn that the court is satisfied as to jurisdiction merely from the fact that the scheme in question has proceeded beyond the first stage.[142]

2.2.3.2.2 Practical matters In addition to determining the composition of the creditor and member meetings at the convening hearing, the court has a wide discretion to order these meetings on such terms as it thinks fit.[143] Meetings under Part 26 of the Companies Act 2006 are meetings of the relevant members/creditors, or classes thereof, and not meetings of the company. As a result, the provisions of the Companies Act 2006 in relation to meetings do not, in general, apply to meetings of members or creditors convened under the scheme jurisdiction.[144] The articles of the company, in so far as they relate to meetings of the company, are also irrelevant for the same reason. The basis on which the meetings are to be conducted is therefore a matter for the court.[145] The order convening the meeting will generally identify the chairman of the meeting and any substitutes, will order the time and place of the meeting, and the court will generally give directions about matters such as the date by reference to which rights to vote will be determined, and the forms of proxy.[146]

The Covid-19 pandemic caused the court to consider the construction of the word 'meeting' where it appears in Part 26 of the Companies Act 2006, and in particular whether it requires all members/creditors to be able to attend a physical meeting in the same place.[147] If yes, then scheme

[142] *Re Stronghold Insurance Company Limited* [2018] EWHC 2909 (Ch) at [33].

[143] See *Re Dorman, Long and Co Ltd* [1934] Ch 635; *Re Dee Valley Group plc* [2017] EWHC 184 (Ch) at [50].

[144] Companies Act 2006, Part 13.

[145] See e.g. *Re RhythmOne plc* [2019] EWHC 967 (Ch) in which Norris J accepted that the court has an inherent jurisdiction to give directions as to how the meeting should be held and conducted, and an inherent jurisdiction to waive any non-compliance with the directions given (at [14]). He held that this does not come to an end with the making of the order for the convening of meetings and thus at the sanctioning hearing he held that, although there had not been strict compliance with the initial order, the omission to send the scheme documents to five shareholders who purchased shares on the record date had no serious impact and that accordingly there was no need to go to the trouble of convening further meetings.

[146] The right to vote by proxy is specified by the Companies Act 2006, s. 899(1).

[147] *Re Castle Trust Direct plc* [2020] EWHC 969 (Ch).

meetings would not be able to take place during a period of national lockdown.[148] In *Re Castle Trust Direct plc*, Trower J held that

> the word 'meeting' has to be construed in the context of the purpose for which it is used. The purpose is the mechanism by which creditors or shareholders are able to come together and consult with each other, should they choose to do so, in order to make a collective decision on the rearrangement or compromise of their rights against the company. It follows that the question is whether what is proposed enables that to happen by a process which has the essential characteristics of a meeting. In my judgment those essential characteristics are a coming together sufficient to enable a consultation to take place.[149]

Accordingly, it is possible for a scheme meeting to be held electronically, whether via some form of video link[150] or by a combination of telephone and webinar, as was proposed in that case. The judge stressed, rightly, that what is key is whether the proposed meeting is sufficient to amount to 'a coming together' with the ability to consult.[151] However, where a meeting is held by electronic means the court will be particularly concerned to ensure at the sanction stage that the meeting did in fact constitute a coming together for the purposes of a consultation. The court is likely to require evidence as to how the technology worked and whether or not there were any difficulties for participating creditors in their ability to hear, ask questions or express opinions at the meeting and whether their ability to contribute to the business of the meeting was otherwise impaired. If such difficulties do occur, it may be that the court at the sanctioning hearing would be unable to conclude that there had indeed been a coming together of creditors, albeit electronically, in a manner sufficient to amount to a meeting. The judge also stated that remote meetings will not necessarily be appropriate in the future in relation to other companies: each case will have to be decided on its own facts having full regard to the effect of any social distancing measures then in force.

It is notable that in other jurisdictions that have schemes of arrangement the statutory provisions sometimes contain less detail regarding the procedural aspects of schemes than is found in the English

[148] See The Health Protection (Coronavirus Restrictions) (England) Regulations 2020 (SI 350/2020).

[149] *Re Castle Trust Direct plc* [2020] EWHC 969 (Ch) at [38].

[150] See *Byng* v. *London Life Association Ltd* [1990] Ch 170.

[151] *Re Castle Trust Direct plc* [2020] EWHC 969 (Ch) at [42].

legislation. In Canada,[152] for example, the legislative provisions are drafted with a high level of generality.[153] The extent to which meetings are required, the majorities required at those meetings and the information required to be disclosed are all matters left for the court to determine, with little or no legislative guidance provided. The CLR considered a similar option for UK schemes, namely 'to remove the reference to meetings of classes from the legislation and empower the court to decide what meetings or other procedure shall be used to ascertain the wishes of creditors and members'.[154] This more flexible procedure is used elsewhere in UK corporate law.[155] However, there was little support for this suggestion, and the CLR did not press ahead with this recommendation.[156]

In general, there is little reason to make this change in relation to English schemes. The statutory provisions are sensible and do not seem to create any difficulties in practice. The legal certainty they provide is also beneficial. In Canada, where statutorily prescribed procedures are absent, the courts have developed standard procedures of their own that are applied to schemes, which mean that, in practice, the steps required to implement a scheme in these jurisdictions are not dissimilar to those required for an English scheme.[157] There are some benefits that can flow

[152] Canadian Business Corporations Act 1985, s. 192.

[153] However, many other overseas jurisdictions follow the more prescriptive approach of English schemes. See e.g. Australia (see Australian Corporations Act 2001, s. 411) and Hong Kong (Hong Kong Companies Ordinance, Cap 622, s. 674). New Zealand adopted a similar approach to Canada until the New Zealand Companies Amendment Act 2014, which entered into force on 1 July 2015 and introduced a number of changes for schemes of arrangement that effect changes of control of certain defined companies, including a statutory approval test (see s. 236A(4)), a requirement that code company shareholders vote in classes and legislative guidance on how classes should be determined.

[154] CLR, *Completing the Structure*, note 117 above, para. 11.33.

[155] See e.g. Insolvency Act 1986, s. 195.

[156] It is also notable that the requirement of class meetings is retained for Part 26A restructuring plans, discussed at section 5.8.

[157] In general, the approval required will be the support of two-thirds in value of the members and creditors present and voting. This is the approval requirement for special resolutions under most Canadian corporate statutes; see Industry Canada, 'Policy on arrangements – Canada Business Corporations Act, section 192', 8 January 2014, at 3.10. In New Zealand there is a division between the rules applied to 'code companies' in change of control scenarios (see section 3.7.1), in which case requirements are laid down regarding procedural matters such as approval requirements, and other scenarios in which there are fewer legislative procedural rules (see New Zealand Companies Act 1993, s. 236) although in practice the courts have created procedural norms, such as an approval requirement of 75 per cent of the members or creditors, as the case may be, without the requirement of a headcount test.

from this more flexible approach. For example, although the courts in Canada have developed standard approval thresholds that contain a requirement for a majority by value, they do not require an additional headcount test. Since it is argued later in this chapter that the headcount test in the English scheme should be abolished, this approach has some attractions. However, the abolition of the headcount test can be tackled more directly in relation to English schemes, without the need to remove the other procedural requirements relating to schemes.

The current approach of English schemes, for the legislation to be reasonably prescriptive about these issues of procedure, is therefore broadly appropriate. As is clear from the decision in *Re Castle Trust Direct plc*, the English courts are able to be flexible when the circumstances require it.

2.2.3.3 Adequacy of notice

One of the purposes of the procedural requirements set out in the 2020 Practice Statement is to enable the scheme creditors/members to have an opportunity to appear at the convening hearing at which the constitution of the classes and relevant jurisdictional issues are determined. This is intended to minimise the risk of a successful challenge only being raised at the sanction hearing. The aim is to avoid the waste of time and money that would occur if scheme meetings were convened and held on an incorrect basis or were there to be some other fundamental roadblock to the scheme.[158] The importance of adequate notice is made clear in the Practice Statement, which emphasises the importance of giving persons affected by a scheme 'sufficient time to enable them to consider what is proposed, to take appropriate advice and, if so advised, to attend the convening hearing'.[159] The Practice Statement does not indicate any fixed time periods but rather states that adequate notice will depend on the circumstances.

The essential question is whether in all the circumstances of the case, including the complexity of the scheme, the degree of prior consultation with creditors and the urgency of the scheme, creditors have been given sufficient notice of the basic terms of the scheme and an effective opportunity to raise any concerns:

[158] *Re Telewest Communications plc (No. 1)* [2004] EWHC 924 (Ch) at [14] *per* David Richards J; *Re T & N Ltd (No. 3)* [2006] EWHC 1447 (Ch) at [18]–[20] *per* David Richards J.

[159] Practice Statement (Companies: Schemes of Arrangement under Part 26 and Part 26A of the Companies Act 2006) [2020] 1 WLR 4493, [8].

> The more complex or novel the scheme, and the less consultation that has taken place with creditors as a whole before the scheme is launched, the longer the notice should generally be. That said, if the scheme is being put forward as a matter of great urgency when the company is in real financial distress, there may not be time to give very much notice to creditors if a default is to be avoided. In such a case the scheme company may well be able to persuade the court that there is good reason to shorten the period of notice or depart altogether from the Practice Statement; and in such a case, any opposing creditor would have a good reason why he had been unable to raise a class or jurisdictional question prior to the sanction hearing.[160]

A further factor that may be relevant is the nature and degree of sophistication of the scheme creditors, particularly any creditors that have not been party to a lock-up agreement with the company.[161] In *Re ColourOz Investment 2 LLC*,[162] Snowden J noted that, although it has become customary for creditors to be alerted to a forthcoming restructuring through the publication of lock-up agreements, this should not be taken to supersede the requirements of the Companies Act 2006 and the Practice Statement, given that lock-up agreements tend to focus on commercial terms rather than issues of class and jurisdiction.

In the absence of 'real urgency',[163] a sufficient notice period should be given to enable scheme creditors/members to consider the matter, take advice and participate at the hearing, if that is what they wish to do. This is an area where judges are alert to attempts by those proposing schemes to 'bounce' creditors or members into a convening hearing in relation to a complex or novel scheme on inadequate notice.[164] Judges have also emphasised that adequate time must be provided to enable the scheme judge to have a realistic opportunity for pre-reading and the scheme timetable should not presume that the court will give its decisions immediately. The court should not be presented with a metaphorical 'gun to the head'.[165]

The method of disseminating the notice of the meeting may also be relevant. In *Re Indah Kiat International Finance Company BV*,[166] for

160 *Re Indah Kiat International Finance Company BV* [2016] EWHC 246 (Ch) at [29] *per* Snowden J. See also *Re NN2 Newco Ltd* [2019] EWHC 1917 (Ch) *per* Norris J at [22]–[23]; *Re Thomas Cook Group Treasury plc* [2019] EWHC 2494 (Ch); *Re House of Fraser (Funding) Ltd* [2018] EWHC 2663 (Ch).

161 For discussion of lock-up agreements see section 5.3.1.

162 [2020] EWHC 1864 (Ch).

163 *Re Indah Kiat International Finance Company BV* [2016] EWHC 246 (Ch) at [30].

164 See e.g. *Re Noble Group Limited* [2018] EWHC 2911 (Ch) at [173].

165 Ibid. at [179].

166 [2016] EWHC 246 (Ch).

example, Snowden J held that the fourteen-day notice period was inadequate given the complex nature of the scheme in that case, the fact that there was no good reason for urgency and, moreover, that the dissemination of the notice was achieved via the clearing system and involved the notice being passed down the intermediary chain before arriving at the ultimate beneficial owner, a process which added significantly to the time and uncertainty involved.

2.3 Meeting(s) of the members or creditors

The next stage of the scheme process requires those members and creditors affected by the scheme to meet and vote to approve it. This section will consider a number of issues, including who needs to consider the scheme (and in particular whether certain members and creditors can be excluded from it), the issue of determining whether separate class meetings will be required, and the approval thresholds for majority voting at these meetings.

2.3.1 Who needs to consider the scheme?

2.3.1.1 Legal, not beneficial, owners

In both creditor schemes and member schemes it is the person who is the legal rather than the beneficial owner of the economic interest that will be party to the scheme. For equity securities this is the person on the register of members.[167] As regards debt securities it is the person who is the legal owner of those securities; for example, in a scheme that compromises the rights attached to debentures, it is the person whose name is on the register as the debenture holder that is party to the scheme and not the person who is the beneficial owner of the debentures.[168]

This potential disjunction between the economic interest and the legal interest in a security can be problematic. It is very common for the legal and economic interest in securities to be split. Even though the economic owners are not formally parties to the scheme, it is clearly preferable to facilitate the representation of their views on the scheme. Some jurisdictions have specifically dealt with this concern. In the Cayman Islands, for example, when the court considers whether the proposed time and place of the meetings and the method of giving notice are appropriate, it is also

[167] For discussion see section 3.2.
[168] For discussion see section 5.2.

specifically required to consider whether the views of those with an economic interest will be taken into account: 'the test is whether the parties having the economic interest, which is typically not the registered holder of the shares or debt instruments, will have sufficient time in which to consider the scheme documentation and make an informed decision'.[169] The applicant for directions in relation to meetings must satisfy the court that the scheme documentation will provide to the person with the economic interest all of the information reasonably necessary to enable that person to make an informed decision about the merits of the proposed scheme.

This approach has not been adopted in relation to the English scheme. However, the courts have been prepared to approve voting arrangements that allow the person with the economic interest to dictate how their vote should be cast in a scheme.[170] For example, where they are faced with a company in which all, or nearly all, of the shares are held as depository interests, the courts have readily approved arrangements for voting that enable the depositories to direct how the legal owner is to formally cast the votes attached to the shares held by way of depository interest. In *Re Equitable Life Assurance Society*,[171] for example, Lloyd J held that split voting was allowed for scheme purposes. This acknowledges the fact that those being asked to vote are often representing a number of underlying interests and that in order to properly represent the views of those underlying economic-right holders it might be necessary for a nominee to vote partly for and partly against the scheme.[172]

The 2020 Practice Statement specifically provides for situations where a scheme company wishes to count as its 'creditors' for voting purposes the indirect holders of debt interests (i.e. the beneficial holders), rather than intermediate legal holders. In these cases, the Practice Statement requires that appropriate evidence of the proposed process for voting by

[169] Cayman Islands Practice Direction No. 1/2002, *Schemes of Arrangement and Compromise under the Companies Law, Section 86*, para. 3.3 and see *Re Uni-Asia Holdings Ltd*, unreported, FSD 34 of 2017 (28 March 2017) at [5].

[170] The court will be alert to situations where the special voting arrangements suggested have the effect of distorting the expression of opinion by members or creditors of the relevant class, rather than facilitating the communication of views by those with an economic interest. See *Re PCCW Ltd* [2009] 3 HKC 292 CA, discussed by C. Bryant in 'Schemes of arrangement' in D. Prentice and A. Reisberg (eds.), *Corporate Finance Law in the UK and EU* (Oxford University Press, 2011) 59–86.

[171] [2002] EWHC 140 (Ch); [2002] BCC 319.

[172] This issue is discussed further in sections 2.3.3.1 and 5.2.4.

these indirect holders be submitted at the convening hearing.[173] This reflects market practice that allows for beneficial holders of interests in bonds and notes to vote on a scheme where legal title is held by a trustee or common depositary.

However, it remains clear that it is the views of the legal owners that count for scheme purposes. This was reiterated in *Re Sirius Minerals plc*,[174] which involved a takeover scheme. The shareholder meeting to approve the scheme was held in March 2020. At the meeting, 812 of the 1,314 members present voted to approve the scheme, with 502 members voting against the scheme. Both the headcount test and the majority-in-value test were therefore satisfied for scheme purposes.[175] In common with many other companies, the company in this case contained a large number of underlying investors: 'it is believed that tens of thousands of small investors acquired a beneficial interest in shares in the company held by ... nominees'.[176] The proposed scheme was controversial because some underlying beneficial owners had purchased their shares in 2019 for more than 20 pence per share, whereas the offer was for 5.5 pence per share. When the company applied to sanction the scheme, concerns were expressed that the beneficial owners were not able to vote on the scheme because they were not included on the company's register of members. In sanctioning the scheme, the judge stated that the fact that many beneficial investors did not have the opportunity to vote was not 'directly relevant to an assessment of fair representation of members, because beneficial shareholders are not members for the purposes of Part 26 of the Act'.[177]

The judge pointed out that if sufficient numbers of beneficial shareholders had given instructions to their nominees to vote against the scheme, the outcome of the vote might have been different, but the company could not be blamed for that. While this is true, it perhaps ignores some of the difficulties which beneficial owners can face. The ability of the beneficial owner to instruct its nominee will depend on the arrangements between the nominee and the beneficial owner, and these arrangements are a function of the nominee's appointment terms and can vary considerably. Where one nominee is positively required to consult the

173 Practice Statement (Companies: Schemes of Arrangement under Part 26 and Part 26A of the Companies Act 2006) [2020] 1 WLR 4493, [13].

174 [2020] EWHC 1447 (Ch).

175 See Companies Act 2006, s. 899(1) and see section 2.3.3.

176 [2020] EWHC 1447 (Ch) at [2].

177 Ibid. at [22].

beneficial holder regarding how they should vote at a shareholder meeting, another may only be required to wait and see whether the beneficial holder will exercise their right to instruct them. Even then, they might have discretion to act contrary to such instructions. Similarly, the lengths to which a nominee must go to forward information to the beneficial holder can differ from one nominee appointment to another. The beneficial owners in this case argued not only that the shareholder meeting to approve the scheme did not represent their views but also that, in some cases, they had received little information from their nominees regarding the takeover and had little time in which to instruct them regarding how to vote on the scheme. The outcome in this case is likely to fuel calls for a reform in this area, to give greater rights to underlying investors.[178]

2.3.1.2 The right to vote on a scheme of arrangement

A company is generally free to decide with whom it proposes any particular compromise or arrangement.[179] This principle can be used to exclude from the scheme any members or creditors who would simply vote against it if an attempt was made to vary their rights. For example, the airline Garuda proposed a scheme that would force some creditors to accept a reduction in their debt, but it excluded certain trade creditors from the scheme, specifically the engine manufacturers whose continued support was believed to be essential to the continuation of the airline's business. This scheme was approved, on the basis that there was no reason why different groups of unsecured creditors should not be dealt with in different ways.[180] However, as Lloyd J held, it was also significant that Garuda could demonstrate a commercially rational basis for including some creditors but excluding others. Similarly, in *Re The Co-Operative Bank plc*, Snowden J confirmed that it is possible to exclude certain creditors from a scheme despite them having the same or sufficiently similar rights against the company, provided a rational commercial justification exists, other than simply a desire to arrange matters so as to achieve the required statutory majorities of those who are included.[181] Where members or

[178] See Law Commission, *Intermediated Securities: Who owns your shares? A scoping paper*, November 2020.

[179] *Re British & Commonwealth Holdings plc (No. 3)* [1992] 1 WLR 672; *Re The Co-Operative Bank Plc* [2017] EWHC 2269 (Ch).

[180] *Perusahaan Perseroan (Persero) PT Perusahaan Penerbangan Garuda Indonesia*, unreported, 4 October 2001.

[181] [2017] EWHC 2269 (Ch). Snowden J held that there had been a rational commercial justification for excluding the retail noteholders from the creditor scheme in that case, including that it might not be in the retail noteholders' interests to be issued with new

creditors are excluded from the scheme, their rights are (naturally) unchanged by the scheme. In general, then, it is not necessary for the company to consult with (or obtain the approval of) any class of members or creditors whose rights are unaffected by the scheme. It is particularly common to make use of the ability to exclude creditors from creditor schemes; typically creditor schemes will not involve all of a company's creditors.[182] The ability to exclude members and creditors is a potentially very valuable feature of the scheme procedure and stands in contrast to other mechanisms that may sometimes appear to be functionally similar.[183] One of the ways in which the ability to exclude creditors in this way has been utilised in recent years is in the development of de facto cross-class cramdowns, discussed further in section 5.4.3.

2.3.2 Separate class meetings

Once it is determined which groups are included in the scheme, and therefore whose consent is required, the next question is whether those groups should meet and vote to approve the scheme at a single meeting,[184] or at separate class meetings. The definition of 'class' for

equity in an unlisted company with no certainty of any return, and that it was not possible for the bank to offer a 'cash-out' option to all noteholders given its financial resources. Moreover, the proposals in respect of retail noteholders were intended to result in a certain and more favourable cash return than the benefits available to ordinary non-retail noteholders under the creditor scheme. One reason given by the scheme company for the differential treatment was held to have been 'closer to the margin' by the judge, namely a concern that there would be an execution risk if the retail noteholders had been included from the scheme given the very large number of noteholders holding each a small number of notes. Nonetheless, even here the court held that the decision to exclude the noteholders was a commercially rational decision and did not amount to anything which might be regarded as 'gerrymandering the composition of classes for any illegitimate purpose' (at [42]).

182 The ability to exclude creditors also exists in relation to Part 26A restructuring plans: *Re Virgin Atlantic Airways Ltd* [2020] EWHC 2376 (Ch).

183 For example, in Australia, creditor schemes (see s. 411 of the Australian Corporations Act 2001) can be organised to affect only certain creditors, in the same way as the English scheme, whereas deeds of company arrangement (see Part 5.3A of the Australian Corporations Act 2001) require all creditors to be included, and to consider and approve the plan. For discussion see T. Damian and A. Rich, *Schemes, Takeovers and Himalayan Peaks: The Use of Schemes of Arrangement to Effect Change of Control Transactions* (3rd ed., Sydney: Centre of Commercial, Corporate and Taxation Law, University of Sydney, 2013) 9.11.4.

184 In general, a meeting of a class of creditors or members under a scheme must consist of more than one person (this is in accordance with the general law on meetings: see e.g. *Palmer's Company Law* (London: Sweet & Maxwell, looseleaf), chs. 7.5 and 7.6). However, the need,

this purpose does not necessarily correspond with the definition of this term for other purposes in company law.[185] It is possible for a class to consist of a single member or creditor.[186]

The general test to determine whether members or creditors should meet as a whole or as separate classes is relatively easily stated, although it has proved difficult to apply in practice.[187] It is notable that this test does not appear in the statutory provisions regarding schemes, and has therefore been developed by the courts.[188] The accepted test was set out by Bowen LJ in *Sovereign Life Assurance Co* v. *Dodd*:

> It seems plain that we must give such a meaning to the term 'class' as will prevent the section being so worked as to result in confiscation and injustice, and that it must be confined to those persons whose rights are not so dissimilar as to make it impossible for them to consult together with a view to their common interest.[189]

A balancing act is required. A class with genuinely different rights requires the protection of a separate meeting, but if too many artificial distinctions are drawn then the scheme will be at the mercy of a veto by any one of the separate meetings that are held. It is easy to see that the fewer meetings that are held, the more schemes will be approved, but this has potential consequences for the protection of minorities. In recent years, there has been a shift of emphasis in applying this test, away from

where appropriate, to divide members or creditors into different classes for the purposes of a scheme means that in some cases a class may contain only one person. In such circumstances it is not essential to convene a meeting of that class because it is well established that by their individual consent a member or creditor may agree to be bound by a scheme: *Re Altitude Scaffolding Ltd* [2006] EWHC 1401 (Ch); [2006] BCC 904.

185 *Re Robert Stephen Holdings Ltd* [1968] 1 WLR 522.

186 *Re RMCA Reinsurance Ltd* [1994] BCC 378; *Re Noble Group Limited* [2018] EWHC 2911 (Ch) (although in the latter case Snowden J acknowledged that it is more common for that creditor to undertake to the court to be bound by the terms of the scheme (at [94])).

187 See e.g. *Re Codere Finance 2 (UK) Ltd* [2020] EWHC 2441 (Ch).

188 This is also the case in other jurisdictions that have introduced schemes, e.g. Australia, Hong Kong, Singapore and India (see e.g. *Infrastructure Leasing & Financial Services Ltd* v. *BPC Ltd* (2015) 3 SCC 363 (Supreme Court)). By way of contrast, when the New Zealand Companies Amendment Act 2014 introduced a requirement that for certain schemes (namely those effecting a change of control of 'code companies') the shareholders should be divided into classes to vote, legislative guidance was also introduced on how classes should be determined: New Zealand Companies Act 1993, Sch. 10A. In practice these appear to be very similar to the provisions in *Sovereign Life Assurance Co* v. *Dodd* [1892] 2 QB 573.

189 [1892] 2 QB 573 at 583 *per* Bowen LJ. The same test is applied in schemes elsewhere, see e.g. in Singapore *Wah Yuen Engineering Pte Ltd* v. *Singapore Cables Manufacturers Pte Ltd* [2003] 3 SLR 629 at [11].

overzealous distinctions that give minorities strong veto rights. As Nourse J has commented, '[i]f one gets too picky about potential different classes, one could end up with virtually as many classes as there are members of a particular group'.[190] Clearly, the composition of class meetings cannot be allowed to operate in a way that permits majority oppression either. As Bowen LJ said of schemes in *Sovereign Life*:

> It makes the majority of the creditors or of a class of creditors bind the minority; it exercises a most formidable compulsion upon dissentient, or would-be dissentient, creditors; and it therefore requires to be construed with care, so as not to place in the hands of some of the creditors the means and opportunity of forcing dissentients to do that which it is unreasonable to require them to do, or of making a mere jest of the interests of the minority.[191]

In *Re Hawk Insurance Co Ltd* Chadwick LJ refined the test set out in *Sovereign Life*. That test, he said, must be applied in the context of the question 'with whom is the compromise or arrangement to be made?':

> In each case the answer to that question will depend upon analysis (i) of the rights which are to be released or varied under the scheme and (ii) the new rights (if any) which the scheme gives, by way of compromise or arrangement, to those whose rights are to be released or varied. It is in the light of that analysis that the test formulated by Bowen LJ in order to determine which creditors fall into a separate class – that is to say, that a class 'must be confined to those persons whose rights are not so dissimilar as to make it impossible for them to consult together with a view to their common interest' – has to be applied.[192]

Although *Hawk Insurance* involved creditors, this statement applies equally to schemes involving shareholders. Rather than asking whether the rights of members and creditors are sufficiently different as to require them to be treated as a separate class, the question following *Hawk Insurance* is whether the rights are sufficiently similar as not to require such separation. The effect of *Hawk Insurance* is therefore to cause a shift in emphasis. While those with genuinely dissimilar rights should be protected, fine-grained distinctions that provide the minority with a veto should be avoided. The class test does not require identical

[190] *Re Anglo American Insurance Co Ltd* [2001] 1 BCLC 755 at 764.
[191] [1892] 2 QB 573 at 582–3.
[192] [2001] EWCA Civ 241; [2002] BCC 300 at [30].

treatment. The court will ask whether the rights and entitlements of the different groups viewed in the totality of the scheme's context are so dissimilar as to make it impossible for them to consult together with a view to their common interest. The court will take account of the scheme in the context of other arrangements entered into collaterally with it,[193] and the alternative should the scheme not go ahead.[194] On this analysis, the focus of minority protection shifts towards the court's sanctioning role.

The approach suggested by Chadwick LJ has been criticised,[195] but it has subsequently been applied by the courts.[196] In terms of timing, the relevant moment for applying this test, and assessing the rights of the members and/or creditors for this purpose, is at the time of the court-convened meetings at which the scheme is voted upon.[197]

2.3.2.1 Rights and interests

In determining the issue of whether separate meetings should be held for members and creditors, the courts have focused on the rights of those involved, not their interests.[198] To illustrate the importance of the distinction between rights and interests, two cases can be considered: *Re Hellenic & General Trust Ltd*[199] and *Re BTR plc*.[200] *Re Hellenic* concerned a scheme that was effecting a change of control. The court in that case regarded it as necessary to separate the ordinary shareholders into two classes. Templeman J held that one shareholder in the target company, which was a wholly owned subsidiary of the bidder, needed to be treated as

193 See e.g. *Re Baltic Exchange Ltd* [2016] EWHC 3391 (Ch) at [17].

194 *Re Apcoa Parking Holdings GmbH* [2014] EWHC 3849 (Ch); *First Pacific Advisors LLC v. Boart Longyear Ltd* [2017] NSWCA 116.

195 See e.g. CLR, *Final Report*, note 117 above, para 13.8; R. Sykes, 'Schemes of arrangement: the Hawk that muddied the waters' (2001) 12(5) *Practical Law Company* 6. For discussion see section 2.3.2.3.

196 See e.g. *Re Equitable Life Assurance Society* [2002] EWHC 140 (Ch); [2002] BCC 319; *Re Telewest Communications plc (No. 1)* [2004] EWHC 924 (Ch) and [2004] EWCA Civ 728; *Re MyTravel Group plc* [2004] EWHC 2741 (Ch); [2005] 1 WLR 2365.

197 See e.g. *Re British Aviation Insurance Co Ltd* [2005] EWHC 1621 (Ch) at [111].

198 *Sovereign Life Assurance Co v. Dodd* [1892] 2 QB 573 at 583 *per* Bowen LJ; *Re Hawk Insurance Co Ltd* [2001] EWCA Civ 241; [2001] 2 BCLC 480 at [23] *per* Chadwick LJ; *Re SABMiller plc* [2016] EWHC 2153 (Ch); *Re Realm Therapeutics Plc* [2019] EWHC 2080 (Ch); *Re Codere Finance 2 (UK) Ltd* [2020] EWHC 2441 (Ch). A similar approach is followed elsewhere; see e.g. in Hong Kong *Re Industrial Equity (Pacific) Ltd* (1991) 2 HKLR 614; *Re UDL Holdings Ltd* [2002] 1 HKC 172.

199 [1976] 1 WLR 123.

200 [1999] 2 BCLC 675.

being in a separate class from the other shareholders in the target. Although the rights held by all of the shareholders were identical their interests in the scheme were different. The wholly owned subsidiary shared interests with the bidder company that the other shareholders did not. According to Templeman J, these different interests meant that they should meet separately.

In *Re BTR plc* a scheme was proposed for the merger of BTR with Siebe, effectively by way of the takeover of BTR by Siebe. BTR had only one class of ordinary shares, all of which were to be treated equally under the scheme. The court was asked by an objecting shareholder not to sanction a scheme on the basis that more than one meeting of shareholders should have been held, given that the shareholders considering the scheme had different interests. In particular, some of the shareholders already held shares in the bidder company, and their interests might therefore be regarded as being different to those of other shareholders. In *Re BTR*, Jonathan Parker J restricted the decision in *Hellenic* to deciding only that a subsidiary's shares should be discounted at the sanctioning stage.[201] This was on the basis that the financial position of the parties was the same whether or not the subsidiary accepted the offer. He rejected the proposition that members with different *interests*, rather than different *rights*, should form a separate class:

> Shareholders with the same rights in respect of the shares which they hold may be subject to an infinite number of different interests and may therefore, assessing their own personal interests (as they are perfectly entitled to do), vote their shares in the light of those interests. But that in itself, in my judgment, is simply a fact of life: it does not lead to the conclusion that shareholders who propose to vote differently are in some way a separate class of shareholders entitled to a separate class meeting. Indeed a journey down that road would in my judgment lead to impracticality and unworkability.[202]

This approach does not deny that interests of this kind might be relevant to the court, but envisages the court taking account of such interests, together with other relevant factors, when determining whether to sanction the scheme. As Chadwick LJ has acknowledged, '[p]arliament has recognised that it is for the court . . . to hold the ring between the different interests; and to decline to sanction a scheme if satisfied that members

[201] Ibid.

[202] Ibid. at 682–3.

having one interest have sought to take advantage over those having another'.[203]

There are a number of practical advantages to the *Re BTR* approach.[204] The rights of the members or creditors will generally be easier for the company to identify and apply than their interests. In the words of Nazareth J: 'Is every interest to constitute a different class? Clearly not, but where then is the line to be drawn? The difficulties in identifying shareholders with such interests . . . could raise in terms of practicality virtually insuperable difficulties.'[205] It will generally be difficult for the company to assess the different interests of its members, without requiring a considerable amount of personal information from them. Requiring that type of information would lead to 'a wholly unworkable, and highly undesirable, situation'.[206] In addition, unless a practical approach of this kind is adopted, there is a danger that 'one could end up with virtually as many classes as there are members of a particular group'.[207]

A consequence of the *Re BTR* approach, however, is that fewer class meetings are likely to be held, and there is less chance of a veto of the scheme by the minority at this stage. The potential reduction in minority protection at this point means that the court's role in scrutinising the scheme prior to sanctioning it becomes more important.

Consequently, it is clear that it is the rights of creditors and members that are important. Assessing members' and creditors' rights for this purpose, while easier than assessing their interests, is not always straightforward. In member schemes, for example, while the existence of class rights provides a useful starting point in deciding whether shareholders have different rights for scheme purposes, it will not be determinative of this issue. So, different classes of shareholders (e.g. ordinary and preference shareholders) will typically have different rights to income and capital, and many reorganisations of share capital within the company will impact differently on these groups so that separate meetings become necessary. However, in other circumstances even different classes of shareholders might be regarded as having the same rights for the purposes of a scheme. For example, where the company is hopelessly

[203] *Re BTR plc* [2000] 1 BCLC 740 at 748.
[204] See also the decision of the Hong Kong courts in support of the 'rights' rather than 'interests' approach: *Re Industrial Equity (Pacific) Ltd* (1991) 2 HKLR 614.
[205] Ibid. at 635 *per* Nazareth J.
[206] *Re BTR plc* [1999] 2 BCLC 675 at 683 *per* Chadwick LJ.
[207] *Re Anglo American Insurance Co Ltd* [2001] 1 BCLC 755 at 764 *per* Neuberger J.

insolvent all classes of shareholders might be regarded as having the same (essentially valueless) rights.

Differentiating between the rights and interests of creditors and members will not always be straightforward. In relation to member schemes, for example, while the issue of the bidder or its subsidiary holding shares in the target has largely been settled a number of other questions have arisen,[208] such as whether members with shareholdings across different classes should require the constitution of a separate class,[209] and a similar issue arises where some of the members in a takeover scheme have given irrevocable undertakings to the bidder.[210] These issues are discussed in the context of member schemes in section 3.5.2. Similar issues arise in relation to creditor schemes. For example, where some creditors have signed lock-up agreements whereby they will receive a fee, conditional on the scheme taking effect, should the fact that they receive a benefit in return for their agreement to vote be sufficient to require the constitution of a separate class?[211] If the creditors are deemed to have merely different interests they will not constitute a separate class (but their different interests might be relevant at the sanctioning stage), whereas if they have different rights this might be relevant for the purpose of constituting separate classes.[212]

In addition, for both member and creditor schemes, the mere fact that prior to the scheme the rights of members or creditors are identical does not necessarily mean that they should be treated as one class for the purposes of the scheme. If the scheme itself proposes to treat different groups of members within a particular class differently, then it may well be that there will need to be separate classes within these groups.[213] However, in some circumstances the difference in treatment may not be such as to require them to hold separate meetings. In *Re Telewest Communications plc*,[214] for example, the sterling bondholders and the dollar bondholders were treated differently, in terms of the exchange rate mechanism adopted under the scheme, but the difference was held not to make their rights so different that they should form separate classes.

[208] See section 3.5.2.5 for further discussion.
[209] See section 3.5.2.2.
[210] See section 3.5.2.4.
[211] For discussion see section 5.3.1.
[212] This is discussed further in the context of creditor schemes in section 5.3.
[213] *Re Anglo American Insurance Co Ltd* [2001] 1 BCLC 755.
[214] [2004] EWHC 924 (Ch); [2004] BCC 342 and [2004] EWCA Civ 728; [2005] BCC 29.

As discussed, following *Hawk Insurance*, the test is not merely whether the members or creditors have different rights but whether the rights are so different as to make it impossible for the creditors/ members put together into a class to consult together in their common interest. The decision in *Re Hawk Insurance* illustrates this point forcefully as regards the creditor scheme in that case. *Hawk Insurance* involved the question whether different types of unsecured creditor, some with vested claims and some with contingent claims, should be treated as being part of the same class for the purposes of voting on a proposed scheme. At first instance Arden J held that these creditors should be treated as comprising different classes.[215] Those with vested claims should be treated as being in the same class as other unsecured creditors, since they all had an accrued claim against the company that they have an immediate right to sue for in full. By contrast, those with contingent claims had no such immediate right and the structure of the scheme was such that those whose claims had not yet accrued would have those claims scaled down to proportions less than 100 per cent. Although these creditors would rank equally on insolvency (as they were all unsecured creditors) these differences, in Arden J's opinion, meant that they should not all be treated as one class for scheme purposes. The Court of Appeal disagreed with this approach. Applying the restated *Sovereign Life* test, Chadwick LJ held that all of the unsecured creditors, including therefore those with contingent rights and those with vested rights, could meet as a single class for this purpose.[216] To understand this decision it is necessary to bear in mind that the court must apply the correct comparator when deciding the rights of the members or creditors that matter for the purpose of separating them into different classes.

2.3.2.2 The correct comparator

The courts need to consider the correct comparator when determining the similarity or dissimilarity of members'/creditors' rights. In *Re Apcoa Parking (UK) Ltd* Hildyard J stated that this issue 'will necessarily inform, and in many if not most cases be the most important factor' in the

[215] [2001] 2 BCLC 480.

[216] This broad approach to the analysis of classes for scheme purposes has subsequently been followed: see e.g. *Re Telewest Communications plc* [2004] EWHC 924 (Ch) and [2004] EWCA Civ 728; *Re UDL Holdings Ltd* [2002] 1 HKC 172.

discussions about proper class composition.[217] This is for two reasons. First, a fair comparison between members'/creditors' rights if there is no scheme and its rights under the proposed scheme depends on ascertaining the nature and quality of the right in the 'non-scheme world', and the latter depends on the appropriate comparator. Second, only by identifying the comparator can the likely practical effect of what is proposed be assessed and the likelihood of sensible discussion between the holders of rights so affected and between them and others with different rights be weighed fairly.[218] This issue is of particular importance for creditor-focused schemes.

In *Hawk Insurance* Chadwick LJ stated that, where a company is insolvent, the starting point for determining separate classes will be the rights of those creditors on winding up. Some groups, such as secured creditors and preferred creditors, should therefore meet separately, since their rights on a winding up are clearly differentiated. In addition, where subordinated creditors have an interest in the company that could be affected in a different way from that of other creditors, their rights will constitute a separate class.[219] This might arise, for example, in different tranches of a securitised bond issue, or in a leveraged buy-out. In such cases it is the rights of creditors on an insolvent liquidation that will be relevant in determining whether they should meet as a separate class.[220] By contrast, all of the unsecured creditors in *Hawk Insurance* had the same rights on a winding up, namely to submit their claims in the winding up, and to have those claims accepted or rejected. The only difference would be that those with contingent claims held debts without a certain value, and therefore those debts would be subject to an estimate. However, in Chadwick LJ's view this did not mean that they should be treated as a separate class for scheme purposes. As expressed by Hildyard J in *Re Apcoa Parking Holdings GmbH*:

> The modern approach, which the practice established pursuant to *re Hawk* both reflects and requires, is to break the question into two parts, and ask first whether there is any difference between the creditors in point of strict legal right, and only to proceed to the second question, at the

217 [2014] EWHC 997 (Ch) at [32]. See also *Re British Aviation Insurance Co Ltd* [2005] EWHC 1621 (Ch).

218 *Re Stronghold Insurance Company Limited* [2018] EWHC 2909 (Ch) at [49].

219 *Re British & Commonwealth Holdings plc (No. 3)* [1992] 1 WLR 672; *Soden* v. *British & Commonwealth Holdings plc (in administration)* [1998] AC 298; *Re MyTravel Group plc* [2004] EWHC 2741 (Ch); [2005] 1 WLR 2365.

220 *Re Telewest Communications plc* [2004] EWHC 924 (Ch).

> Convening stage, if there is; and if there is, to postulate, by reference to the alternative if the scheme were to fail, whether objectively there would be more to unite than divide the creditors in the proposed class, ignoring for that purpose any personal or extraneous interest or subjective motivation operating in the case of any particular creditor(s).[221]

Thus, where the comparator of a winding up is used, the courts tend to adopt a broad approach to class composition, and the rights of all unsecured creditors will generally be treated as forming one class.[222] However, the courts have warned that insolvency cannot 'be used as a solvent for all class differences'.[223] Clearly some categories of creditors will still require division. For example, within the category of secured creditors further division will generally be required where securities differ. A creditor whose claim is protected by a fixed charge is far less vulnerable than one whose security is a floating charge. Even creditors whose claims are secured over the same property may have divergent interests. A scheme that proposes the sale of a security and a transfer of the rights of the secured creditors to a substituted security might be acceptable to the first but not the second chargee.

By contrast, where a company is solvent the rights of the creditors on insolvency are unlikely to be the appropriate comparators.[224] In *Re British Aviation Insurance Co Ltd*, for example, Lewison J held that the appropriate comparator was a continuing solvent run-off.[225] This will often have an impact on the decision of the court as to the appropriate number of class meetings to be held. In *British Aviation*, where the company was solvent, liquidation was not a realistic alternative to the scheme. The valuation and immediate satisfaction of contingent claims under the solvent scheme in *British Aviation* involved a clear variation of the claimants' rights to prove in

221 [2014] EWHC 3849 (Ch) at [52].

222 A similar approach has been followed elsewhere; see e.g. *First Pacific Advisors LLC* v. *Boart Longyear Ltd* [2017] NSWCA 116; *Ocean Rig UDW Inc*, Cayman Islands Grand Court, 18 September 2017.

223 *Re Apcoa Parking Holdings GmbH* [2014] EWHC 3849 (Ch) at [117].

224 *Re British Aviation Insurance Co Ltd* [2005] EWHC 1621 (Ch); [2006] BCC 14; *Re Sovereign Marine & General Insurance Co Ltd* [2006] EWHC 1335 (Ch); [2007] 1 BCLC 228; *Re Stronghold Insurance Company Limited* [2018] EWHC 2909 (Ch); *Re Equitable Life Assurance Society* [2019] EWHC 2345 (Ch). For discussion of the appropriate time to switch from a solvent to an insolvent comparator see *Re Premier Oil plc* [2020] CSOH 39.

225 [2005] EWHC 1621 (Ch); [2006] BCC 14 at [88].

liquidation. In contrast to *Hawk Insurance*, separate class meetings were required.[226]

Identifying different classes of creditors' rights is particularly challenging in insurance cases because some creditors may have matured claims (which might be established as to liability and quantum, or liability might have been admitted but damages as yet unquantified, or an actionable condition, such as asbestosis, may have arisen but liability and damages have yet to be established) or the conditions for the claim have been incurred but not yet reported (IBNR).[227] In asbestos claims, for example, a policyholder's exposure to asbestos may have occurred during the policy coverage years, but generally the resulting personal injury claim will only arise some time later. In *British Aviation*, creditors with matured and contingent claims were grouped separately from those with IBNR claims and it was determined that separate meetings should be held. As a result of these difficulties (amongst other issues) Lewison J did not sanction the scheme in *British Aviation*. A further difficulty that might arise is where the future outcome of the company remains genuinely uncertain. In *Re Stronghold Insurance Company Limited*,[228] for example, the court struggled to ascertain the relevant comparator (solvent liquidation, insolvent liquidation or continued solvent run-off). This was due in large part to the regulators' silence on their intended course of action (if any) owing to a breach of the company's regulatory capital requirements. Hildyard J ultimately looked at the position in the 'near and mid-term'[229] and agreed with the company that the correct comparator was a continued solvent run-off, albeit with a risk of liquidation in the future.

As far as member schemes are concerned, the company will be solvent. In general terms the comparison is therefore between the rights that the members will have if the scheme goes ahead (i.e. the rights under the scheme) and those held by the members if the scheme does not go ahead, whether those rights arise under the articles of the company, or the general law or under some specialist provisions such as takeover regulation.

226 See also *Re Stronghold Insurance Company Limited* [2018] EWHC 2909 (Ch).

227 For discussion of whether IBNR claims should always form a separate class see *Re Stronghold Insurance Company Limited* [2018] EWHC 2909 (Ch), and also see section 6.2.

228 [2018] EWHC 2909 (Ch).

229 Ibid. at [63].

2.3.2.3 Comments on the courts' approach to class composition

Lord Millett in *Re UDL Holdings Ltd* summarised the state of the authorities on this issue as follows:

> Persons whose rights are so dissimilar that they cannot sensibly consult together with a view to their common interest must be given separate meetings. Persons whose rights are sufficiently similar that they can consult together with a view to their common interest should be summoned to a single meeting . . . The test is based on similarity or dissimilarity of legal rights against the company, not on similarity or dissimilarity of interests not derived from such legal rights. The fact that individuals may hold divergent views based on their private interests not derived from their legal rights against the company is not a ground for calling separate meetings . . . The question is whether the rights which are to be released or varied under the scheme or the new rights which the scheme gives in their place are so different that the scheme must be treated as a compromise or arrangement with more than one class.[230]

A number of general comments can be made about the state of the law in the light of the decisions in *Sovereign Life*, as applied in *BTR* and *Re Hawk Insurance* and in more recent cases.

First, it may be seen that the trend, when balancing concerns of minority oppression against the possibility of majority oppression, is to give greater weight to the latter danger at the class meeting stage. Rather than the question being whether members' and creditors' rights are sufficiently different as to require them to form a separate class, the question following *Hawk Insurance* is whether they are sufficiently similar as not to. These decisions also emphasise rights rather than interests. The effect has been to reduce the number of separate class meetings.

Concerns were raised after *Hawk Insurance* that the court's approach in this regard had perhaps gone too far. After all, the result in *Hawk Insurance* was a single meeting of all the unsecured creditors, notwithstanding that they did, in one sense, have different rights. The CLR stated that '[u]nless this decision is confined to its special facts, we consider that the position should be restored to that which it was thought to be before this decision, namely that separate meetings would have to be held if the creditors or members who are sought to be bound into a scheme have different legal rights'.[231] The CLR suggested that one way to deal with this issue would be to include a definition of 'class' within the legislation. It

230 *Re UDL Holdings Ltd* [2002] 1 HKC 172 (Final Court of Appeal of Hong Kong), at 184–5.
231 CLR, *Final Report*, note 117 above, para. 13.8

proposed that the only persons entitled to attend and vote at a scheme meeting should be 'persons whose rights are not so dissimilar as to make it impossible for them to consult together with a view to acting in their common interest'.[232] Additionally, the CLR proposed that the court should not sanction a scheme where such meetings had not been held, unless it sees fit to dispense with the requirement for separate meetings, or is satisfied that any difference between the rights of the various classes is immaterial. The CLR noted that this latter requirement would have the advantage of enabling the court to waive the requirement for separate meetings in appropriate cases, thereby removing 'one of the problems' caused by the legislation.[233]

These changes were not introduced in the Companies Act 2006.[234] Neither are these reforms necessary. Once the correct comparator is factored in, the decision in *Hawk Insurance* should not be a matter for concern or alarm. In a situation where the company is insolvent, as it was in *Hawk Insurance*, the fact that some of the unsecured creditors are contingent creditors does not prevent them all being regarded as having the same rights in a winding up. The CLR accepted that the court could dispense with the requirement for a separate meeting if it is 'satisfied that any difference between the rights of the various classes is immaterial'.[235] *Hawk Insurance* should be analysed in these terms, that is, on the basis that the rights of the unsecured creditors are different, but that those differences are immaterial once the company is insolvent and when those rights are viewed through the prism of winding up. However, it is preferable, and more in keeping with *Sovereign Life*, to regard the situation in *Hawk Insurance* as one in which the rights of all of the unsecured creditors in that situation are the same, namely the right to submit their claims in the winding up and to have those claims accepted, or rejected.

Second, the decisions in *Hawk Insurance* and *Re BTR* shift the focus of minority protection away from the consideration of separate meetings, at the first court hearing, and towards the courts' discretion to sanction the scheme at the second hearing. If members or creditors at a particular meeting have interests that are unrepresentative of the class as a whole then, as Chadwick LJ makes clear in *Re BTR*, the correct mechanism for the court to address these concerns is at the sanctioning stage. At that stage a court will be concerned to determine whether the votes necessary

[232] Ibid.

[233] Ibid.

[234] This is despite initial support for these changes: DTI, *Company Law Reform*, note 127 above, para. 4.14.

[235] CLR, *Final Report*, note 117 above, para. 13.8.

to secure the approval were cast in order to promote a special interest of some members that was not shared by the class as a whole.[236] As Hildyard J said in *Re Apcoa Parking Holdings GmbH*,

> the inclination of judges [is] to prefer the more flexible tool of discretion and an overall appreciation of fairness tested by reference to the real alternatives rather than the straight-jacket of jurisdiction, especially where rigidity may result in fragmentation of classes to avoid jurisdictional issues, but at the cost of enabling a small group to hold out unfairly against a majority.[237]

Minorities will, as a result, be more reliant on the court's scrutiny function at the sanctioning stage, as discussed in section 2.4.[238]

2.3.3 Approval at the class meetings

The company needs to obtain the approval of all members or creditors, or classes thereof, who will be affected by the scheme. There is no quorum requirement for a vote on a scheme, and the vote is on a poll rather than by a show of hands. The level of approval required at the meeting is a majority in number, representing three-fourths in value of its creditors or members present and voting in person or by proxy.[239] Non-voting shareholders, and those that do not turn up at the meeting, are therefore excluded for the purposes of calculating the majority.[240]

2.3.3.1 The majority-in-value test

Unlike the majority-in-number requirement, discussed in section 2.3.3.2, the majority-in-value test has proved relatively uncontroversial.

Under a member scheme, since each share has a nominal value, it is usually relatively straightforward to apply this test. However, one issue that has arisen in relation to takeover schemes is whether 75 per cent is a large enough majority.[241] The 75 per cent requirement aligns the

236 *Re BTR plc* [1999] 2 BCLC 675.
237 [2014] EWHC 3849 (Ch) at [54].
238 See section 2.4.
239 Companies Act 2006, s. 899(1).
240 It is also worth noting that treasury shares are discounted at all stages of the scheme. This is because the company cannot exercise any rights in respect of such shares and any purported exercise of such a right is void: ibid., s. 726(2).
241 By way of contrast, in Canada there is no statutorily imposed approval threshold, and the courts generally impose a lower approval threshold than in relation to English schemes, namely 66⅔ per cent.

decision taken by members to approve a scheme with other significant corporate decisions, such as altering the company's articles.[242] However, in takeovers that occur by way of a traditional offer, if the bidder wishes to acquire 100 per cent of the target, it would need the consent of 90 per cent of the shareholders in the target company.[243] Concerns have therefore been voiced that the minority can effectively be bound by a lower percentage of the members in a scheme (75 per cent of the shares by value and a majority in number of them) than in a takeover (where the minority could not be forced to sell their shares unless 90 per cent of the other shareholders had already accepted the offer).[244] It has been suggested that approving a scheme of arrangement in such circumstances should require a very high standard of proof.[245] However, the current approach of the English courts is to regard whether a company proceeds by way of a scheme of arrangement or through an offer as a matter of choice.[246] English courts have rejected the argument that where a scheme is used as an alternative to a takeover, the court should insist on a 90 per cent approval of the scheme by shareholders.[247] On this view the lower threshold in a scheme is countered by the fact that the members need to meet in classes and also, crucially, that the court needs to sanction the scheme.[248]

In the case of a creditor scheme, to apply the majority-in-value test requires working out in advance the amount (or a formula) in respect of which each creditor will be allowed to vote. This will depend on the value of the debt.[249] For this reason, only debts that can have an estimate placed upon them can be claimed.[250] Given that future and contingent creditors are included within the definition of a creditor, for the purposes of a scheme,[251] this can give rise to difficult issues in valuing their claims for the purpose of determining whether the requisite majority is present.

242 Companies Act 2006, s. 21.

243 Once the bidder has acquired 90 per cent of the target shares it can then squeeze out the remaining target shareholders: Companies Act 2006, s. 979, discussed further in section 3.3.1.2.

244 For discussion see J. Payne, 'Schemes of arrangement, takeovers and minority shareholder protection' (2011) *Journal of Corporate Law Studies* 67–97.

245 *Re Hellenic & General Trust* [1976] 1 WLR 123.

246 *Re BTR plc* [1999] 2 BCLC 675, affirmed [2000] 1 BCLC 740; *Re TDG plc* [2008] EWHC 2334 (Ch); [2009] 1 BCLC 445.

247 *Re National Bank Ltd* [1966] 1 WLR 819; *Re TDG plc* [2008] EWHC 2334 (Ch); [2009] 1 BCLC 445.

248 For further discussion of this point see section 3.7.

249 *Re British Aviation Insurance Co Ltd* [2005] EWHC 1621 (Ch); [2006] BCC 14.

250 *Re Midland Coal, Coke and Iron Co*, [1895] 1 Ch 267.

251 See section 5.2.

One issue of general interest to both member and creditor schemes is how the majority-in-value test is to be applied where, as is increasingly common, the individual in question interacts not directly with the company but via a nominee. For example, shares may be held beneficially for a number of reasons. The desire for shares in publicly traded companies to be held and traded electronically has led to the development of a variety of systems around the world. In the UK, for example, the shift from certificated to uncertificated issues and transfers has been effected through the CREST computer system, operated by Euroclear UK & Ireland.[252] Although investors in this system still have the option of holding an account directly, many choose to hold shares via an intermediary, for reasons of convenience.[253] In this situation it is the intermediary that is the registered holder of the shares, and entitled to vote. The rise of intermediated holdings has led to a recognition that in some circumstances it might be helpful to enfranchise the underlying beneficial owner.[254] The same point arises in relation to creditor schemes where, similarly, there may be a nominal creditor that is entitled to vote, but that creditor may hold for numerous underlying beneficial owners that might have conflicting interests or conflicting wishes on a matter on which the actual creditor is entitled to vote.

The courts have noted that this can result in the views of the beneficial owners being unrecognised.[255] The courts have therefore been prepared to tackle this issue by making appropriate adjustments, for example by allowing split voting arrangements to be put in place.[256] The Companies Act 2006 includes a number of provisions which seek to enfranchise beneficial owners, including instructing the intermediary how to vote on their behalf, and enabling the intermediary to delegate the right to vote to the beneficiary, usually by appointing the beneficiary as a proxy.[257] The

252 See the Uncertificated Securities Regulations 2001 (SI 2001/3755 as amended), supplemented by the CREST terms and conditions (see CREST Reference manual (September 2009), available at www.euroclear.com). CREST is named after the CrestCo corporation, which has been owned and operated by Euroclear since 2002.

253 See generally L. Gullifer and J. Payne (eds.), *Intermediation and Beyond* (Oxford: Hart, 2019).

254 For a discussion of these issues see J. Payne, 'Intermediated securities and the right to vote in the UK' in L. Gullifer and J. Payne (eds.), *Intermediated Securities: Legal Problems and Practical Issues* (Oxford: Hart, 2010) and P. Davies, 'Investment chains and corporate governance' in L. Gullifer and J. Payne (eds.), *Intermediation and Beyond* (Oxford: Hart, 2019).

255 *Re Equitable Life Assurance Society* [2002] EWHC 140 (Ch); [2002] BCC 319.

256 See e.g. ibid.

257 Companies Act 2006, ss. 145, 146, 152, 324. For discussion see Payne, 'Intermediated securities and the right to vote in the UK', note 254 above, and Davies, 'Investment

2020 Practice Statement recognises this issue, stating that '[w]here interests in the applicant's debt are held indirectly, for example through intermediaries, if it is proposed that the votes to be cast at the meetings should by some method reflect the views of persons holding such indirect interests, the evidence should set out the applicant's proposals in that respect and any facts justifying those proposals'.[258]

2.3.3.2 The headcount test

2.3.3.2.1 General The majority-in-number requirement for approval at a class meeting, or headcount test, has proved controversial. There have been calls for its repeal both in England and in other jurisdictions that have imported schemes of arrangement, although it remains in place in the English scheme procedure at present. It is suggested in this section that the arguments in favour of its repeal are compelling and that this reform would be a beneficial change to the scheme procedure.

This test was first introduced in 1870,[259] and was intended to provide 'a check on the ability of creditors with large claims to carry the day'.[260] When schemes were extended to members in 1908, the headcount test was retained.[261] The rationale behind this retention for member schemes is unclear. Presumably, the idea was that the protection given to small creditors should be extended to small shareholders.

The headcount test has been criticised. In 2001 the CLR stated that the headcount test was 'irrelevant and burdensome',[262] and recommended its removal. However, this recommendation was not adopted by the government.[263] The Attorney General stated that although the abolition of the test would facilitate schemes for companies and large creditors and members, this would be at the expense of small creditors and members and the government was not persuaded that the abolition would strike

chains and corporate governance', note 254 above. These provisions relate to member rights rather than creditor rights.

258 Practice Statement (Companies: Schemes of Arrangement under Part 26 and Part 26A of the Companies Act 2006) [2020] 1 WLR 4493, [13].

259 Joint Stock Companies Act 1870, s. 2.

260 CLR, *Completing the Structure*, note 117 above, at para. 11.34.

261 Companies (Consolidation) Act 1908, s. 120.

262 CLR, *Completing the Structure*, note 117 above, at 207 and *Final Report*, note 117 above, at para. 13.10. The CLR noted that this is a requirement that is not found elsewhere in the Companies Act.

263 This is despite initial support for these changes: DTI, *Company Law Reform*, note 127 above, para. 4.14. No explanation for this change of direction is to be found in the Explanatory Notes accompanying the Companies Act 2006.

'the right balance'.[264] As a result, the headcount test remains intact in the Companies Act 2006.

It is notable that some of the jurisdictions that have imported the scheme of arrangement from England do not include a requirement for the headcount test, that is, the approval in scheme meetings is simply by a majority in value of the relevant members or creditors. This is the case in Canada,[265] India,[266] Malaysia,[267] South Africa (for member schemes)[268] and New Zealand (for creditor schemes and certain member schemes).[269] The headcount test, or some form of it, does appear in legislation in Singapore,[270] Hong Kong,[271] Australia,[272] the Cayman Islands,[273] the British Virgin Islands (BVI),[274] Bermuda,[275] New Zealand (for certain member schemes)[276] and South Africa (for creditor

264 *Hansard*, HL, col. GC326 (28 March 2006).

265 Canadian Business Corporations Act 1985, s. 192.

266 Indian Companies Act 2013, s. 230.

267 See Malaysian Companies Act 2016, s. 366(2) and *Sham Chin Yen* v. *Mansion Properties Sdn Bhd* [2019] 1 LNS 781 (CA); *Re TH Heavy Engineering Bhd* [2018] MLJU 466 (High Court – Kuala Lumpur) (but see Malaysian Code on Takeovers and Mergers 2016, Sch. 3, para. 2(f) with regard to takeover schemes).

268 South Africa Companies Act No. 71 of 2008, ch. 5. However, the headcount test is retained for creditor schemes (South Africa Companies Act No. 71 of 2008, ch. 6).

269 For creditor schemes and member schemes other than those involving a change of control of a 'code company' (see New Zealand Companies Act 1993, s. 236A), the New Zealand legislation does not specify the test by which the meetings should approve the scheme (see New Zealand Companies Act 1993, s. 236). This is left for the courts to determine. However, when the courts do so, the usual practice is for the court's direction to require an approval level of 75 per cent of the members or creditors (as the case may be), but without the requirement of a headcount test.

270 Singapore Companies Act, s. 210(3AB), which provides the court with the ability to waive the majority-in-number requirement if necessary.

271 Hong Kong Companies Ordinance, Cap 622, s. 674 which provides that for creditor schemes and member schemes that do not involve a general offer or takeover offer, the approval requirement includes both a majority by value requirement and a headcount test, but the court is given a discretion to dispense with the headcount test. However, for a member scheme that involves a general offer or a takeover offer, the headcount test is replaced with the requirement that the votes cast against the scheme do not exceed 10 per cent of the voting rights attached to all disinterested shares.

272 Australian Corporation Act 2001, s. 411(d).

273 Cayman Islands Companies Law, as revised, s. 86.

274 BVI Business Companies Act 2004, s. 179A(3).

275 Bermuda Companies Act 1981, s. 99(2).

276 See New Zealand Companies Act 1993, s. 236 as amended by New Zealand Companies Amendment Act 2014 which introduced a statutory approval test for schemes effecting a change of control of certain companies ('code companies'), namely that such schemes must be approved by a 75 per cent in value plus 50 per cent of those entitled to vote (s. 236A(4)). This is therefore different from the headcount test for English schemes (and

schemes).[277] However, in a number of these jurisdictions this test has been amended, and in others there are ongoing discussions about whether it should be amended or abolished.

In Australia, for example, the headcount test has been amended for member schemes, so that the court has discretion to approve a scheme if it has been approved by a 75 per cent majority, even if the headcount test has not been met.[278] Despite this amendment, a review by the Corporations and Markets Advisory Committee (CAMAC) in Australia subsequently recommended the removal of the headcount test altogether, leaving only the voted shares test, namely that 75 per cent of the shares voted on the resolution. This would bring this decision-making vote into line with decisions on other fundamental corporate matters, such as changes to the company's constitution.[279]

Singapore introduced a reform to the headcount test in 2014 that affects both member and creditor schemes. Although the initial intention was to amend only member schemes, in order to tackle the concerns about share splitting, discussed in section 2.3.3.2.2.1, the amended provisions apply equally to creditor schemes.[280] Stopping short of abolition,

indeed the headcount test as employed in other jurisdictions) which requires 50 per cent by number of those voting on the resolution to approve the scheme. The formulation of the New Zealand headcount test is potentially problematic. In widely held public companies, voter turnout is often very low and it might not be practically possible to achieve 50 per cent of total voting rights in the company.

277 South Africa Companies Act No. 71 of 2008, Ch. 6.

278 Australian Corporations Act 2001, s. 411(4)(a)(ii)(A) (this applies only to member schemes and not to creditor schemes). For discussion see *Re Boart Longyear Ltd* [2019] FCA 62 in which the Australian Federal Court found that the court's power to dispense with the headcount test was not limited to preventing share splitting. Instead, it was Parliament's intention that it should be used, albeit rarely, where the vote had been 'unfairly influenced' at [160] *per* Farrell J (although Farrell J did not ultimately dispense with the headcount test in that case).

279 CAMAC, *Members' Schemes of Arrangement*, Report, December 2009, 77–94, available at www.camac.gov.au. To date the Australian government has not taken up this suggested reform.

280 See Ministry of Finance, *Report of the Steering Committee for the Review of the Companies Act: Consultation Paper* (June 2011), 3-35 to 3-38. Creditor schemes of arrangement in Singapore have subsequently undergone a substantial reform, to incorporate many aspects of the US Chapter 11 regime, but these changes have not included any further reform of the headcount test. See Singapore Companies (Amendment) Act 2017, which came into force on 23 May 2017 (and for background see Ministry of Law *Public Consultation on Proposed Amendments to the Companies Act to Strengthen Singapore as an International Centre for Debt Restructuring*, 2016). For discussion, see Wee Meng Seng, 'Whither the Scheme of Arrangement in Singapore: More Chapter 11, Less Scheme?' available at https://papers.ssrn.com/sol3/papers.cfm?abstract_id=2922956.

the reform nevertheless recognises the possibility of abuse arising from the majority-in-number test. It provides that the court may prescribe a different majority for the headcount test, although it must still represent three-fourths in value.[281]

In Hong Kong, the government published a consultation paper in 2009 seeking views on whether the headcount test should be kept, or abolished, or whether the court should be given discretion to sanction a scheme even where the headcount test is not met, similar to the Australian position.[282] In the end, the Hong Kong Companies Ordinance 2012 introduced a series of tests for different kinds of scheme: in schemes that involve a general offer or a takeover offer, the headcount test is replaced with the requirement that the votes cast against the scheme do not exceed 10 per cent of the voting rights attached to all disinterested shares; for other member schemes that do not involve a general offer or takeover offer, the headcount test is retained, but the court is given a new discretion to dispense with the headcount test; for creditor schemes, the headcount test is retained.[283]

In the UK, it is notable that the restructuring plan introduced into Part 26A of the Companies Act 2006 by the Corporate Insolvency and Governance Act 2020 does not include a headcount requirement as part of its approval test for votes in class meetings.[284] This is despite the fact that the restructuring plan is closely modelled on the scheme of arrangement, particularly regarding procedural issues, so that, for example, the 2020 Practice Statement applies to both restructuring plans and schemes. It is also despite the headcount test being part of the Insolvency Service's initial proposals for restructuring plans.[285] In its response to the

[281] Singapore Companies Act s. 210(3AB)(a),(b).

[282] Financial Services and Treasury Bureau, *Consultation Paper: Draft Companies Bill First Phase Consultation* (December 2009) ch. 6.

[283] Hong Kong Companies Ordinance, Cap 622, s. 674.

[284] Companies Act 2006, s. 901F(1) discussed at section 5.8. Similarly, the Dutch Act on the Confirmation of Private Plans (*Wet homologatie onderhands akkoord*) contains no headcount test.

[285] See BEIS, *Insolvency and Corporate Governance: Government Response*, August 2018, para. 5.155; Insolvency Service, *A Review of the Corporate Insolvency Framework: A Consultation on Options for Reform*, May 2016, para. 9.19. The Explanatory Notes accompanying the Corporate Insolvency and Governance Act 2020 do not explain this change. It is also, perhaps, telling that the EU Restructuring Directive (EU) 2019/1023 does not require a headcount requirement as part of its approval process for restructuring plans, given that the English scheme of arrangement was undoubtedly a significant influence behind the development of this Directive, although such a requirement remains an option for Member States (Art. 9(6)).

Insolvency Service's proposals, the government stated that it was 'attracted by respondents' reasoning on why a majority in number of creditors should not be needed'[286] but felt the need to ensure that minority interests are protected and so suggested that the headcount test could be replaced with a requirement that more than half of the total value of 'unconnected creditors' vote in support of the scheme. As it turns out, the approval requirements for restructuring plans include neither the headcount test nor an 'unconnected creditors' test; they rely, instead, on the court's discretion to protect small creditors and members.[287]

In 2019 the Law Commission included the possible reform of the headcount test for schemes of arrangement in its Call for Evidence regarding intermediated securities.[288] In its 2020 follow-up paper the Law Commission states: 'We think that there is a strong argument for removing the headcount test in section 899 of the CA 2006.'[289] There seems to be an increasing recognition that this test is not beneficial and may indeed be problematic.

2.3.3.2.2 Problems arising from the headcount test There are two main problems to which the headcount test gives rise: the first relates to concerns about abuse, while the second is a result of intermediation in the holding of securities.

2.3.3.2.2.1 The possibility of abuse It is possible to circumvent the headcount test by the use of share splitting. A Hong Kong decision, *Re PCCW Ltd*,[290] illustrates this point.[291] In that case a scheme was proposed to privatise a company, PCCW Ltd. At the court-appointed meeting, there was, ostensibly, a sufficient number of votes in favour of the scheme to satisfy the headcount and share value tests. However, allegations were made that some shareholders were given PCCW shares to

[286] BEIS, *Government response: Insolvency and Corporate Governance* (2018) para. 5.155.

[287] Corporate Insolvency and Governance Act 2020, Explanatory Notes, para. 190.

[288] Law Commission, *Call for Evidence: Intermediated Securities*, August 2019, paras. 2.24–2.30.

[289] Law Commission, *Intermediated Securities*, note 178 above, para. 4.56. This appears to be the Law Commission's preferred option in the paper, but the paper does discuss alternatives, including a discretionary regime akin to the Australian system (at paras. 4.61–4.66).

[290] [2009] 3 HKC 292 CA. See S. H. Goo, 'Headcount test and scheme of arrangement' (2010) LQR 517.

[291] For an Australian case on the same issue see *Re MIM Holdings Ltd* (2003) 45 ACSR 559.

induce them to vote in favour of the scheme to meet the headcount test. At first instance, the judge found evidence of share splitting to boost the headcount.[292]

It is clear that in sanctioning a scheme the court is not just concerned with the factual question of whether the statutory provisions have been complied with; it also has discretion to refuse a scheme even if this factual issue is satisfied where, for example, it finds that the majority voting on the scheme did not fairly represent the class.[293] The Hong Kong Court of Appeal in *Re PCCW Ltd* was clear that, while, factually, the threshold had been achieved, the use of share splitting to achieve a majority in headcount was a form of manipulation of the vote, and that a court should not exercise its discretion to sanction a scheme that was approved only through such vote manipulation. Further, the court emphasised that the burden rests with the petitioner, and if there are matters that cast serious doubt on the extent to which a statutory majority fairly reflects the interest of the class, the court has to take this into account in deciding how much weight it could attach to the opinion of this majority.

Despite the potential dangers posed by share splitting, in the UK the Attorney General has stated that the theoretical possibility of 'a picture of abuse taking place, with people splitting their shareholdings up into a series of nominee companies' is not a good enough reason to do away with the headcount test.[294] To a certain extent, the concerns about share splitting that arise can be dealt with by a court at the sanctioning stage since the court can take account of share splitting and refuse to sanction where manipulation of this kind has occurred, as indeed occurred in *Re PCCW Ltd*. This might be said to alleviate some of the potential abuse to which share splitting can lead, as long as the courts remain vigilant towards this issue. However, the courts in general have no discretion to sanction a scheme where share splitting has been used to boost the position of those opposed to a scheme. This concern was one of the reasons behind the introduction in Australia of the court's discretion to sanction a scheme despite the headcount test not being passed:

> A members' scheme could be defeated by parties opposed to the scheme engaging in 'share splitting', which involves one or more members transferring small parcels of shares to a large number of other persons who are

[292] *Re PCCW Ltd*, unreported, HCMP 2382/2008, 6 April 2009.

[293] See e.g. *Re Alabama, New Orleans, Texas & Pacific Junction Railway Co* [1891] 1 Ch 213 at 238–9. For further analysis see section 2.4.

[294] *Hansard*, HL col. 217 (16 May 2006).

> willing to attend the meeting and vote in accordance with the wishes of the transferor. By splitting shares to increase the number of members voting against the scheme, an individual or small group opposed to the scheme may cause the scheme to be defeated. This may occur even though a special majority is achieved in terms of voting rights attaching to share capital, and if the share split had not occurred, the majority of members were in favour of the scheme.[295]

This issue arose for consideration in *Re Dee Valley Group plc*[296] in which the English court was asked to consider the validity of splitting shareholdings in order to defeat the headcount test in a scheme designed to effect a takeover. The company, Dee Valley Group plc, was the subject of competing takeover bids. One of the bidders, Severn Trent Water, eventually succeeded in securing the recommendation of the board and it was proposed to effect the takeover by means of a scheme. Just before the court-appointed meeting to approve the scheme, the board became aware of a series of transfers of the ordinary voting shares. An employee opposed to the takeover bought shares in the company and 'split' the shareholding by transferring one share each to 445 individuals by gift with the intention of defeating the headcount test. The board obtained a direction of the court to allow the chairman of the court-appointed meeting to ignore the transferred shares in circumstances where the split votes would have meant that the headcount test would not be satisfied and the scheme would thus fail. This meant that the scheme could proceed to the sanctioning hearing and the court then had the opportunity to consider whether the split shares should have been counted.

Therefore, unlike the position in *Re PCCW Ltd*, where the shares were split to allow shareholders to vote in favour of the scheme, in *Dee Valley* the share splitting was intended to prevent the scheme from going ahead. In *Dee Valley* the court held that the votes of shareholders who had acquired their shares from a person splitting his holding with the sole purpose of defeating the scheme were invalid as they could not be voting in the interests of the class. In allowing such a meeting to be summoned, the court is effectively directing the chairperson to take all appropriate steps to hold that meeting fairly. This includes disregarding votes where appropriate. In this case, the court's decision was not based on an examination of the motives of the shareholders concerned; rather, the

[295] Explanatory Statement to the Exposure Draft of the Corporations Amendment (Insolvency) Bill 2007, November 2006 para. 4.170 available at http://archive.treasury.gov.au/documents/1302/PDF/ES_to_the_Bill.pdf.

[296] *Re Dee Valley Group plc* [2017] EWHC 184 (Ch).

court accepted that the chairman is permitted to have regard to existing, objective evidence and to draw inferences from it. On the facts, the court held that the chairperson of the Dee Valley scheme meeting had sufficient evidence to conclude that the only explanation for the conduct of the 'new' shareholders was that they were furthering a share manipulation strategy to defeat the scheme through the majority-in-number jurisdiction requirement. It was therefore proper for the chairperson to reject those votes as he was entitled to protect the integrity of the meeting against such manipulative practices.[297] The scheme was sanctioned.

Although the outcome of the decision in *Dee Valley* is to be welcomed, as it reduces the opportunity for the headcount test to be manipulated in this way, there remain reasons to be concerned. One concern relates to the way in which the court needed to reach its decision. Ideally, any issues about the way in which court-convened meetings arrive at their decision should simply be factors taken into account at the court sanctioning decision, in the exercise of the court's discretion, as occurred in *Re PCCW*. Because this option was not available, the court needed to apply a less satisfactory approach, holding instead that a meeting of members convened by a court in relation to a scheme is of a different nature from a general meeting of the shareholders of a company and therefore the principle that a shareholder is entitled to exercise their unconstrained right of property in their shares by voting them in accordance with their own motives or individual wishes does not apply. Accordingly, in *Dee Valley* it was held that members voting at a class meeting directed by the court must exercise their power to vote for the purpose of benefitting the class as a whole and not merely individual members. This is a pragmatic solution to the situation, but it potentially sits uncomfortably with ordinary company law principles, arguments about the differences between a court-sanctioned meeting and a general meeting notwithstanding.

A second but related concern relates to the application of this test. The facts in *Dee Valley* were very stark. This was a very significant increase in the size of the shareholding, immediately before the relevant meeting,

[297] While, on the facts of the case, the chairman had been granted permission by a registrar, Vos J was clear that no such directions from the court were required since in 'directing the chairman to hold a court meeting, the court is effectively directing him to take all appropriate steps to hold a fair meeting for the purpose of ascertaining the votes of the class for or against the scheme' ([2017] EWHC 184 (Ch) at [51]). It seems likely, however, that most chairmen would prefer to have the court's blessing before disregarding votes in the future.

and none of the new members had any significant economic interest. If the facts are less stark in the future it might be more difficult for a chairman to disregard the votes at the court-convened meeting. The decision also leaves a number of difficult questions unanswered such as the nature of the test to be applied by the chairman (is it objective or subjective, and how should a chairman weigh non-financial considerations being taken into account by members, some of which may be perfectly proper, as well as the difficulty of balancing long-term and short-term considerations?) and what the effect will be of the chairman making a mistake in excluding votes (could the court still exercise its discretion to sanction the scheme?).

For these reasons, although the courts in *PCCW* and *Dee Valley* dealt creatively with the problems generated by the headcount test, and the outcomes are to be welcomed, the problems created by this test have not gone away and the need to remove the test remains.

This section has focused on the problems arising for member schemes from share splitting. Similar issues may come into play as regards creditor schemes.[298] Debts (or part of them) can potentially be assigned in order to boost the headcount.[299] However, there are some practical difficulties that can impact on the ease of assignment.[300] For example, the terms of the original agreement may not permit assignment, and only rights can be assigned, not obligations. In addition, for small creditors opposing the scheme, there is another practical barrier, namely the chances of finding assignees willing to take on the debts, since the chances of recovery may be relatively slim. This particular issue may therefore be less acute in creditor schemes than in member schemes.

2.3.3.2.2.2 Problems arising from intermediation Another argument that is sometimes raised against the headcount test in relation to member schemes is the fact that many shares in listed companies tend to be held by an intermediary. In calculating the majority-in-number requirement,

[298] See e.g. *SK Engineering* v. *Conchubar Aromatics* [2017] SGCA 51. On the facts the Singapore Court of Appeal held that the assignments were not made bona fide and declined to sanction the scheme.

[299] Statutory assignment is governed by the Law of Property Act 1925, s. 136(1) (this requires that the assignment is in writing, is absolute (not by way of a charge only) and that written notice of the assignment has been given to the obligor). Debts can also be assigned in equity: Gullifer and Payne, *Corporate Finance Law*, note 85 above, at 8.2.2.1.

[300] See e.g. ibid. at 8.2.2.

only registered members are relevant.[301] It is the intermediary, being the legal owner of the shares, that appears on the share register, and that is therefore the relevant person for this purpose. The concern is sometimes raised that in such circumstances the headcount test is not indicative of the decisions of the beneficial owners of the shares. The courts have taken a pragmatic approach to dealing with this difficulty, allowing vote splitting where the purpose is to ensure that genuine independent beneficial owners are effectively enfranchised.[302] This demonstrates an awareness of the problem of registered owners holding for multiple beneficial owners. However, these arrangements also cause difficulties for the headcount test that are not so easy to resolve. Where a nominee votes both for and against a scheme, using these vote-splitting arrangements, it will count as two people for the headcount test, one voting for and the other against:

> That does, in a sense, produce an oddity, because if you had, let us say, in an extremely simple case, ten members, one of whom wished to cast a split vote, you would really have to count that person on the headcount both for and against. So you would have on the face of it eleven members voting. But since the person would be on both sides of the head count, both in the 'yes' and 'no' lobbies, that makes no difference to the calculation of the majority in number, whereas it permits an appropriate way to achieve and calculate the true majority in value.[303]

This seems reasonable, although difficulties may arise in some scenarios. Take the situation where all of the shares are held by nominees, and they all engage in split voting of the kind described, then they would all cancel one another out under the headcount test and it would be very difficult to see how a majority in number could be achieved.

It may seem unlikely for these sorts of difficulties with the headcount test to arise in the context of member schemes, but they can happen. In the Law Commission's Call for Evidence regarding the need for reform in this context, it cited the Unilever scheme in 2018 in which the application of the headcount test to a situation where many of the shareholders held their shares through intermediaries was said to be one of the factors leading to the cancellation of the scheme.[304] This was a potentially controversial scheme and shareholder advocacy groups criticised the potentially dilutive impact of the headcount test on the voting power of

[301] *Re Abbey National plc* [2004] EWHC 2776 (Ch); [2005] 2 BCLC 15.

[302] *Re Equitable Life Assurance Society* [2002] EWHC 140 (Ch); [2002] BCC 319.

[303] Ibid. at 327 *per* Lloyd J.

[304] Law Commission, *Call for Evidence: Intermediated Securities*, August 2019, paras. 2.28–2.29.

the ultimate investors.[305] The headcount test can also be relevant in dealing with the situation in which only one or two members attend the meeting, as occurred, for example, in Jersey in *Atrium European Real Estate Limited* v. *NB*[306] in which only two shareholders were able to attend and vote on the scheme.

The impact of intermediation on the headcount test in creditor schemes is more of a problem. The vast majority of bonds are now held through global custodian arrangements.[307] As discussed in section 5.2.4, this results in the bondholder, the ultimate beneficial owner, holding its interest via an intermediary, or more usually a tier of intermediaries.[308] Applying the headcount test to this situation requires analysis of who should be regarded as the 'creditor' for this purpose. If the ultimate beneficial owners are treated as the creditors then the headcount test can be applied, but if, instead, the creditor is the 'holder' of the bonds and is better regarded as the depository holding for the first-tier intermediaries (Euroclear and/or Clearstream in Europe) then there is only one creditor and it will be impossible to satisfy the majority-in-number test in any scheme which seeks to compromise the bond.

It has become standard practice to avoid this problem by treating bondholders as contingent creditors (even without them holding definitive notes), in order to allow them to vote in the scheme directly.[309] This is a good outcome from a practical perspective. If they are not regarded as creditors for scheme purposes then unfortunate consequences can follow.[310] To determine whether there is support for the scheme, a meeting is needed, whereby a majority in number and 75 per cent in value of the creditors or class of creditors present and voting in person or by proxy agree to the compromise.[311] Imagine a company, A plc, which

[305] See also the example of *Re Sirius Minerals plc* [2020] EWHC 1447 (Ch), discussed by the Law Commission in its scoping paper: Law Commission, *Intermediated Securities*, note 178 above, paras. 4.17–4.23.

[306] [2019] JRC 198 (Royal Court, Jersey).

[307] See section 5.2.4 for detailed discussion.

[308] The orthodox analysis is to see this tier of intermediaries taking effect via a chain of trusts: See e.g. *Re Lehman Brothers International (Europe) (in Administration)* [2010] EWHC 2914 (Ch); *SL Claimants* v. *Tesco plc* [2019] EWHC 2858 (Ch).

[309] See e.g. *Re Castle Holdco 4 Ltd* [2009] EWHC 1347 (Ch); *Re Gallery Capital SA and Gallery Media Group Ltd*, unreported, 21 April 2010; *Re Magyar Telecom BV* [2013] EWHC 3800 (Ch); *Re Zlomrex International Finance SA* [2013] EWHC 3866 (Ch); and *Re New World Resources NV* [2014] EWHC 3143 (Ch). In Singapore see *Re Swiber Holdings Ltd* [2018] SGHC 211.

[310] See e.g. *Re Swiber Holdings Ltd* [2018] SGHC 211 at [34].

[311] Companies Act 2006, s. 899(1).

raises £100 million in a bond issue and subsequently proposes a scheme of arrangement to compromise this bond. If it cannot treat the ultimate investors as creditors then it would have only one creditor (the entity acting as 'holder' of the bonds). It is therefore impossible for the majority-in-number test to be met.[312]

However, the argument that bondholders are contingent creditors in such circumstances is problematic for the reasons set out in section 5.2.4 and the headcount test creates problems in practice for bondholder schemes.[313] Abolishing the headcount test would avoid these difficulties.[314]

2.3.3.2.3 Summary As discussed in this section, the headcount test is problematic as it is subject to manipulation and the application of the test is difficult where the individual holds via a nominee.[315] As regards member schemes, it may additionally be pointed out that the headcount test is at odds with the mechanism otherwise adopted for fundamental corporate matters, which relates to the number of shares voted and not to the number of shareholders. The predominant argument in favour of the headcount test is that it provides protection for smaller shareholders and creditors. It aims to prevent a scheme that does not enjoy broad-based support amongst members and/or creditors nevertheless being forced through by a small number of individuals who between them hold a large stake in the company, or have large claims against it. On this analysis, a benefit of the headcount test is that it gives minority shareholders and creditors an opportunity to have a significant say in the future nature and structure of a company under a scheme.[316]

312 This is despite the fact that there are mechanisms that can be put in place to allow the vote to be split as to value in accordance with the wishes of the ultimate account holders: C. Maunder, 'Bondholders' schemes of arrangement: playing the numbers game' (2003) *Insolvency Intelligence* 73. Whilst this can give rise to information about the value of the debts of those supporting the scheme, the headcount test cannot be satisfied since this does not affect the definition of 'creditor' for scheme purposes.

313 City of London Law Society, Response of the Joint Working Party of the City of London Law Society Company Law, Financial Law and Regulatory Law Committees to the Law Commission's Consultation on Intermediated Securities, 8 November 2019, 9.

314 For discussion see J. Payne, 'Intermediation and bondholder schemes of arrangement' in L. Gullifer and J. Payne (eds.), *Intermediation and Beyond* (Oxford: Hart, 2019).

315 This view is supported by City of London Law Society, Response of the Joint Working Party of the City of London Law Society Company Law, Financial Law and Regulatory Law Committees to the Law Commission's Consultation on Intermediated Securities, 8 November 2019, 9.

316 CAMAC, *Members' Schemes of Arrangement*, Discussion Paper, June 2008, para. 4.2.4.

However, while the test might be seen as adding some protection for small shareholders and creditors, it has the potential to result in a scheme being blocked even where the holders of the overwhelming number of shares in a company have voted in favour. On this view, the headcount test places significant veto power in the hands of small shareholders, out of proportion to their financial involvement in the company. It can result in a group of persons, who together have contributed only a small proportion of the company's equity or debt capital, having the capacity to block a scheme that is supported by shareholders or creditors that have contributed a much larger portion of the capital. It is important to note that small shareholders and creditors have other protections, such as the duties of directors when proposing the scheme and, ultimately, the fact that the court has to sanction the scheme, discussed in section 2.4. At the sanctioning stage, the court has a general discretion to take into account the number of investors who vote for and against a scheme, overall turnout and other factors it considers relevant,[317] which could include the number of ultimate investors on whose behalf an intermediary holds shares. It seems to have been accepted that the role of the court provides adequate protection to minority members/creditors in a Part 26A restructuring plan, and the same approach should be adopted in relation to schemes. It is hoped that the Law Commission's reform recommendations will bear fruit in this regard.

2.4 The sanction of the court

Following the approval of the scheme in the separate class meetings,[318] application is made to the court to sanction it.[319] This section will consider the matters taken into consideration by the court when

[317] See e.g. *Re Old Mutual Group plc* [2018] EWHC 1875 (Ch); *Re Stellar Diamonds plc* [2018] EWHC 1152 (Ch).

[318] It is clear under the Companies Act 2006, s. 899 that the English court cannot sanction a scheme of arrangement unless all of the classes have approved it by the requisite majorities. This is distinct from the position in relation to the Part 26A restructuring plan (see section 5.8) and from the position regarding schemes in some other jurisdictions (see e.g. the Canadian provisions in s. 192 of the Canadian Business Corporations Act 1985, the terms of which provide the court with a broad discretion to approve a plan of arrangement even if the approval levels have not been met).

[319] Companies Act 2006, s. 899(2). The application may be from the company, any member or creditor or, if appointed, a liquidator or administrator.

determining whether to exercise its discretion to approve the scheme.[320]

The Companies Act 2006 contains no details about what matters the court should take into account when deciding whether to sanction a scheme. It merely states that a compromise or arrangement, if agreed by the members' and creditors' meetings, as relevant, will be binding on all members/creditors or classes thereof, if sanctioned by the court.[321] It has been for the courts themselves to determine how they should exercise their discretion to give or withhold this sanction.

The court is not obliged to sanction a scheme and there is no entitlement to get the scheme sanctioned.[322] In recent years there has been renewed focus on the fact that the court will not simply 'act as a rubber stamp',[323] and an emphasis on the need for the proponent of any scheme to draw to the court's attention all matters relevant to jurisdiction and the exercise of the court's discretion.[324] This approach is entirely appropriate. Schemes of arrangement are often proposed in pressured circumstances and frequently involve unopposed hearings. In addition to the obligation of a scheme proponent to deal with the court with the utmost candour, it is important that the courts provide the appropriate level of scrutiny to uphold the integrity of schemes of arrangement as a valid, and internationally recognisable, process.

In relation to schemes involving a foreign company, the court will wish to satisfy itself that it has jurisdiction to sanction the scheme. This issue may well have been raised at the convening hearing,[325] but many, if not most, issues regarding the court's jurisdiction will be left to the sanctioning hearing. In particular, issues involving a discretionary element or

[320] Similar tests are applied in other jurisdictions though the language used to describe the test can sometimes differ: in New Zealand see *Weatherson* v. *Altus Property Investments Limited* (2001) 9 NZCLC 262 (CA); in Canada see *BCE Inc* v. *1976 Debentureholders*, 2008 SCC 69 at [137], *Re Stelco Inc* [2007] OJ No. 4234 (SCJ) at [2], *Re TrizecCorp* [1994] AJ No. 577 (QB) at [13], *St Lawrence & Hudson Railway Co* [1998] OJ No. 3934 (SCJ); in Hong Kong see *Re UDL Holdings Ltd* [2002] 1 HKC 172; in Singapore see *Daewoo Singapore Pte Ltd* v. *CEL Tractors Pte Ltd* [2001] 4 SLR 35 at 51, *The Royal Bank of Scotland NV* v. *TT International Ltd* [2012] SGCA 9; and in Bermuda see *Re APP China Group Ltd* [2003] no. 381.

[321] Companies Act 2006, s. 899(3).

[322] See e.g. *Scottish Lion Insurance Co Ltd* v. *Goodrich Corp* [2010] CSIH 6 (Inner House of the Court of Session); 2010 SC 349 at [36] *per* Lord Hamilton.

[323] See *Re Easynet Global Services Ltd* [2018] EWCA Civ 10 at [15].

[324] *Re Van Gansewinkel Groep BV & Ors* [2015] EWHC 2151 (Ch) at [6] *per* Snowden J.

[325] See section 2.2.3.2.1.

value judgement will be left to this stage.[326] In determining this issue, the court will take account of whether there is sufficient connection between the scheme and England and a reasonable prospect of the scheme being effective, having regard in particular to the prospects for the scheme's recognition in other relevant jurisdictions.[327] This issue is discussed further in Chapter 7.

For all schemes, the court will consider a range of issues when determining whether to sanction it. Morgan J summarised the court's approach in *Re TDG plc*[328] as follows:

(i) the court must be satisfied that the provisions of the statute have been complied with;
(ii) the court must be satisfied that in relation to the class of shareholders, the subject of the court meeting, was fairly represented by those who attended the meeting, and the statutory majority are acting *bona fide* and not coercing the minority in order to promote interests adverse to those of the class they purport to represent;
(iii) an intelligent and honest person, a member of the class concerned and acting in respect of his own interest, might reasonably approve the scheme; and
(iv) there must be no blot on the scheme.

These considerations may be divided into three aspects. The first is that the procedural requirements have been complied with, for example that the requisite majority approvals were met (see (i)). The second goes to the fairness of the scheme and encompasses points (ii) and (iii).[329] The third acknowledges that, even if all of the other aspects of the scheme have been satisfied, there may be a technical or legal defect in the scheme such that it does not work according to its own terms, or it would otherwise infringe some mandatory provision of the law (see (iv)).

The role of the court at this stage is important.[330] The potential for minority oppression in schemes is significant given that minority rights can be altered or removed without the consent of the individual member

[326] *Re Stronghold Insurance Company Limited* [2018] EWHC 2909 (Ch).
[327] For a full discussion see Chapter 7.
[328] [2009] 1 BCLC 445 at [29].
[329] Although these two issues are often referred to as separate tests, it is clear that they are part of an overarching consideration of fairness and the outcome of one test is likely to impact on the outcome of the other; see e.g. *Re Realm Therapeutics Plc* [2019] EWHC 2080 (Ch) at [52].
[330] For discussion see J. Payne, 'The role of the court in debt restructuring', note 110 above, 124.

or creditor (as long as the class to which that member/creditor belongs consents, along with all other member/creditor classes). The division of members and creditors into classes is therefore an important form of minority protection, but, as discussed in section 2.3.2.3, there has been a shift towards fewer classes and for minority protection to be dealt with at the sanctioning stage. The exercise of the court's discretion at this stage is therefore a key form of protection for minorities. Although the courts do not refuse to sanction schemes very often,[331] this fact does not undermine the importance of the role of the court. The provision of a clear steer regarding difficulties at an early stage means that deficiencies can be corrected before sanctioning is sought and that problematic schemes often do not proceed to the sanctioning hearing.[332]

The application to the court for the scheme to be sanctioned can be opposed by members and creditors who object to the scheme.[333] However, there are no statutory provisions restricting those who can oppose a scheme,[334] and legitimate concerns of third parties can also be taken into account by the court.[335] This can include creditors or

331 See e.g. *Re Sunbird Business Services Ltd* [2020] EWHC 2493 (Ch); *Puma Brandenburg Ltd* v. *Aralon Resources and Investment Company Ltd and Nortrust Nominees Ltd* (18 May 2017, judgment 27/2017, Guernsey Court of Appeal).

332 See e.g. *Re Indah Kiat International Finance Company BV* [2016] EWHC 246 (Ch).

333 Some jurisdictions place limitations on this right, see e.g. Indian Companies Act 2013, s. 230(4) which stipulates that any objection to the scheme at the sanctioning hearing can only be made by shareholders with not less than 10 per cent of the shareholding or creditors with not less than 5 per cent of outstanding debt. No such limitations exist in English schemes.

334 See *Re BAT Industries plc*, unreported, 3 September 1998, in which Neuberger J allowed objections from prospective litigants against the company. The claimants were contingent creditors to a dividend proposed to be paid outside the scheme, and the scheme was in fact between the company and its members. The matter objected to was therefore outside the scheme (but would inevitably have followed the scheme). Cf. the approach of David Richards J in *Re Telewest Communications plc (No. 2)* [2004] EWHC 1466 (Ch). In *Re RAC Motoring Services Ltd* [2000] 1 BCLC 307, when faced with objections by possible claimants against the company's assets, Neuberger J emphasised that the court was not undertaking a roving commission at the suit of any objector alleging prejudice from the scheme.

335 The court has complete discretion as to whether to award costs for or against an objector, or to make no costs award at all: Civil Procedure Rules, r. 44.3(2)(b). See e.g. *Re Inmarsat plc* [2020] EWHC 776 (Ch). The instances in which the court may make such an order are likely to be where there is a collateral motive, or where the objector is a speculative investor seeking to leverage a better deal, and where the scheme is otherwise fundamentally sound. However, unless the objections are wholly improper or irrelevant or obviously collaterally motivated, there is little likelihood of an adverse costs order since the court will not wish to deter parties who have genuine issues to raise (see also *Re Stronghold Insurance Company Limited* [2018] EWHC 2909 (Ch); *Re Ophir Energy plc* [2019] EWHC 1278 (Ch)).

shareholders that have not been given the right to vote on a scheme (because their interests are unaffected by the scheme) but who nevertheless seek to object to the scheme at this stage on the basis that the scheme is unfair to their interests.[336] There is a balance to be struck, however. While the courts emphasise the importance of potential opponents to a scheme appearing at the court hearing(s), they look unfavourably upon those who seek to disrupt a scheme without legitimate cause.[337] Fundamentally, although it is open to any member or creditor to raise objections at the sanctioning stage, in the absence of oppression the mere fact that a minority shareholder is unhappy with the outcome of the scheme is not sufficient reason for the court to refuse to sanction: 'If the required majority decide that, for better or worse, this is an offer that they would wish to accept, and the deal was acceptable to them, then it is inherent in the whole scheme of arrangement regime that the minority prima facie has to go along with that, no matter how disgruntled they may be.'[338]

2.4.1 Have the statutory provisions been complied with?

The court will want to ensure that the statutory requirements set out in Part 26 of the Companies Act 2006 have been complied with. This has a number of elements. For instance, the court will want to ensure that the explanatory statement provided in relation to the scheme was adequate.[339] If not, or if the explanatory statement is defective in some other way, the court will not sanction the scheme. In addition, it will want to see that the resolutions at the class meetings are passed by the statutory majority of each class. If this has not occurred then the court cannot approve the scheme even if the court considers it to be fair and the scheme would, otherwise, have been approved. Consequently, the cramdown of an entire class of members or creditors is not possible under a scheme of arrangement,[340] although it is possible in a Part 26A restructuring plan, introduced by the Corporate Insolvency and Governance Act 2020.[341]

[336] See e.g. *Re Bluebrook Ltd* [2009] EWHC 2114 (Ch) discussed further at section 5.4.3.

[337] See e.g. *Re Ophir Energy plc* [2019] EWHC 1278 (Ch).

[338] *Re Carpetright plc* [2020] EWHC 342 (Ch) at [6] *per* Mann J.

[339] E.g. the court may reject the scheme where it feels that the disclosures made are inadequate: *Re C. M. Banks Ltd* [1944] NZLR 248.

[340] It is, however, possible to achieve the de facto cramdown of entire classes if the right transaction structure is developed. A good example of this is the use of a scheme twinned with pre-pack administration to effectively sideline the junior creditors in the financial restructuring of a company (see section 5.4.3).

[341] See section 5.8.

Determining whether the classes of members/creditors have approved the scheme by the requisite majority has two elements. The first is to ensure that the approval requirements have been met. The somewhat peculiar way in which approval must be obtained at these meetings, that is, the majority in number, representing three-fourths in value of the company's creditors or members present and voting in person or by proxy,[342] makes this task more complicated than it might otherwise be. In recent years the majority-in-number requirement has created some problems in this regard, particularly around the issue of share splitting.[343]

The second relates to the question of whether the correct class meetings have been held.[344] As discussed in section 2.2.3, following the introduction of the Practice Statement, issues regarding the composition and summoning of class meetings should be resolved at an earlier stage in proceedings. Members, or creditors, who feel unfairly treated can still raise objections to the scheme at the sanctioning stage, but the court will expect them to show good reason why they did not raise any concerns (e.g. regarding the composition of classes) at the earlier stage.[345] The court has acknowledged that it might not always be possible to provide members of creditors with full details of the scheme (including details of class constitution) before the convening hearing, in which case it is not reasonable to expect them to raise objections at that hearing.[346]

A question arises as to whether the court should have power to sanction a scheme of arrangement despite some technical defect regarding compliance with the statutory procedure, for example where classes were wrongly constituted. If the court believes that, despite these defects, the scheme is nevertheless fair and that it would have been approved anyway then there would seem to be good reasons for allowing the court to sanction the scheme. To refuse to sanction the scheme in these circumstances seems unnecessary, potentially costly and to have little policy benefit attached to it.[347] It was a recommendation of the CLR that the court should be given discretion to sanction a scheme of arrangement

342 Companies Act 2006, s. 899(1).

343 See section 2.3.3.2.

344 See e.g. *Re British Aviation Insurance Co Ltd* [2005] EWHC 1621 (Ch); [2006] BCC 14.

345 See Practice Statement (Companies: Schemes of Arrangement under Part 26 and Part 26A of the Companies Act 2006) [2020] 1 WLR 4493.

346 *Marconi Corporation plc* v. *Marconi plc* [2003] EWHC 663 (Ch).

347 See e.g. the comments of David Richards J in *Re Telewest Communications plc (No. 1)* [2004] EWHC 924 (Ch).

where it is satisfied that the incorrect composition of classes did not have any substantive effect on the outcome.[348] However, the government did not follow this recommendation, despite initial suggestions that this proposal would be implemented.[349] Although no public explanation exists for this change of approach, the government's decision not to make this change appears to have been based on a concern for minority rights. When the Attorney General addressed this issue in the House of Lords Grand Committee debating the Companies Bill, he stated:

> The amendment would weaken another safeguard for individual creditors and members that is contained in the current law. Under the amendment, they could be deprived of their rights without a properly constituted class meeting on the basis of what the court considers to be 'fair'. That would give the court an extremely wide discretion and, in some cases, allow the court to override the wishes of the minority creditors or shareholders.[350]

However, these concerns appear unfounded, and it is unfortunate that the courts do not have the flexibility to sanction a scheme in circumstances where the defects are technical and have no substantive effect on the outcome.[351]

2.4.2 *The bona fide test*

In addition to these practical procedural issues, the courts have stressed that they have a broad supervisory jurisdiction over schemes of arrangement.[352] Even where the classes are appropriately configured and the statutory majorities have voted in favour of the scheme, the court will still want to ensure that the class is fairly represented by those who attend the meeting and that the statutory majority act bona fide and do not coerce the minority in order to promote interests adverse

[348] CLR, *Final Report*, note 117 above, para. 13.7. A similar argument for a curative power for the court, to allow it to sanction schemes in such circumstances, has also been considered in Australia, and CAMAC did recommend that such a reform be introduced: CAMAC, *Members' Schemes of Arrangement*, Report, December 2009, ch. 5, esp. 91.

[349] DTI, *Company Law Reform*, note 127 above, para. 4.14.

[350] *Hansard*, HL, col GC 326 (28 March 2006) (Lord Goldsmith).

[351] Some jurisdictions go even further in this regard. In Canada, for example, the court has a broad discretion to set the level of voting approval required by members/creditors to approve a scheme, and then to sanction it even if that mandated voting threshold has not been reached.

[352] *Re Alabama, New Orleans, Texas & Pacific Junction Railway Co* [1891] 1 Ch 213 at 238–9 *per* Lindley LJ.

to those of the class whom they purport to represent.[353] It is clear that the court need not simply endorse the majority vote,[354] and if there are reasons to doubt that the vote represents the views of the class as a whole, the court can refuse to sanction the scheme.

The court will be concerned to ensure that the votes necessary to secure the approval of the class were cast bona fide and not in order to promote a special interest of some members or creditors that was not shared by the class as a whole.[355] If the court considers that the meeting is unrepresentative, or that those voting at the meeting have done so to promote a special interest that differs from the interest of the ordinary, independent and objective member/creditor, then the court can refuse to sanction the scheme. Consequently, the votes of the majority are not treated by the court as conclusive. Bowen LJ has explained the reasoning behind this requirement as follows:

> [A]lthough in a meeting which is to be held under this section it is perfectly fair for every man to do that which is best for himself, yet the Court, which has to see what is reasonable and just as regards the interests of the whole class, would certainly be very much influenced in its decision, if it turned out that the majority was composed of persons who had not really the interests of that class at stake.[356]

This hurdle can operate as a real protection for minorities. In *Re NFU Development Trust Ltd*,[357] Brightman J refused to sanction the scheme even though it had been passed by the requisite majority of the members. The scheme there involved the members surrendering their membership rights. Brightman J therefore held that this was not an 'arrangement' for these purposes since there was no element of give and take; however, he went on to say that a further problem with the scheme was that 'no member voting in the interests of members as a whole' could reasonably approve it.[358]

Hildyard J in *Re Lehman Bros International (Europe) Ltd* summarised the relevant questions as follows:

[353] *Re Anglo-Continental Supply Company Limited* [1922] 2 Ch 723 at 736; *Re National Bank Ltd* [1966] 1 WLR 819; *Re Anglo American Insurance Co Ltd* [2001] 1 BCLC 755 at 762.

[354] See e.g. *Re BTR plc* [2000] 1 BCLC 740 at 747 *per* Jonathan Parker J; *Re TDG plc* [2008] EWHC 2334 (Ch); [2009] 1 BCLC 445.

[355] *Re BTR plc (Leave to Appeal)* [2000] 1 BCLC 740.

[356] *Re Alabama, New Orleans, Texas & Pacific Junction Railway Co* [1891] 1 Ch 213 at 244.

[357] [1972] 1 WLR 1548.

[358] Ibid. at 1555.

> (a) whether the majority creditors had some 'special interest(s)' different from and adverse to the other members of the [relevant] class by which it is shown (b) they were predominantly motivated in voting as they did; if so, (c) whether their votes are to be (i) disregarded or (ii) discounted, and (d) what effect that should have in terms of whether or not the court should decline to sanction the scheme.[359]

In *Re Realm Therapeutics Plc*,[360] Norris J reiterated that it is class members' rights as opposed to their interests which are important. A class consists of those who have to face the same issue, not those who think the same way about the issue. When addressing the issue faced by the class, a member is entitled to vote in accordance with their own economic interests. What is not legitimate is to vote in accordance with economic interests in relation to some matter *other* than the issue raised for decision, some matter not shared by the class as a whole. Where there are two possible explanations for the casting of votes, the question is whether it is the illegitimate one that predominates.

One scenario in which some members of a class might have special interests of the kind envisaged here is in a takeover scheme. Take the situation in which the bidder's subsidiaries hold shares in the target company and vote those shares in favour of the scheme at the court-convened members' meeting.[361] The courts now take a broad view of the concept of 'class' for scheme purposes.[362] If the bidder's subsidiaries have the same rights as the other shareholders (e.g. if they all hold ordinary shares in the target company and are not being treated differently in the scheme) then the bidder's subsidiaries could be regarded as forming part of the same class as the other target shareholders for the purpose of meeting to approve the scheme. However, the bidder's subsidiaries clearly have a different interest from the rest of the class when deciding whether to approve the scheme. Where the majority is reached only with the votes of the bidder's subsidiaries, the court would be likely to refuse to sanction the scheme.[363] In

[359] [2018] EWHC 1980 (Ch) at [88]. The Singaporean courts have taken a similar approach. For example, in *The Royal Bank of Scotland NV* v. *TT International Ltd* (2012) SGCA 9 it was held that the votes of creditors related to the company may be discounted by the court as their interests may differ from 'ordinary, independent and objective creditors of the same class' (at [26]).

[360] [2019] EWHC 2080 (Ch).

[361] For further discussion see section 3.5.2, especially section 3.5.2.5.

[362] See section 2.3.2.

[363] However, in some circumstances the courts have been prepared to sanction the scheme even where such a conflict of interest exists, provided full disclosure has been made to the rest of the class: *Goodfellow* v. *Nelson Line (Liverpool) Ltd* [1912] 2 Ch 324.

determining this issue, the court will assess not just the scheme in a narrow or limited sense but all of the allied documents and arrangements that are entered into pursuant to the scheme and which might give rise to concerns about members or creditors having special interests that affect their vote in the class meetings.[364]

However, the mere fact that the scheme confers significant benefits on those voting for it is not of itself a reason for the court to call into question the fairness of the scheme, as long as those voting for the scheme are acting bona fide.[365] In *Re Lehman Bros International (Europe) Ltd*,[366] the court held that 'the mere fact that the majority creditors have a special interest in supporting the scheme does not, without more, entail that the class was not fairly represented'.[367] To impugn class representation, any special interest would need to be opposed to the interest of the remaining members of the class. Further, there must be a 'strong and direct causative link'[368] between the adverse interest and the voting decision. In *Re Lehman Bros*, Hildyard J continued to favour the 'but for' test he put forward in *Re Apcoa Parking Holdings GmbH*[369] as a useful means for demonstrating the necessary causal link:

> I continue to think that with suitable caution or nuance in its application, the 'but for' test may be helpful in conveying the extent to which the special interest must be demonstrated to be an adverse one before the vote of a member of a class at a duly constituted class meeting is to be discounted or even disregarded.[370]

On the facts, the special interest was simply an additional reason, not the dominant or causative reason, for voting in favour of the scheme; therefore, the special interest did not undermine the representation of the class.

In assessing these issues, the court will take account of the level of voting and the voting outcomes and also the nature and the quality of the information provided to the class of members/creditors: the class must

364 *Re Telewest Communications plc (No. 1)* [2004] EWHC 924 (Ch) at [54]; *Re Stemcor Trade Finance Limited* [2015] EWHC 2662 (Ch) at [17]–[18]; *Re Baltic Exchange Ltd* [2016] EWHC 3391 (Ch).

365 *Re The Co-Operative Bank Plc* [2017] EWHC 2269 (Ch).

366 [2018] EWHC 1980 (Ch).

367 Ibid. at [89] *per* Hildyard J.

368 Ibid. at [90].

369 [2014] EWCH 3849 (Ch) at [130] but see *Ocean Rig UDW Inc*, Cayman Islands Grand Court, 18 September 2017 at [95], and *Re Boart Longyear Ltd (No. 2)* (2017) 122 ACSR 437 at [134].

370 [2018] EWHC 1980 (Ch) at [102] *per* Hildyard J.

have been 'properly consulted'.[371] Where the level of support from the unconnected members or creditors is significant, there may still be good reasons for the court to sanction the scheme even where there are concerns about some members/creditors having a special interest.[372] By contrast, low levels of voting might tip the balance in the other direction.[373] This is because the court might have concerns about whether the notification process had resulted in shareholders not receiving adequate notice of the court meeting or because of concerns that a low turnout might be indicative of a meeting that was unrepresentative of the membership as a whole.[374] As Morgan J stated in *Re TDG plc*,[375] a low turnout at the meeting is not itself a valid reason for a court to refuse to sanction the scheme since the fact that shareholders do not attend the meeting might be attributable to a variety of causes[376] and is not an indicator of opposition to the scheme.[377] Nevertheless, the size of turnout might be relevant in considering whether the result of the vote could have been affected by collateral factors, that is, by those members or creditors with special interests.[378] This is an issue that might play out differently in creditor and member schemes. In *Re Stellar Diamonds plc*,

371 See David Richards J in *Re Telewest Communications plc (No. 2)* [2004] EWHC 1466 (Ch) at [20]–[22] and *Re Sunbird Business Services Ltd* [2020] EWHC 2493 (Ch) (in which the 'paucity of information' provided to creditors was a core reason for the refusal of the judge to sanction that scheme).

372 See e.g. *Re The Co-Operative Bank Plc* [2017] EWHC 2269 (Ch). This argument is particularly strong where the level of support from the unconnected creditors would satisfy the 75 per cent by value test, but it might still be made where the unconnected creditors form more than a simple majority (see e.g. *Re TT International Ltd* [2010] SGHC 177).

373 See e.g. *Re Cape plc* [2006] EWHC 1316 (Ch); [2006] 3 All ER 1222 (in which the low turnout was not held to be a problem); *Re Osiris Insurance Ltd* [1999] 1 BCLC 182.

374 See e.g. *Re Stellar Diamonds plc* [2018] EWHC 1152 (Ch) at [14]. A low turnout may cause the court to look critically at the composition of the statutory majority. In *Re Realm Therapeutics plc* [2019] EWHC 2080 (Ch), for example, only twenty-four scheme shareholders attended the meeting: by headcount this represented just 5.61 per cent of the total shareholder population, although by value it represented 70.98 per cent of the shares in issue. So, large shareholders were heavily represented, but Norris J also noted that there were nineteen attendees with modest shareholdings (valued at about £7,500 or less), as part of his assessment in sanctioning the scheme.

375 [2009] 1BCLC 445 at [25].

376 For example, a large number of small creditors or members who are unlikely to be motivated to take an interest in the scheme. In member schemes the court may also take account of the level of turnout at ordinary company meetings. For discussion see *Re Stellar Diamonds plc* [2018] EWHC 1152 (Ch); *Re Patagonia Gold plc* [2019] EWHC 2688 (Ch).

377 See *Re TDG plc* [2009] 1 BCLC 445 at [25].

378 *Re British Aviation Insurance Co Ltd* [2005] EWHC 1621 (Ch); [2006] BCC 14 at [117].

Snowden J gave the following as one of his reasons for sanctioning the transfer scheme in that case despite the low turnout:

> Moreover . . . this is a members' scheme which, by reference to the market price of the scheme shares and the consideration shares, confers a considerable premium on all shareholders. It is not a complex creditors' scheme where, for example, there might be cause for greater concern as to how a limited fund was being divided up between different groups of creditors who were required to accept a reduction in their claims, or as to how different groups of creditors might share in a variety of potential future benefits from a restructured enterprise.[379]

The final issue is what the effect will be if the court concludes that a member's or creditor's special interest was the dominant causative reason for it having voted in favour of a proposed scheme. In particular, the question arises as to whether the court could or should nevertheless exercise its discretion to sanction the scheme. In practice, the court has two options for dealing with situations where a special interest has been found to be the dominant causative reason for the member's/creditor's vote: the court may either (a) discount the weight given to the majority vote and consider the fairness of the scheme without adopting any particular presumption in favour of the majority or (b) altogether disregard the relevant votes of 'special interest' creditors so that the relevant votes are void and do not count at all towards the statutory majority, in which case if the requisite majorities are not achieved the scheme must fail.[380] It is clear, however, that the treatment of an unrepresentative vote is a matter of discretion for the court.[381] It is therefore for the court to take account of all the circumstances, including the level of support from unconnected members/creditors, and the court's view of the balance of benefit offered by the scheme when determining whether and to what extent to discount or disregard votes and whether to exercise its discretion to sanction the scheme.

2.4.3 *The 'intelligent and honest' person test*

The courts have stressed that the scheme must be one that 'an intelligent and honest man, a member of the class concerned and acting in respect of

[379] Ibid. at [24].

[380] *Re UDL Holdings Ltd* [2002] 1 HKC 172 (Final Court of Appeal of Hong Kong), 155 *per* Lord Millett. See also *Re Realm Therapeutics Plc* [2019] EWHC 2080 (Ch) at [47] *per* Norris J.

[381] *Re Alabama, New Orleans, Texas & Pacific Junction Railway Co* [1891] 1 Ch 213 at 244 *per* Bowen LJ. The same approach is adopted elsewhere e.g. *Re Boart Longyear Ltd (No.2)* (2017) 122 ACSR 437) at [152].

his interest might reasonably approve'.[382] However, the court has emphasised that its role is not to usurp the views of those who have properly voted in favour of the scheme, and it will be strongly influenced if there is a substantial majority vote in favour of the scheme.[383] The test is not 'is this a reasonable scheme?' but rather 'could the class of creditors/members reasonably have approved it?' It is clear that the scheme proposed need not be the only fair scheme or even, in the court's view, the best scheme.[384] Necessarily, there may be reasonable differences of view on these issues.[385] The court has also recognised that in commercial matters members or creditors are generally the best judges of their own interests and that accordingly the court 'will be slow to differ from the meeting'.[386] There is necessarily some overlap with the previous test, namely whether the requisite majorities acting bona fides have voted in favour of the scheme. If this is the case, the court will be loath to overturn the decision of these groups.

The court will assess the question of whether an intelligent and honest person, a member of the class concerned, acting in their own interest, could reasonably approve the scheme by reference to the time at which the scheme meetings were held. This issue arose for consideration in *Re Cobham plc*,[387] in which the scheme was promulgated in August 2019, the scheme meeting took place in September 2019, but the sanction hearing occurred only in January 2020. In the interim there had been a period of political and economic uncertainty, including the calling of a general election, and it was claimed by a dissenting shareholder at the sanctioning hearing that if the scheme meeting were to be held again, the outcome would be different. Zacaroli J held that even at the time of the scheme meetings in September 2019 there was considerable economic and political uncertainty and that 'the shareholders were in a position to take into account (when voting on the scheme) whether it would be better to vote against the Scheme on the basis that if and when the uncertainty was resolved, the share price (and thus the likely offer on the table) might improve'.[388] In circumstances where an

[382] *Re Alabama, New Orleans, Texas & Pacific Junction Railway Co* [1891] 1 Ch 213 at 238–9 *per* Lindley LJ; *Re TDG plc* [2009] 1 BCLC 445 at [29].

[383] *Re Equitable Life Assurance Society* [2002] EWHC 140 (Ch); [2002] BCC 319; *Re TDG plc* [2008] EWHC 2334 (Ch); [2009] 1 BCLC 445. See also *Re Premier Oil plc* [2020] CSOH 39.

[384] See e.g. *Re Realm Therapeutics Plc* [2019] EWHC 2080 (Ch).

[385] See e.g. *Re Telewest Communications Plc (No. 2)* [2004] EWHC 1466 (Ch).

[386] Ibid. at [22] *per* David Richards J. See also *Re Premier Oil plc* [2020] CSOH 39.

[387] [2020] EWHC 320 (Ch).

[388] Ibid. at [11].

unexpected and unforeseeable event intervenes between the convening meeting and the sanctioning meeting, the court should consider whether there is a sufficient possibility that the vote which occurred would be different and whether the statutory majority would still have been achieved if the members/creditors had been aware of the intervening event.[389]

The court will consider the full commercial and factual context of the scheme. The central issue will be whether the scheme is fair amongst the various interests involved and so could reasonably have been approved at the meetings.[390] It will also be relevant, as part of this analysis, what percentage of the members/creditors voted in favour of the scheme. In *Re Realm Therapeutics Plc*,[391] for example, Norris J acknowledged that some of the criticisms of the scheme in that case had weight and merit in some respects. However, he could not ignore the fact that an experienced board and a 78.49 per cent majority by value of experienced investors considered that this was a transaction that an honest and intelligent shareholder could approve. Accordingly, although approving the deal involved a gamble, the court was not as well-placed as the investors to make this pure commercial judgement, and Norris J sanctioned that scheme.

Providing that the scheme is fair and equitable, the court will not judge its commercial merits.[392] The function of the court is not to determine how it would have voted on the scheme.[393] The court should be very slow to interfere with the expression by the scheme creditors of what they believe to be in their best interests.[394] It will therefore be extremely rare for the court to exercise its discretion to refuse to sanction a scheme that has been approved by the correct majorities of members/creditors, where the classes are correctly constituted and where there is no suggestion that the majority did not represent the class.[395] However, the detailed and deeply considered judgments given in relation to these issues show that the court will rigorously put to the test the question of whether the proposed scheme is genuinely fair and appropriate.[396]

389 See e.g. *Re Nisa Retail Ltd* [2018] EWHC 1183 (Ch) at [26]–[29].

390 *Re Cape plc* [2006] EWHC 1316 (Ch); [2006] 3 All ER 1222.

391 [2019] EWHC 2080 (Ch).

392 The same approach is adopted in other jurisdictions e.g. *Re APP China Group Ltd* [2003] no. 381 (Bermuda).

393 See e.g. *Re Telewest Communications Plc (No. 2)* [2004] EWHC 1466 (Ch).

394 *Re Global Investment House KSC* [2012] EWHC 3792 (Ch).

395 *British Aviation Insurance Co Ltd* [2005] EWHC 1621 (Ch)[*per* Lewison J at [75]–[76].

396 See e.g. *Re Lehman Bros International (Europe) Ltd* [2018] EWHC 1980 (Ch).

2.4.4 *A blot on the scheme*

In addition to the considerations set out so far in this section, the court generally will not sanction a scheme if it finds a 'blot', such as illegality or material mistake, in the scheme: 'Put another way, the court is unlikely to approve a scheme that does not have the effect that the company and creditors intend.'[397] Snowden J considered whether such a blot existed in *Re Van Gansewinkel Groep BV & Ors.*[398] In that case the possible blot related to the release by scheme creditors of a third-party guarantor. It is accepted that such releases can fall within the concept of an 'arrangement' where such a release is necessary to give legal or commercial effect to the compromise or arrangement between the scheme company and its creditors.[399] That test clearly applied on the facts of *Gansewinkel*: the release of the third-party guarantor was part and parcel of the compromise between scheme creditors and the scheme companies. However, the necessary deed of release was not expressly provided for in the scheme documents. In the end, the judge was satisfied that the scheme documentation could be interpreted to include such a release and that the scheme creditors clearly intended the release to occur as part of the scheme. The court ordinarily will not sanction a scheme which contains or provides for significant new or different terms that have not been drawn to the attention of creditors prior to their voting upon the scheme, so if the judge had not been satisfied that the scheme creditors had contemplated this release, further scheme meetings would have been needed before the scheme could progress.

2.5 Delivery to the Registrar of Companies

The order sanctioning the scheme takes effect once a copy is delivered to the Registrar of Companies.[400] It is clear therefore that although the scheme resembles a contract between a company and its members/creditors, in fact a scheme has binding force only by virtue of

[397] *Re Van Gansewinkel Groep BV & Ors* [2015] EWHC 2151 (Ch) at [61] *per* Snowden J.

[398] [2015] EWHC 2151 (Ch). Another example was given by Zacaroli J in *Re Cobham plc* [2020] EWHC 320 (Ch), namely, if the scheme involves a reduction of capital and no special resolution is proposed to approve that reduction (at [5]). For examples relating to member schemes see *Re RhythmOne plc* [2019] EWHC 967 (Ch) at [18] and *Re Vernalis plc* [2018] EWHC 3898 (Ch) at [13]–[16]. See also *Re Royal London Mutual Insurance Society Ltd* [2018] EWHC 2215 (Ch) at [33].

[399] See section 2.1.1.

[400] Companies Act 2006, s. 899(4). If the order amends the company's articles or any constitutional resolution or agreement, a copy of the amended articles/resolution/agreement must then be sent to the Registrar: s. 901.

statute.[401] Once the court has sanctioned the scheme and the sanction order is delivered to the Registrar of Companies,[402] it becomes binding on the company (including the liquidator/administrator if the company is in liquidation/administration)[403] and on all the relevant members and creditors. Crucially, therefore, the scheme also binds any dissenters.

The court will set aside the scheme subsequently only on very limited grounds, for example if the consent has been obtained by fraud.[404] Similarly, schemes once sanctioned cannot be amended unless the scheme itself provides for amendment in future.[405] It has been suggested that the court's sanction overrides any illegality, such as unlawful financial assistance, in the scheme.[406] It is unclear whether the court can later withdraw its sanction if it subsequently emerges that there was some defect or irregularity in the proceedings leading up to the order, but the preferable view is that it should not.[407]

2.6 Summary

This chapter has sought to provide an analysis of the mechanics of schemes of arrangement. The provisions set out in this chapter generally apply to all schemes, whether they are member-focused or

401 *Kempe* v. *Ambassador Insurance Co* [1998] 1 WLR 271.

402 When the court is considering whether to sanction a scheme, it has complete discretion as to consequential directions. In *Re Allied Domecq plc* [2000] BCC 582, for example, the court approved a proposed scheme but, as there were differences between the proposal then before it and that which had been approved earlier by the shareholders, the court's sanction was made conditional upon the company undertaking to ensure that the shareholders reaffirmed their support by the appropriate resolution.

403 Companies Act 2006, s. 899(3). The courts have rejected the argument that a scheme that satisfies the requirements of the Act might nevertheless amount to a deprivation of possessions contrary to Art. 1 of the First Protocol of the European Convention on Human Rights: *Re Equitable Life Assurance Society* [2002] EWHC 140 (Ch); [2002] BCC 319; *Re Waste Recycling Group plc* [2003] EWHC 2065 (Ch); [2004] 1 BCLC 352.

404 Even where the judgment is obtained by fraud the court will not set it aside if it is satisfied that the result would have been the same in the absence of fraud: *Fletcher* v. *Royal Automobile Club Ltd* [2000] 1 BCLC 331; *British and Commonwealth Holdings plc* v. *Barclays Bank plc* [1996] 1 BCLC 1.

405 See *Sport Financiera SA* v. *Olympic Gold Holdings Ltd*, ECSC-BVI (Comm), 19 September 2013.

406 It was suggested by Harman J in *British and Commonwealth Holdings plc* v. *Barclays Bank plc* [1996] 1 BCLC 1 that the court's sanction would override such illegality.

407 See *Sovereign Life Assurance Co* v. *Dodd* [1892] 2 QB 573 (where a creditor was held not bound by the approved scheme); cf. *Chief Commissioner of Payroll Tax* v. *Group Four Industries Ltd* [1984] 1 NSWLR 680.

creditor-focused. It is clear that there are three broad stages involved in any scheme, namely (i) the proposal of a scheme between the company and its members/creditors followed by an application to court to summon the necessary meetings; (ii) meetings of the members/creditors (in classes where required) to consider and vote on the scheme; and (iii) the sanctioning of the scheme by the court, and the delivery of a copy of the order to the Registrar of Companies. The legislative provisions regarding schemes are relatively brief, covering just a few sections of the Companies Act 2006. Much of the detail of how schemes operate in practice has therefore been developed by the courts.

The role of the courts in this regard is very significant. It is the courts that have helped to develop schemes of arrangement into a flexible and valuable tool for companies. For example, it is the courts that have consistently defined the concept of 'arrangement' very broadly and have overcome some of the difficulties associated with organising members and creditors into classes by moving away from overzealous distinctions, concentrating on rights rather than interests, and by shifting the focus of the court's protection of minorities to the sanctioning hearing. These developments are to be welcomed. Although the decision in *Hawk Insurance* has been criticised, along with the consequent change in the approach to determining classes in this context, shifting the focus on minority protection from the class meeting stage to the sanctioning hearing is a sensible and pragmatic development which should not be viewed as diminishing or undermining minority protection. The English court has demonstrated a keen awareness of the need to exercise its role in a way that will protect members and creditors, at both the convening and the sanctioning hearings, not least in ensuring that adequate disclosure is provided to members/creditors, in sufficient time for them to consider the proposals, and in scrutinising the fairness of the scheme at the sanctioning stage.

The commercially sensible approach taken by the English courts in this regard goes a long way to explaining the rise in popularity of schemes of arrangement in recent years. However, there are limits to what the courts can do, and statutory reform of a number of aspects of scheme procedure would be desirable. In particular, there is no way for the courts to remove or amend the legislative requirement for a headcount test; only Parliament is able to do this. This is a reform that is long overdue and the arguments in favour of the removal of this requirement are compelling. Second, it is also recommended in this chapter that the courts be provided with the power to sanction a scheme where technical defects in the statutory procedure have occurred but the court nevertheless believes that the scheme is fair. This was a reform recommended by the CLR but, unfortunately, not taken forward by the government.

3

Member schemes of arrangement: takeover schemes

3.1 Introduction

The purpose of this chapter, and the next, is to consider member schemes. This chapter will focus on the most common use of member schemes, namely the use of a scheme to effect a takeover of a company, as an alternative to a takeover offer.[1] However, other types of member scheme are possible, and examples of these schemes are discussed in Chapter 4.

Although schemes of arrangement, when first introduced, were exclusively for arrangements between a company and its creditors, the possibility of member schemes was introduced in 1900,[2] and since that time the use of member schemes has become commonplace.[3] Perhaps the first point to consider is what is meant by a member scheme. There is no sharp division between member schemes and creditor schemes. Often schemes will need to be considered and approved by both members and creditors. The use of the term 'member schemes' is not meant to suggest that only members will ever consider and approve such schemes. Some of the member schemes described in this chapter and the next might well involve creditors. For example, in a takeover scheme, described in this

[1] For the purposes of this chapter, a takeover may be defined as a transaction in which a person (or persons acting in concert) acquire(s) control of a company to which the City Code on Takeovers and Mergers (the Takeover Code) applies: Takeover Code, Introduction, s. 3(a). Control for these purposes means the holding of shares carrying 30 per cent or more of the voting rights of the company: ibid. Definitions section.

[2] Companies Act 1900, s. 24 extended schemes to members and Companies Act 1907, s. 38 extended schemes to companies outside the course of liquidation. For further discussion of the historical development of schemes see section 1.2.

[3] In this book, the terms 'member' and 'shareholder' are used interchangeably since most member schemes will involve companies that have issued share capital.

chapter, creditors may play a role. The bidder's offer might include share options, the holders of which are considered to be creditors for scheme purposes,[4] and/or the offer might include convertible securities such as convertible bonds. However, the bidder's purpose is to acquire control of the company and therefore the scheme may still be regarded as member-focused. These are schemes that occur in solvent companies, the predominant purpose of which is to enable a change in control of the company or to facilitate some restructuring of the company or its equity capital. Schemes involving financially distressed companies, even where the company is still technically solvent, will be discussed in Chapters 5 and 6. For this reason, schemes effecting debt–equity swaps, which will generally involve members and creditors, will be dealt with in those chapters, which describe creditor schemes.[5]

There has been some discussion as to whether a takeover can be effected by way of a scheme of arrangement.[6] Part 26 of the Companies Act 2006 applies where a compromise or arrangement is proposed between a company and its members/creditors or any class of them.[7] Given that generally the company's only role in a takeover scheme is to register the shares of the new owner, the question arises whether this can be regarded as an arrangement between the company and its members. This issue was discussed in *Re Savoy Hotel Ltd*.[8] The courts have interpreted the phrase 'compromise or arrangement' broadly,[9] and Nourse J was clear that a takeover should be regarded as an 'arrangement' for scheme purposes.[10] This issue arose again in

4 See sections 3.2 (definition of a member for scheme purposes) and 5.2 (definition of a creditor for scheme purposes).

5 See Chapters 5 and 6.

6 In an early Australian case, the argument was raised that the legislature cannot have intended the scheme provisions to be used to effect a change of control (*Re City of Melbourne Bank Ltd (in liquidation)* (1897) 19 ALT 80). The judge dealt with this swiftly, stating that the legislative provisions were clearly broad enough to encompass this use (at 382).

7 Companies Act 2006, s. 895.

8 [1981] Ch 351.

9 See section 2.1.1.

10 *Re Savoy Hotel Ltd* [1981] Ch 351 *per* Nourse J, approving *Singer Manufacturing Co* v. *Robinow*, 1971 SC 11. One further limitation that has been suggested is that a court has no power to sanction a scheme involving a third party that is not the company, its liquidator or a member or creditor within the relevant class or classes. No such limitation appears on the face of the statute. As a result, it is clear that the court has the power to sanction a scheme under which, for example, the bidder is not an existing member of the company: *British & Commonwealth Holdings plc* v. *Barclays Bank plc* [1996] 1 WLR 1; *Re Glendale Land Development Ltd (No. 2)* (1982) 7 ACLR 171.

Re Jelf Group plc[11] in which the scheme involved the entire shareholding of the company being transferred to another company in a straightforward transfer scheme arrangement, the only form of takeover scheme that is possible following a change in the law in March 2015.[12] Despite transfer schemes being a common occurrence, Mann J had concerns as to whether they fell within the ambit of this phrase. As there was clearly no compromise involved on the facts, he focused on the term 'arrangement'. Given that the scheme involved an offer to the members, which they had accepted, and a transfer of their shares to the purchaser, with the company's only role being to register the transfer, he stated that 'the company seems hardly to participate in the scheme'.[13]

Ultimately Mann J did classify the transfer scheme in *Re Jelf Group* as an arrangement. In order to do so, he noted the existence of authority on this point, such as *Re Savoy Hotel Ltd*, and the fact that this authority had been relied upon for decades. Mann J was clearly of the view that interpreting the term 'arrangement' in this way potentially involved a 'stretching' of that term[14] and stated that he might have come to a different decision were he considering this point 'afresh'.[15] When this was raised as an argument in *Re SABMiller plc*,[16] Snowden J found that the transfer scheme in that case fell within the term 'arrangement', stating that there was a long history of schemes being used to facilitate takeovers and that, although there might be doubts should the matter be considered afresh, it would not be right to differ from the weight of authority and the clear understanding of the position. This is clearly the right approach. Snowden J also took account of the change of law in 2015 which restricted reduction schemes; he found it compelling that Parliament would have taken this step only on the basis of a clear understanding that transfer schemes remained available. This analysis seems to have been accepted, with courts called on to consider transfer schemes since *SABMiller* accepting that transfer schemes do fall within the statutory language.[17]

[11] [2015] EWHC 3857 (Ch).
[12] For discussion see section 3.3.1.1.
[13] [2015] EWHC 3857 (Ch) at [4].
[14] Ibid. at [10]
[15] Ibid. at [7].
[16] [2016] 10 WLUK 31, 4 October 2016.
[17] See e.g. *Re Hargreave Hale Ltd* (unreported) 15 September 2017 (Morgan J); *Re Imagination Technologies Group plc* [2017] EWHC 2934 (Ch) at [3]; *Re Stellar Diamonds plc* [2018] EWHC 1152 (Ch) at [11]; *Re Elegant Hotels Group plc* [2019] EWHC 3699 (Ch) at [6]; *Re Inmarsat plc* [2019] EWHC 3470 (Ch) at [36]; *Re*

Over recent years, the use of schemes of arrangement as a mechanism for effecting a takeover in the UK has become increasingly common, particularly in widely held companies.[18] In the financial year ended March 2002, for example, around 10 per cent of offers regulated by the Panel were effected through schemes; this grew to 41 per cent for the year ended March 2008[19] and in the year ended March 2020, of the sixty-five firm offers, nineteen were structured as a contractual offer and forty-six as a scheme of arrangement at the time of the firm offer announcement, that is, schemes accounted for 70 per cent of offers.[20] Schemes are generally the structure of choice for recommended bids.

The remainder of this chapter proceeds as follows. The definition of 'member' for scheme purposes is discussed in section 3.2. The reasons why a bidder might choose to structure a takeover by way of a scheme rather than a more traditional offer are discussed in section 3.3. Where a scheme involves a target company that is subject to the Takeover Code, the rules of the Takeover Panel will apply to takeovers effected via schemes of arrangement, and in section 3.4 issues of procedure relating to takeover schemes are considered, including the implications for a scheme of the application of the Takeover Code.[21] In section 3.5 the issue of class meetings in a takeover scheme is discussed. As we saw in Chapter 2, determining the class meetings that need to be held is one of the trickier aspects of a scheme, and there are a number of difficult issues that arise in takeover schemes. The issue of class meetings is closely bound up with the issue of minority protection more broadly, and in section 3.6 the level of minority protection available in a scheme is considered and compared to the minority protection available in an offer. Finally, section 3.7 addresses the question of whether it should be possible to effect takeovers via a scheme and, if so, whether special

Patagonia Gold plc [2019] EWHC 2688 (Ch); *Re Lonmin plc* [2019] EWHC 1702 (Ch) at [12]; *Re RhythmOne plc* [2019] EWHC 967 (Ch) at [12]; *Re Realm Therapeutics Plc* [2019] EWHC 2080 (Ch) (in which the point was accepted without discussion, at [43]).

18 For example, in *Practical Law Company*, 'Public M & A trends and highlights from the first half of 2019': twenty-five of the firm offers announced in the first half of 2019 for main market or AIM companies subject to the Takeover Code were structured as a scheme of arrangement (76 per cent) and eight as contractual offers (24 per cent).

19 Takeover Panel, Annual Report and Accounts for the year ended 31 March 2008, 13.

20 Takeover Panel, Annual Report and Accounts for the year ended 31 March 2020, 19.

21 Although the Takeover Panel has always applied its rules to takeovers effected via a scheme of arrangement, the practice of using schemes to effect this result has now become so common that the Panel introduced an Appendix to the Takeover Code (App. 7) to deal specifically with this issue. For further discussion see section 3.4.1.

provisions need to be adopted into the standard scheme procedure described in Chapter 2. It is suggested that there is no reason to be sceptical about the use of schemes in this context and that no additional safeguards need to be put in place beyond those that the law currently provides.

3.2 The definition of 'member' for the purpose of a scheme of arrangement

There is no specific definition of 'member' provided by Part 26 of the Companies Act 2006. In the case of a company registered under the Companies Act, the members are the subscribers and the other persons who agree to become members, and whose names are on the company's register of members.[22] It is clear that 'member' therefore refers to the legal and not the beneficial owners of the company's shares.

It is well established that option holders and persons holding other securities that are convertible into shares are not regarded as members of the company for scheme purposes.[23] The term 'creditor' is not defined for scheme purposes, but the courts have stated that this term should be given a wide meaning, to include any person having any monetary claim against the company that, when payable, will constitute a debt (including unliquidated, prospective or contingent claims).[24] The courts have therefore treated option holders and the holders of other convertible securities as 'creditors' for scheme purposes. This is on the basis that an option is a conditional contract that, at the time the contract is entered into, creates a liability on the relevant company to issue shares. If the company were to fail to issue the shares, the option holder would have a claim for damages against it.[25]

[22] Companies Act 2006, s. 112. Various provisions of the Act include a wider definition of 'member' than this. For example, Companies Act 2006, s. 994(2) states that the provisions of Part 30 of the Act are to apply to a person who is not a member of a company but to whom shares have been transferred or transmitted by operation of law, as if they were a member of the company. No such extension has been made in relation to Part 26.

[23] *Re Compania de Electricidad de la Provincia de Buenos Aires Ltd* [1980] 1 Ch 146 at 183.

[24] *Re Lehman Brothers International (Europe) (in administration)* [2009] EWCA Civ 1161; [2010] 1 BCLC 496; *Re Alabama, New Orleans, Texas & Pacific Junction Railway Co* [1891] 1 Ch 213; *Re Midland Coal, Coke and Iron Co* [1895] 1 Ch 267. For discussion see section 5.2.

[25] In other jurisdictions the courts have expressed reservations as to the correctness of this analysis: see e.g. the approach of the Australian courts, discussed in T. Damian and A. Rich, *Schemes, Takeovers and Himalayan Peaks: The Use of Schemes of Arrangement to Effect Change of Control Transactions* (3rd ed., The Ross Parsons Centre of Commercial, Corporate and Taxation Law, University of Sydney, 2013) at section 3.4.1.

3.3 The use of a scheme of arrangement as an alternative to a takeover

3.3.1 The structure of a takeover effected by a scheme as compared to a traditional offer

Although traditional takeover offers and schemes of arrangement can be used to achieve the same end, namely a shift in control of the target company, they are structurally quite different. The distinctions between the two have implications for a number of issues, including which transaction is likely to suit a bidder better (discussed in this part of the chapter), the procedure of the transaction (discussed in section 3.4), issues of minority protection (discussed in sections 3.5 and 3.6) and, potentially, also the policy issues around the use of schemes to effect changes of control (discussed in section 3.7).

3.3.1.1 A takeover effected by a scheme

In Chapter 2 the procedure for a scheme was set out in detail. Broadly, where the scheme is being used to effect a takeover, it will first involve an arrangement being proposed between the company and its members,[26] that proposal generally coming from the board. An application will then be made to court for an order that meetings of members be summoned.[27] Members will then meet in classes to consider and approve the scheme, by a majority in number representing 75 per cent in value of the members, or class thereof.[28] Application must then be made to court to sanction the scheme.[29] The order sanctioning the scheme takes effect once a copy is delivered to the Registrar of Companies.[30] Thereafter the court will set aside a scheme only on very limited grounds, such as where the consent to the scheme was obtained by fraud.

Until 2015 a takeover effected by a scheme of arrangement could occur in one of two ways: by a cancellation scheme or by a transfer scheme. A change in the law in 2015 means that only transfer schemes are now possible for this purpose.[31] In a transfer scheme, the effect of a successful

[26] On occasion a takeover scheme might also involve creditors. This point is discussed in section 3.1.

[27] Companies Act 2006, s. 896.

[28] Ibid., s. 899(1).

[29] Ibid.

[30] Ibid., s. 899(4).

[31] The Companies Act 2006 (Amendment of Part 17) Regulations 2015 (SI 472/2015). Cancellation schemes can still be used for other purposes; see sections 4.2.2.1 and 4.2.2.2.

scheme is that all of the shares of the target not already owned by the bidder are transferred to the bidder. The only material steps to be taken by the target company are, typically, the registration of the bidder as shareholder in place of existing shareholders, and the issue of new share certificates to the bidder.[32]

Even though the scheme provides for a transfer of shares, no contractual offer for those shares is made to the target shareholders by the bidder.[33] A scheme is a statutory mechanism whereby the members can agree to the proposal, put forward by the target board, that the target shares be transferred to the bidder on the proposed terms. If the scheme is approved by the requisite majorities in the relevant meetings, and the court sanctions the scheme and the order is delivered to the Registrar, then all of the members are bound to transfer their shares in accordance with the terms of the scheme, even if they voted against it. The bidder deals not with the target shareholders but with the target company.

In a cancellation scheme, by contrast, the shareholders of the target agree to the cancellation of their shares in the target company. The reserve created in the target company as a result of this arrangement is then used to pay up in full new target shares that are issued to the bidder.[34] The shareholders of the target then receive, in exchange for their cancelled shares, cash or shares in the bidder company.[35] Use of a scheme in this way does not bypass the requirements of companies legislation or other relevant law.[36] In addition to the scheme procedure set out in Chapter 2, therefore, in a cancellation scheme the target

[32] See *Re Savoy Hotel Ltd* [1981] Ch 351; *Re Jelf Group Ltd* [2015] EWHC 3857 (Ch).

[33] Although this is treated as an offer for the purposes of the Takeover Code: see the definition of 'offer' in the Definitions section of the Code.

[34] Where the target company is a public company the provisions of Companies Act 2006, s. 593ff. must be taken into account. These provide that, where a public company allots shares that are fully or partly paid up otherwise than in cash, the consideration for the allotment must be independently valued under s. 596. The simplest way around this is to take advantage of the exemption in s. 593(2) (which applies to the issue of shares to members out of a company's reserve accounts) by ensuring that the bidder is a member of the target before the cancellation and allotment, and that its shares are not cancelled as part of the scheme.

[35] This is sometimes known as a 'reduction scheme' as it combines a scheme with a reduction of capital, although this reduction is fictitious in the sense that the reserve arising in the company's accounts following the reduction is immediately applied in paying up new shares in the company, so that no creditor protection issue arises.

[36] *Re Guardian Assurance Company* [1917] 1 Ch 431. In addition to the reduction of capital rules, therefore, the company will have to comply with other aspects of the Companies Act 2006, such as the financial assistance rules (see section 3.3.2.4) and the general law, so

company needs to comply with the requirements of the Companies Act 2006 regarding reductions of capital.[37]

Despite the fact that the need to satisfy the reduction of capital provisions in the Companies Act 2006 added time and cost to a cancellation scheme, compared to a transfer scheme, cancellation schemes were far more common as a means of effecting a change of control prior to 2015,[38] owing to the stamp duty saving involved. Stamp duty is payable on share transfers, but on a cancellation scheme no shares are actually transferred. Particularly in large transactions, this stamp duty saving could be substantial and could therefore justify the extra time and expense involved in a cancellation scheme.[39] It was this stamp duty loophole which led to the change in the law in 2015.

The aim of the Companies Act 2006 (Amendment of Part 17) Regulations 2015[40] was to equalise the stamp duty treatment of takeovers effected by way of a takeover offer and scheme of arrangement. The Regulations amend section 641 of the Companies Act 2006 to prohibit a company from reducing its share capital as part of a scheme of arrangement where the purpose of the scheme is to acquire all the shares of the company, except where the acquisition amounts to

that, for example, an arrangement proposed by way of a scheme must be *intra vires* the company (*In re Oceanic Steam Navigation Co Ltd* [1939] Ch 41).

37 This added a number of procedural requirements to the typical scheme process. The Companies Act allows public companies to reduce their capital by way of a special resolution that is subsequently confirmed by the court: ss. 641(1), 645–9 (a private company can follow this route or use a special resolution coupled with a solvency statement from the directors: ss. 641(1), 642–4). In a cancellation scheme a general meeting of the company is required to consider and vote on this special resolution, either at the same time as the class meetings or at a separate meeting. At the sanctioning stage, the court additionally needs to consider and confirm the reduction of capital (s. 648) and the reduction becomes effective upon registration of the order and a statement of capital (approved by the court) by the Registrar of Companies (s. 649).

38 This is not the case in all jurisdictions in which both transfer schemes and cancellation schemes are available; e.g. in Australia transfer schemes are far more common than cancellation schemes as a result of the impact of different tax provisions: Damian and Rich, *Schemes, Takeovers and Himalayan Peaks*, note 25 above, at 3.2.4.

39 In *Re Rylands-Whitecross Limited*, 21 December 1973, unreported, Brightman J held that the use of a cancellation scheme solely for the purpose of avoiding stamp duty was a misuse of the time of the court and the provisions of companies legislation. However, in that case the company had only three shareholders who had all agreed the transaction terms in advance. Brightman J made it clear that he distinguished other cancellation schemes which did not involve a pre-arranged sale. Where there are other features to the scheme, such as the need to bind potential dissenters to the terms of the transaction, the use of cancellation schemes to avoid stamp duty was accepted by the courts.

40 SI 472/2015.

a restructuring that inserts a new holding company into the group structure.[41] All takeover schemes are therefore now carried out by way of a transfer scheme. This change in the law does not appear to have significantly impacted on the use of schemes as an alternative to recommended bids. In 2019, there were a total of sixty-six firm offers involving UK public companies, with 71 per cent of the offers being structured by schemes of arrangement.[42]

A scheme involving a company falling within the ambit of the Takeover Code will be subject to the provisions of the Code. This adds some specific procedural issues to a scheme effecting a takeover offer. These are discussed further in section 3.4.

3.3.1.2 A takeover effected by an offer

In contrast to a scheme of arrangement, in a takeover offer the bidder deals first and foremost not with the target company but with the target shareholders. The bidder makes an offer to the target shareholders to buy their shares. The relationship is fundamentally one of contract between the bidder and the target shareholders, and the bidder prima facie has no relationship with the target company. Of course, overlaying this contractual relationship is a significant layer of regulation. Although the core transaction is between the bidder and the target shareholders, a takeover will have significant implications for others in the target company because the purpose of a takeover is not merely to transfer shares but, crucially, to transfer control of the company. Those affected include the directors, the minority shareholders and the non-shareholder stakeholders, and it can also have implications for the bidder shareholders and the stakeholders. There is a detailed regulatory regime for takeovers, including Part 28 of the Companies Act 2006 and the Takeover Code, that is overseen by the Panel on Takeovers and Mergers (the Takeover Panel), a statutory body.[43]

[41] Companies Act 2006, ss. 641(2A)(2B)(2C). For a discussion of the continued use of cancellation schemes see sections 4.2.2.1 and 4.2.2.2.

[42] See LexisNexis, UK public M&A deals in 2019 – Market Tracker Trend Report, 10 February 2020.

[43] Companies Act 2006, ss. 942–54. For a discussion of the development of takeover regulation in the UK see J. Armour and D. A. Skeel Jr, 'Who writes the rules of hostile takeovers, and why? – The peculiar divergence of US and UK takeover regulation' (2007) *Georgetown Law Journal* 1727.

An overview of the procedure of an offer is given here in order to enable a comparison with schemes to be made. The dominant policies at work regarding the procedure of an offer in the UK are the objectives, first, to allow the shareholders of the target to have the decision-making role and for that decision to be as undistorted as possible and, second, that the target company should not be subject to an offer, or speculation regarding an offer, for an excessive period of time.[44] It may, therefore, seem surprising that the Takeover Code requires the offer from the bidder to be put forward in the first instance not to the shareholders of the target but to the target board or its advisors.[45] The target directors must then obtain competent independent advice on the offer, which is made known to the target shareholders,[46] and must also make the board's opinion on the offer known to the target shareholders.[47] The contents of the independent advice received by the target directors and their opinions on the offer are commonly contained in the bidder's offer circular, in the event of a recommended offer, or in a defence document, if such offer is hostile.[48]

Once a 'firm intention' announcement is made, the bidder becomes obliged to post a formal offer document to the shareholders within twenty-eight days.[49] The formal offer must provide

[44] Takeover Code, GP 6 provides that '[a]n offeree company must not be hindered in the conduct of its affairs for longer than is reasonable by a bid for its securities'. While the UK remained aligned with EU law, the source of the General Principles was Takeover Directive 2004/25/EC, Art. 3. Following the UK's exit from the EU and the end of the transition period, after 31 December 2020 they are replicated in domestic legislation: Companies Act 2006, Sch 1C, Part 1, as inserted by the Takeovers (Amendment) (EU Exit) Regulations 2019 (SI 217/2019).

[45] Ibid., r. 1(a). Bidders may wish to make an informal approach before committing themselves to a formal offer. Changes introduced in 2010 constrain the ability of bidders to do so, in response to concerns about 'virtual bids' whereby bidders signal an interest in the company, but no firm offer is made. Consequently, the Takeover Code provides that, except with the consent of the Panel, any publicly named potential bidder must, within twenty-eight days, announce a firm intention to make an offer, or announce that it will not make an offer, or apply for an extension of the deadline (jointly with the target company): rr. 2.6–2.8.

[46] Ibid., r. 3.1.

[47] Ibid., r. 25.2.

[48] The Takeover Code sets out the requirements for the content of the target board's circular: r. 25.

[49] Takeover Code, r. 24.1 (the only exceptions being that the offer is subject to a specific precondition which has not been met (r. 2.7(b)) or the consent of the Takeover Panel has been obtained). As a result of changes introduced in Takeover Panel RS 2017/2, there is now a minimum period for bidders to make this offer, i.e. a bidder now cannot publish an offer document for at least fourteen days from the announcement of its firm intention to make an offer, without the consent of the board of the target company.

shareholders with a significant amount of information about the bid, the intention being that '[s]hareholders must be given sufficient information and advice to enable them to reach a properly informed decision as to the merits or demerits of an offer'.[50] The Takeover Code sets out in detail the financial and other information that must be made available to the shareholders in order to put them in this position.[51] As a general principle, all documents and statements made during the course of an offer 'must be prepared with the highest standards of care and accuracy and the information given must be adequately and fairly presented'.[52]

The Takeover Code imposes significant restrictions on the ability of the bidder to place conditions on the offer, since one aim of the Code is that the shareholders should have a clear offer to accept or reject.[53] However, one condition that will always be present in a bid, because it is required by the Takeover Code, relates to when an offer will become unconditional. The Code provides that an offer for voting securities will be conditional on acceptances being secured by the bidder sufficient to give it, together with securities already held, more than 50 per cent of the voting rights in the target.[54] However, it is possible for the bidder to set a higher level.[55] An important stage in any bid is therefore when it becomes 'unconditional as to acceptances', which means that it has satisfied all of its conditions (including passing the 50 per cent hurdle – or such higher hurdle as the bidder has imposed on the bid) and has effectively succeeded. Once the formal offer documents have been posted to the shareholders, the bid is open to acceptance by the

50 Ibid., r. 23.

51 Ibid., rr. 24, 25.

52 Ibid., r. 19.1. Misstatements in these documents are capable of giving rise to a negligent misstatement claim at common law by the target shareholders, to whom these documents are clearly addressed (see *Caparo Industries plc* v. *Dickman* [1990] 2 AC 605; *Morgan Crucible Co plc* v. *Hill Samuel & Co Ltd* [1991] Ch 295 cf. *Partco Group Ltd* v. *Wragg* [2002] EWCA Civ 594; [2002] 2 BCLC 323). The Takeover Panel also has the power to award compensation: Companies Act 2006, s. 954.

53 See Takeover Code, r. 13. The Code Committee of the Takeover Panel has launched a substantial consultation on offer conditions: Takeover Panel, Public Consultation by the Code Committee, Conditions to Offer and the Offer Timetable, PCP 2020/1, 27 October 2020.

54 Ibid., r. 10.

55 If the bidder wants to ensure that it can obtain 100 per cent of the target, it will set this level at 90 per cent, at which point it will be able to squeeze out the remaining 10 per cent: Companies Act 2006, ss. 979–82.

shareholders to whom it is addressed. The offer must be kept open for acceptance for at least twenty-one days.[56] After an offer has become unconditional as to acceptances, the offer must then remain open for at least a further fourteen days.[57]

One common event in many bids is the need for a bidder to revise its initial offer to the shareholders, either because its original offer proves unattractive to them or to take account of an offer from a rival bidder. At this point, the Takeover Code provides that the revised offer must be kept open for a further period of at least fourteen days,[58] and any shareholders who had accepted the original offer are entitled to the revised consideration.[59]

In some circumstances the bidder will want to acquire total control of the target. The squeeze-out rules can help in this situation.[60] They provide that, where a single class of shares has been bid for, the bidder is entitled to acquire compulsorily the shares of the non-acceptors if the offer has been accepted by at least 90 per cent in value of the shares to which the offer relates.[61] The successful bidder triggers the squeeze-out procedure by giving notice to the non-accepting shareholders, accompanied by a statutory declaration of its entitlement to do so,[62] within three months of the last day on which the offer could be accepted.[63] The effect of the notice is that the bidder becomes entitled and bound to acquire the shares on the final terms of the offer.[64] From the bidder's point of view the squeeze-out right is valuable as it prevents the minority from exploiting their hold-up power in circumstances where the bidder

56 Takeover Code, r. 31.1 (this can subsequently be extended). The maximum length of time that the offer may remain open for acceptance is until the sixtieth day after the offer was posted: r. 31.6.

57 Ibid., r. 31.4.

58 Ibid., r. 32.1.

59 Ibid., r. 32.3.

60 Companies Act 2006, Part 28, Ch. 3. These rules implemented Art. 15 of the Takeover Directive 2004/25/EC which required some amendments to the existing law governing squeeze-outs.

61 Companies Act 2006, s. 979(2)(a). If the shares are voting shares, the acceptances also have to represent at least 90 per cent of the voting rights carried by those shares: s. 979(2)(b). Where more than one class is bid for, the 90 per cent test is applied to each class separately: s. 979(3)(4).

62 Ibid., s. 979(4)–(8). The bidder must also send the documents to the target company: s. 980(4)–(8).

63 Ibid., s. 980(2)(3). Where the offer is not governed by the Takeover Code, so that there is no fixed closing date for the offer, the period is six months from the date of the offer.

64 Ibid., s. 981(2).

has good reasons to require 100 per cent ownership. It can therefore be regarded as an incentive to bidders. Non-accepting shareholders can appeal to the court, objecting to the bidder's right to acquire their shares or asking for the terms of the acquisition to be amended.[65]

The squeeze-out right is mirrored by a sell-out right, which allows the last 10 per cent of shareholders to leave the company rather than to remain as minority shareholders.[66] The bidder must give each non-accepting shareholder notice of their entitlement to be bought out within one month of the end of the offer period, and shareholders then have three months to take up this right.[67] The effect of the notice is that the bidder is bound to acquire the shares on the final terms of the offer.[68] Either the bidder or a non-accepting shareholder may apply for the court to determine the terms of the offer.[69] However, in practice, the sell-out remedy is not used a great deal since the Takeover Code requires the bidder to keep the offer open for a further fourteen days once the offer has become unconditional as to acceptances.[70] This gives shareholders an opportunity to change their mind and accept the offer, without the need to demonstrate that the bidder has reached the 90 per cent threshold and without the possibility of court intervention.

Where an offer has not been successful, that is, where it has not become wholly unconditional within the bid timetable or been withdrawn or lapsed, neither the bidder nor any person acting in concert with it may make another offer for the target company within the next twelve months.[71] Further, if a person or concert party holds 50 per cent or more of the voting rights, it must not, within six months of the closure of the offer, make a second offer or acquire any

[65] Ibid., s. 986(1). The expropriatory nature of these provisions has meant that the courts have tended to construe them strictly when determining whether the bidder has met the requirements for a squeeze-out to occur: *Re Bugle Press Ltd* [1961] Ch 270; *Re Chez Nico (Restaurants) Ltd* [1992] BCLC 192; *Fiske Nominees Ltd* v. *Dwyka Diamond Ltd* [2002] EWHC 770 (Ch); [2002] 2 BCLC 123.

[66] Companies Act 2006, s. 983.

[67] Ibid., s. 984(1)–(4). There are criminal sanctions for the bidder and any officer in default: s. 984(5)–(7).

[68] Ibid., s. 985.

[69] Ibid., s. 986.

[70] Takeover Code, r. 31.4.

[71] Ibid., r. 35.1.

shares from the shareholders on better terms than those under the previous offer.[72]

3.3.2 *A comparison of schemes and offers as mechanisms for effecting a takeover*

There are a number of advantages and disadvantages to a scheme of arrangement, as compared to a traditional offer, that might incentivise the parties to choose one rather than the other as the mechanism for effecting a change of control on a particular set of facts.

3.3.2.1 Tax

Until 2015, tax was one of the reasons to choose a scheme of arrangement rather than a takeover offer. Stamp duty is payable at 0.5 per cent of the consideration on the transfer of shares in the target company.[73] In a traditional offer, which involves the individual shareholders in the target accepting the offer and transferring their shares to the bidder, stamp duty is paid on that transfer. Similarly, a transfer scheme attracts stamp duty on the shares transferred to the bidder. However, cancellation schemes require no transfer of shares, and therefore no stamp duty is payable. Prior to 2015, this tax saving was a significant reason for recommended bids to proceed by way of a cancellation scheme rather than a traditional offer. However, the change to the law in 2015 brought an end to cancellation schemes being used in this way, and so this tax advantage has dropped away.[74]

3.3.2.2 Acquiring 100 per cent control of the target

A successful scheme of arrangement will always involve the bidder acquiring 100 per cent control of the target. Once the scheme has been approved by the court, and the order delivered to the Registrar, the bidder has certainty that it can acquire 100 per cent control of the target.[75] By contrast, in an offer the bidder's offer must be conditional on acceptances being secured by the bidder sufficient to give it (together

[72] Ibid., r. 35.3.

[73] Finance Act 1999, Sch. 13, para. 3. Where the target shares are held in CREST, stamp duty reserve tax is payable instead of stamp duty, but at the same rate (Finance Act 1999, s. 87).

[74] The Companies Act 2006 (Amendment of Part 17) Regulations 2015 (SI 472/2015), discussed at section 3.3.1.1.

[75] Only on very limited grounds can the court set aside the scheme subsequently; for example, if the consent has been obtained by fraud.

with securities already held) more than 50 per cent of the voting rights in the target.[76] The bidder can choose to make the offer conditional on a level of acceptances greater than the 50 per cent threshold, but it need not do so. A takeover offer can therefore involve the bidder acquiring less than 100 per cent of the target. Only when the acceptance level reaches 90 per cent can the bidder make use of a squeeze-out right to acquire compulsorily the remaining 10 per cent of the shares.[77]

If it is important for the bidder to acquire 100 per cent control of the target company, then a scheme of arrangement will be more attractive. There may be a number of reasons why a bidder wants to secure 100 per cent ownership of the target company. For example, if it wants to use the target company's assets as security for loans made to the bidder to finance the bid, it will be important for the bidder to acquire all of the target's shares. This is particularly common in private equity transactions. Alternatively, the bidder may plan to re-register the target as a private company, perhaps to avoid the prohibition on the provision of financial assistance that applies to public companies[78] or to allow the target to benefit from the less onerous administrative requirements applicable to private companies under the Companies Act 2006. The acquisition of 100 per cent of the shares will avoid giving the minority scope to object to this re-registration.[79] Another reason why the bidder may want 100 per cent control of the target is to avoid sharing the planned gains with any remaining minority. This might be because the bidder is intending to extract cash from the target by way of dividend payments or because it intends to amalgamate its business with that of the target, thereby creating synergies and costs savings. There may be many other commercial, taxation or accounting reasons why the bidder might want to acquire all of the shares in the target. If the bidder wants to acquire 100 per cent control, a scheme will be particularly valuable where the target has many shareholders (often individuals) who might not respond to an offer. Bidders for companies that have been privatised or demutualised, and so have many small shareholders, may find it easier to use a scheme for this reason.

[76] Takeover Code, r. 10.

[77] Companies Act 2006, s. 979(2)(a). A corresponding right to sell out exists for minority shareholders at this point: ss. 983–5.

[78] Ibid., s. 678. Discussed further in section 3.3.2.4.

[79] Ibid., ss. 97–8: s. 98 allows the holders of not less than 5 per cent of the nominal value of a company's issued share capital, or not fewer than fifty members, to apply to court to object to the re-registration.

It is not impossible to obtain 100 per cent of the target using a traditional offer, though it is more difficult. Where the acquisition of 100 per cent of the shares is key, some takeover offers will set the minimum level of acceptances at 90 per cent so that the bidder can then make use of the squeeze-out rules. However, this requires acceptance by the holders of 90 per cent of the shares to which the offer relates, rather than the lower level required for a scheme (a majority in number representing 75 per cent in value of the members or class thereof). The fact that the scheme approval level relates only to those present and voting (in person or by proxy) can reduce this percentage further. If only 50 per cent of the votes are cast at the meeting, for example, then a vote in favour by 40 per cent of shareholders (i.e. 80 per cent of those attending and voting) will suffice.[80]

This difference in approval thresholds is therefore another significant advantage for schemes, from the bidder's point of view. However, it has also given rise to a certain level of controversy regarding the use of schemes to effect takeovers, which is discussed further in section 3.7.

3.3.2.3 Speed

The timetable for an offer is more fluid than that for a scheme. Because of the need to fit in two court hearings and members' meetings to vote on the scheme, the timetable for a scheme is usually seven to eight weeks from posting. By contrast, the minimum time period from posting to declaring an offer unconditional is twenty-one days,[81] and the maximum is eighty-one days.[82] It may be faster to use an offer than a scheme, especially where the offer is straightforward, no competing offer emerges and the bidder only needs to obtain, say, 50 per cent ownership of the target. However, in other circumstances a scheme will be quicker, in particular where the bidder wants to acquire 100 per cent control of the target. Under a scheme the bidder knows that seven to eight weeks after posting it will have control, if the scheme is successful. Under an offer, the bidder has no such certainty. Furthermore, if the bidder has to rely on the use of the squeeze-out process to acquire the rump 10 per cent shareholders, this process can add a substantial delay.

[80] If the turnout at the meeting is very low, this might be a factor for the court to take into account when determining whether to sanction the scheme at the sanctioning hearing: see sections 2.4.2 and 2.4.3. For discussion see e.g. *Re Vernalis plc* [2018] EWHC 3898 (Ch); *Re Stellar Diamonds plc* [2018] EWHC 1152 (Ch).

[81] Takeover Code, r. 31.1.

[82] Ibid., r. 31.7.

3.3.2.4 Financial assistance

The financial assistance rules have the potential to cause difficulties for bidders in some circumstances. Section 678(1) of the Companies Act 2006 prohibits a company or any subsidiary from giving financial assistance, directly or indirectly, for the purpose of acquiring shares in a public company before or at the same time as the share acquisition takes place. This prohibition no longer applies to private companies.[83] The concept of 'financial assistance' is construed broadly.[84] Where financial assistance is given, certain exceptions may still exempt the transaction, including where the company's principal purpose in giving the assistance is not to facilitate any such acquisition or alternatively where giving the assistance for that purpose is only an incidental part of some larger purpose of the company.[85] These exceptions are subject to a requirement that such assistance be given in good faith in the company's interests.

Where a target company is a public company, these provisions would certainly prevent a bidder from using cash in the target to finance the offer prior to, or at the time of, the offer. Cash resources in the target can be extracted only after the offer has been completed and the company has been re-registered as a private company.

In a scheme, the financial assistance rules still apply. An example of the court's approach to this issue is to be found in *Re Uniq plc*.[86] In that case, David Richards J considered a scheme of arrangement involving financial assistance as part of a restructuring to resolve financial difficulties within a group of companies. A solvent company was restructured in such a way as to release it from its obligations under a pensions scheme that was in deficit. This was felt to be the only way for the company to remain financially viable.

[83] Cf. Companies Act 1985, ss. 151–5. However, the rules on maintenance of capital continue to apply to private companies, and there is a danger that some corporate actions planned as part of a takeover might involve a breach of some other company law obligation, such as an illegal reduction of capital.

[84] See Companies Act 2006, s. 677(1). *Chaston* v. *SWP Group plc* [2002] EWCA Civ 1999; [2003] 1 BCLC 675, cf. *MT Realisations Ltd* v. *Digital Equipment Co Ltd* [2002] EWHC 1628 (Ch); [2002] 2 BCLC 688. See generally E. Ferran, 'Corporate transactions and financial assistance: Shifting policy perceptions but static law' (2004) 63 *Cambridge Law Journal* 225. So, for example, 'financial assistance' includes not only assistance that directly or indirectly helps to pay the price but also other steps that merely smooth the path, e.g. the payment of concurrent benefits such as accountants' fees.

[85] Ibid., ss. 678(2), 678(4), 679(2) and 679(4).

[86] [2011] EWHC 749 (Ch); [2012] 1 BCLC 783. For discussion see e.g. K. J. Leivesley, 'Financial assistance: Why a Uniq approach may overcome Chaston' (2011) *Journal of Business Law* 725.

The restructuring in *Re Uniq* was achieved by apportioning the pensions liabilities to a special purpose vehicle (newco) and was conditional upon a series of transactions effected under the scheme of arrangement. This involved, inter alia, Uniq issuing and allotting 90.2 per cent of its shares to newco, to be held for the benefit of the pensions scheme. In return for the allotment of these shares, newco undertook to pay to Uniq the shares' nominal value (approximately £66.6 million). To assist newco in fulfilling this undertaking, a series of transfers were planned, to place it in funds. Thus, Uniq agreed to transfer a total of £66.6 million to newco via its subsidiaries. The potential for these payments to contravene section 678(1) of the Companies Act 2006 was clear.[87]

David Richards J considered whether these payments should properly be characterised as financial assistance. He considered that there was reason to doubt this, looking at the commercial realities of the situation.[88] In particular, the judge took account of the ultimate consideration received in exchange for the loans (the release of the Uniq group companies from a joint liability of approximately £473 million) and the genuine purpose of the transaction: to advance each of the company's interests. Ultimately, however, he determined that the transfers did constitute financial assistance within section 677(1)(c) of the Companies Act 2006. However, he went on to hold that the loans were permitted under the principal purpose exception: the principal purpose of the £66.6 million transfer to newco was to achieve the release from liabilities attached to the defined benefit section of the pensions scheme and, correspondingly, to avoid the insolvency of the Uniq group companies. This is a sensible, commercial approach to the assessment of financial assistance that is to be welcomed.

Where a transaction does involve financial assistance, the benefit of organising the takeover by way of a scheme, rather than an offer, is clear. Section 681(2)(e) of the Companies Act 2006 provides an unconditional exception to the financial assistance provisions. It permits anything done in pursuance of an order of the court under Part 26 of the Companies Act 2006, which sanctions a compromise or arrangement with members or creditors. In other words, actions that would otherwise be prevented by the prohibition may be approved by the court as part of the scheme.

[87] Ibid. at [35] *per* David Richards J.

[88] The 'commercial realities' test was proposed by Hoffmann J in *Charterhouse Investment Trust Ltd* v. *Tempest Diesels Ltd* [1986] BCLC 1.

An example of the use of section 681(2)(e) can be seen in *Re Uniq*. An issue of financial assistance in that case arose in respect of indemnities, expenses and professional services that Uniq agreed to provide and pay to newco under the terms of the restructuring agreement. David Richards J did not examine these methods of assistance in any detail but indicated that some of the assistance could relate to the share acquisition and could therefore constitute financial assistance. However, he held that 'they will not be unlawful, if done in pursuance of an order under s. 681(2)(e)'.[89] To avoid any doubt, he confirmed that reliance on section 681(2)(e) was not conditional upon other criteria. In particular, he stated that there was no need to satisfy the criterion used in the former 'whitewash' procedure under sections 155–8 of the Companies Act 1985. These criteria were (i) a statutory declaration that there were no grounds on which the company could be found unable to pay its debts and (ii) the financial assistance either did not reduce the net assets of the company or, to the extent that it did, the reduction was covered by distributable profits. However, in circumstances where these conditions are satisfied, the judge stated that 'there would in general be no reason not to exercise the power'.[90] David Richards J refused to attempt to set down a general test for the exercise of this discretion. However, he was satisfied in this case that the indemnities and costs provided by Uniq were commercially necessary and in the interests of the creditors and members. He therefore exercised his power to approve them under section 681(2)(e).

3.3.2.5 US shareholders

A difficult issue can arise for bidders where the target has US shareholders and where the offer is a securities exchange offer. As a result of the potentially broad ambit of the US rules,[91] the possibility arises that the consideration securities will need to be registered under the US Securities Act of 1933. This registration process is an expensive and time-consuming exercise; as a result, bidders for UK companies frequently seek to avoid this requirement.

One possibility is to attempt to exclude the US shareholders from receiving securities in securities exchange offers for UK companies, and to sell the shares to which they would otherwise have been entitled, with

89 [2011] EWHC 749 (Ch); [2012] 1 BCLC 783 at [43].

90 Ibid. at [45].

91 The Williams Act of 1968, which amended the US Securities Exchange Act of 1934 to provide for the regulation of tender offers, states that it applies to all offers made in the USA or to US security holders, regardless of where the target is incorporated.

the proceeds of sale being remitted to them instead. However, the starting point in the Takeover Code is that all holders of the securities of an offeree company must be afforded equal treatment.[92] Although the Takeover Code contains a general derogation from this requirement where foreign shareholders are concerned, this derogation is narrowly drawn and of limited benefit in practice.[93] Useful exemptions do exist in the US rules, and may be beneficial to bidders, but only where the US shareholder base is small. In particular, if the US shareholding is less than 10 per cent of the total, the offer will be exempt from most registration and specific disclosure requirements, under a 'Tier 1' exemption. Above this level, filing requirements will apply.[94]

However, where a scheme is used, provisions in the US legislation allow bidders to circumvent the US registration requirements entirely.[95] There are a number of conditions that a bidder must satisfy to utilise this exemption: inter alia, that the securities must be issued in exchange for securities, claims or property interests (not cash); and that a court or authorised governmental entity must approve the fairness of the terms and the conditions of the exchange. The reviewing court/authorised governmental entity must hold a hearing before approving the fairness of the terms and conditions of the transaction and must find, before approving the transaction, that the terms and conditions of the exchange are fair to those to whom securities will be issued. The hearing must be open to everyone to whom securities would be issued in the proposed exchange and adequate notice of the hearing must be given to all those persons.[96] It is clear that these conditions are satisfied by the scheme procedure.

Therefore, where a significant proportion of the shares in the target company are held by persons in the USA, there may be an advantage to using a scheme. However, if US shareholders are excluded from receiving securities under the terms of an offer that is being implemented by way of a scheme of arrangement, and are therefore at a disadvantage compared

[92] See Takeover Code, General Principles, especially GP 1.

[93] The derogation has two limbs. First, there must be a significant risk to the bidder of civil, regulatory or, particularly, criminal exposure, and second, less than 3 per cent of the target company shares must be held by the shareholders in the relevant jurisdiction: Takeover Code, note to r. 30.4.

[94] Above 40 per cent, the full registration and filing requirements apply. Between 10 per cent and 40 per cent there are limited (Tier 2) exemptions from some filing requirements.

[95] Securities Act 1933, s. 3(a)(10).

[96] Ibid. See e.g. *Re Ladbrokes Coral Group plc* [2018] EWHC 1382 (Ch).

to other shareholders (for example, because the value of the securities being issued is greater than the value of any cash consideration being offered as part of the offer), they might be considered to constitute a different class, with the result that a separate class consent will be required. The requirement to obtain the approval of a separate class of shareholders that might feel aggrieved at not being entitled to the same consideration as non-US shareholders could jeopardise the success of the scheme. A scheme of arrangement should not, therefore, be seen as a method of excluding US shareholders from any securities offer.

3.3.2.6 Lost and untraceable shareholders

In situations where there are lost and untraceable shareholders, it may be beneficial to proceed by way of a scheme. This is because such shareholders cannot be taken into account when calculating the acceptance level for an offer, unless permission is sought from the court. By contrast, in a scheme, these shareholders will not be relevant when determining whether the 75 per cent acceptance level has been reached. This is because, in a scheme, only 75 per cent of those present and voting (whether in person or by proxy) need to vote in favour.[97]

In addition, in a scheme, once the shareholder approval thresholds are met, the court has sanctioned the scheme and the order has been delivered to the Registrar, there is no need for the company to try to trace any untraceable shareholders: they are bound by the scheme. By way of contrast, in an offer, these untraceable shareholders can only be dealt with as part of the squeeze-out regime once the 90 per cent threshold has been reached.[98]

3.3.2.7 Ability of dissenting shareholders to block a bid

It is easier for the bidder to reach the 75 per cent threshold needed to gain 100 per cent control in a scheme than to reach the 90 per cent level that would be needed in an offer to ensure the same result. However, it is also easier for a dissenting shareholder to block a bid that is effected by means of a scheme of arrangement than to block one effected through an offer. In an offer, opposing target shareholders need to have 50 per cent of the shares to block the bid completely, since a bidder is able to declare its offer unconditional as to acceptances as soon as the level of acceptances exceeds 50 per cent. In contrast, with just 25 per cent of the shares,

[97] Companies Act 2006, s. 899(1).

[98] Ibid., s. 986(9).

dissentient shareholders can block a scheme. Indeed, the power of the dissentient shareholders may be even greater than this. Since it is only those shares actually voted at the meeting that are taken into account, and since any shares held by the bidder are generally not voted at the shareholder meeting,[99] the holder of a stake of less than 25 per cent may well have the power to vote down the scheme.[100]

A good example of this scenario arose in the bid by Dickson Poon to take Harvey Nichols private in 2002. A scheme was originally proposed to effect the bid. However, a shareholder holding around 15 per cent of the shares was able to ensure that the scheme was voted down. This was because Mr Poon already held a stake of 50.1 per cent, which was excluded from the vote. Accordingly, the 15 per cent stake represented 30 per cent of the shares that could be voted at the members' meeting, and so the holder was able to block the scheme. Mr Poon subsequently switched to an offer to effect the takeover. Therefore, if a bidder is willing to go ahead with less than 100 per cent control of the target and there is a concern about dissentient shareholders, it may be better to use an offer.

3.3.2.8 Hostile bids

An important consequence of the structural differences between schemes of arrangement and offers, highlighted in section 3.3.1, is that in a scheme the process is controlled by the target rather than the bidder. It is the target and its directors that are responsible for the scheme. It is the target company shareholders that must approve the arrangement. It is also the target company that has to produce the scheme document to be sent to members. A scheme will generally be completed only if it is recommended by the target directors.[101] Accordingly, if the bid is to be hostile, a bidder is likely to opt for an offer rather than a scheme. Since an offer is a corporate action by the bidder, it can be either hostile or recommended. By contrast, it is sometimes said that a scheme can only be used to effect an agreed or friendly transaction.

This statement is not quite accurate. As a technical matter, a hostile bidder can use its position as a shareholder in the target to launch

[99] For discussion see section 3.5.2.5.

[100] If the members need to be divided into separate classes to vote, the total percentage of the members in the company that can prevent a bid going forward may be even smaller since all classes need to approve a bid, i.e. 25 per cent of those voting in a class meeting (excluding any shares held by the bidder) would be enough to block the bid.

[101] See section 2.2.1.1 for a discussion of the possibility of hostile schemes of arrangement.

a scheme, after consultation with the Takeover Panel.[102] However, there are practical difficulties in implementing a hostile scheme, so that, despite a number of examples of such unsolicited change-of-control transactions being announced and proposed as schemes of arrangement, there seems to be no case where such a scheme has been successful in practice to date.

As discussed in Chapter 2, the application for the order giving directions for the meetings to approve a scheme can be made by a member of the company as well as by the company itself.[103] In the context of takeovers, this raises the possibility of a bidder acquiring shares in a target and then seeking a court order convening meetings to approve a scheme whereby the target shares are purchased by the bidder. The courts have acknowledged that they do have discretion to direct that members' meetings be held in such circumstances.[104] The Takeover Panel has recognised this possibility and the Takeover Code now requires that the target board be consulted in advance before such a proposal is announced.[105] However, a hostile bidder faces a number of difficulties that render this scenario rather unlikely.

First, as Nourse J stated in *Re Savoy Hotel Ltd*,[106] although the court has discretion to direct that meetings be held in such circumstances, the court does not have jurisdiction to sanction a scheme that does not have the approval of the company. Therefore, the court will not convene meetings on the application of a member if it is clear that the scheme will not secure the approval of the company. A good example of this issue in practice arose in a Bermudan case, *Validus Holdings Ltd* v. *IPC Holdings Ltd and Max Capital Group Ltd.*[107] Validus Holdings announced a hostile scheme to acquire IPC Holdings. It acquired 100 shares in IPC and applied to the court for orders convening a scheme meeting to vote on the proposed scheme. The court noted that it remained an unprecedented course to embark on a scheme in the face of opposition from the target board and that there were severe practical difficulties in implementing such a scheme. The court accepted that it did have the power to order the convening of the meeting. However, the

102 Takeover Code, App. 7, s. 13.

103 Companies Act 2006, s. 896(2). See section 2.2.1.1.

104 See e.g. *Re Savoy Hotel Ltd* [1981] Ch 351.

105 Takeover Code, App. 7, s. 13. HgCapital LLP's offer for Goldshield Group plc, announced on 25 September 2009, provides at least one precedent for the attempted use of a scheme in a hostile bid. However, the success of such an approach was not tested as the offer was ultimately recommended by Goldshield.

106 [1981] Ch 351.

107 [2009] SC (Supreme Court of Bermuda) 25 Civ (13 May 2009) Ground CJ.

court ultimately decided that it was not appropriate to convene the meeting in this case as there was no evidence that the scheme would have the support of the company in general meeting.

Second, there are also a number of practical difficulties that arise in the hostile bid scenario, in particular lack of information on the hostile member's part. The scheme process involves information being disclosed by the company, to satisfy the relevant disclosure obligations. For example, the Companies Act 2006 imposes significant obligations in terms of the explanatory statement that must accompany the scheme proposal, setting out, inter alia, the effect of the scheme, any material interests of the directors and the effect of those interests on the scheme.[108] It is not clear that a member proposing a hostile scheme would necessarily have all of the information needed to complete the explanatory statement.

To deal with these issues it is possible to announce a hostile offer in which the bidder reserves the right to implement the takeover by way of a scheme, provided a recommendation is forthcoming or if shareholders in general meeting approve the scheme by the appropriate resolution. It is also possible to launch a bid by way of a scheme that is preconditional on obtaining a board recommendation.

3.3.2.9 Contested bids

The fact that it is the target rather than the bidder that is in control of the process in a scheme of arrangement also has an important consequence for the bidder regarding the terms being offered to the target shareholders. In a takeover offer it is the bidder who is in control, and it is relatively easy for the bidder to change the terms of the bid during the offer process, for example to respond to a competing bid that arises. This competing bid may arise by way of an offer or even by way of another scheme.[109]

It is potentially more difficult for the bidder to change the terms of a scheme of arrangement than to change the terms of an offer, and it may be necessary to restart the scheme timetable. In particular, if a bidder wishes to increase the amount that it is willing to pay, the concern is that a new shareholder meeting may have to be convened, with all the delay

[108] Companies Act 2006, s. 897.

[109] For example, competitive bids were made by Tata Steel and CSN for Corus Group plc in 2006. The acquisition of Corus by CSN, to be implemented by way of a scheme, was preconditional on the withdrawal of Tata Steel's offer for Corus, which was also to be implemented by way of a scheme.

that this would entail. However, the courts may be prepared to allow an increase in price, without starting the court process again, provided that the terms other than the price stay the same and the shareholders have sufficient time to consider any new information before the meeting takes place.[110] This is only likely to apply where the change is more favourable to shareholders. Any revision to a scheme with fewer than fourteen days' notice before the date of the meeting(s) to approve the scheme, or indeed any revision after the date of the meeting, will require the consent of the Takeover Panel.[111]

However, there is a risk that the target company will simply adjourn the shareholders' meeting(s) if a competing bid is submitted. Since the target, and not the bidder, has control of the scheme process, the bidder cannot prevent this. Alternatively, if the competing bid arises after the shareholders' meetings have been held, further meetings may have to be convened and held.

Therefore, if a competing bid is possible, or likely, it may be that an offer will be more suitable than a scheme. Historically, concerns about the loss of control experienced by the bidder in a scheme have been mitigated by the target and the bidder concluding a transaction or implementation agreement that imposed obligations on both parties to implement the scheme (e.g. to meet agreed timetables), but changes to the Takeover Code have prohibited any arrangements that require the target to give undertakings in the context of a takeover offer except in certain limited circumstances. However, concerns relating to the bidder's lack of control over the scheme process and timetable may still be mitigated in two important ways. First, if the bidder is concerned that a scheme might be adjourned by the target for a significant period of time, the Takeover Panel will allow conditions to be inserted within the scheme causing the bid to lapse if the scheme is not effective by a certain long-stop date.[112] Second, if a competing bid does arise it is possible to switch to an offer.[113]

110 This was allowed, for example, in the Debenhams plc scheme of arrangement in 2003 in which the successful bidder increased its price after the notice convening the shareholder meetings to approve the scheme had been sent out. The court allowed the bidder to increase its price and still use the same shareholder meeting to approve the scheme on condition that the bidder sent out another circular and put out an advertisement in the *Financial Times*.

111 Takeover Code, App. 7, s. 7.

112 Takeover Code, App. 7, s. 3(b). See e.g. *Re Inmarsat plc* [2019] EWHC 3470 (Ch).

113 Bidders must obtain the consent of the Panel before switching from a scheme to an offer (Takeover Code, App. 7, s. 8) but do not need to reserve the right to do so in their offer conditions.

3.3.2.10 The involvement of the court

In a takeover offer in the UK there will generally be no court involvement. Indeed, this is regarded as one of the strengths of the UK system, as compared, say, with the system of takeover regulation in the USA.[114] In the UK the takeover is governed by the rules set out in the Takeover Code, and to the extent that rulings are required during the course of the bid these are made by the Takeover Panel. Although the Panel's decisions are subject to judicial review, the courts have established narrow limits within which any judicial review of a Takeover Panel decision will operate.[115] It is expected that parties will still have to abide by Takeover Panel rulings, even where they have indicated an intention to seek judicial review.[116] Crucially, the courts to date have been content to carry out a retrospective review of the Takeover Panel's decisions. The courts will only intervene after a bid has been concluded and will only act to provide guidance as to how the Takeover Panel should proceed in future cases, or to relieve individuals of disciplinary sanctions. Importantly, the courts have not interfered in the course of an existing bid.[117] On this basis there is very little to be gained by a party making use of litigation in the course of a takeover.[118]

By contrast, in a scheme there are two compulsory court hearings. This has two implications. First, a scheme can be more expensive than a traditional offer because of the more complex process and the fact that it is a court procedure. Second, there are consequences for the timetable and the flexibility of the process. As a scheme meeting cannot be convened without an order of the court, and the date of the meeting is set by an order of the court, any adjournment will need a further application to the court. Similarly, the abandonment of a scheme meeting is likely to require an application to court. The scheme process, therefore, is

[114] See e.g. Armour and Skeel, 'Who writes the rules for hostile takeovers, and why?', note 43 above.

[115] *R* v. *Panel on Takeovers and Mergers ex p Datafin* [1987] QB 815.

[116] Ibid. at 840–1.

[117] Ibid.; *R* v. *Panel of Takeovers and Mergers ex p Guinness plc* [1990] 1 QB 146; *R* v. *Panel of Takeovers and Mergers ex p Fayed* [1992] BCC 524. See also *Panel* v. *King* [2018] CSIH 30 in which the court continued to apply the deferential approach that is in evidence in *R* v. *Panel on Takeovers and Mergers ex p Datafin* [1987] QB 815.

[118] Of course, the court can have a role in both squeeze-out and sell-out (see Companies Act 2006, s. 986), but since this occurs only once the bidder has obtained 90 per cent, in practice this does not provide an opportunity for the court involvement to frustrate the bid.

not ideal for dealing with new information, whether that be details of a rival bid or simply new material information of a more general type.

It is also notable that, unlike an offer, court approval is required before a scheme can go ahead. This might make a bidder nervous as it potentially provides a forum for disgruntled minority shareholders to object. A scheme might also add an element of completion risk that does not exist in relation to offers. It was mentioned in Chapter 2 that the court, in deciding whether or not to sanction the scheme, is not bound by the members' decision. The sanctioning stage is not a rubber-stamping exercise and the courts do, on occasion, exercise their discretion to refuse a scheme even where it has been approved by the members and/or creditors.[119]

3.3.2.11 Structural flexibility

Although schemes are procedurally less flexible than traditional offers, they are structurally more flexible. For example, it may be that rather than the bidder company taking over the target, both bidder and target are acquired by a newco, using two schemes of arrangement that are inter-conditional. This may be done to increase the perception that the transaction is a merger of equals rather than a takeover of one company by another. An example of this situation was the merger of Halifax and Bank of Scotland in 2001 in which a new holding company, HBOS, was formed.

As any arrangement between a company and its members can be effected by way of a scheme, a takeover by way of a scheme also affords the companies involved an opportunity to effect a reorganisation at the same time. It is therefore relatively common to see, as part of a takeover scheme, some reorganisation of the resulting group companies.

3.3.2.12 The need to separate the members into classes in schemes

Another issue that makes schemes potentially more cumbersome than offers is the need to separate the members into classes in order for them to consider and approve the scheme. If the target gets the classes wrong, this can be a reason for the court to refuse to sanction the scheme at the sanctioning hearing. However, the definition of classes for this purpose is

[119] See e.g. *Re NFU Development Trust Ltd* [1972] 1 WLR 1548; *Puma Brandenburg Ltd* v. *Aralon Resources and Investment Company Ltd and Nortrust Nominees Ltd* (18 May 2017, judgment 27/2017, Guernsey Court of Appeal). For discussion see section 2.4.3.

not straightforward. This was discussed in Chapter 2[120] and will be discussed further in the context of takeover bids later in this chapter.[121]

3.3.2.13 Summary

There are both advantages and disadvantages to progressing with a takeover by way of a scheme rather than an offer, and schemes will not be suitable in all cases. They may be slower and more costly than a takeover offer in some circumstances and can give rise to complex issues (such as the need to consider whether separate class meetings are required) that do not arise in an offer. A hostile bidder will often find it easier to proceed by way of an offer than a scheme, though a hostile scheme is technically possible, and a bidder that anticipates competing bids may also prefer to utilise an offer rather than a scheme. However, the lower voting threshold in schemes makes it easier for a bidder to obtain 100 per cent control of the target, and there are other benefits that schemes can offer, such as their structural flexibility. These issues help to explain why schemes are now the mechanism of choice for recommended bids.

3.4 The impact on takeover schemes of the Takeover Code and the involvement of the Takeover Panel

3.4.1 The role of the Takeover Panel and the Takeover Code in schemes

The procedure for schemes was described in detail in Chapter 2 and this procedure applies to all kinds of scheme, including takeover schemes. However, the purpose of this section is to highlight a number of additional procedural issues that arise in takeover schemes as a result of the involvement of the Takeover Panel and the Takeover Code.[122]

The first set of rules governing the regulation of takeovers was published in 1959,[123] followed by the first City Code on Takeovers and Mergers (Takeover Code) in 1968. The purpose of the Takeover Code is set out in its introduction:

[120] See section 2.3.2.

[121] See section 3.5.

[122] The ambit of the Takeover Code applies only to changes of control of certain companies: Takeover Code, Introduction, s. 3. Transfer schemes of companies falling outside this section are therefore outside the ambit of the Takeover Code; see e.g. *Re Realm Therapeutics Plc* [2019] EWHC 2080 (Ch).

[123] See Issuing Houses Association, *Notes on the Amalgamation of British Businesses* (London: 1959).

> The Code is designed principally to ensure that shareholders in an offeree company are treated fairly and are not denied an opportunity to decide on the merits of a takeover and that shareholders in the offeree company of the same class are afforded equivalent treatment by an offeror. The Code also provides an orderly framework within which takeovers are conducted. In addition, it is designed to promote, in conjunction with other regulatory regimes, the integrity of the financial markets.
>
> The Code is not concerned with the financial or commercial advantages or disadvantages of a takeover. These are matters for the offeree company and its shareholders. In addition, it is not the purpose of the Code either to facilitate or to impede takeovers. Nor is the Code concerned with those issues, such as competition policy, which are the responsibility of government and other bodies.
>
> The Code has been developed since 1968 to reflect the collective opinion of those professionally involved in the field of takeovers as to appropriate business standards and as to how fairness to offeree company shareholders and an orderly framework for takeovers can be achieved.[124]

Also in 1968, a new body was established with the task of adjudicating disputes about the application of the rules: the Takeover Panel. Until 2006 the Takeover Panel had no statutory authority but relied for its authority on the fact that its membership represented the main parties with a material interest in takeovers, although there was also a threat of public censure against those that breached the provisions of the Takeover Code. However, the Companies Act 2006 placed both the Takeover Panel and the Takeover Code on a statutory footing.[125]

Initially the operation of the Takeover Code was based on the premise that takeover offers would occur by way of a contractual offer capable of acceptance by target shareholders. The provisions of the Takeover Code were drafted with traditional contractual offers in mind, but the Code applies to all takeover transactions, however structured, including schemes. However, as described in section 3.3, schemes and offers are fundamentally different transactions, and some of the provisions of the Takeover Code do not map exactly onto the scheme process. Although the fact that the Code applied to schemes was not doubted, for some time the exact application of parts of its provisions was difficult to discern. During this period, the application of the Takeover Code to the workings of a scheme of arrangement was established by a series of rulings and a Practice Statement.[126] In

[124] Takeover Code, Introduction, s. 2(a).

[125] Companies Act 2006, Part 28, which implements the Takeover Directive, Dir 2004/25/EC, [2004] OJ L142/12.

[126] Takeover Panel, Practice Statement No. 14, *Schemes of Arrangement*, 9 November 2005.

light of the increasing popularity of schemes, the Takeover Panel decided to formalise the position for schemes of arrangement in 2008:

> Historically, the Code was applied to schemes on a case-by-case basis, with a flexible approach being adopted where necessary. In view, however, of the increasing number of schemes, the Code Committee decided to codify the application of the Code to schemes in order to provide greater transparency and certainty in this area. The Committee decided not to amend the Code on a rule-by-rule basis so that, except where specified, the provisions of the Code continue to apply equally to contractual offers and schemes. However, significant flexibility has been retained in relation to the application of the Code to schemes, bearing in mind the speed at which market practice in relation to schemes continues to develop.[127]

This formalisation by the Takeover Panel involved a clarification of the extent to which the Takeover Code applies to schemes and the addition of a new Appendix 7 to the Code, which deals specifically with schemes.[128] It is clear that where schemes are used to effect takeovers of companies within the jurisdiction of the Takeover Panel,[129] the Takeover Code will apply. The Takeover Code states unequivocally that its provisions 'apply to an offer effected by means of a scheme of arrangement in the same way as they apply to an offer effected by means of a contractual offer' except as set out in Appendix 7 of the Code.[130]

The importance of synchronising the approach towards takeovers by way of schemes with those by way of offers was confirmed in *Re Expro International Group plc*.[131] The facts of this case bear consideration in some detail as they provide a good illustration of the issues that can arise in practice. On 17 April 2008 Umbrellastream announced a recommended offer for Expro, of £14.35 per Expro share. The offer was to be implemented by way of a scheme of arrangement. The next day Halliburton announced that it was conducting due diligence, with a view to making a competing offer. The company applied to court for

[127] Takeover Panel, Annual Report and Accounts for the year ended 31 March 2008, Director General's Report, at 13.

[128] See e.g. Takeover Panel, 'Schemes of arrangement: Statement by the Code Committee of the Panel following the external consultation process on PCP', 2007/1, RS 2007/1, 29 November 2007. These changes were effective from 14 January 2008. This appendix has subsequently been amended; see e.g. Instrument 2011/2, 21 July 2011; Instrument 2017/2, 13 April 2017.

[129] See Takeover Code, Introduction, s. 3(a).

[130] Takeover Code, App. 7, s. 1.

[131] [2008] EWHC 1543 (Ch); [2010] 2 BCLC 514.

directions to convene a meeting of shareholders to consider the scheme, and a date for the shareholders' meeting was fixed for 2 June 2008. On 23 May Halliburton announced its intention to make an offer of £15.25 per share, but this proposal did not amount to a firm intention, and was subject to preconditions. Umbrellastream increased its offer to £15.50 on the same day. On 27 May the company announced that it would seek an adjournment of the shareholders' meeting to 9 June, and a further circular was sent to shareholders with the new terms offered by Umbrellastream. The company also agreed not to seek to postpone either the meeting on 9 June or the court hearings fixed for 23 and 25 June (to sanction the scheme and confirm the reduction of capital). However, this was subject to an independent competing bidder not announcing a higher cash offer before 20 June, a date imposed by the Takeover Panel (and agreed by Halliburton), in order to inject 'some degree of certainty'[132] into the process. In short, Halliburton was put under an obligation to 'put up or shut up', that is, to make a firm offer or announce the withdrawal of its offer by 20 June.

On 9 June, no higher offer from Halliburton being forthcoming, the Expro shareholders met and approved the scheme by the requisite majority. A further increase in price was offered by Umbrellastream on 13 June, to £16.15, and a circular was sent to shareholders to this effect. Only at 11.03 p.m. on 20 June did Halliburton clarify that it wished to make an offer of £16.25 per Expro share, on the basis that the company would cooperate with this proposal being put to the shareholders in a scheme of arrangement. However, the independent members of the Expro board, who had conduct of the bid, considered that the addition of 10p to the Umbrellastream offer price was insufficient to cause them to agree to Halliburton's proposal.[133] Halliburton then withdrew its offer, though it reserved its right to make an offer for Expro, inter alia, if the court refused to sanction the Umbrellastream scheme at the sanctioning hearing or if there was a delay of fourteen days or more in the sanctioning of that scheme. A number of shareholders appeared at the sanctioning hearing

[132] Ibid. at [10] *per* David Richards J.

[133] Two reasons were put forward. First, the Halliburton payment would be made in September whereas Umbrellastream's payment would arrive in July: the board considered that even depositing the Umbrellastream payment in an ordinary bank account would yield more in the intervening period. Second, the Halliburton offer was subject to conditions (e.g. US anti-trust clearance) while the Umbrellastream scheme was not, rendering it at greater execution risk.

to ask for the scheme to be adjourned by fourteen days, in order to bring the Halliburton offer back into consideration.

David Richards J refused this request for adjournment and sanctioned the Umbrellastream scheme. He noted his support for the Expro board's assessment of the relative benefits and strengths of the competing offers. He held that no material change in circumstances had occurred since the Expro shareholders had approved the scheme on 9 June: the shareholders had approved it knowing of Halliburton's interest and the deadline of 20 June for Halliburton to make a firm offer. To order an adjournment would therefore be going against the shareholders' wishes as expressed on 9 June and the wishes of the independent board of Expro.

Of particular interest, however, are the comments that the judge went on to make about the relationship between the Takeover Code and schemes of arrangement. The importance of this issue is highlighted by the fact that the Takeover Panel was '[u]nusually . . . perhaps uniquely'[134] represented in the proceedings. Having introduced new provisions to the Takeover Code in January 2008, to codify the Takeover Panel's practice and to clarify the Takeover Code timetable in relation to schemes, the Panel was concerned that a successful application for an adjournment by the dissentient shareholders in this case might create just the kind of uncertainty that the Takeover Code changes were intended to reduce. One of the primary purposes of the Takeover Code is to provide greater certainty for market participants, whether the takeover is effected by way of a traditional offer or a scheme. The judge agreed with the Takeover Panel that allowing the requested adjournment would be counterproductive and would perpetuate the uncertainty being faced by the Expro shareholders:

> I have approached this application by the shareholders . . . entirely on its own merits and in accordance with the established principles applicable to the consideration of schemes of arrangement. I nonetheless should say that I have concern that there should, if possible, be a common approach to the conduct of bids, whether they are structured as an offer or as a scheme. I would not think it desirable that the court procedure involved in a scheme should allow in an undesirable level of uncertainty which the provisions of the Code have successfully reduced or eliminated in the case of ordinary offers.[135]

134 [2008] EWHC 1543 (Ch); [2010] 2 BCLC 514 at [52] *per* David Richards J.

135 Ibid. at [55].

The other issue raised by the *Expro* case was the possibility of a two-track system for takeovers effected by way of schemes. In takeovers effected by offers, it is the Takeover Panel that has the primary decision-making responsibility, and indeed there has been a desire to restrict the role of the court in takeovers in order to prevent the possibility of litigation being used as a defensive tactic, as discussed in section 3.3.2.10. However, in schemes the court has a significant role to play: '[i]n the case of a scheme . . . there is dual jurisdiction as it might be described of both the Panel and the court'[136] and there is therefore the possibility that this court process could undermine the function of the Takeover Panel and the Takeover Code in setting the timetable and process for takeovers effected by schemes. It is clear from the decision in *Expro* that the judge was keen for the court's involvement in schemes not to create a two-track process, one for contractual offers and one for schemes, nor for the court to be used to undermine the role of the Panel and the Code in schemes. The Takeover Panel clearly took some comfort from the *Expro* decision in relation to this issue: 'On this evidence, it does not appear that there is any current likelihood of the Courts playing a more active role in determining the outcome of offers.'[137]

3.4.2 Substantive provisions

In general the provisions of the Takeover Code apply to an offer effected by means of a scheme of arrangement in the same way as they apply to an offer effected by means of a contractual offer, except as set out in Appendix 7 of the Takeover Code.[138] Appendix 7 is important for clarifying how the Takeover Code is adapted to apply to schemes, but also for specifying the ways in which the Takeover Code does not apply to schemes. For example, it explains that a mandatory offer under rule 9 of the Takeover Code cannot be satisfied by way of a scheme of arrangement except with the prior consent of the Takeover Panel.[139]

3.4.2.1 Announcement

A scheme effecting a takeover is announced in the same way as an offer, in accordance with rule 2.7 of the Takeover Code. The announcement

136 Ibid. at [24].
137 Takeover Panel, Annual Report and Accounts for the year ended 31 March 2008, Director General's Report, 14.
138 Takeover Code, App. 7, s. 1.
139 Ibid., App. 7, s. 2.

will refer to the fact that the acquisition will be implemented by means of a scheme.

Once a bidder has announced a firm intention to make an offer by way of a scheme, it will normally be obliged to proceed with that offer, just as it would a contractual offer. However, there are a number of situations in which a bidder will normally be released from that obligation, including those in which the requisite majorities are not obtained at the shareholder meeting, or a competing offer or scheme is effective.[140] If the bidder decides to switch from a scheme structure to an offer, it will normally have to proceed with the offer, but not with its scheme. There may be other circumstances in which the Panel will not force the bidder to proceed with its scheme; for example where the target board withdraws its support for the scheme and intends to take steps to terminate the scheme process. However, the mere fact that the target board withdraws its recommendation of an offer to be implemented by way of a scheme will not normally of itself be sufficient to terminate the bidder's obligation to proceed with the scheme, or end the offer period.

3.4.2.2 Scheme circular and disclosures

Chapter 2 sets out the general disclosures that the court requires to be included in the scheme circular.[141] The fact that the Takeover Code applies to a particular scheme will mean that, in addition, the usual disclosures required by the Code will apply to the scheme circular.[142] For example, rule 24.2 of the Takeover Code requires the offer document (and therefore the scheme circular) to include the bidder's intentions with regard to the future business of the target company plus, inter alia, the bidder's plans for the continued employment of employees and management, its strategic plans for the target company, its intention with regard to the target's research and development functions, the balance of the skills and functions of the target's employees and management and the location of the target's headquarters and details of its headquarters functions.[143] In addition, the

[140] For discussion see Takeover Panel, 'Schemes of arrangement: Statement', note 128 above.

[141] See section 2.2.2.

[142] Takeover Code, r. 24.

[143] Ibid. r. 24.2(a). See also Takeover Panel, *Statements of Intention and Related Matters*, RS 2017/2, 11 December 2017, which addressed the issue of timing, so that these statements of intention provided by bidders should be made earlier in the process (at the time of the firm intention to make an offer rather than in the offer document) in order to provide employees and their representatives with more time to digest this information.

financial and other information of both the bidder and the target company must be disclosed in detail.[144]

In addition, the Takeover Code requires the target to make a number of public announcements as the scheme progresses. For example, the target is required to make a public announcement of the results of the first court meeting and of the general meetings of members (or any separate class meetings) that gather to consider the scheme.[145] Any adjournments of the court meeting to approve the scheme (or any delay to the timetable published in the scheme document) must also be announced.[146] The target is also required to make a public announcement of the outcome of the sanctioning hearing, and the sanctioning of the scheme, and a further announcement when the scheme becomes effective.[147]

It is notable that, although the disclosures required of the bidder are broadly similar whether a scheme or an offer is involved, the two processes differ in regard to other documentation requirements. One of the advantages of effecting a takeover involving a securities exchange by way of a scheme is that it avoids the need to produce a prospectus, insofar as it does not constitute an offer to the public.[148] The Financial Services Authority (FSA) (precursor to the Financial Conduct Authority (FCA)) indicated its support for such a view,[149] but this had remained an area of uncertainty. The FCA published a draft technical note in 2020 in which it confirmed that the issue of new securities pursuant to a scheme of arrangement does not constitute an offer of transferable securities to the public requiring the need for a prospectus.[150] However, the FCA also indicated that the position is different for a scheme with a 'mix and match' facility offering a choice between shares and cash; such a scheme involves a shareholder being asked to make a choice between different forms of consideration and about whether to buy or subscribe for the

[144] Ibid., r. 24.3.
[145] Ibid., App. 7, s. 5.
[146] Takeover Code, App. 7, s. 6. The Panel should be consulted to determine whether notice of such adjournment or delay should be posted to shareholders in addition to such an announcement.
[147] Ibid.
[148] A prospectus may still be required, however, for the purposes of admission to trading.
[149] UKLA List! Issue No. 10, June 2005.
[150] FCA, Primary Market Bulletin Issue No. 30, 19 August 2020 and FCA, Primary Market/TN/606.1, August 2020.

securities in question and therefore would require a prospectus, if there is no exemption.[151]

3.4.2.3 Scheme timetable

The fact that the Takeover Code applies has implications for the timetable of a scheme.[152] For example, following rule 30.1 of the Takeover Code, the scheme document must normally be posted within twenty-eight days of announcement.[153] Shareholder meetings should normally be held at least twenty-one days after the date of the scheme circular.[154] This is despite the fact that the Companies Act 2006 allows for company meetings with a shorter notice period than this (fourteen clear days).[155] The Takeover Panel decided that because a contractual offer must remain open for at least twenty-one days under rule 31.1 of the Takeover Code, the time to obtain shareholder approval for a scheme should mirror this.[156]

By contrast, the Panel decided that there should be no maximum time for the holding of shareholder meetings and/or the fulfilment of other scheme conditions, in the absence of a competitive situation. This means that there is no equivalent of the customary sixty-day limit for gaining sufficient acceptances for an offer.[157] Also, target shareholders are not 'locked in' to the scheme. In contrast to a contractual offer where accepting shareholders may not be able to withdraw their acceptances

151 FCA, Primary Market/TN/606.1, August 2020.

152 A number of provisions that regulate the timetable of an offer are disapplied for schemes because they have no relevance. So, for example, since a scheme of arrangement does not have a 'closing date' that may be extended in the same way as in a contractual offer, r. 31.3 of the Takeover Code, which provides that a bidder has no obligation to extend an offer the conditions of which are not met by a closing date, is disapplied in a scheme. Similarly, r. 31.4 of the Takeover Code, which states that a contractual offer that has become or been declared unconditional as to acceptances must remain open for acceptance for not less than fourteen days after the date on which it would otherwise have expired, is also disapplied in a scheme. A full list of the provisions of the Takeover Code that are disapplied in a scheme is set out in App. 7, s. 16.

153 Takeover Code, App. 7, s. 3(a).

154 Ibid., App. 7, s. 3(b).

155 Companies Act 2006, s. 307A.

156 Takeover Panel, 'Schemes of arrangement: Statement', note 128 above, at para. 3.10. However, it was recognised that circumstances might arise in which it would be appropriate to grant a derogation from the strict application of a twenty-one-day notice period. The Takeover Code therefore provides that the notice period for the shareholder meetings in relation to a scheme should 'normally' be at least twenty-one days from the date of the scheme circular, to allow for derogation from this rule: Takeover Code, App. 7, s. 3(d)(iii).

157 Takeover Code, r. 31.6.

in order to sell their shares, shareholders in a target company that is the subject of a scheme are generally free to sell their shares until shortly before the effective date of the scheme.[158]

One important issue, when considering how the Takeover Code should apply to schemes, is the definition of 'offer period' for scheme purposes. The start of an offer period for these purposes is relatively straightforward. The Takeover Code provides that an offer period commences 'when the first announcement is made of an offer or possible offer for the company, or when certain other announcements are made'.[159] For scheme purposes this will presumably be when the announcement of the scheme is made. The Takeover Code provides that the end of the offer period for schemes occurs 'when the scheme of arrangement has become effective'.[160] Whilst obtaining shareholder approval at the shareholders' meeting(s) and the sanction of the court are both essential to a scheme's success, a scheme will become legally binding and effective only on the date when a copy of the court order sanctioning the scheme is filed with the Registrar of Companies.[161] Therefore, in the normal course of events, provisions in the Takeover Code that apply during an 'offer period' or 'during the course of an offer' (or similar) will be interpreted as applying until the scheme has been sanctioned by the court and a copy of the order filed with the Registrar, or it has lapsed or been withdrawn.

The consideration offered by the bidder for the purposes of the takeover (whether cash, shares in the bidder, loan notes or other securities) must be dispatched to the target shareholders within fourteen days of the scheme becoming effective.[162]

3.4.2.4 Takeover Panel consents and consultations

There are a number of matters that must go to the Takeover Panel for approval if they arise during a scheme effecting a takeover. So, for example, the Panel's approval is required for any revision to the scheme

[158] In practice, trading in the shares will be suspended and the register of members will be closed to allow for the registrars to calculate entitlements to consideration.

[159] Takeover Code, Definitions section, definition of 'offer period'.

[160] Ibid.

[161] Companies Act 2006, s. 899(4) and see section 2.5.

[162] Takeover Code, App. 7, s. 10. In addition, the terms of the scheme should reflect this so that it may be enforced by target shareholders.

with fewer than fourteen days' notice before the date of the court meeting to approve the circular or after the date of the court meeting.[163]

Also, Panel consent is required before a bidder can switch its structure from a scheme to a contractual offer or vice versa.[164] In practice, although bidders often expressly reserve the right to do so, there is no specific need to reserve the right to switch or to include the level of acceptance condition that would apply in the circumstances of a switch to a contractual offer.

Where the bidder is considering a hostile scheme, that is, a scheme without the support of the target board, Appendix 7 states that the Panel should be consulted first.[165]

3.5 Class meetings in a takeover scheme

3.5.1 General

One of the most difficult issues in relation to a scheme is the separation of members and creditors into classes, which then consider and approve the scheme. A failure to separate members and creditors into the correct classes will result in the court being unable to sanction the scheme.[166] The test for determining classes for scheme purposes was discussed in Chapter 2,[167] and the 2020 Practice Statement makes it clear that the issue of dividing shareholders into the correct classes should be undertaken at the convening hearing.[168] The application of this test to takeover

163 Ibid., App. 7, s. 7.

164 Ibid., App. 7, s. 8. There are a number of examples of such switches occurring in practice. For an example of a switch from an offer to a scheme, see the offer by Baroness Retail Ltd for Debenhams plc in 2003, and as an example of a switch from a scheme to an offer, see the consortium bid for Canary Wharf Group plc in 2003.

165 Ibid., App. 7, s. 13.

166 See section 2.4. This is the case even if the court takes the view that the incorrect constitution of the classes would have had no effect on the outcome of the vote. However, Practice Statement (Companies: Schemes of Arrangement under Part 26 and Part 26A of the Companies Act 2006), [2020] 1 WLR 4493 aims to ensure that these matters are dealt with at an earlier stage in the scheme process (for discussion see section 2.2.3).

167 See section 2.3.2.

168 Practice Statement (Companies: Schemes of Arrangement under Part 26 and Part 26A of the Companies Act 2006) [2020] 1 WLR 4493, discussed in section 2.2.3. The previous Practice Statement had on its face applied only to creditor schemes (see Practice Statement *Ch D: Schemes of Arrangements with Creditors* [2002] 1 WLR 1345) but it had been accepted by the courts that the approach set out in that Practice Statement could be applied by analogy to member schemes in appropriate circumstances.

schemes is not straightforward and will be considered further in this section.

Before doing this, a number of general points can be made. First, not all members and creditors of the target company will necessarily need to consider and approve the scheme. As discussed in section 2.3.1.2, a company is free to decide with whom it proposes any particular compromise or arrangement. It is therefore possible for a company to exclude certain members or creditors from the scheme. Such members'/ creditors' rights would therefore be unaffected by the scheme. It is common for any shares held by the bidder to be excluded from the scheme, for example.

Second, it is not necessary for the company to consult with any class of members or creditors that is unaffected by the scheme.[169] In general, in schemes that effect change-of-control transactions, the bidder will want every class of members to have a vote on, and to be bound by, a scheme of arrangement as it will not wish to acquire control of a target company with outstanding minority interests. However, it is possible that in some circumstances some members might have no vote on a takeover scheme, where their interests are unaffected by the scheme. For example, if a company has a class of non-voting shares, and the bidder does not propose to acquire those shares in the scheme, then those shareholders' rights may be regarded as unaffected by the scheme, in which case they would have no vote.[170]

As regards the position of creditors in takeover schemes, in general it is the members, and not the creditors, whose rights will be affected by such schemes.[171] However, in some instances takeover schemes will affect creditors' interests, and therefore their consideration and approval will be required. This will be the case where the scheme relates to a company in which there are those holding share options or convertible securities,

[169] *Re Tea Corporation Ltd* [1904] 1 Ch 12. For discussion see section 2.3.1.2.

[170] See e.g. *Re Advance Bank Australia Ltd* (1997) 22 ACSR 513. In this case Santow J stated that, where their rights are affected by the scheme, the mere fact that they have constraints on their voting rights in the company's constitution would be unlikely to prevent them voting at court-convened scheme meetings (at 528). Where the court determines that such shareholders are affected, and do have a vote, the next question is whether they comprise a separate class for scheme purposes.

[171] Even when cancellation schemes were possible and thus the scheme involved a reduction of capital (see section 3.3.1.1), generally creditors' interests were unaffected. Although reductions of capital are generally regarded as a creditor protection issue, in cancellation schemes the reduction of capital is entirely fictitious since the reserve created is immediately applied in paying up new shares (with an equal capital).

since such option holders are treated as creditors rather than members for scheme purposes.[172] The Takeover Code requires any offer to include appropriate proposals to deal with such securities. These proposals will generally provide that the holders of such options or securities will be permitted to exercise their conversion rights and/or options conditional upon the court sanctioning the scheme.[173]

Third, although the fact that shareholders have interests that are distinct from the other shareholders is not sufficient to require a separate class to be formed (the court is interested in whether shareholders have different rights, not different interests, in determining class meetings),[174] in considering whether to approve a scheme the court is entitled to take account of the existence of those interests in exercising its general fairness discretion.[175] In appropriate cases the court has the power to discount or disregard the votes of certain members at the sanctioning stage, on the basis that they have an interest separate to that of others in the class. The court will not exercise this power lightly. However, takeover schemes do provide some examples of situations in which a court may exercise this discretion, for example where the shareholder in question controls the bidder or forms part of the corporate group to which the bidder belongs.

3.5.2 The division of members into classes for the purpose of a takeover scheme

When members meet to consider and vote on a scheme, they must do so in classes. This was discussed in detail in section 2.3.2. The definition of a class for scheme purposes was set out by Bowen LJ in *Sovereign Life Assurance Co* v. *Dodd*[176] and refined by Chadwick LJ in *Re Hawk Insurance Co Ltd*:[177]

> In each case the answer to that question will depend upon analysis (i) of the rights which are to be released or varied under the scheme and (ii) the new rights (if any) which the scheme gives, by way of compromise or

172 *Re Compania de Electricidad de la Provincia de Buenos Aires Ltd* [1980] 1 Ch 146, and see section 3.2.
173 Takeover Code, r. 15.
174 See section 2.3.2.1.
175 See section 2.4.3.
176 [1892] 2 QB 573.
177 [2001] EWCA Civ 241; [2001] 2 BCLC 480. See section 2.3.2.

> arrangement, to those whose rights are to be released or varied. It is in the light of that analysis that the test formulated by Bowen LJ in order to determine which creditors fall into a separate class – that is to say, that a class 'must be confined to those persons whose rights are not so dissimilar as to make it impossible for them to consult together with a view to their common interest' – has to be applied.[178]

Chadwick LJ recognised the need for a balance to be struck: those with genuinely different rights require the protection of a separate meeting, but if too many artificial distinctions are drawn then the scheme will be at the mercy of a veto by any one of the separate meetings.[179] This helps to explain the emphasis on 'rights' rather than 'interests' in determining the division of shareholders into classes.

The facts of *Re BTR plc*[180] are a good illustration of the court's approach to these issues. BTR had only one class of shares, ordinary shares, all of which were to be treated equally under the scheme. It was nevertheless suggested by an objecting shareholder that the court should take account of the likelihood of the shareholders voting in different ways in the meeting, because of their separate interests. Indeed, it was suggested that about forty separate class meetings were needed to accommodate all of these different interests. Chadwick LJ rejected this approach. The court does, however, have the ability to take account of these issues as part of its fairness assessment at the sanctioning stage, to determine whether the approval of the meetings has been reached only by the majority promoting a special interest, separate from the rest of the class.[181]

The court has also held that, in considering class composition, the court must be concerned with the rights held by the members and not with how members perceive those rights. In *Re Waste Recycling Group plc*,[182] the court rejected an argument by a minority shareholder that his shares should be treated as forming a separate class because he held his shares in the company as a means of holding the board to account on environmental matters rather than, as most other shareholders, as a mere financial investment.

178 Ibid. at [30].

179 See also *Re UDL Holdings Ltd* [2002] 1 HKC 172 (Final Court of Appeal of Hong Kong).

180 [1999] 2 BCLC 675. For a more recent example see e.g. *Re Imagination Technologies Group plc* [2017] EWHC 2934 (Ch).

181 *Re BTR plc (Leave to Appeal)* [2000] 1 BCLC 740 at 748.

182 [2003] EWHC 2065 (Ch); [2004] 1 BCLC 352.

The current state of the law is therefore relatively easily stated: only different rights (not different interests) should be taken into account when separating members into classes. Instead, interests can be taken into account by the court at the sanctioning hearing.[183] However, the application of these principles is not always straightforward.

This test does not require *identical* treatment of members before they can be regarded as forming a single class. Instead, the focus is on the extent to which the relevant rights are dissimilar, and whether it is impossible for the relevant members to consult together in their common interest. However, it is clear that where the rights of members differ significantly, they will need to be separated into different classes in order to consider and approve the scheme. For example, it is sometimes the case that a scheme effecting a takeover might include separate proposals for ordinary shareholders and holders of convertible securities.[184] In such circumstances the ordinary shares and the convertible securities will form two separate classes for scheme purposes.

Schemes may be used to effect takeovers of targets with separate classes of shares in issue, for example ordinary and preference shares. These different classes might also constitute different classes for scheme purposes, although 'class' for scheme purposes does not necessarily mean a class as defined in the articles of the company.[185] Thus, for example, the ordinary shareholders of a target company might comprise two (or more) classes for the purposes of considering a scheme. Often, shares that are in different classes in the articles will comprise different classes for scheme purposes, but this will not always be the case, and the exact class composition will depend on the particular circumstances.

3.5.2.1 Different treatment of members of the same class

Even where shares are of a single class in the articles, where shareholders are treated differently under the scheme they may nevertheless constitute separate classes for scheme purposes. So, in *Re BTR*, when Chadwick LJ refers to the similarity of the rights of members, those members will need to have the same rights under the company's constitution *and* under the

[183] For comment on the current test see section 2.3.2.3.

[184] See e.g. the scheme of arrangement for Kunick plc, completed July 2002.

[185] See e.g. *Re Robert Stephen Holdings Ltd* [1968] 1 WLR 522.

scheme in order for them to be able to meet together as a single group to consider and approve the scheme.[186]

One situation in which this issue arises is where there are overseas shareholders in the target company. Where the scheme involves the target shareholders receiving bidder securities, the scheme may provide that those bidder securities instead be sold for the benefit of overseas shareholders, that is, for the overseas shareholders to receive the cash instead.[187] This is in order to avoid difficulties with overseas jurisdictions that might prohibit the issue of such securities, or permit it only subject to costly or time-consuming procedures. Provided the same terms are offered to shareholders in different overseas jurisdictions (or any differences are required to comply with differences of overseas securities legislation) and the overseas shareholders comprise a small minority, the courts will usually be sympathetic to such an arrangement. However, such arrangements may mean that, although all of the target shareholders hold shares with the same rights (e.g. they are all ordinary shares), their different treatment under the scheme will result in different classes being required for the purpose of considering and voting on the scheme.

3.5.2.2 Members with shareholdings across different classes

Members may have shareholdings across different classes. In some circumstances this might influence them to support a proposal for one class so as to benefit themselves in their capacity as holders of another, separate, class. One issue that therefore arises in the takeover scheme context is whether the shares of such members should form a separate class.[188] In general this is regarded as a difference in interests rather than rights and therefore, following *Re Hawk Insurance* and *Re BTR*, it does not necessitate such shares forming a separate class. However, this is something that the court can take into account at the sanctioning stage, especially where there are significant numbers of persons with cross-holdings. The court may wish to examine whether cross-shareholdings of this kind influenced voting behaviour to such an extent that it cannot be said that the majority vote fairly represented the views of the class as a whole. If the court is not satisfied on this point, it may be appropriate for it to disregard some or all of the votes of those with cross-holdings, to see

[186] *Re BTR plc* [2000] 1 BCLC 740 at 747 *per* Chadwick LJ. This also follows from Chadwick LJ's judgment in *Re Hawk Insurance Co Ltd* [2001] EWCA Civ 241; [2001] 2 BCLC 480 at [30].

[187] See e.g. the scheme of arrangement for Safeway plc, completed March 2004.

[188] See e.g. *Re Alabama, New Orleans, Texas & Pacific Junction Railway Co* [1891] 1 Ch 213.

whether the scheme would still have been approved if those persons had been excluded from the vote. If the scheme would not have been approved, the court might consider it appropriate to refuse to sanction the scheme.[189]

In a similar vein, a person should not be excluded from a class merely because they hold shares in the target and are also one of its creditors. However, the court might again wish to take account of this extraneous interest at the sanctioning stage, when considering whether to approve the scheme.

3.5.2.3 Members with shares in the bidder

One particular example of a situation in which target shareholders might be regarded as having a conflicting class interest is where members of the target also hold shares in the bidder. Following the analysis set out earlier in this section, however, this fact will generally not require those shares to be treated as forming a separate class (after all, it is relatively common for this to arise where a class member is an index fund), but this is something that the court can take into account at the sanctioning stage.[190] Alternatively, the relevant member(s) could commit not to vote on the scheme so as to avoid jeopardising the court exercising its discretion to approve the scheme.

A twist on this arose in *Re Realm Therapeutics Plc*,[191] in which one of the objections raised at the sanctioning hearing was that a target shareholder (BVF) that was also a minority shareholder of the bidder continued to buy shares in the target. Picking up on a statement by Templeman J in *Re Hellenic & General Trust Ltd*[192] that a class meeting was incorrectly constituted because it contained a party that was acting both as a vendor and as a purchaser, it was suggested that the class meeting in *Realm* was defective on the same basis: it was suggested that BVF was both a vendor of the target shares (because it was exchanging its shares in the target for shares in the bidder pursuant to the scheme) and a purchaser (because it bought the target shares from other target shareholders). Norris J dismissed this argument. BVF was a vendor and a purchaser under different transactions and, unlike the situation in

[189] E.g. *Re A. W. Allen Ltd* [1930] VLR 251.

[190] *Re BTR plc* [1999] 2 BCLC 675; *Re BTR plc (Leave to Appeal)* [2000] 1 BCLC 740; *Re Primacom Holdings GmbH* [2012] EWHC 164(Ch) at [48]-[50]; *Re Realm Therapeutics Plc* [2019] EWHC 2080 (Ch).

[191] [2019] EWHC 2080 (Ch).

[192] [1976] 1 WLR 123, 126.

Hellenic, BVF was a distinct entity from the bidder company: the one was not under the control of the other. Consequently, the fact that a class member has acquired voting shares after the announcement of the transaction which is eventually embodied in the circular and is to be voted on at the scheme meeting does not fracture the class, though it might constitute a relevant factor at the subsequent sanctioning hearing.

3.5.2.4 Irrevocable undertakings

It is common for a bidder to seek irrevocable undertakings (or 'lock-up' arrangements) from target shareholders in advance of the bid, in order to ensure its success.[193] In the context of a takeover offer, these will generally consist of an undertaking to sell shares to the bidder. In a scheme, they will amount to an undertaking to vote in favour of the scheme. The question arises whether the shares of target shareholders that provide such undertakings should be treated as being in a separate class for scheme purposes.

Again, following the decisions in *Re BTR* and *Re Hawk Insurance*, such shareholders may be regarded as having different interests from the other target shareholders, rather than different rights. On the whole, therefore, it is accepted that such shares do not need to be placed in a separate class. Only if different terms are offered to those providing irrevocable undertakings will the shares be regarded as forming a separate class.

However, the court can still take account of such undertakings at the sanctioning hearing. It is possible that if the scheme received the relevant class approval solely because of the voting of shares in accordance with such an undertaking, then the court might refuse to sanction it.[194] This will depend on the facts of the particular scheme. In *Re Waste Recycling Group plc*,[195] the court approved a scheme in which irrevocable undertakings to vote in favour of the scheme had been given by the holders of nearly 50 per cent of the ordinary shares. There was no suggestion that the irrevocable undertakings had influenced the voting. As a general rule, where the terms of these irrevocable undertakings are not such as would reasonably have caused the person having the vote to vote differently in the absence of the agreement, they are unlikely to give rise to class issues or to prevent the court sanctioning the scheme.[196]

[193] For a discussion of this issue in the context of creditor schemes see section 5.3.1.

[194] See e.g. *Re BTR plc (Leave to Appeal)* [2000] 1 BCLC 740 at 746.

[195] [2003] EWHC 2065 (Ch); [2004] 1 BCLC 352.

[196] See e.g. *Re Telewest Communications plc (No. 1)* [2004] EWHC 924 (Ch) and *Re Telewest Communications plc (No. 2)* [2004] EWHC 1466 (Ch) *per* David Richards J (in the

The court's view of this matter will also depend on the precise nature of the undertaking. The court is unlikely to be overly concerned by statements of intention to vote in favour of a scheme that are not legally binding.[197] The court may also be less concerned about undertakings that fall away if circumstances change, for example if a higher offer emerges or if the board of the target ceases to recommend the scheme.

3.5.2.5 The position of the bidder and its subsidiaries

Generally, the bidder will exclude its own shares from the scheme so that any shares it holds in the target are not transferred under the scheme.[198] As a result, the shares of the bidder will not be part of the relevant class of shares at the court-convened member meetings. If the excluded bidder's shares are intended to be treated in the same way as the scheme shares, the bidder should agree to treat them in the same way. If they are not to be treated in the same way, they will simply be left alone outside the scheme.

However, a question arises as to what would happen if the bidder did not exclude its shares in this way. Will the shares of the bidder be part of the same class as all of the other shares in the target company for the purposes of considering and approving the scheme? It could be argued that an application of the *Hawk Insurance* and *Re BTR* principles would suggest that it is only the bidder's interests that are distinct from those of the other shareholders, not its rights. Therefore, all of the target shares (including the bidder's shares) should form a single class, with any concerns about the different interests of the bidder being dealt with at the sanctioning hearing.[199]

However, it is often assumed that the bidder's shares should not be part of the same class as the other target shares. It is difficult to see how it could be concluded that the bidder could consult together with the other shareholders with a view to their common interest in such a situation. It also seems clear that the court would have difficulty sanctioning the scheme at the sanctioning hearing if the bidder shares had been counted towards the 75 per cent level for approval purposes. What seems most

context of a creditor scheme); *Re Elegant Hotels Group plc* [2019] EWHC 3699 (Ch); *Re Smith & Williamson Holdings Ltd* [2019] EWHC 3021 (Ch).

197 See e.g. *Re Jessel Trust Ltd* [1985] BCLC 119; *Re Stockbridge Ltd* (1993) 9 ACSR 637.

198 See e.g. *Re National Bank Ltd* [1966] 1 WLR 819; *Singer Manufacturing Co* v. *Robinow* 1971 SC 11; *Re Hellenic & General Trust Ltd* [1976] 1 WLR 123.

199 See e.g. *Rosen* v. *Bruyns NO* [1973] 1 SALR 815 (where the participation of the bidder in the class of creditors voting on a scheme was allowed); *Re Jax Marine Pty Ltd* [1967] 1 NSWR 145.

likely is that, as a matter of course, the court at the sanctioning hearing would exclude the votes of the bidder when determining whether the class had approved the scheme by the requisite majority. It is therefore pragmatic to take the view that the bidder will not be able to include any shares in the target company that it already holds towards that 75 per cent level.

The question of the treatment of shareholdings of the bidder's subsidiaries in the target has also arisen. In *Re Hellenic &General Trust Ltd*, Templeman J held that the scheme failed because the classes had been improperly constituted.[200] In particular, target company shares held by a wholly owned subsidiary of the bidder should have been treated as constituting a separate class. The scheme would have failed to achieve the requisite approval without the positive vote of the subsidiary. This decision has been criticised.[201] In *Re BTR*, the decision in *Hellenic* was restricted to deciding only that the subsidiary's shares should be discounted. This was on the basis that the financial position of the parties was the same whether or not the subsidiary accepted the offer. The subsidiary's rights were the same, even though its interests were not, and the court was in a position to deal with the difference in the interests at the sanctioning stage.[202] The court will therefore have regard to this issue at the sanctioning hearing and might simply exclude the votes of the bidder's subsidiaries in determining whether the class has in fact reached the requisite majority when voting to approve the scheme. If not, then, as in *Hellenic*, the scheme will not be sanctioned. For these reasons it is usual to exclude target shares held by the bidder's subsidiaries, and indeed companies in the bidder's group more generally, from the scheme.[203]

Other jurisdictions have dealt with this issue in other ways. For example, the authorities in Hong Kong have adopted an additional regulatory requirement, to supplement the member approval

200 [1976] 1 WLR 123.

201 See e.g. J. A. Hornby, 'Class membership in a company's scheme of arrangement' [1976] 39 MLR 207; D. D. Prentice, 'Corporate arrangements – protecting minority interests' [1976] 92 LQR 13.

202 Lord Millett in *Re UDL Holdings Ltd* [2002] 1 HKC 172 took a slightly different approach to this issue. He was of the view that the subsidiary's shares could justifiably be treated as forming a separate class, not because its rights or interests were distinct from those of other shareholders but rather because the fact of the relationship between the bidder and its subsidiary might mean that the subsidiary and the other shareholders would receive different treatment under the scheme.

203 See e.g. *Re Greene King plc* [2019] EWHC 3173 (Ch).

requirements that otherwise apply in relation to schemes of arrangement.[204] The Takeover Code in Hong Kong provides that, unless the regulator consents to the contrary, a scheme of arrangement may be implemented only if (i) the scheme is approved by at least 75 per cent of the votes attaching to the 'disinterested shares' that are cast either in person or by proxy at a duly convened meeting of the holders of 'disinterested shares' and (ii) the number of votes cast against the resolution to approve the scheme of arrangement at such meeting is not more than 10 per cent of the votes attaching to all 'disinterested shares'.[205] 'Disinterested shares' for this purpose are defined to mean shares of the target company other than those owned by the bidder or persons acting in concert with it.[206]

The treatment of a bidder and its subsidiaries, as described here, raises an interesting contrast between the positions in a scheme and those in a takeover offer. In an offer, a bidder will usually seek to build a tactical stake in the target, directly and/or via a subsidiary. Any acquisition of the target shares by the bidder will help it towards the 50 per cent level required for majority control. In contrast, since under a scheme the votes of a bidder and its subsidiary will be excluded when determining whether the approval level has been reached, there will generally be limited benefits to the bidder from stake building on a bid that is to be implemented by way of a scheme. Any stake building may act against the bidder's interests because it will give more power to any dissentient shareholder(s), enhancing the voting power of any such minority and increasing the chances that the minority will be able to block the scheme. However, the limited benefits to the bidder in stake building when proposing to implement the bid by way of a scheme are that it may acquire sufficient shares to allow it to block a competing scheme and, in the event that there is a successful competing bidder, it might benefit from any increase in the price offered by any successful rival bidder to the extent that it would have acquired a stake at a price below the successful offer price.

3.5.3 *Participation and voting in class meetings*

It is for shareholders to decide whether or not they wish to participate in the scheme meetings. If a particular member or creditor is included in

204 Companies Ordinance, Cap 32, s. 166.
205 Hong Kong Takeovers Code, r. 2.10.
206 Ibid., note 6 to r. 2.

a class for scheme purposes, the court cannot compel that member or creditor to attend and vote. In *SABMiller plc*,[207] certain large shareholders agreed to be excluded from the single class meeting and gave undertakings to be bound by the outcome of the scheme. As Snowden J stated:

> where a member or creditor is not acting under compulsion, and is willing to give his consent voluntarily by agreeing to give an undertaking to be bound by the proposal, there is no confiscation of his property or rights, and no injustice to him if he is not summoned to a scheme meeting. Nor is there any injustice to other members or creditors if the consenting member or creditor simply agrees not to be included in the scheme meeting. Those other members or creditors have no rights to force him to attend and vote; and far from creating injustice for the dissentients, the consequence of the consenting member or creditor agreeing not to be included in the category of persons summoned to the meeting is that the votes of the dissentient members or creditors may well carry more weight at the meeting.[208]

This is a sensible approach. In reaching this decision, Snowden J emphasised the importance of schemes in facilitating compromises or arrangements between a company and its members/creditors, and as such sections 895 and 896 of the Companies Act 2006 should be interpreted flexibly and purposively so as to permit the court, where appropriate, to accept undertakings of the kind being offered by the shareholders in this case. Furthermore, the outcome here aligns with the common practice of members or creditors voluntarily excluding themselves from a class to which they might otherwise be said to belong in order to avoid giving dissentient members/creditors the opportunity to attack a vote at the sanctioning hearing.[209] The shareholders offering the undertaking in *Re SABMiller* had entered into arrangements with the company which could possibly have provided grounds for challenge at the sanctioning stage on the basis of those shareholders holding different interests from other shareholders in the single class meeting, and therefore this arrangement was a way of avoiding this possibility.

In terms of voting at the class meeting, a class member is entitled to vote in accordance with their economic interests in relation to that issue, even if those economic interests differ from the economic interests of

[207] [2016] EWHC 2153 (Ch).
[208] Ibid. at [49].
[209] For an example relating to a creditor scheme see *Re Stemcor Trade Finance Ltd* [2015] EWHC 2662 (Ch).

other members of the class. For instance, a class member can take a longer- or shorter-term approach to their decision-making or their risk appetite may be greater or less than that of other members of the class. To that extent, a member is free to vote with regard to its own individual interests at a scheme meeting, even if those interests are not shared by other members of the relevant class.[210] What is not legitimate, of course, is for a class member to vote in accordance with economic interests in relation to some matter that is not shared by the class as a whole, such as where the class member holds shares in the bidder and votes as it does because it is complicit with the bidder and seeking to further the bidder's goals. In such circumstances the member would be using its vote not for the purpose it was given (i.e. in relation to the issue facing the class as a whole) but for some collateral purpose. The court can take account of this at the sanctioning stage: if there is a 'strong and direct causative link'[211] between the adverse interest and the voting decision, the court can either discount the weight given to the majority vote or disregard altogether the relevant votes of the 'special interest' members.

In terms of the conduct of the court-convened class meeting, meetings under Part 26 of the Companies Act 2006 are meetings of the relevant members/creditors or classes thereof, and not meetings of the company. This has various implications. The conduct of scheme meetings is governed by the court rather than rules set out in Part 13 of the Companies Act 2006 or the company's articles of association.[212] It also has implications for voting at these meetings. Unlike company meetings where the general rule is that a vote is a piece of property and that members can vote as they wish,[213] it was stated in *Re Dee Valley Group plc*[214] that members'/creditors' votes in a scheme meeting must be exercised for the purpose of benefitting the class as a whole and not for any collateral purpose[215] and, moreover, that the consequences of not doing so would not merely be taken account of at the court sanctioning stage[216] but could also lead to the chairman of the relevant meeting discounting the votes for the

210 See *Re Alabama, New Orleans, Texas & Pacific Junction Railway Co* [1891] 1 Ch 213 at 243–4.
211 *Re Lehman Bros International (Europe) Ltd* [2018] EWHC 1980 (Ch) at [90] *per* Hildyard J. See further section 2.4.2.
212 See section 2.2.3.2.2.
213 There are obvious exceptions to this, e.g. *Allen* v. *Gold Reefs of West Africa Ltd* [1900] 1 Ch 656; *Citco Banking Corp NV* v. *Pusser's Ltd* [2007] UKPC 13.
214 [2017] EWHC 184 (Ch).
215 Ibid. at [47].
216 See section 2.4.2.

purposes of determining whether the statutory majority approved the scheme. Prior to *Dee Valley*, any doubt regarding the bona fides of those voting at the class meeting would have been dealt with at the sanctioning stage. However, in *Dee Valley* the court was faced with a split voting strategy whereby a shareholder opposed to the scheme transferred shares to others who would vote against it with the goal of defeating the scheme. The court faced a difficulty, namely that if the votes of the transferees of this split voting strategy were taken into account by the chairman of the meeting, the class meeting would not approve the scheme and therefore the court would not be able to consider whether to sanction it; the court's sanctioning discretion arises only where all of the relevant class meetings have approved the scheme.[217] In *Dee Valley*, the judge was clearly keen to find a way to ensure that legitimate schemes are not defeated at the class meeting stage in this way. Sir Geoffrey Vos C stated: 'If that were to occur regularly, the undoubted utility of schemes of arrangement to facilitate takeovers that were much in the financial interests of the majority would be damaged.'[218]

In an ideal world, the issue of bona fides would be left to be dealt with by the court at the sanctioning stage, when it can take account of all of the circumstances in determining whether to exercise its discretion rather than requiring the chairman to consider the motivations of members/creditors at the scheme meeting itself.[219] Unfortunately, a combination of the headcount test[220] and the application of section 899, which requires each class meeting to have approved the scheme before the court can consider it at the sanctioning stage, makes this option impossible in a *Dee Valley* situation. The removal of the headcount test as advocated in section 2.3.3.2 would solve the problem, but in the meantime the solution proposed by Vos C is a practical response to it. It should, however, be

[217] Companies Act 2006, s. 899.

[218] [2017] EWHC 184 (Ch) at [40].

[219] On the facts of *Dee Valley* it is notable that the judge held that the chairman did not need to inquire into the particular motivations of the members in order to decide whether to discount their votes: 'In my judgment, the Chairman's knowledge of the circumstances in which the Individual Shareholders had acquired their shares gave him sufficient evidence to conclude that the votes of the Individual Shareholders at the … Meeting were not being cast for the purpose of benefitting the class as a whole. That was not specifically because their imputed or expressed motives fell outside the band of what is permissible. It was because the only possible explanation for the conduct of the Individual Shareholders was to further a share manipulation strategy to defeat the Scheme by use of the majority in number jurisdictional requirement' (at [58]).

[220] See section 2.3.3.2.

confined to those situations in which the more usual approach (namely leaving these issues to the sanctioning stage) cannot be utilised.

3.6 A comparison of minority protection in schemes and offers

Schemes of arrangement allow the minority shareholders to be bound by the majority so that, in a takeover scheme, even if they dissent, they will be bound to sell their shares to the bidder in accordance with the terms of the scheme. This raises obvious issues of potential minority abuse. However, when the minority protections put in place in a scheme are compared with those in place in an offer, it is clear that substantially more protection is provided in an offer. The reasons for this differential treatment need to be examined.

3.6.1 Minority protection in a scheme

There are, broadly, two protections put in place for minority shareholders in a scheme.[221] The first is the fact that shareholders meet in

[221] It is notable that other jurisdictions sometimes include different forms of minority protection in their scheme arrangements. Under the South Africa Companies Act No. 71 of 2008, Ch. 5, for example, members need to approve the scheme by a 75 per cent majority (with no headcount requirement), but do not meet in classes to do so (s. 115(1) and (2)). The role of the court is greatly reduced compared to that in an English scheme as there is no convening hearing, a court sanction is required in only a narrow range of circumstances (s. 115(3) and (6)), and if the court is asked to approve the transaction, its discretion is more limited than in an English scheme (s. 115(7)). However, the 2008 Act introduced two other forms of protection for members: the requirement that a report on the commercial merits of the proposed scheme be provided by an independent expert and distributed to the shareholders (s. 114(2) and (3)) and the introduction of an appraisal right which entitles a member to force the company to buy it out at fair value in certain circumstances (s. 164). Given that in most change of control transactions the members' shares will be transferred to the bidder, the value of this provision lies not in the exit right per se but in the right to exit at 'fair value' and therefore much depends on the court's interpretation of what this means, i.e. whether it is analogous to the value determined pursuant to the scheme or has some other value attached to it. For a discussion of how fair value should be determined see e.g. *Loest v. Gendac and Another* 2017 (4) SA 187 (GP). See also Canadian Business Corporations Act 1985, s. 190 (in which court consent is required for a member to utilise this right). Some jurisdictions offer this as an alternative to schemes; see e.g. the British Virgin Islands (BVI) in which the scheme of arrangement sits alongside plans of arrangement (see BVI Business Companies Act 2004, ss. 177–9, 179A) and whereas the former contains the same forms of minority protection as an English scheme, the latter are distinct in a number of respects including the right for dissenting shareholders to receive payment of fair value for their shares.

classes to consider whether to vote in favour of the scheme. The company needs to obtain the approval of all classes of members or creditors that are affected by the scheme. Only if each class meeting approves will the court be able to sanction the scheme, that is, the cramdown of a whole dissenting class is not possible.[222] The courts can therefore protect minorities by ensuring that they have all of the information they need to determine whether to attend and how to vote at the meetings,[223] and by ensuring that correctly constituted class meetings are held. In theory, the fact that different class meetings are held means that shareholders should vote alongside others with similar concerns and interests, and this should make it more likely that the minority voice will be heard. However, the level of protection will depend in large part on how many class meetings are held. The more class meetings there are, the more minority shareholders will have veto rights in relation to the proposed scheme. There has been a shift in recent years away from large numbers of class meetings that can give minorities strong veto rights. Although it is still important to divide shareholders and creditors into different classes, many distinctions between members and creditors (especially those that may more properly be characterised as different interests rather than different rights) will instead be taken into consideration by the court at the sanctioning stage.

The second form of protection for minorities, then, is the scrutiny of the court, particularly at the sanctioning hearing. The court has wide discretion at this stage to refuse to sanction a scheme if minority oppression is present. The court will pay particular attention to whether the statutory requirements are met (e.g. that the votes are passed by the requisite majorities) and the judge will also apply a fairness test. In particular, the court may wish to examine whether different interests held by the majority shareholders influenced their voting behaviour to such an extent that it cannot be said that the majority vote fairly represented the views of the class as a whole.[224] Examples of this given in section 3.5 include situations in which the majority includes the bidder or its subsidiaries, or members hold shareholdings across different classes. If the court is not satisfied as to this matter, it may be appropriate for it to discount or disregard some or all of the votes of those with different interests to see whether the scheme would still have been approved if

[222] This is distinct from the position in creditor schemes under a Part 26A restructuring plan, discussed in section 5.8.

[223] See section 2.2.2.

[224] See generally section 2.4.

those persons had been excluded from the vote. If the scheme would not have been approved, the court might consider it appropriate to refuse to sanction the scheme.

3.6.2 *Minority protection in an offer*

The aims of UK takeover regulation are twofold: first, to regulate the relationship between the target directors and the target shareholders, and resolve this potential conflict in favour of the shareholders; and second, to regulate the relationship between the bidder and the target shareholders. Concentrating on the latter, UK takeover regulation has put in place a raft of measures designed to ensure shareholder protection. These issues were barely affected by the UK's implementation of the Takeover Directive in 2006.[225]

At the centre of these measures is the concept of shareholder equality enshrined in General Principle 1 of the Takeover Code.[226] As a result, rules are in place regarding the need for the same offer to be made to all shareholders of the same class[227] and, where a target company has more than one class of equity share capital, for a 'comparable' offer to be made for each class, whether it carries voting rights or not.[228] If the offer is subsequently increased by the bidder then even those who accepted the original offer are entitled to the new, higher price.[229] However, the Takeover Code requires not only equality of treatment of shareholders within the bid but also equality between offerees and sellers outside the bid.[230] The Code seeks to prevent the bidder from doing favourable deals with a few selected

[225] The Takeover Directive 2004/25/EC was implemented via Companies Act 2006, Part 28. For discussion see DTI, *Implementation of the EU directive on Takeover Bids: Guidance on the changes to the rules on company takeovers* (London: April 2006).

[226] While the UK was a member of the EU, and during the transition period, the General Principles within the Takeover Code were taken from the Takeover Directive 2004/25/EC, Art. 3. After 31 December 2020 they are replicated in domestic law: Companies Act 2006, Sch 1C, part 1, inserted by the Takeovers (Amendment) (EU Exit) Regulations 2019 (SI 217/2019).

[227] Takeover Code, GP 1. The definition of class for these purposes has been determined strictly: see e.g. the Takeover Panel Appeal Board's decision in relation to Eurotunnel plc, www.thetakeoverappealboard.org.uk/wp-content/uploads/2016/12/2007-02.pdf.

[228] Takeover Code, r. 14. The Takeover Code has in place rules designed to prevent the bidder offering disguised enhanced deals to only some of the shareholders: r. 16.

[229] Ibid., r. 32.3.

[230] For discussion see P. Davies, 'The notion of equality in European takeover regulation' in J. Payne (ed.), *Takeovers in English and German Law* (Oxford: Hart, 2002).

shareholders, either before the offer period[231] or during the offer period.[232] In addition, there are rules in place to ensure that the target shareholders have adequate information upon which to make a decision,[233] and that they have enough time within which to reach a decision.[234]

The squeeze-out and sell-out rules also have built-in protection for the minority. These rules allow the shares of the 'rump' 10 per cent shareholders to be bought out at the option of the bidder (squeeze-out), or sold by the rump shareholders to the bidder (sell-out), once the bidder has acquired at least 90 per cent by value of the shares to which the offer relates.[235] The sell-out rules give the rump shareholders the right not only to exit the company, rather than to remain as minority shareholders, but, crucially, to be bought out at the offer price.[236] The squeeze-out rules allow the bidder to acquire the shares of the rump shareholders, but oblige the bidder to buy the shares on the final terms of the offer.[237] The rump shareholders can object, by application to court.[238] Generally, the court will allow the squeeze-out where it is on the same terms as the final offer, unless the rump shareholders can demonstrate that the final offer is not indicative of fairness, for example where the 90 per cent shareholders are not independent of the bidder.[239]

Last, but not least, there is the mandatory bid rule that states that once a person, together with anyone with whom they are acting in concert, acquires 30 per cent of the shares carrying voting rights, or holds between 30 and 50 per cent and acquires additional shares carrying voting rights,

231 Takeover Code, r. 6.1.

232 Ibid., r. 6.2.

233 Ibid., rr. 23, 24, 25.

234 The offer must be kept open for acceptance by the shareholders for at least twenty-one days (Takeover Code, r. 31.1). Any revised offer must be kept open for a further period of fourteen days (Takeover Code, r. 32.1) and any shareholders who accepted the original offer are entitled to the revised consideration (r. 32.3).

235 Squeeze-out and sell-out rules have been present in companies legislation since 1929. The current rules are located in Companies Act 2006, Part 28, Ch. 3. These rules also implement Art. 15 of the Takeover Directive 2004/25/EC, which required some amendments to the existing law governing takeovers. For discussion of the reforms in the 2006 Act see also the Company Law Review Steering Group, *Modern Company Law for a Competitive Economy: Final Report* (July 2001) URN 01/942–3 (CLR, *Final Report*) 282–300.

236 Companies Act 2006, ss. 983–5.

237 Ibid., s. 981(2).

238 Ibid., s. 986.

239 *Re Bugle Press Ltd* [1961] Ch 270; *Re Chez Nico (Restaurants) Ltd* [1992] BCLC 192; *Fiske Nominees Ltd* v. *Dwyka Diamond Ltd* [2002] EWHC 770 (Ch); [2002] 2 BCLC 123.

then a mandatory bid is required.[240] That person must extend offers to the holders of any class of equity share capital (voting or non-voting) and also to the holders of any other class of transferable securities carrying voting rights.[241] The offer must be a cash offer, or with a cash alternative, and must be at the highest price paid by the offeror or a member of its concert party within the twelve months prior to the commencement of the offer.[242]

3.6.3 A comparison of these minority protection provisions

The minority protection available in a scheme is substantially more limited than that available in an offer. This can be justified once the different reasons for the existence of minority protection in a scheme and in an offer are understood.

3.6.3.1 Justifications for minority protection in an offer

It is important to understand why the principle of shareholder equality is enshrined in UK takeover regulation. The idea of equality amongst shareholders in a bid situation is in contrast to general UK company law principles, in which shareholders must be treated fairly but not necessarily equally.[243] Indeed, it is generally accepted that controlling shares in a company are worth more than non-controlling ones,[244] which contradicts the idea of all shareholders being paid rateably in a takeover scenario.

There seem to be two principal concerns at work in this context: the need to ensure that the decision taken by the shareholders is as undistorted as possible, and a desire to protect the minority shareholders from abuse. As regards undistorted choice, the idea is, broadly, that the shareholders' decisions should be made in a manner that is distorted as little as possible by any actions of the bidder. In the absence of specific takeover regulation, bidders could offer different deals to different shareholders or make offers with very short periods for acceptance. Bidders would have the opportunity to 'divide and conquer', skewing the offer in order to acquire the company at the lowest possible price. The collective action problems faced by the target shareholders potentially increase the

[240] Takeover Code, r. 9.1.
[241] Ibid.
[242] Ibid., r. 9.5. The Panel can agree to an adjusted price.
[243] See e.g. *Mutual Life Insurance Co of New York* v. *Rank Organisation Ltd* [1985] BCLC 11.
[244] *Short* v. *Treasury Commissioners* [1948] AC 534.

bargaining strength of the bidder at the expense of the target shareholders.[245]

If the decision on the outcome of the bid is given primarily to the shareholders rather than the target board, as it is in the UK, it is crucial that the shareholders' decision-making is as undistorted as possible. A result of the pressure to tender might be that the bidder will succeed in gaining control over a target even if the value-maximising course of action for the target shareholders would be to reject the bid. Undistorted choice is therefore about allocative efficiency,[246] and is a crucial aspect of UK takeover regulation.

Two arguments can be made in favour of providing minority shareholders with additional protection in a bid situation. The first is that the bidder, once successful and in control of the target, may engage in oppressive acts towards the minority, and that the minority needs protection from that potential oppression. The second is that shareholders should be entitled to a right of exit when a change of control occurs following a takeover. Both are based on the idea that, without this protection, the minority might become 'trapped' in the target company under the control of the bidder and therefore the minority shareholder needs to be provided with the opportunity to exit, and furthermore to exit at the bid price.

While the need to ensure undistorted choice is undisputed, the arguments in favour of minority protection in order to prevent oppression or to provide an exit are more problematic. As regards the prevention of oppression, for example, it is argued that shareholders require a remedy because they might suffer oppression in the future, not because they have already suffered oppression at the hands of the new controller. In general, however, remedies in company law are provided to minority shareholders on the basis that they have suffered actual abuse, and a remedy is likely to be denied to a minority shareholder who relies on merely the potential for abuse to occur in the future.[247] It is not clear why the position should be so markedly different in relation to takeovers.

245 L. Bebchuk, 'The pressure to tender: An analysis and a proposed remedy' (1987) 12 *Delaware Journal of Corporate Law* 911.

246 Ibid.; L. Bebchuk, 'Towards an undistorted choice and equal treatment in corporate takeovers' (1985) 98 *Harvard Law Review* 1693.

247 See e.g. *Re Astec (BSR) plc* [1998] 2 BCLC 556 (involving an unfair prejudice petition under s. 459 Companies Act 1985, now restated as s. 994 Companies Act 2006), where the perceived premature nature of the petition was a contributory factor in the dismissal of the petition.

Furthermore, UK company law already provides remedies for minority shareholders faced with actual abuse, in particular section 994 of the Companies Act 2006. This remedy is of most use in the context of small, quasi-partnership companies,[248] and is rare in large public companies since the most common remedy awarded by the court (an exit via a buy-out of the petitioner's shares) is available to a shareholder in a publicly listed company via a sale in the market. However, in a takeover situation, a minority shareholder in a publicly listed company is not trapped in any meaningful sense since the opportunity to sell the shares in the market always exists. A minority shareholder might argue that the market price for the shares in those circumstances does not reflect a fair price, since the actions of the new controller have depressed the market value of the shares, but shareholders in a publicly traded company know, or ought to, that the value of their shares may go down as well as up.[249]

The second argument, that minority shareholders in a takeover bid need a right of exit at the bid price, seems to be based not on the view that the new controllers will behave oppressively or illegally, or have the potential to do so, but rather on the idea that the position of shareholders in a company depends to a significant extent on the identity of the controllers of a company. Even if the new controllers are not per se oppressive towards the minority, nevertheless the change of control has the potential to affect the minority shareholders adversely. For example, the new controllers might implement a new, less successful business strategy. However, changes of control can occur in a number of ways, and other events that trigger a change of control could result in changes of policy, such as a change in the company's business activities, and could also have a detrimental effect on the minority shareholders. If this argument were valid then it might be expected that minority shareholders would have the right to exit on any change of control, however it came about, but that is not what we see in practice.

In addition, the ability of the minority to exit at the bid price means that there is no control premium available in takeovers. This is at odds with other areas of company law where it is accepted that the holders of a majority stake in a company should obtain a premium on the sale of their shares since they are selling control of the company. Moreover, this rule has the effect of making bids more expensive, which is likely to

248 For discussion see *O'Neill* v. *Phillips* [1999] 1 WLR 1092 (HL).

249 One situation where the minority may need protection is where the new controller takes the company private, following the change of control, in which case there will be no ready market for the minority's shares.

reduce the number of bids made overall.[250] Whether this is a cause for concern depends on whether you take the view that takeovers should be encouraged or not.

In summary, while the arguments regarding the need to provide minority shareholders with a right to exit at the bid price can be questioned, the need to ensure undistorted choice in a bid scenario is a strong justification for the raft of measures put in place in an offer.

3.6.3.2 Justifications for minority protection in a scheme

Unlike a takeover offer, a scheme involves a decision of the company, taken by the shareholders in a meeting or meetings. As a consequence, there is no opportunity for the bidder to divide and conquer.[251] There are no individual contracts for the sale and purchase of shares being entered into between the bidder and individual shareholders. There is no collective action problem akin to that which faces the dispersed shareholders in the majority of UK publicly traded companies confronted with a takeover offer. The concerns regarding distorted choice therefore do not arise in the context of a scheme.

The issue in the scheme context is simply one of minority protection. Again, though, it is important to distinguish the position regarding takeover offers. There is no need to worry about the minority shareholders needing a right of exit. All shareholders are bound by a successful scheme to transfer their shares to the bidder. The bidder acquires 100 per cent of the shares and there is therefore no possibility of any shareholders being left behind who might wish to exit the target company after the bid.

As regards the danger of oppression, the issues are also different. In the scheme scenario, the concern is not about oppression after the bid since, again, there will be no target shareholders left in the company at that point as the bidder will hold 100 per cent of the shares. Rather, it is about oppression in the process of deciding whether to accept the scheme. Since a successful scheme binds all shareholders, the effect is that even dissenting shareholders will be required to sell their shares to the bidder for the price agreed as part of the scheme. This can be regarded as triggering the need for some kind of a protective response. However, in line with other

[250] F. H. Easterbrook and D. R. Fischel, 'The proper role of a target's management in responding to a tender offer' (1981) 94 *Harvard Law Review* 1161 at 1174–80; Bebchuk, 'Toward an undistorted choice', note 246 above, at 1740–2.

[251] As a belt and braces, the Takeover Code does restrict the way in which a bidder can acquire interests in a target: Takeover Code, rr. 5, 11 and 16.

areas of UK company law, the response adopted in this regard is relatively laissez-faire. In general, UK law has taken the view that shares can be expropriated as long as a fair price is paid for them. A good example of this is the squeeze-out rules, discussed in section 3.3.1.2, which generally do allow shareholders' shares to be purchased as long as the price is fair (and, broadly, the bid price will be regarded as a good indication of fairness).[252]

In fact, the potential for oppression in a scheme is most akin to that facing the rump shareholders in a takeover who are required by the squeeze-out rules to sell their shares to the bidder. In both scenarios, the minority shareholders are being required to sell their shares at a price that is imposed upon them. In squeeze-outs, the minority can apply to court for an order that there should be no acquisition or that the offer price be amended. It is for the petitioner to establish that the squeeze-out is unfair. Generally, the fact that 90 per cent of the shareholders have accepted the offer will be taken as evidence that the offer is fair unless the petitioner can demonstrate unfairness despite this 90 per cent acceptance level, for example, where the 90 per cent acceptors are not independent of the bidder.[253] These instances are rare, however. Usually, the court will not intervene to prevent the squeeze-out occurring on the final terms of the offer. This seems appropriate. A shareholder has no intrinsic right to retain its shares, and expropriation should be allowed if the price is fair. In general, the fact that the remainder of the shareholders have accepted the price will be a good indication of fairness. Only in exceptional circumstances, where this is not the case, should the court interfere.

As a result, the lower level of minority protection available in a scheme should not be a cause for concern. The protections in place in a scheme perform a fundamentally different function from most of the rules put in place in an offer. The concern that is raised in a scheme, namely the possibility of expropriation at an unfair price, is dealt with appropriately by the courts in this regard.

It is sometimes suggested that bidders should not be allowed to make use of schemes to effect takeovers (since this allows them to bypass the rigorous regulatory regime in place in relation to takeover offers) or, at least, if a scheme is used in this regard, additional regulatory requirements should be put in place to ensure that bidders do not gain an

[252] *Allen* v. *Gold Reefs of West Africa Ltd* [1900] 1 Ch 656; *Citco Banking Corp NV* v. *Pusser's Ltd* [2007] UKPC 13 (PC); [2007] 2 BCLC 483.

[253] *Re Bugle Press Ltd* [1961] Ch 270; *Re Chez Nico (Restaurants) Ltd* [1992] BCLC 192; *Fiske Nominees Ltd* v. *Dwyka Diamond Ltd* [2002] EWHC 770 (Ch); [2002] 2 BCLC 123.

unscrupulous advantage by bypassing takeover regulation in this way. This will be explored further in section 3.7, but the discussion in the present section suggests that the lower minority protections available in a scheme should not be seen as a cause of concern.

3.7 Should takeovers be allowed by way of a scheme of arrangement?

3.7.1 The English approach compared to that of other jurisdictions

This chapter has explained that English schemes are now very commonly used to effect takeovers. However, some disquiet about the use of schemes in this context continues to exist. Other jurisdictions that have imported the English scheme have specifically regulated the relationship between schemes and takeover offers, owing to concerns about the use of schemes in this context.[254] For example, in Australia, section 411(17) of the Australian Corporations Act 2001 provides that a court will have jurisdiction to approve a scheme of arrangement only where either (i) it is satisfied that the scheme has not been proposed to avoid the operation of the takeovers legislation or (ii) a statement is received from the Australian Securities and Investment Commission (ASIC) indicating that it has no objection to the arrangement.[255]

[254] In India, similar concerns seem to be behind Indian Companies Act 2013, s. 230(11)–(12). By contrast, a number of other jurisdictions that have imported the English scheme have adopted the same basic approach to this issue as the English courts; see e.g. BVI (see Business Companies Act 2004, s. 179A), Bermuda (see Bermuda Companies Act 1981, s. 99), the Cayman Islands (see Companies Law, as revised, s. 86). See also Singapore where in 2011 the Company Law Reform Steering Committee considered whether to introduce a provision dealing with this issue, akin to s. 411(17) of the Australian Corporations Act 2001, but rejected this proposal: Ministry of Finance, Report of the Steering Committee for the Review of the Companies Act: Consultation Paper 2011, paras. 165–7. Although the scheme provisions in South Africa have moved away from their English origins somewhat, it remains the case that South Africa does not specifically legislate the relationship between schemes and takeovers (see Companies Act No. 71 of 2008, Ch. 5).

[255] The courts have held that the mere fact that a deal could have been structured under takeover legislation does not mean that it was structured as a scheme for the purpose of avoiding takeover legislation: *Re ACM Gold Ltd* (1992) 7 ACSR 231; *Re Stockbridge Ltd* (1993) 9 ACSR 637; *Re Capilano Honey* (2018) 132 ACSR 332 at [36]. In *Capilano* the Australian Securities and Investment Commission (ASIC) argued that the transaction had been structured to avoid takeover legislation in future transactions involving the holdco as opposed to the scheme itself being such an avoidance, but Farrell J rejected this argument, holding that the plain words of s. 411(17) showed that it did not apply to this kind of 'future avoidance' (at [58]–[60]). Even if the Australian court is satisfied that

In New Zealand, concerns about transactions being structured by way of schemes in order to avoid the operation of the New Zealand Takeover Code led to legislative changes in 2015.[256] The changes relate to schemes of arrangement that affect the voting rights of 'code companies'.[257] Code companies are defined as companies that (i) are a party to a listing agreement with a registered exchange and have securities that confer voting rights quoted on the registered exchange's securities market; (ii) were within paragraph (i) at any time during the twelve-month period before the date or the occurrence of an event referred to in the Takeovers Code; or (iii) have fifty or more shareholders and fifty or more share parcels.[258] These changes include a provision similar to section 411(17) of the Australian Corporations Act 2001, as a result of which the court must approve a scheme that would affect the voting rights of shareholders of a company falling within the ambit of the Takeovers Code only if it is satisfied that the shareholders of that company would not be adversely affected by the transaction not being undertaken under the Takeovers Code or the promoters of the scheme produce to it a 'no-objection' letter from the Takeovers Panel.[259] This is not identical to section 411(17) of the Australian legislation. In particular the New Zealand provision does not contain a specific anti-avoidance provision, opting instead for an assessment of the effect on shareholders. Nevertheless, the genesis for the New Zealand provision is clearly a similar concern about the (potentially) inappropriate use of schemes to effect change-of-control transactions.

either condition (i) or (ii) is met, it is not compelled to sanction the scheme. It still has an overriding fairness discretion that it must exercise in determining whether to approve the scheme: see e.g. *Re ACM Gold Ltd* (1992) 7 ACSR 231 at 239–40.

256 New Zealand Companies Amendment Act 2014 which entered into force on 1 July 2015 and inserted new sections 236A–236B into the New Zealand Companies Act 1993. Prior to the adoption of the New Zealand Takeovers Code in 2001, it was accepted in New Zealand that a scheme of arrangement was an appropriate method for carrying out a takeover, but the introduction of the Takeovers Code in 2001 made changes to this view (see e.g. S. Clune, 'Amalgamations, schemes of arrangement and takeovers regulation: Concerns of the Takeovers Panel and the need for reform' (2007) 13 *Canterbury Law Review* 91) and the 2015 changes continue this trend.

257 New Zealand Takeovers Panel, *Schemes of arrangement and amalgamations involving code companies – Recommendations to the Minister of Commerce* (Wellington: Takeovers Panel, 19 August 2008) and *Schemes of arrangement and amalgamations involving code companies – Explanatory statement* (Wellington: Takeovers Panel, 19 August 2008).

258 New Zealand Takeovers Code Approval Order 2000, r. 3A.

259 New Zealand Companies Act 1993, s. 236A(4) and see New Zealand Takeover Panel, *Guidance Notes: Schemes of Arrangement*, 9 September 2019.

In Canada, scheme provisions state that 'where *it is not practicable* for a corporation that is not insolvent to effect a fundamental change in the nature of an arrangement under any other provision of this Act, the corporation may apply to a court for an order approving an arrangement proposed by the corporation'.[260] The legislation says nothing specifically about the use of schemes to effect change-of-control transactions, but the interpretation of the phrase 'it is not practicable' is potentially key in this regard since a rigid interpretation of this term could be used to restrict the use of schemes to effect change-of-control transactions in practice. In the event, while this phrase has been interpreted to mean something less than 'impossible', nevertheless the parties need to demonstrate that it would be inconvenient or less advantageous for a change-of-control transaction to proceed by way of another mechanism (such as a takeover offer). This is subject to the overriding concern to ensure that the scheme provisions 'not be utilized to subvert the procedural or substantive safeguards applicable to other sorts of transactions possible under [the Canada Business Corporations Act]',[261] such as takeover legislation. As a result, although the position is less overtly regulated than the position in Australia or New Zealand, the Canadian approach still seems to demonstrate a concern about the use of schemes in this context.

A slightly different approach is adopted in the Hong Kong legislative provisions dealing with schemes.[262] There is nothing equivalent to section 411(17) of the Australian Corporations Act or the provisions in New Zealand. However, in 2014 changes were introduced to the approval thresholds for schemes effecting change-of-control transactions. Specifically, the headcount test (i.e. the requirement that approval be by a majority in number as well as 75 per cent by value) does not apply to a scheme used to effect a takeover offer. Instead, such a scheme requires the approval of at least 75 per cent of the votes of the members present and voting in person or by proxy *and* that the votes cast against the scheme must not exceed 10 per cent of the total voting rights attached to the 'disinterested shares' in the company.[263] Disinterested shares are broadly those not held by the bidder or its associates. This latter requirement appears to be an attempt to recognise that the minority can

[260] Canadian Business Corporations Act 1985, s. 192(3), emphasis added.

[261] Industry Canada, Policy Statement 15.1, 'Policy concerning arrangements under section 192 of the Canada Business Corporations Act', 8 January 2014, at 2.06.

[262] In relation to Malaysia, see Malaysian Code on Takeovers and Mergers 2016, Sch. 3, para. 2(f).

[263] Hong Kong Companies Ordinance, Cap. 622, s. 674(2).

generally be bound by a lower percentage of the members in a scheme (75 per cent after these reforms were implemented) than in a takeover (90 per cent of shareholders need to agree to the offer before the bidder can squeeze out the remainder). The additional requirement of not more than 10 per cent of the disinterested shareholders voting against the scheme mirrors this 90 per cent requirement in a takeover offer, and seems to reflect a perceived need for increased minority protection where a scheme is used to effect a change-of-control transaction.

These concerns give rise to the question of whether the current English approach to this issue, namely neutrality as to whether a change of control occurs by way of a scheme or of a takeover, is correct. Should this issue be regulated in order to reduce the frequency of takeover schemes in some way, whether that is by making schemes in this context harder to achieve (perhaps by raising the approval threshold for such schemes) or by requiring such transactions to proceed by way of a traditional takeover offer, unless the parties can show a good reason why not?

A number of criticisms are levelled at the use of schemes in this context, which will be considered in turn. These are:

(i) that the approval threshold for a bidder to obtain 100 per cent ownership of a company via a scheme is lower than that required for a takeover offer;
(ii) that schemes may be used to bypass the detailed requirements of the takeover regime; and
(iii) that schemes do not maximise shareholder value for the target shareholders.

It is suggested that none of these concerns justifies a change to the current English practice regarding takeover schemes.

3.7.2 *Approval thresholds*

The first concern relates to the approval threshold required for schemes. In particular, concerns have been voiced that the minority can effectively be bound by a lower percentage of the members in a scheme (75 per cent of the shares and a majority in number of them) than in a takeover (where the minority cannot be forced to sell their shares unless 90 per cent of the other shareholders have already accepted the offer). It has been suggested that approving a scheme of arrangement in such circumstances should require a very high standard of proof.[264] In Hong Kong, as discussed, there is a different, higher approval threshold for schemes involving a change of control, namely a requirement that, in addition to 75 per cent by value voting in favour, less than 10 per cent of the total voting rights attached to the 'disinterested shares' in the company may vote against it,[265] if the approval threshold is to be reached. The question arises whether the English scheme needs to modify the approval threshold for schemes that effect a change-of-control transaction, in order to recognise a perceived disparity between the approval threshold that currently exists for schemes and that which exists for traditional takeover offers.

Two points can be made in this regard. The first point is a practical one. Although the approval level for schemes appears to be lower than that for takeover offers, in practice the effect might be less dramatic. This is for a number of reasons. First, in a scheme, the members vote in classes and every class must approve a scheme before a court can consider whether to sanction it, so if a dissenting minority of a class of members opposes the scheme, the scheme cannot go ahead. Second, the addition of the headcount test for schemes, which does not exist for takeover offers, can add a significant additional hurdle for those attempting to get a scheme approved.[266] Third, the operation of the court's fairness discretion means that the votes of the bidder and its subsidiaries will not be counted in determining whether the appropriate majorities have been met.[267] Fourth, in a scheme, it is only the votes of those that attend and vote (in person or by proxy) that count for these purposes and, given shareholder apathy in many listed companies, this may mean that relatively few shareholders actually attend and vote at the meeting. The typical levels of those attending and voting at scheme meetings is low.[268] In *Re Stellar Diamonds plc*,[269] for example, the fifty-seven scheme shareholders who attended and voted

264 See e.g. *Re Hellenic & General Trust Ltd* [1976] 1 WLR 123.

265 Hong Kong Companies Ordinance, Cap. 622 s. 674(2).

266 For discussion of the headcount test see section 2.3.3.2.

267 See section 3.5.2.5.

268 This is not per se problematic. The courts have held that the fact that the scheme meeting was not attended by a significant number of small shareholders does not necessarily signify anything: 'They chose not to vote, or overlooked voting, or felt incapable of voting, or were content to leave the matter to rest with the majority of the shareholders. No inference can be drawn from their non-participation' (*Re Patagonia Gold plc* [2019] EWHC 2688 (Ch) *per* Norris J at [6]). The same approach has been adopted in Australia; see e.g. *Re Matine Ltd* (1998) 28 ACSR 268 at 295 *per* Santow J. Of course, it is possible that a low turnout is indicative of other concerns, such as the fact that those voting were unrepresentative of the class as a whole; see section 2.4.2.

269 [2018] EWHC 1152 (Ch).

represented only 5.68 per cent in number of the company's shareholders. The turnout by value was 59.84 per cent.[270] These last two points are particularly important. Disinterested minorities holding relatively few votes, who turn up and vote at a meeting, might be in a position to block a scheme.[271] So, for example, even with only one class meeting, and assuming that all shareholders attend and vote at the meeting, if the bidder and its subsidiaries hold 60 per cent of the shares in the target company, 10 per cent of the shareholders (i.e. 25 per cent of the 'disinterested' shares) would be able to block the scheme. If only half of the disinterested shareholders attend and vote then 10 per cent of the disinterested shareholders could block a scheme in which the bidder and its associates hold just 20 per cent of the voting shares in the target.[272] Schemes might therefore put more power in the hands of a dissenting minority than appears from the approval threshold stated in the legislation, and, accordingly, the disparity between this threshold and that in takeover offers might not be as significant as is sometimes claimed.

The second point is a more general one, about whether any difference between the approval threshold for schemes and that for takeover offers (of whatever size) is something that the court ought to take into account. The English courts have considered on a number of occasions whether the approval threshold for schemes should be raised to bring it into line with the position regarding takeovers, and have always rejected this approach. For example, Plowman J considered this argument in relation to the predecessor to section 895 of the Companies Act 2006, and stated:

> I cannot accede to that proposition. In the first place, it seems to me to involve imposing a limitation or qualification either on the generality of the word 'arrangement' . . . or else on the discretion of the court under that section. The legislature has not seen fit to impose any such limitation in terms and I see no reason for implying any. Moreover, the two sections, [dealing with schemes and with squeeze-outs], involve quite different

[270] Similar patterns are evident elsewhere. For example, there is evidence in Australia which suggests that only 62 per cent of shares are voted on a scheme and only 22 per cent of members vote on a scheme: Corporations and Markets Advisory Committee, 'Members' schemes of arrangement', Discussion Paper, June 2008, at 56–7.

[271] See section 3.3.2.7.

[272] For discussion see Damian and Rich, *Schemes, Takeovers and Himalayan Peaks*, note 25 above, at 701–9. The authors assess the actual percentage of votes required to defeat any of the twenty-five largest schemes of arrangement used to effect a change of control in Australia in the period 2005–12 at significantly below 25 per cent, and in fact the average percentage of votes required to defeat these schemes at 14.34 per cent (at 706).

> considerations and different approaches. Under [the statutory provisions dealing with schemes] an arrangement can only be sanctioned if the question of fairness has first of all been submitted to the court. Under [the statutory provisions dealing with squeeze-out], on the other hand, the matter may never come to the court at all. If it does come to the court, then the onus is cast on the dissenting minority to demonstrate the unfairness of the scheme. There are, therefore, good reasons for requiring a smaller majority in favour of a scheme ... than the majority which is required under [the squeeze-out provisions] if the minority is to be expropriated.[273]

The approach of the English courts is that whether a company proceeds by way of a scheme of arrangement or an offer is a matter of choice for that company.[274] The courts have rejected the argument that where a scheme is used as an alternative to an offer the court should insist on a 90 per cent approval of the scheme by shareholders.[275] On this view, the lower threshold in a scheme is countered by the fact that the court needs to sanction the scheme. Minority protection should therefore be ensured at that stage in the proceedings.

This seems entirely correct. There are different approval thresholds in place for schemes and offers, but those different levels are justifiable. Schemes have a number of protective safeguards that an offer does not, the two most significant being the requirement for the members to consider and approve the scheme in classes (which increases the minority protection) and the involvement of the court both in approving the meetings of members and/or creditors and then in sanctioning the scheme. The role of the court at the sanctioning hearing operates as a particularly important protective device. Minorities are able to air their views at the sanctioning hearing, and the exercise of the court's fairness discretion can operate as a significant safeguard. The court's role in taking account of these issues and determining whether to sanction the scheme is an important counterbalance to the lower approval threshold in place for schemes, which justifies the different approval levels required for these different change-of-control mechanisms.

As a result, the lower approval level for schemes is appropriate. It is argued elsewhere in this book that in one aspect the approval level for schemes should be reformed, namely by the removal of the headcount

273 *Re National Bank Ltd* [1966] 1 WLR 819 at 829–30.

274 *Re BTR plc* [1999] 2 BCLC 675; *Re BTR plc (Leave to Appeal)* [2000] 1 BCLC 740; *Re TDG plc* [2008] EWHC 2334 (Ch); [2009] 1 BCLC 445.

275 *Re National Bank Ltd* [1966] 1 WLR 819; *Re TDG plc* [2008] EWHC 2334 (Ch); [2009] 1 BCLC 445; *Re Realm Therapeutics Plc* [2019] EWHC 2080 (Ch) at [63].

test.[276] This would mean that the approval threshold for schemes would simply be 75 per cent by value, which would bring the decision on a scheme into line with other significant member decisions such as whether to alter the articles of the company.[277]

3.7.3 *The use of schemes to bypass the takeover regime*

A second criticism sometimes raised in relation to schemes in this context is that they allow bidders to effect a takeover without having to comply with the detailed disclosure and other requirements of the takeover regime. This concern seems to explain the introduction of section 411(17) of the Australian Corporations Act, with the specific anti-avoidance provision attached to it, and the approach adopted in Canada. These concerns also seem to explain the provisions in New Zealand that, while not specifically anti-avoidance in form, nevertheless seem to be based on concerns about the use of schemes to bypass minority protection.

However, it will be clear from this chapter that schemes used to effect the takeover of a company subject to the Takeover Code in the UK must comply with that regime just as much as a more traditional offer.[278] Many of the obligations under the Takeover Code, for example disclosure requirements, apply identically to offers and schemes.[279] Where differences do exist, there are good reasons for their existence, mostly based on the structure and operation of a scheme as compared to an offer. One example of this was discussed in section 3.6. Many of the rules in the Takeover Code that provide for equality amongst target shareholders in an offer are not necessary in a scheme because there is no opportunity for the bidder to 'divide and conquer' in the same way and there is no possibility of minority shareholders being left in the target company following a successful scheme.[280] The protections that are put in place for minority shareholders in schemes, described in section 3.6, are adequate and appropriate for the dangers that face those shareholders.

For English schemes, both the courts and the Takeover Panel play a significant role in overseeing the use of schemes to effect change-of-control transactions and ensuring that minority protection is upheld.

[276] See section 2.3.3.2.
[277] Companies Act 2006, s. 21.
[278] See, in particular, section 3.4.
[279] See section 3.4.2.2.
[280] See section 3.6, particularly 3.6.3.1.

One way to understand the introduction of the provisions in New Zealand in 2015 is to appreciate that the New Zealand legislation dealing with schemes has traditionally been structured somewhat differently from the English provisions.[281] Broadly, the New Zealand provisions were drafted with a higher level of generality and provide the court with a much wider discretion than their English counterparts regarding some of the procedural aspects of a scheme.[282] Specifically, the New Zealand provisions contain significantly fewer minority protections on the face of the legislation, compared to the English scheme provisions. There is no statutory requirement that members or creditors be provided with all material information necessary for them to assess the merits of the scheme.[283] Prior to 2015, there was no requirement that the members or creditors meet in separate classes[284] and the legislation provided no specific voting thresholds,[285] although these requirements were then

281 New Zealand Companies Act 1993, s. 236.

282 This flexibility can perhaps be explained by the reform process that led to the New Zealand Companies Act 1993. The scheme provisions under the prior act, ss. 205–7 of the New Zealand Companies Act 1955, contained similar requirements to the English scheme, including the requirement for two court meetings (one to convene the meetings and one to sanction the scheme), an obligation on the company to make significant disclosures regarding the details of the scheme, the need for class meetings (where relevant) and a statutory approval threshold of 75 per cent (though no headcount test). When considering the reform of the Companies Act 1955, the New Zealand Law Commission discussed whether court intervention was required in all cases of company reorganisation, and concluded that this was neither efficient nor desirable. As a result, it recommended that the regime under the 1955 Act should be split into two different procedures: a prescriptive option, under which a 75 per cent vote at a meeting of shareholders and/or creditors could bring about an amalgamation without court sanction, and a broad backup procedure allowing the High Court to sanction an amalgamation or compromise without a vote where the prescriptive option was not practical: New Zealand Law Commission, *Company Law: Reform and Restatement* (Wellington: June 1989) at 26–7. Although the initial intention was for this court approval route to operate as a backup option, during the parliamentary process the court-sanctioned scheme of arrangement provision was transformed from a backup into a true alternative to the amalgamation provisions. For discussion see Clune, 'Amalgamations, schemes of arrangement and takeovers regulation', note 256 above, at 91.

283 New Zealand Companies Act 1993, s. 236(2)(c) provides that this is something that the court may require, but need not.

284 New Zealand Companies Act 1993, s. 236(2)(b) provides that, again, this is something that the court may require, but there is no obligation to do so. In 2015 this changed, and a new s. 236A(4) was introduced, providing that for certain companies ('code companies') there is now a legislative requirement for voting to be in classes.

285 This was also changed in 2015: s. 236A(4) was introduced which provides that the vote must be '(a) by a resolution approved by a majority of 75% of the votes of the shareholders in each interest class entitled to vote and voting on the question; and (b) by a resolution approved by a simple majority of the votes of those shareholders entitled to vote'.

introduced for change-of-control schemes involving code companies. There has also been less attempt to regulate schemes alongside takeovers, within existing takeover regulation; there is no equivalent of Appendix 7 of the UK Takeover Code, for example.[286] This might help to explain why it was felt necessary to bolster the position of minority shareholders with the additional legislative provision, described in section 3.7.1, when a scheme is used to effect a takeover.[287]

The position in Australia appears to provide the strongest counterpoint to the English position. Australia's scheme provisions are otherwise very similar to those in the English scheme.[288] The levels of disclosure requirements and minority protection in Australian schemes are essentially the same as those in English schemes. The Australian courts perform the same role of scrutinising schemes and upholding minority protection (particularly through the exercise of their discretion at the sanctioning hearing) and the Australian regulator (ASIC) and the Australian Takeovers Panel appear to provide a similar supervisory role in schemes to that provided by the Takeover Panel and the FCA in the UK. Should the existence of section 411(17) of the Australian Corporations Act therefore lead us to doubt the current English position? In short, it should not.

286 The New Zealand Takeover Panel states its approach to schemes as follows: 'The Panel views schemes as a legitimate and valuable means for undertaking corporate transactions in New Zealand. The ability to carry out corporate transactions under a Companies Act process, rather than under the Code, provides economically sensible commercial flexibility' (see New Zealand Takeover Panel, Guidance Notes: Schemes of Arrangement, 9 September 2019, at [1.6]). The main role for the Takeover Panel is therefore to determine whether to provide the 'no objection' letter referred to in s. 236A.

287 One other explanation put forward by the New Zealand Takeovers Panel is a concern that the court hears only from the promoters of the scheme and that, in the absence of an 'interested' third party application to the Court, there is no hearing and the scheme proceeds before a judge 'on the papers' – and that leaves a judge in a difficult position (see New Zealand Takeovers Panel, 'Law Changes for Schemes of Arrangement Moves Forward Guidance', Code Word Issue 28). This issue would not arise in an English scheme since there will be a court hearing even if no objector turns up to the sanctioning hearing. Furthermore, in the absence of an objector, the English courts take on an additional scrutiny role themselves.

288 The same three-stage process is required for schemes in Australia as that set out in Chapter 2 for English schemes: a scheme is proposed on behalf of the company and an application is made to court for meetings to be held (Australian Corporations Act 2001, s. 411(1)); the members and/or creditors meet in classes to consider and approve the scheme (s. 411(4)(a)); then a second court hearing is required to sanction the scheme (s. 411(4)(b)) and, if sanctioned, the order of the court becomes effective once lodged with the Australian Securities and Investment Commission (ASIC) (s. 411(10)) (rather than the Registrar of Companies, under the English provisions).

It was initially unclear how section 411(17) should be interpreted. The language of the section, which specifically refers to the avoidance of any of the takeover provisions, opened the way for challenges to change-of-control transactions that were effected by way of a scheme of arrangement. However, it now appears to be accepted that schemes of arrangement and takeover offers should be treated as true alternatives, and that there is no legislative preference for one procedure over another.[289] In the case of *Re ACM Gold Ltd*,[290] for example, two companies that were both part of a large group sought to become wholly owned subsidiaries of a third company, Poseidon. The scheme envisaged the transfer of a small portion of the two companies' shares to Poseidon and the cancellation of the rest, in exchange for shares in Poseidon and a payment of 10 cents per share by way of a reduction of capital. ASIC opposed the application, on the ground that Poseidon sought to avoid the takeover regulation provisions in Chapter 6 of the Australian Corporations Act. O'Loughlin J stated that Chapter 6 does not take automatic precedence over Chapter 5 (which contains the scheme provisions), and that section 411(17) was to be given a liberal and practical interpretation in view of the elements of the relevant transaction. The judge rejected a wider interpretation of section 411(17) that, because the deal could have been structured to accord with Chapter 6, the use of a scheme to carry it out was prohibited. This reasoning has been followed in a number of subsequent cases.[291]

The approach of both ASIC[292] and the Australian Takeovers Panel[293] also appears to be that, despite the existence of section 411(17), schemes of arrangement and takeover offers should be treated as genuine alternatives in effecting a change of control. Nevertheless, difficulties still remain. In particular, ASIC will not issue a 'no-objection' letter until the final court hearing sanctioning the scheme (or just before),[294] leaving the parties facing a considerable period of uncertainty while they wait for this letter to emerge. Even if

[289] For discussion see Damian and Rich, *Schemes, Takeovers and Himalayan Peaks*, note 25 above, ch. 11.

[290] (1992) 7 ACSR 231.

[291] See *Re Stockbridge Ltd* (1993) 9 ACSR 637; *Nicron Resources Ltd* v. *Catto* (1992) 10 ACLC 1186; *Re Capilano Honey* (2018) 132 ACSR 332.

[292] ASIC has provided guidance as to the circumstances in which it will issue a 'no-objection' letter: ASIC Regulatory Guide 60, 'Schemes of arrangement', September 2011, at [60.17].

[293] *Re St Barbara Mines Ltd and Taipan Resources NL* (2000) 18 ACLC 913 at 917; Takeovers Panel, Guidance Note 15, 'Trust Scheme Mergers', 2nd issue, 6 May 2011 at [8].

[294] ASIC Regulatory Guide 60, 'Schemes of Arrangement', September 2011, at [60.106].

ASIC does issue such a letter, the court can still take account of whether the scheme has been proposed to avoid the operation of the takeover legislation when applying its fairness discretion at the sanctioning hearing.[295] The courts have stated that they are likely to do so only where this issue is raised by an objector as a factor that the court should take into account when exercising its discretion.[296] Exactly how the courts should determine this matter, if an objector raises it as an issue, remains somewhat obscure. The precise operation of section 411(17) 'remains a source of lingering uncertainty and adds an unquantifiable and unacceptable element of completion risk to any scheme of arrangement' in Australia.[297] As a result, there have been strong arguments made for the repeal of section 411(17) by the Corporations and Markets Advisory Committee (CAMAC), amongst others.[298] In light of this, it is clear that adopting a provision akin to section 411(17) for English schemes is neither necessary nor desirable.

3.7.4 Maximising value for the target shareholders

A further concern that is sometimes raised regarding the use of schemes is that they do not facilitate auctions for control, and therefore do not maximise shareholder value for the target shareholders. However, if a scheme is announced, there is nothing to prevent a subsequent bidder from launching a rival offer or a rival scheme. Indeed, it is not uncommon to see competing bids being introduced after a scheme is announced.[299] There have also been occasions on which rival offers for a target have been made by way of schemes.[300] The restrictions introduced into the Takeover Code to deal with break fees and other lock-up devices, which aim to give companies greater protection against protracted 'virtual bids', apply equally to schemes and to takeover offers, and are intended to foster an auction-for-control environment.[301]

[295] Australian Corporations Act 2001, s. 411(17).
[296] See e.g. *Re Macquarie Private Capital A Ltd* (2008) 26 ACLC 366.
[297] Ibid.
[298] CAMAC, *Members' Schemes of Arrangement*, Report, December 2009, 95–108, available at www.camac.gov.au. For further discussion of this issue see Damian and Rich, *Schemes, Takeovers and Himalayan Peaks*, note 25 above, at 15.2.
[299] See section 3.3.2.9.
[300] See e.g. the rival bids made by Tata Steel and CSN for Corus Group plc in 2006.
[301] Changes were introduced in September 2011, adopting proposed amendments set out in Takeover Panel, *Consultation Paper Issued by the Code Committee of the Panel, Review of*

The fact that, generally, bidders will not seek to purchase large stakes in the target company prior to a scheme (because these shares will not be counted towards the approval threshold)[302] means that the way is left more open for competing bids to arise, as compared to the scenario in a takeover offer, where the bidder will generally have locked up a large stake in the target company in advance. If a rival bidder wishes to proceed by way of a takeover offer, there will be a larger pool of shares available for it to purchase as a springboard into its offer. If the rival bidder wishes to proceed by way of a scheme then there is no requirement for it to purchase a large stake in the target before it can do so. Either way, it may be argued that commencing a change of control by way of a scheme does not stifle the market for corporate control in any way, and may even facilitate it in some circumstances. It is also possible for the court at the sanctioning hearing to take account of changes of circumstances between meetings and the sanctioning hearing that could have an effect on price.[303]

Finally, there is no evidence that companies are sold at a lower premium under a scheme than under a takeover bid.[304] All in all, there seems little support for the view that schemes have a dampening effect on the market for corporate control, or the proposition that they do not maximise shareholder value for the target shareholders, when compared to traditional offers.

3.8 Summary

This chapter has examined the most common form of member schemes, namely a scheme designed to effect a change-of-control transaction as an alternative to a takeover offer. After considering the meaning of 'member' for scheme purposes, the chapter discussed the advantages and disadvantages of schemes and offers to effect a change of control. Schemes will not always be the right mechanism for achieving a change of control, but it is striking how often they are chosen in practice for recommended bids.

Certain Aspects of the Regulation of Takeover Bids, Proposed Amendments to the Takeover Code, PCP 2011/1, 21 March 2011, Part A and Part B.

302 See section 3.5.2.5.

303 *Re Cobham plc* [2020] EWHC 320 (Ch).

304 See (in the context of Australian deals) Damian and Rich, *Schemes, Takeovers and Himalayan Peaks*, note 25 above, at 712–13.

One issue that arises in this context is whether schemes should be used to effect change-of-control transactions in this way. Concerns are sometimes raised as to whether schemes allow bidders to bypass takeover regulation that is put in place to protect minorities, or to acquire a target more easily than via an offer (as a consequence of the lower approval threshold) in a way that is inappropriate. These concerns have led to legislative changes in overseas jurisdictions that have imported the English scheme. However, in the UK, the Takeover Code covers change-of-control transactions that are effected by schemes as well as those effected by offers. In addition, while the minority protection available to shareholders in a scheme and in an offer are distinct (and the protections available to minorities in a scheme are lower than those in an offer), these differences are entirely explicable when the purpose of these different mechanisms are considered. Where the parties decide to use a scheme rather than an offer, there is no reason to be concerned about the use of a scheme, or to insist on additional safeguards being put in place beyond those that the law currently provides. Supervision by the English courts and, where appropriate, the Takeover Panel operates to provide sufficient safeguards and protections for dissenting and minority shareholders and other parties concerned about the impact of the transaction on their rights.

4

Member schemes of arrangement: other examples

4.1 Introduction

In Chapter 3 some general issues regarding member schemes were discussed, including the definition of 'member' for the purpose of schemes of arrangement, and there was detailed examination of the most common use of member schemes, namely to effect a change of control of a target company as an alternative to a takeover offer. However, as discussed in Chapter 1, the legislative provisions are not prescriptive about the uses that can be made of schemes, and member schemes can therefore be used to give effect to any compromise or arrangement that the company and its members could properly agree between themselves.[1] The list of examples provided here is intended to be illustrative rather than exhaustive. Some of the alternatives to the use of schemes in these circumstances are also considered.

4.2 The introduction of a new holding company (holdco schemes)

4.2.1 The use of holdco schemes

One of the most common uses of member schemes, other than takeover schemes, is to reorganise a corporate group. This is typically done by way of a scheme between a company and its members, which creates a new holding company for the group (a holdco scheme).[2] There are a number

[1] See the definition of 'member' for these purposes in section 3.2. For the definition of 'compromise' and 'arrangement' see section 2.1.1.

[2] For recent examples of holdco schemes see *Re Home Retail Group plc* [2016] EWHC 2072 (Ch); *Re The Co-operative Bank plc* [2017] EWHC 2269 (Ch); *Re Old Mutual Plc* [2018]

of reasons why holdco schemes are used, but two of the most common are to redomicile the group to a different jurisdiction and to create additional distributable reserves that can then be returned to the shareholders. The new holding company created in this way may be a UK company, but need not be, and may be a private company or a public company.[3]

4.2.1.1 Redomicile of a corporate group

The domicile of a company is the country under whose laws that company is registered or incorporated. In some circumstances there may be a wish to change the domicile of the group to a different jurisdiction, perhaps to take advantage of a more beneficial tax regime or more favourable regulatory requirements. There is no mechanism within the Companies Act 2006 by which companies can achieve this. The addition of a new holding company domiciled in the new jurisdiction can, however, achieve this goal.[4]

4.2.1.2 The creation of additional distributable reserves

The addition of a new holding company by way of a scheme can also be used to increase the availability of distributable reserves within a group, as described in section 4.2.2.1. There are a number of reasons why companies might want to increase their distributable reserves in this way. It may be that in the existing structure there are very low distributable reserves, and the group wishes to unlock previously undistributable reserves in order to return capital to the shareholders, perhaps by way of

EWHC 1875 (Ch); *Re Euroclear plc* [2018] EWHC 3484 (Ch); *Re Unilever plc* [2018] EWHC 2546 (Ch); *Re Galliford Try plc* [2019] EWHC 3252 (Ch); *Re Tethyan Resources Plc* [2019] EWHC 3244 (Ch); *Re Man Group plc* [2019] EWHC 1392 (Ch).

[3] This will depend on considerations such as whether the intention is that securities of the company be publicly traded (a private company may not offer its securities to the public: Companies Act 2006, s. 755(1)). Where the securities are intended to be offered to the public, or the admission of the securities to trading on a regulated market will be requested, a prospectus will generally be required: Financial Services and Markets Act 2000, s. 85(1)(2). The general view is that schemes of arrangement do not constitute an offer of securities to the public (see section 3.4.2.2 for discussion) but where it is intended that the shares are listed on a regulated market, a prospectus will be needed.

[4] See e.g. *Re Euroclear plc* [2018] EWHC 3484 (Ch); *Re Steris plc* [2019] EWHC 751 (Ch); *Re Tethyan Resources plc* [2019] EWHC 3244 (Ch). Schemes are also used elsewhere in the world to redomicile corporate groups; see e.g. in Australia, *Re James Hardie Industries Ltd* (2001) 39 ACSR 552; *Re Allied Gold Ltd* [2011] QSC 108; *Re Allied Gold Ltd (No. 2)* [2011] QSC 194; *Re Marengo Mining Ltd* [2012] FCA 1220; *Re Marengo Mining Ltd (No. 2)* [2012] FCA 1498.

a payment of dividends or a share buyback.[5] Companies wishing to pay dividends to shareholders will face a fundamental problem if they have insufficient distributable reserves to allow them to do so since, of course, companies may pay dividends only out of distributable reserves,[6] and a holdco scheme may therefore be beneficial. A good example of this form of holdco scheme is that effected by Mann Group plc in 2012.[7] The intention of that scheme was to enhance the group's access to distributable reserves in order to allow the group to continue its previously stated dividend policy. Alternatively, the group might use a holdco scheme to return to the shareholders cash that has arisen from the sale of some of the group's businesses.[8]

4.2.2 The usual form of a holdco scheme

4.2.2.1 Transfer schemes and cancellation schemes

Member schemes can be used to add a new holding company in one of two ways: by way of a transfer scheme or via a cancellation scheme.[9] A transfer scheme involves the members in the company that is proposing the scheme (oldco) transferring their shares in oldco to the new holding company, in exchange for shares in the new holding company in a predetermined ratio. In a cancellation scheme the members agree to have their existing shares in oldco cancelled in consideration for the issue to them of shares in the new holding company, again in a predetermined ratio. Of the two, cancellation schemes are far more common because they do not require the payment of stamp duty by the new holding company. By contrast, in a transfer scheme the new holding company has to pay stamp duty of 0.5 per cent on the transfer to it of the shares of the existing shareholders.

The scheme procedure for a holdco scheme follows the process described in Chapter 2. The members will need to be divided into classes

[5] See e.g. Rolls-Royce Holdings plc scheme of arrangement in 2011; AEA Technology plc scheme of arrangement in 2010.

[6] See Companies Act 2006, s. 830(1).

[7] See *Re Mann Group plc* [2012] EWHC 4089 (Ch).

[8] An example of this kind of scheme is that of United Utilities plc in 2008. This scheme was intended to create additional distributable reserves in order to enable the group to return a significant amount of capital to its shareholders, arising from the sale of United Utilities Electricity. See also Melrose plc scheme of arrangement, in 2012.

[9] Both discussed in detail in section 3.3.1.1.

in order to meet and approve the scheme.[10] The court will then need to sanction the scheme and the order will be delivered to the Registrar.[11] However, in a cancellation scheme the scheme needs to be combined with the procedure for a reduction of capital by oldco, since in these schemes the capital of oldco will be reduced, and the reserve created in oldco is then applied in paying up in full new shares in the new holding company. Both private and public companies tend to achieve this by way of a special resolution confirmed by the court,[12] despite the fact that private companies have the option of making use of the solvency statement route, which avoids the need to go to court.[13] Given that the scheme procedure involves two court hearings in any case, it is generally simpler to combine the reduction of capital and the scheme, and to comply with the requirements of both processes.[14]

Therefore, in addition to the requirements of the scheme, described in detail in Chapter 2, in a cancellation scheme the company must satisfy the court that it has complied with the requirements for the reduction of capital. As a result, the creditors' consent must have been obtained, or the debt discharged, determined or secured in relation to every creditor of the company entitled to object to the reduction.[15] In general, reductions of this kind do not prejudice creditors, since the reserve arising in the company's accounts following the reduction is immediately applied in paying up and issuing new shares in the new holding company. Following the cancellation of shares in oldco, new shares in this company are issued to the new holding company so that it becomes the holding company of oldco, and therefore of the group as a whole. Finally, in

[10] The issue of dividing members into classes for scheme purposes is discussed in detail in section 3.5.2.

[11] In a member scheme that does not involve a reduction or cancellation of capital, the scheme becomes effective on delivery of the court order sanctioning the scheme to the Registrar of Companies (s. 899(4)). Where the scheme involves a reduction of capital, the scheme will not be fully operative until the court order confirming the reduction, together with the required statement of capital, is delivered to the Registrar (s. 649(3)(a)). In practice the two are delivered at the same time, if the sanction and the reduction occur at the same court hearing.

[12] Companies Act 2006, s. 645.

[13] Ibid., ss. 642–4. This route requires a special resolution supported by a solvency statement from the directors.

[14] A cancellation scheme may involve a reduction of oldco's share capital to zero, although only temporarily as it is immediately recapitalised. Nonetheless, the solvency statement procedure does not allow a company to reduce its share capital to zero (s. 641(2)) which is another reason why the solvency statement procedure may not be suitable for a cancellation scheme.

[15] Companies Act 2006, s. 648(2).

consideration for the cancellation of their shares in oldco, the shareholders receive shares in the new holding company. This may be in the ratio one new holding company share for each oldco share, or in some other agreed ratio.[16]

Where the holdco scheme is intended to facilitate the creation of additional distributable reserves, it is then necessary for an additional step to be taken once the holdco scheme becomes effective. In order to create those distributable reserves, a reduction of capital by the new holding company is required.[17] This reduction of capital will generally be subsequent to and conditional upon the holdco scheme becoming effective. The reserve created by a reduction of capital is treated as a distributable reserve of the company unless the court orders otherwise.[18]

4.2.2.2 Cancellation schemes after 2015

As discussed in Chapter 3,[19] a change in the law in 2015 brought an end to cancellation schemes being used as a means of effecting a change of control.[20] All takeover schemes are now carried out by way of a transfer scheme. The purpose of the introduction of this change in the law was to

[16] Where the new holding company is a public company, this raises the question of whether the company needs to comply with the requirements for independent valuation, given that the shares are issued for non-cash consideration (Companies Act 2006, s. 593). However, it will generally be possible to make use of the exception within s. 594(1)(2), i.e. where the allotment of shares by a company is in connection with an arrangement providing for an allotment of shares in that company, on terms that the whole or part of the consideration for the allotted shares is to be provided by either the transfer to that company or the cancellation of all or some of the shares in another company. Schemes of arrangement are specified as falling within this exception (s. 594(6)(a)(i)). However, the exception will apply only where the issue of shares is open to all shareholders in the other company (oldco in our scenario), or, if the arrangement applies only to a particular class of shares, to the holders of that entire class: s. 594(4).

[17] The procedure for a reduction of capital is simplified in this instance by reason of the fact that the new holding company will often have no creditors. As a result, the creditor protection issues that usually arise when the court considers whether to confirm a reduction of capital do not tend to arise here. The court might therefore dispense with the usual requirement that a list of creditors be settled (s. 646(2)) and will generally approve a reduction where there is a bona fide commercial reason for the reduction and creditors are adequately protected. See e.g. *Re Ratners Group plc* [1988] BCLC 685. Reductions of capital in order to create additional distributable reserves, therefore, will usually be approved by the court, as long as there is a genuine commercial purpose and any creditors are protected.

[18] Companies Act 2006, ss. 610, 612.

[19] See section 3.3.1.1.

[20] The Companies Act 2006 (Amendment of Part 17) Regulations 2015 (SI 472/2015).

close a specific tax loophole in relation to the use of a reduction of capital in a cancellation takeover scheme so as to avoid the payment of stamp duty on a transfer of shares to the bidder. However, the legislature did not intend to outlaw or restrict reductions of capital used in conjunction with holdco schemes.[21] Consequently, although section 641(2A) of the Companies Act 2006 now states that a company may not reduce its share capital as part of a scheme by virtue of which, broadly, one or more people are to acquire all the shares in the company, section 641(2B) provides for an exception:

> Subsection 2A does not apply to a scheme under which –
> (a) the company is to have a new parent undertaking;
> (b) all or substantially all of the members of the company become members of the parent undertaking; and
> (c) the members of the company are to hold proportions of the equity share capital in the parent undertaking in the same or substantially the same proportions as they hold the equity share capital of the company.

This differentiation between allowed and not-allowed cancellation schemes raises an important issue, namely whether the boundary between the two is sufficiently clearly delineated.

This is something with which the courts have had to grapple.[22] Two issues in particular have arisen. The first relates to whether the exception in section 641(2B) can be utilised where the cancellation scheme involves more than one class of shares. This issue arose in *Re Steris plc*[23] in which it was proposed to redomicile the parent company of the group by inserting a new group holding company incorporated in the Republic of Ireland, with a view to mitigating the uncertainties of Brexit. The company had both ordinary shares and redeemable preference shares, but the cancellation scheme applied only to the company's ordinary share capital. Snowden J noted that there was a potential disconnect between the language of section 641(2A), which includes in the prohibition a scheme for the acquisition of all of a class of shares in a company, and that of section 641(2B)(b), which disapplies the prohibition in the

[21] See BIS, Explanatory memorandum to the Companies Act 2006 (Amendment of Part 17) Regulations 2015 No. 472, paras. 7.3–7.4.

[22] In some cases, companies involved in a restructuring have sought guidance from the court at the convening hearing as to whether a cancellation scheme falls within the exemption created by s. 641(2B). See e.g. *Re Home Retail Group plc* [2016] EWHC 2072 (Ch); *Re Old Mutual plc* [2018] EWHC 873 (Ch).

[23] [2019] EWHC 751 (Ch).

case of a scheme under which 'all or substantially all of the members of the company become members of the parent undertaking'. Read literally, this might prohibit a cancellation scheme such as the one in this case where the scheme did not replicate in the new parent the holdings of shares that formed part of the share capital of the company (i.e. the preference shares). However, the judge held that it was clear from the inclusion of the words 'substantially all', and from the government's Explanatory Memorandum accompanying the enactment of the prohibition,[24] that Parliament intended that a cancellation scheme could be permitted notwithstanding that there might be a small difference in the identity of the members of the company and of the new parent undertaking before and after the scheme. In sanctioning the scheme, the judge took account of the fact that the preference shareholders represented a very small proportion of the membership in number and by value (so that the ordinary shareholders who would become members of the new parent clearly comprised 'substantially all' of the members of the company) and also that section 641(2B) was clearly focused on equity share capital (and the preference shares did not constitute equity share capital for the purposes of section 548 of the Companies Act 2006).

The decision in *Re Steris* seems sensible, but it evidences the fact that the courts may well have difficult decisions to make about whether differences in the identity of the members of the company and in the new parent undertaking are sufficiently small as to allow the 'substantially all' test to be satisfied. Clearly, the situation becomes more difficult if it involves excluded shares that do constitute equity capital, as occurred in *Re Man Group plc*,[25] or where the scheme provides that some number

[24] See BIS, Explanatory memorandum to the Companies Act 2006 (Amendment of Part 17) Regulations 2015 No. 472.

[25] In *Re Man Group plc* [2019] EWHC 1392 (Ch), in contrast to *Re Steris*, the two categories of shares involved ordinary shares which were included in the scheme and 50,000 deferred shares which were excluded from the scheme but which *did* fall within the definition of equity share capital under s. 548 of the Companies Act 2006, because they carried a right to participate as regards capital beyond a specified amount in a distribution. In sanctioning the scheme, Snowden J noted: 'In reality . . . the specified level for participation is so high that the Deferred Shares will never be able to participate' (at [18]) and furthermore that the proportion of shares comprised by the deferred shares was even smaller than that in *Re Steris*. In *Re Man Group*, Snowden J also considered the availability of the exemption in s. 641(2B) given that newco already had two issued ordinary shares which were the original subscribers' shares at the date of the scheme. Snowden J held that these did not prevent the application of the section: 'Those shares will represent an insignificant proportion of the equity share capital of [newco] once the Scheme becomes effective, and the intention is that they will be bought back by [newco]

of the shareholders may be excluded from the scheme for legal or regulatory reasons (which is not uncommon).[26] There is clearly an element of uncertainty created in these circumstances and companies may therefore seek to address this issue at the convening stage to ensure that the scheme falls within the exception in section 641(2B) before progressing further.

A second problem arises where the holdco scheme forms part of a broader set of transactions which, viewed as a whole, might infringe section 641(2A). In *Re Home Retail Group plc*,[27] for example, the company announced that it had agreed to sell its Homebase business and that it would make a capital return to its shareholders of the net cash proceeds of the sale, amounting to some £200 million. Shortly afterwards, and before the Homebase sale had been completed, the company reached agreement in principle on a takeover by Sainsbury. The company therefore designed a series of transactions intended to facilitate both the promised return to shareholders and the takeover by Sainsbury. First there was a scheme under which a company, newco, would become the company's holding company, with the company's existing shareholders essentially obtaining corresponding holdings in newco. Second, there would be a reduction of capital to effect the previously announced return to shareholders. Finally, the shares in newco would be compulsorily transferred to Sainsbury in accordance with provisions in newco's articles of association. The judge was clear that section 641(2B) applied if the subsection was read literally, but the question arose as to whether this remained the case if all parts of this transaction were viewed as a whole. Newey J considered the *Ramsay* principle and its requirement to give a purposive construction to legislation, referring to a passage in the judgment of Ribeiro PJ in *Collector of Stamp Revenue* v. *Arrowtown Assets Ltd*:[28]

> The driving principle in the *Ramsay* line of cases continues to involve a general rule of statutory construction and an unblinkered approach to the analysis of the facts. The ultimate question is whether the relevant

and cancelled once [newco] has issued the new ordinary shares to the members of the Company. I am satisfied that these factors mean that the exception in s 641(2B) will still be available: the members of the Company will still become members of [newco], and any difference in their proportional shareholdings in [newco] caused by the existence of the subscriber shares will be both insignificant and temporary' (at [25]).

26 See e.g. *Re Man Group plc* [2019] EWHC 1392 (Ch).

27 [2016] EWHC 2072 (Ch).

28 [2003] HKCFA 46.

> statutory provisions, construed purposively, were intended to apply to the transaction, viewed realistically.

Newey J concluded that even if the *Ramsay* principle is capable of applying to section 641(2B), it would not 'bite on a cancellation scheme which is part of a real world transaction having a clear commercial and business purpose' such as the transaction in that case.[29] Accordingly, the court permitted the cancellation scheme to be used to insert a new holding company, even though soon afterwards a bidder would acquire the holding company. A similar approach was followed by Snowden J in *Re Old Mutual plc.*[30]

Notably both *Home Retail* and *Old Mutual* involved the cancellation scheme being used as part of an acquisition, and so it is perhaps unsurprising that the dividing line between allowed and not-allowed cancellation schemes arose as an issue. However, this difficult dividing line can also arise in cases where there is no outside acquirer at all, such as in *Re Unilever plc.*[31] This case involved the creation of a new holdco to enable the company to be restructured, with the previous dual parent structure being replaced with a new single holding company incorporated in the Netherlands. The scheme was part of wider arrangements which were intended to implement this simplification. The scheme was preceded by the mandatory transfer of legal title to most of the ordinary shares in the company to a nominee, which took place under an amendment to the company's articles. The scheme itself was a cancellation scheme and involved the new holdco issuing ordinary shares to those previously holding ordinary shares in the company, including therefore to the mandatory transfer nominee holding for the underlying shareholders. On the face of it, section 641(2B) was satisfied since (a) the company was to have a new parent undertaking; (b) all or substantially all of the members of the company were to become members of the parent undertaking – if one looked at the position immediately before the scheme, once most of the ordinary shares had been transferred to the mandatory transfer nominee; and (c) the members of the company were to hold proportions of the equity share capital of the parent undertaking in the same proportions as they held the equity share capital of the company. However, although that was the case if one looked at the scheme in isolation, if one viewed the previous step and the scheme as forming

[29] [2016] EWHC 2072 (Ch) at [14] *per* Newey J.

[30] [2018] EWHC 1875 (Ch). See also *Re Galliford Try plc* [2019] EWHC 3252 (Ch).

[31] [2018] EWHC 2546 (Ch).

one composite transaction, it could not be said that all or substantially all of the members of the company before the mandatory transfer would become members of the parent undertaking, and hence section 641(2B) was not satisfied. At the moment before the mandatory transfer, the shareholders in the company consisted of a very large number of shareholders, but most of those would not become members of the new parent undertaking. It was for that reason, indeed, that the mandatory transfer had not been made part of the scheme but had instead been dealt with outside and prior to the scheme by way of an amendment of the articles. The question for the judge, though, was whether the mandatory transfer step should be treated as part of a scheme for the purposes of applying section 641(2B). The judge held that it should not, and that the exception created by section 641(2B) therefore applied. In reaching this conclusion the judge was satisfied both that the mandatory transfer was not part of the scheme, and was to be properly treated as a separate step, and that the present scheme fell within the spirit of the exemption created by section 641(2B).

The courts have adopted a pragmatic approach to the ban on cancellation schemes and in particular to the application of sections 641(2A) and (2B). The first question for the courts is to determine which transactions constitute the scheme in question. The modern approach is not to look simplistically at the terms of the document entitled 'scheme of arrangement' but to have regard to the other arrangements entered into pursuant to the terms of the scheme.[32] However, in applying section 641(2B) in these complex transactions, the courts generally are prepared to view these transactions as a series of separate steps, the key issue being whether the transaction in question falls within the spirit of the section 641(2B) exception, as set out by the government in the Explanatory Memorandum to the introduction of these sections. In particular, the courts are concerned to assess whether the proposed transaction involves any artificial steps designed to avoid paying stamp duty.[33] These policy arguments can only take the courts so far, however. As Snowden J acknowledged in *Old Mutual*, there would potentially have been a problem in that case if it had all been done with one scheme, rather than two.[34] What these cases clearly demonstrate is that the boundary

[32] *Re Stemcor Trade Finance Limited* [2015] EWHC 2662 (Ch) at [18].

[33] *Re Old Mutual plc* [2018] EWHC 1875 (Ch), applying *UBS AG* v. *HMRC* [2016] UKSC 13 at [65] *per* Lord Reed.

[34] [2018] EWHC 1875 (Ch) at [50]–[62].

created by the 2015 legislative changes between allowed and not-allowed cancellation schemes is not a straightforward one.

4.2.3 *Why schemes might be valuable as a tool to reorganise corporate groups*

There are various reasons why a scheme is likely to be valuable to achieve a group reorganisation. First, as discussed, schemes of this kind might facilitate something that in practical terms is difficult, if not impossible, to achieve by other means, such as the redomicile of a group or the creation of additional distributable reserves. Second, there are also legal advantages to using a scheme. Many of these advantages have been discussed in earlier chapters of this book, namely the flexibility of schemes, the ability of schemes to enable the majority within a class to bind the minority and the fact that, after the court has sanctioned the scheme and the order has been delivered to the Registrar, the scheme cannot be challenged unless fraud can be established, providing finality and certainty to the arrangements.[35] However, there are two additional advantages that attach to the use of schemes in this context that need to be mentioned. The first is the additional powers that the court has under section 900 of the Companies Act 2006 in this scenario; the second is the scope to deal with potential financial assistance issues.

4.2.3.1 Additional provisions of the Companies Act 2006: reconstructions and amalgamations

Under section 900 of the Companies Act 2006, where a scheme involves a reconstruction of any company or companies, or the amalgamation of two or more companies, and under the scheme the whole or any part of the undertaking or property of any company concerned in the scheme is to be transferred to another company, then the court has very broad powers to make a variety of ancillary orders.[36]

[35] See section 2.5.

[36] For a discussion of the historical background to these provisions see *Re MyTravel Group plc* [2004] EWCA Civ 1734; [2005] 2 BCLC 123 at [17]. Similar powers exist in other jurisdictions that have imported the English scheme of arrangement; see e.g. in Australia s. 413 of the Australian Corporations Act 2001 (notice, however, that in 2009 the Corporations and Markets Advisory Committee (CAMAC) put forward proposals for a short-form merger procedure within wholly owned corporate groups that would dispense with shareholder involvement and create a reduced role for the court: CAMAC, 'Members' schemes of arrangement', Report, December 2009 at 114).

4.2.3.1.1 The meaning of 'reconstruction' and 'amalgamation' Neither 'reconstruction' nor 'amalgamation' has any definite legal meaning.[37] Neither term is defined by the Companies Act 2006; instead, '[i]n each case one has to decide whether the transaction is such that, in the meaning of commercial men, it is one which is comprehended in the term "reconstruction" or "amalgamation"'.[38] However, the courts have been prepared to provide guidance on the meaning of these terms.

In relation to 'reconstruction', the courts have suggested the following three key features, which are not intended to be exhaustive:

(i) all, or substantially all, of the undertaking is transferred by one company (the transferor company) to another (the transferee company), and the undertaking is then carried on by the transferee company;
(ii) substantially the same business must be carried on by the transferee company as was carried on by the transferor company;[39] and
(iii) the shareholders of the transferee company must be (or, after the reconstruction, become) the same, or substantially the same, as the shareholders of the transferor company.[40] However, there is no need for the transferee company to take over all, or any, of the liabilities of the transferor company.[41]

An example of a situation that failed this test was the scheme in *Re MyTravel Group plc*.[42] In that case a scheme was proposed to effect a debt-for-equity swap. The undertakings of the company, and a limited quantity of the company's liabilities, were to be transferred to a new company (newco) pursuant to the scheme. Under the proposed scheme, the creditors of the company would receive shares in newco in consideration for the forgiveness of their debts. However, as the shareholders of the company would receive only 4 per cent of the shares in newco, Mann J held that the scheme did not involve a reconstruction. The requirement that the shareholders of the transferee company be substantially the same as the shareholders of the transferor company

37 *Re South African Supply and Cold Storage Company* [1904] 2 Ch 268 at 281.
38 Ibid. at 282 *per* Buckley J.
39 Although it is possible for the transferee company to also have other businesses.
40 *Re South African Supply and Cold Storage Company* [1904] 2 Ch 268 at 286; *Brooklands Selangor Holdings Ltd* v. *IRC* [1970] 2 All ER 76 at 86–8; *Re Courage Group's Pension Schemes* [1987] 1 All ER 528 at 541; *Re MyTravel Group plc* [2004] EWCA Civ 1734; [2005] 2 BCLC 123 at 131–41.
41 *Re South African Supply and Cold Storage Company* [1904] 2 Ch 268 at 286.
42 [2004] EWCA Civ 1734; [2005] 2 BCLC 123.

was not satisfied. For this reason, it is unlikely that a debt-restructuring scheme would be able to bring itself within these provisions. The shareholders in a company facing financial difficulties would, at best, expect to see their existing equity interest diluted under the terms of any scheme. In many situations they would be wiped out entirely. The test established in *MyTravel*, however, goes further and suggests that section 900 can be used only where the capital structure of the transferee company is the same as that of the transferor company. On this basis, section 900 cannot be used as a mechanism to override the interests of existing junior creditors who are out of the money.[43]

By the same token, it is unlikely that, as presently interpreted, this aspect of section 900 will be useful where a bidder aims to take control of a target company,[44] since the shareholdings of the transferee and the transferor company will undoubtedly change significantly as a result of the transaction (indeed, that is the point). However, a situation, such as a holdco scheme, in which an undertaking is being carried on by one company and is in substance transferred to another company within a group consisting of substantially the same shareholders, with a view to that undertaking being continued by the transferee company, has been held to constitute a 'reconstruction' for this purpose.[45]

In relation to 'amalgamation', the courts suggest that either (i) all, or substantially all, of the undertakings of one company (or of several companies) are transferred to another (existing) company; or (ii) all, or substantially all, of the undertakings of two (or more) companies are transferred to another (newly incorporated) company.[46] As Buckley J has said, '[y]ou must weld two things together and arrive at an amalgam –

[43] For discussion see section 5.4.3. In 2010, the City of London Law Society suggested that s. 900 be amended to remove the requirement for the transferee and transferor companies to have the same capital structure, in order to enhance the value of schemes as a restructuring tool (see City of London Law Society, *Proposals for a Restructuring Moratorium – A Consultation: Response of the City of London Law Society Insolvency Law Committee*, 18 October 2010, para. 45). This suggestion has not been taken forward. See instead the development of the Part 26A restructuring plan discussed in section 5.8.

[44] For this purpose, the concept of 'amalgamation' is more likely to be useful: see section 4.3.1.

[45] See e.g. *Hooper* v. *Western Counties and South Wales Telephone Co Ltd* (1892) 68 LT 78, 80; *Re South African Supply and Cold Storage Company* [1904] 2 Ch 268, 286.

[46] *Re South African Supply and Cold Storage Company* [1904] 2 Ch 268; *The Citizens and Graziers' Life Assurance Company Limited* v. *Commonwealth Life (Amalgamated) Assurances Limited* (1934) 51 CLR 422.

a blending of two undertakings'.[47] In contrast to a reconstruction, there is no requirement that the shareholders of the transferee company are (or, after the amalgamation, become) the same, or substantially the same, as the shareholders in the transferor company.[48]

An amalgamation essentially requires the transferor company to cease any meaningful operations and to be deregistered or wound up. However, it might still be an amalgamation if the transferor company continues for some special and definite purpose. In *Re South African Supply and Cold Storage Company*, for example, a small sum was retained by the transferor company to cover liquidation expenses. However, a situation in which both the transferor and the transferee companies continue with separate control (i.e. as separate legal entities) and are capable of independent activities would be unlikely to be regarded as an amalgamation.[49] On this basis, while a typical holdco scheme appears to fall within the definition of a reconstruction, it is unlikely to be an amalgamation.

4.2.3.1.2 Ancillary orders Where a scheme involves a reconstruction or an amalgamation, the court has a broad range of ancillary orders that it can make either when approving the scheme of arrangement or later. The ancillary orders available to the court are set out in section 900(2) of the Companies Act 2006 and allow it, for example, to order the transfer of the business or undertaking (including liabilities) of one company to another, or the allotting of shares or debentures of one company to another person, or the dissolution of a company without a winding up.[50] These ancillary powers can be very useful; for example, they may

47 *Re South African Supply and Cold Storage Company* [1904] 2 Ch 268 at 287.

48 Ibid. However, some overseas cases have suggested that the shareholders in the transferor company must have the right to receive shares in the transferee company where they would become shareholders alongside the existing shareholders in the transferee company: *The Citizens and Graziers' Life Assurance Company Limited* v. *Commonwealth Life (Amalgamated) Assurances Limited* (1934) 51 CLR 422; *Re Opes Prime Stockbroking Limited (No. 1)* (2009) 73 ACSR 385. Alternatively, these cases suggest that it would be acceptable for the transferee company to offer a cash sum if the transferor shareholders do not exercise their right to acquire shares in the transferee company.

49 *Re Walker's Settlement* [1935] 1 Ch 567; *The Citizens and Graziers' Life Assurance Company Limited* v. *Commonwealth Life (Amalgamated) Assurances Limited* (1934) 51 CLR 422.

50 Some doubt has been raised about the exact extent of the court's powers under these ancillary provisions. In particular, it has been doubted whether the court has the ability to make an order under these provisions to transfer the rights and obligations under contracts of service with employees: *Nokes* v. *Doncaster Amalgamated Collieries Ltd*

enable a court to transfer a contract even if it contains a provision to the effect that it cannot be assigned without a party's consent.[51] It is not clear, however, why these ancillary orders should be available in the event of an amalgamation or reconstruction but not to other forms of scheme.

These ancillary powers can be beneficial. However, if the company in question is a public company, a court may not sanction a compromise or arrangement by that company unless the requirements of Part 27 of the Companies Act 2006 are satisfied.

4.2.3.1.3 Part 27 of the Companies Act 2006 Part 27 provides additional requirements for the implementation of a scheme of arrangement under Part 26, where the purpose of the scheme is to effect certain types of transfer of assets and liabilities involving public companies.[52] These provisions occupy forty sections of the Companies Act 2006 and add significant additional requirements to a transaction before a court can sanction such a scheme.[53] A major feature of such schemes is that the target company is wound up. However, an important limitation on the scope of these provisions is that they apply only in respect of mergers between companies incorporated in the UK.

There are three situations in which these additional requirements must be complied with. The first is where a public company proposes to transfer all of its undertaking, property and liabilities to another, existing, public company (merger by absorption). The members of the transferor company must receive shares in the transferee company by way of consideration.[54] The transferor company is then dissolved. The second situation is where two or more public companies propose to transfer all of their undertaking, property and liabilities to a new company (merger

[1940] AC 1014, although cf. *Re Royal Victorian Institute for the Blind Ltd* [2004] FCA 735.

51 *Stork ICM Australia Pty Ltd* v. *Stork Food Systems Australasia Pty Ltd* [2006] FCA 1849 at [96]–[99].

52 These provisions originate in EU law: from the Third EC Directive on Mergers (Directive 78/855/EEC of 9 October 1978 based on Article 54(3)(g) of the Treaty and concerning mergers of public limited liability companies) and the Sixth EC Directive on Divisions (Directive 82/891/EEC of 17 December 1982 based on Article 54(3)(g) of the Treaty and concerning the division of public limited liability companies). Directive 78/855/EEC and Directive 82/891/EEC were subsequently consolidated as Directive 2011/35 concerning mergers of public limited liability companies, and were codified with Directive 2005/56 on cross-border mergers of limited liability companies into Directive 2017/1132 as from 20 June 2017, from which date the former directives were all repealed.

53 Companies Act 2006, s. 903.

54 Ibid., ss. 904(1)(a) and 902(1)(c).

by formation of a new company).[55] The transferee company can be either a public or a private company, but it must be a company formed for the purposes of the scheme.[56] The members of the transferor companies must receive shares in the transferee company by way of consideration.[57] The transferor companies are then dissolved. The third situation is where a public company proposes to divide its undertaking, property and liabilities between two or more companies (merger by division).[58] The transferee companies must be either existing public companies or new companies.[59] The members of the transferor company must receive shares in the transferee companies by way of consideration.[60] The transferor company is then dissolved.

There are a number of additional requirements imposed in these scenarios, but there are also a number of exemptions that apply, to add to the complexity of these provisions. First, for mergers by absorption and division, there must be a meeting to approve the scheme not only by each class of members of the transferor companies but also by each class of members of any transferee company, other than a new company formed for the purpose of the scheme.[61] The majority requirements for these meetings are the same as for a scheme,[62] and it is assumed that the same criteria will apply to determining classes.[63] Next, the directors of all merging companies, or all those involved in the division, must prepare a draft of the proposed terms of the scheme.[64] Unless the draft terms are published on a website,[65] the directors of each company must deliver a copy to the Registrar, who will then publish a notice in the *Gazette*.[66] There must be at least one month between the publication of the notice in the *Gazette* and the holding of any scheme meeting.[67]

[55] Ibid., s. 904(1)(b).
[56] Ibid., s. 902(2)(a).
[57] Ibid., s. 902(2)(c).
[58] Ibid., s. 919(1).
[59] Ibid.
[60] Ibid., ss. 919(1), 902(2)(c).
[61] Ibid., ss. 907, 922. However, there are exceptions to these provisions: ss. 916, 917, 918, 932. Since mergers by formation of a new company have transferee companies formed only for the purpose of the scheme, these provisions do not apply to them.
[62] Ibid., ss. 907(1), 922(1). For discussion of the majority required for a scheme see section 2.3.3.
[63] See section 2.3.2.
[64] Companies Act 2006, ss. 905, 920.
[65] Ibid., ss. 906A, 921A.
[66] Ibid., ss. 906, 921. This is subject to an exception: s. 934(1).
[67] Ibid., ss. 906(3), 921(3).

The directors of the merging companies, or those involved in the division, must draw up a directors' report. Furthermore, the explanatory statement that is required to accompany all schemes must include details of the legal and economic grounds for the draft terms,[68] in particular for the share exchange ratio, and specify any valuation difficulties.[69] An independent expert's report is also required for each merging company,[70] or each company involved in the division.[71] In general, for at least one month prior to the first scheme meeting, the draft terms of the merger, the directors' report, the expert's report and certain financial information (such as the annual report and accounts for the previous three financial years) must be available for inspection by the members of each of the merging companies, or those involved in the division.[72] Any material changes to the property or liabilities of one of the relevant companies between the date of adoption of the draft terms and the date of any meeting must be reported to each scheme meeting of that company by the directors.[73] The articles of the newly formed transferee company/companies, in the case of a merger by fusion or division, must be approved by ordinary resolution of each transferor company under the scheme.[74]

4.2.3.2 Financial assistance

It is possible that a group reorganisation might fall foul of the rules within the Companies Act 2006 prohibiting the provision of financial assistance.[75] This would be the case, for example, where a public company provides financial assistance for the acquisition of shares in itself.

[68] See section 2.2.2.

[69] Companies Act 2006, ss. 908(2)(b), 923(2)(b). There are additional requirements for divisions: s. 923(3). There are exceptions to this requirement: ss. 915, 915A, 933, 933A.

[70] Ibid., ss. 936, 937.

[71] Ibid., ss. 909, 924. The minimum content for such reports is specified in ss. 909(5) and 924(5). Again, there are exceptions to this requirement: ss. 915, 915A, 918A, 933, 933A.

[72] Ibid., ss. 911, 926. The members must also be able to obtain copies of these documents free of charge during this period. As an alternative to inspection, the relevant documents may be made available on a website maintained by and identifying the company as long as access to the site is unrestricted and free of charge during the period: ss. 911A, 926A. This is subject to a number of exceptions, e.g. s. 934.

[73] Ibid., ss. 911B, 927.

[74] Ibid., ss. 912, 928.

[75] Companies Act 2006, ss. 677–9. See e.g. British Telecommunications plc scheme of arrangement, November 2001 (though this related to the financial assistance provisions in the Companies Act 1985).

In a scheme, the financial assistance rules still apply. An example of the court's approach to this issue is to be found in *Re Uniq plc*.[76] In that case, David Richards J considered a scheme of arrangement involving financial assistance as part of a restructuring to resolve financial difficulties within a group of companies. A solvent company was restructured in such a way as to release the company from its obligations under a pensions scheme that was in deficit. This was felt to be the only way for the company to remain financially viable, and the court sanctioned the scheme in that case.

However, where a transaction does involve financial assistance, the benefit of organising the transaction by way of a scheme is clear: section 681(2)(e) of the Companies Act 2006 provides an unconditional exception to the financial assistance provisions. It permits anything done in pursuance of an order of the court under Part 26 of the Companies Act 2006 that sanctions a compromise or arrangement with members or creditors. In other words, actions that would otherwise be prevented by the prohibition may be approved by the court as part of the scheme.[77]

4.3 The use of schemes in mergers and demergers

4.3.1 Mergers

The term 'merger' does not describe a technical legal process in English law. This is not the case in other jurisdictions.[78] In the UK, the term 'merger' may be used to describe a number of different types of transaction. It can be used to refer to a transaction in which two separate entities merge into one legal entity, and the assets and liabilities of the target entity are transferred to the surviving entity. An example of this kind of

[76] [2011] EWHC 749 (Ch); [2012] 1 BCLC 783. For further discussion see section 3.3.2.4.

[77] For the avoidance of doubt, David Richards J confirmed that reliance on section 681(2)(e) was not conditional upon other criteria. In particular, he stated that there was no need to satisfy the criterion used in the former 'whitewash' procedure under ss. 155–8 of the Companies Act 1985. However, in circumstances where these conditions are satisfied, the judge stated that 'there would in general be no reason not to exercise the power' (at [45]).

[78] In Delaware, for example, a statutory regime allows for the merger or consolidation of two or more Delaware corporations (Delaware General Corporation Law, § 251) or for the merger and consolidation of one or more Delaware corporations with one or more corporations from other states in the USA (§ 252). The term 'merger' in this context is used to indicate a transaction in which two separate legal entities become one legal entity, with all of the assets and liabilities of the target entity being transferred to the surviving entity. See also the statutory merger regime that exists in the British Virgin Islands, which is similar to the Delaware regime: BVI Business Companies Act 2004, Part IX.

merger in the UK existed pursuant to the Companies (Cross-Border Mergers) Regulations 2007,[79] although these Regulations ceased to apply at the end of the post-Brexit transition period on 31 December 2020.[80] The word 'merger' might also be used more generally to describe a situation in which all of the assets and liabilities of the target are transferred to another company, or even to describe situations in which there is a transfer of shares in the target, as discussed in Chapter 3.[81] This may be particularly important for commercial or presentational reasons, for example where the parties are of roughly equivalent size and wish the transaction to be perceived as a 'merger of equals' rather than as a takeover of the target by the bidder. The use of the term 'merger' therefore needs to be treated with some care.

When 'merger' is used in the narrow sense of two separate entities merging into one legal entity, with the assets and liabilities of the target entity being transferred to the surviving entity, it can be seen that while schemes *can* be used to effect such a change of control, they are rarely used in this way. On the whole, this is for practical rather than legal reasons. In general, changes of control will take place via acquisition by a bidder of sufficient voting shares in a target company to enable the bidder to acquire control of the target company,[82] a process described in detail in Chapter 3, rather than via the acquisition of the assets and liabilities of the target. There are some practical reasons for this. First, a share sale tends to be a more straightforward transaction than an asset

[79] SI 2974/2007. These Regulations implemented into UK law Directive 2005/56 on cross-border mergers of limited liability companies (this Directive was subsequently consolidated into Directive 2017/1132). Due to the British preference for takeovers, the Regulations were not utilised a great deal in the UK, but for an example see *Re Wood DIY Ltd* [2011] EWHC 3089 (Ch).

[80] See the Companies, Limited Liability Partnerships and Partnerships (Amendment etc.) (EU Exit) Regulations 2019 (SI 2019/348). For discussion see *Re Easynet Global Services Ltd* [2018] EWCA Civ 10.

[81] In particular, where the consideration for the purchase of shares in the target company is securities in the bidder (i.e. a securities exchange) rather than cash consideration, the resulting transaction is sometimes described as a merger.

[82] The concept of control will differ according to the circumstances. The definition of control for the purposes of the Takeover Code is the holding of shares carrying 30 per cent or more of the voting rights of a company: Takeover Code, Definitions section. Outside the boundaries of the Takeover Code, the concept of control may well be different. Even for target companies that fall within the Takeover Code, it may well be that a bidder wishes to acquire more than 30 per cent of the shares carrying voting rights, and may in fact want to acquire 100 per cent of those shares. This is common in the case of private equity transactions, where the lending banks want to achieve certainty with regard to taking security over the target's assets following the transaction.

sale. Only shares are transferred, as opposed to all of the underlying assets of the business, for which separate transfers with different formalities may be required. In addition, on a share purchase, all the target's liabilities will automatically pass to the buyer. On an asset purchase, the buyer acquires only agreed and identified assets and liabilities, provided that these can be specified with sufficient precision as a matter of fact and drafting.[83] Second, on a share purchase, the business is transferred as a going concern (subject to change-of-control provisions in relevant contracts). This is not necessarily the case with an asset purchase. Third, the tax treatment of share and asset purchases is also different. Generally, transfer duties are lower on share purchases. There is little or nothing in a scheme of arrangement that can address these issues.

Were a scheme to be used to effect a change of control via a transfer of the undertaking and assets of the target company, section 900 of the Companies Act 2006, discussed in section 4.2.3.1, may be relevant. This section provides a number of additional powers to the court where that transaction involves a 'reconstruction' or an 'amalgamation'. A merger of this kind is unlikely to be a 'reconstruction', given the requirement that the shareholders in the transferee company be substantially the same as the shareholders of the transferor company,[84] but it could well be an amalgamation. However, Part 27 of the Act provides additional regulations where the scheme involves 'mergers and divisions' of a public company,[85] which can add a significant layer of complexity and regulation to the transaction.

4.3.2 Demergers

In contrast to the situation regarding mergers, described in section 4.3.1, demergers are often effected through schemes.[86] Demergers may be

[83] This is subject to exceptions in certain jurisdictions. See e.g. Transfer of Undertakings (Protection of Employment) Regulations 2006 (SI 2006/246); Collective Redundancies and Transfer of Undertakings (Protection of Employment) (Amendment) Regulations 2014 (SI 2014/16).

[84] See e.g. *Re MyTravel Group plc* [2004] EWCA Civ 1734; [2005] 2 BCLC 123.

[85] See section 4.2.3.1.3.

[86] See e.g. *Re Old Mutual Group plc* [2018] EWHC 1875 (Ch); *Re BGEO Group plc* [2018] EWHC 3975 (Ch). The use of schemes to effect demergers is also common in other jurisdictions. See e.g. *Re Arrow Energy Ltd* [2011] FCA 2; *Re Foster's Group Ltd* [2011] VSC 93; *Re Strategic Energy Resources Ltd* [2011] VSC 645; *Re Strategic Energy Resources Ltd (No. 2)* [2012] VSC 75; *Re Alchemia Ltd* [2012] FCA 927; *Re Alchemia Ltd (No. 2)* [2012] FCA 1136; *Re Texon Petroleum Ltd* [2013] FCA 29.

contemplated for a number of reasons, for example to streamline a group whose businesses have become too diverse, or in order to escape regulatory restrictions that affect one part of a business but not others, or as a preliminary step in a sale of one or more of a group's businesses to another company.

There are various options for a group wishing to effect a demerger. One option is the issue by the company effecting the demerger of a dividend to its shareholders in the form of shares in the subsidiary to be demerged. This is possible only where the company effecting the demerger has sufficient distributable reserves, but the addition of the kind of scheme whereby a new holding company is added to the group (described in section 4.2.1.2) can be a mechanism for creating sufficient distributable reserves to enable this to occur. A second option is to reduce the capital of the company effecting the demerger and transfer the business to be demerged to a newly formed company that then issue shares to the demerging company's shareholders. This can be problematic if the holding company has significant creditor protection issues.[87] One possibility, therefore, is using a holdco scheme, whereby a new holding company is created before the reduction of capital is effected since, as described earlier, this has the effect of simplifying creditor protection issues.[88]

Section 110 of the Insolvency Act 1986 might alternatively be used to effect the demerger.[89] This section allows a company to reconstruct itself by means of a voluntary liquidation, that is, section 110 is designed for use when a company is solvent.[90] A typical section 110 demerger involves the company transferring its assets to two or more newly created companies in return for shares in those companies. The shares in the new companies are then distributed to the shareholders of the original company in proportion to their shareholdings in the original company, and that original company is then wound up. The shareholders might continue to own the two companies, or the companies might then be sold.

[87] See e.g. *Re CSR Ltd* (2010) 76 ACSR 454.

[88] See e.g. The Carphone Warehouse Group plc scheme of arrangement in 2010.

[89] Section 110 can be used by any company formed and registered under the Companies Act: Insolvency Act 1986, s. 110(1). The transferee can be either a company or an LLP (s. 110(1)). It need not be a company formed under the Companies Act 2006.

[90] A members' voluntary liquidation is one in which the directors have made a 'declaration of solvency' that all the company's debts will be paid in full within twelve months (see Insolvency Act 1986, s. 89). For the distinction between a members' and a creditors' voluntary liquidation see Insolvency Act 1986, s. 90.

The procedure to put a section 110 arrangement in place starts with a special resolution of the shareholders to wind up the company, to appoint a liquidator, to approve the section 110 reconstruction and to authorise the liquidator to carry out the reconstruction.[91] Following the passing of this special resolution, and subject to the rights of the dissenting shareholders, discussed next, the section 110 arrangement is then binding on all the members of the company.[92] Unlike a scheme of arrangement, therefore, a section 110 reconstruction of this kind does not require court approval.

However, several forms of minority shareholder protection are available. In a members' voluntary winding-up, a special resolution will be required. Those that vote in favour are bound by the scheme, but can still refuse to accept an interest in the transferee.[93] The effect is that all rights in that interest are lost, although if the shares are sold, the member is entitled to the proceeds. However, those that vote against the special resolution have a number of protections. First, they can refuse to accept such interests. Second, they have statutory protection under section 111,[94] which allows a dissentient to write to the liquidator within seven days of the resolution.[95] The liquidator must then either abstain from carrying the resolution into effect or purchase the member's interest in the transferee.[96] Since the former is possible only if there is some barrier to the transaction being carried out, in practice the liquidator will have to buy out the dissentients. The price will be that agreed by the liquidator and the dissentients, or that fixed by arbitration.[97] It should take into account the value of the interest before reconstruction. Although members' rights can be varied using this form of arrangement, it will not generally be possible to make them significantly less attractive. If a number of the members elect to be bought out, the reorganisation under section 110 may well become prohibitively expensive. Finally, a reconstruction can be challenged by a shareholders' action against the company. This action may be

[91] Insolvency Act 1986, s. 110(3)(a). As to the timing of this special resolution see s. 110(6).

[92] Ibid., s. 110(5).

[93] E.g. *Cleve* v. *Financial Corporation* (1873) LR 16 Eq 363.

[94] A shareholder cannot be deprived of the rights afforded by s. 111 as a result of a provision in the company's articles: *Payne* v. *The Cork Co Ltd* [1900] 1 Ch 308.

[95] Insolvency Act 1986, s. 111(1)(2). See also *Brailey* v. *Rhodesia Consolidated Ltd* [1910] 2 Ch 95.

[96] Insolvency Act 1986, s. 111(2).

[97] Ibid., s. 111(4).

brought by any member that dissents, but will be brought on behalf of all shareholders.[98]

As for the protection of creditors, the creditors of the transferor company remain as such, and retain all of their rights against the company. It will normally be part of the arrangement in a members' winding-up that the transferee agrees to meet the liabilities of the transferor, and gives an indemnity to that effect. Alternatively, the transferor may retain sufficient assets to pay its creditors. Creditors can attempt to stop a section 110 demerger from progressing by petitioning the court for a compulsory winding-up order. To succeed, the creditor must demonstrate either that it is just and equitable to wind up the company or that the company is unable to pay its debts.[99] If the court orders the company to be wound up within one year of the special resolution authorising the section 110 scheme, the special resolution is not valid unless sanctioned by the court.[100] As a result, the demerger will remain open to challenge for a year after the transaction, and that challenge can be brought by any creditor with debts that are not discharged.[101] A demerger is therefore subject to a considerable period of uncertainty after the transaction, a situation that does not exist in a scheme.[102]

As a result of these disadvantages, schemes may be used instead of or alongside section 110.[103] In the latter situation, a holdco scheme might be used to add a new holding company into the group, which is then liquidated using the section 110 procedure. Since this new holding company will have no creditors, or relatively few creditors, the effect of introducing a holdco scheme is to reduce the possibility of a challenge by creditors.[104]

[98] See e.g. *Clinch* v. *Financial Corporation* (1868) LR 5 Eq 450; *Re Oriental Commercial Bank, Alabaster's Case* (1868–69) LR 7 273; *Re City and County Investment Co* (1879) 13 Ch D 475.

[99] See Insolvency Act 1986, s. 123.

[100] Ibid., s. 110(6).

[101] See e.g. *Re City and County Investment Co* (1879) 13 Ch D 475.

[102] See section 2.5.

[103] In an early case, *Re General Motor Cab Co Ltd* [1913] 1 Ch 377 (CA), it was suggested that the definition of 'arrangement' for scheme purposes could not encompass a situation that replicated a transfer of assets and that ought to have been carried out under the then equivalent of s. 110. However, subsequent cases have confirmed that a scheme of arrangement may be used to effect a transfer of assets to members if such a transfer could have been effected under s. 110 of the Insolvency Act 1986 in appropriate circumstances: *Re Anglo Continental Supply Company Limited* [1922] 2 Ch 723.

[104] See e.g. General Electric Company scheme of arrangement in 1999.

4.4 The use of schemes to alter class rights

Member schemes can be used within a company to reorganise the company's share capital by, for example, consolidating different classes of shares or dividing the existing shares into different classes. However, if the rights attached to the shares appear in the company's articles, as they commonly do, it will generally be far simpler for the share capital to be reorganised by altering the articles by special resolution.[105] Moreover, it is no longer necessary to use a scheme to alter class rights since a simplified statutory procedure now applies to all such rights: essentially, class rights can be altered as long as 75 per cent of the class consent.[106] In general, therefore, variation of class rights will not be carried out via a scheme, unless the articles specifically state that the rights can only be varied using a scheme, which would be unusual.[107] Nevertheless, there may be circumstances in which a scheme can be useful, for example where there are a number of untraceable shareholders who must be bound by the scheme.[108]

4.5 The use of schemes to remove minority shareholders

In some circumstances the company may wish to remove minority shareholders from the company. There may be a variety of reasons for this, for example where the minority wishes to prevent the majority passing a special resolution, or in order to avoid reporting obligations to regulatory authorities abroad triggered by the existence of foreign shareholders within the company.[109] In some circumstances a scheme may be used to achieve this removal.[110]

[105] Companies Act 2006, s. 21. It might also be necessary to obtain the consent of the separate classes of shareholders if class rights are being altered: Companies Act 2006, s. 630. Where class rights are altered by way of a scheme, however, the meetings convened by the court of each class of members subject to the scheme will suffice to obtain any class approvals that are needed. The statutory regime for separate class sanction of a variation of class rights in the Companies Act 2006 does not apply to schemes: s. 632.

[106] Ibid., ss. 630–5.

[107] Some jurisdictions specifically require that where a scheme is used to vary shareholder rights, it must satisfy the general provisions within company legislation which relate to variation of shareholders rights by resolution: Indian Companies Act 2013, s. 230(7)(a).

[108] E.g. *Re BAT Industries plc*, unreported, 3 September 1998.

[109] See e.g. ITV plc scheme of arrangement in 2005, which was intended to reduce the number of US-resident holders of the company's shares to below 300 in order to suspend the company's obligations to register with and report to the Securities and Exchange Commission.

[110] See e.g. BSB Holdings Ltd scheme of arrangement in 1997.

However, there is a significant potential flaw in this use of schemes, since such schemes are likely to involve the majority and the minority being placed in separate classes for the purpose of considering and voting on the scheme. Even if they hold the same class of shares before the scheme (e.g. ordinary shares), their different treatment within the scheme, with the majority remaining as shareholders in the company and the minority being removed, means that they are likely to be treated as comprising different classes.[111] As a result, if the minority shareholders are opposed to the scheme, they will have a veto right. The use of a scheme to remove the minority can succeed, therefore, only where the majority of the minority support the scheme.

4.6 Summary

The purpose of this chapter, in combination with Chapter 3, is to illustrate the broad range of uses to which member schemes can be put. These examples demonstrate the value and flexibility of schemes in this context. Chapter 3 explored a particularly well-established and well-used form of member schemes, namely the takeover scheme. As this chapter has sought to illustrate, member schemes are not confined to this purpose. In particular, holdco schemes are an important and practical device for companies to achieve various goals, including redomiciling a corporate group, or creating additional distributable reserves, which would be difficult, if not impossible, to achieve by other means. The large number of holdco schemes in recent years are evidence of the value of these schemes.

[111] See section 2.3.2.

5

Creditor schemes of arrangement: debt restructuring

5.1 Introduction

The purpose of this chapter and the next is to consider creditor schemes.[1] When schemes of arrangement were first introduced in 1870,[2] they applied only to arrangements between a company and its creditors, and only to arrangements proposed by companies in the course of being wound up. Both of these constraints were subsequently dropped,[3] but it remains a common use of schemes of arrangement to effect a compromise between the company and its creditors. In particular, schemes for restructuring the debt of financially distressed companies have become very popular.[4] This stems, inter alia, from

[1] As discussed in earlier chapters, there is no hard boundary between creditor and member schemes. However, the schemes discussed in this chapter may be regarded as creditor-focused, in that the predominant purpose is a reorganisation of the company's debt.

[2] Joint Stock Companies Arrangement Act 1870.

[3] The Companies Act 1907 extended schemes to companies not in liquidation and the Companies (Consolidation) Act 1908 extended schemes to arrangements between a company and its members or any class of them. For a discussion of the historical development of schemes see section 1.2.

[4] This is not just the case in English schemes. In many other jurisdictions, schemes are commonly used to restructure the debts of financially distressed companies; see e.g. Singapore, Hong Kong, Malaysia, South Africa, Bermuda, BVI, Cayman Islands and Ireland. In Australia, despite the historic under-utilisation of schemes as a debt-restructuring device, they are increasingly being used for this purpose; see e.g. *Re BIS Finance Pty Ltd* [2017] NSWSC 1713. The use of schemes to restructure debt in Canada also seems to be increasingly common (see e.g. *Re Essar Steel Canada Inc* 2014 ONSC 4285 (CanLII); *Re RGL Reservoir Management Inc* 2017 ONSC 7302 (CanLII)). For a discussion of the use of schemes for financially distressed companies in India see *Y. Shivram Prasad* v. *S. Dhanapal* (National Company Law Appellate Tribunal, 27 February 2019) and U. Varottil, 'The scheme of arrangement as a debt restructuring tool in India: problems and prospects' (2018) *European Company and Financial Law Review* 585.

a growing appreciation of the benefits of schemes by companies and their advisors, coupled with a constructive commercial attitude on the part of the courts in dealing with schemes. The downturn in the economy after 2008 fuelled the development of schemes as an effective restructuring tool, and the economic difficulties for companies arising from the Covid-19 pandemic have again focused attention on this issue and have led to legislative reforms which seek to increase the debt restructuring options for financially distressed companies.

This chapter will consider two issues of relevance to all creditor schemes, namely the definition of a creditor for this purpose and the division of creditors into classes, and will then analyse the most common form of creditor scheme at the present time, namely a scheme designed to restructure the debt of a financially distressed company in order to promote some form of rescue of that company, possibly involving its sale. Other examples of creditor schemes are discussed in Chapter 6. Before getting into the detail of this chapter, though, it is helpful to consider, in general terms, some of the reasons why a creditor scheme might prove valuable to a company. One of the particularly advantageous aspects of a scheme that alters creditors' rights is the ability of the majority to bind the minority. It is possible for creditors' rights to be altered informally, without a scheme, via informal consensual arrangements between a company and its creditors.[5] The difficulty with this mechanism is that no creditor can be bound by a change to which it has not consented, either in advance[6] or at the time of the proposed change. Therefore, for a change to be effective, all of the affected creditors have to agree. In general, the position regarding creditors is therefore distinct from that regarding shareholders. For shareholders, if the rights are in the articles, the 75 per cent majority shareholders can, in principle, bind the minority.[7] For creditors, the usual position is that a single dissenting creditor, even one holding only a very small percentage of the company's debts, can prevent the

[5] See section 5.5.

[6] For example, it is common for bondholders' agreements to contain a clause specifying that a percentage of the bondholders less than 100 per cent (typically 75 per cent) can bind the remainder. See L. Gullifer and J. Payne, *Corporate Finance Law: Principles and Policy* (3rd ed., Hart, 2020) at 8.3.3.

[7] Companies Act 2006, s. 21 (regarding alterations of articles). This is subject to the common law principle that the majority must act bona fide in the best interests of the company: *Allen* v. *Gold Reefs of West Africa Ltd* [1900] 1 Ch 656. The position is different where class rights are involved: Companies Act 2006, ss. 630–2.

compromise.[8] Using a scheme can avoid these difficult issues, since 75 per cent by value, and a majority in number, of a class can bind the minority in a scheme, provided the scheme is subsequently sanctioned by the court.

The flexibility of a scheme, along with the lack of statutorily prescribed content, is another significant advantage. Schemes can therefore be tailored to the specific corporate needs of a particular company.[9] They can be used either alongside or as an alternative to liquidation or administration. They can be used to remove or modify all aspects of the creditor–debtor relationship, including security rights. They can also be used to swap debt for equity, and to reorganise corporate groups. It is also significant that schemes can be used whether the company is solvent or insolvent.[10] Although the company's solvency is one of the factors that the court can take into account at the sanctioning hearing, the fact that a company is solvent does not affect the procedures that are relevant in approving or sanctioning the scheme and, indeed, solvent creditor schemes are very common. An example of a solvent creditor scheme involves settling outstanding or future claims within the reinsurance industry.[11]

The fact that, in relation to creditor schemes, there is no requirement that there be any impending insolvency is a significant benefit of the scheme procedure. The ability to effect a restructuring before insolvency, and head off liquidation, is therefore a potentially valuable aspect of the English scheme. Early attention may be given to corporate difficulties,

[8] However, this position can be varied by contract. In deeds of debt securities, for example, it is common to provide that the trustee can take action against a corporate borrower with the approval of a specified majority less than 100 per cent. As with shareholders' ability to alter the articles, there are common law restrictions on the ability of the majority to exercise its voting power in these situations for an improper purpose: *British America Nickel Corporation* v. *O'Brien* [1927] AC 369. These can obviously bind only the parties to the contract, whereas a scheme can bind other creditors.

[9] In *Re ColourOz Investment 2 LLC* [2020] EWHC 1864 (Ch) Snowden J held that a scheme can validly confer a power of attorney to execute a deed on behalf of scheme creditors (such as a deed of release or variation). The provisions of section 1 of the Powers of Attorney Act 1971, which ordinarily require a power of attorney itself to be executed by deed, do not apply to a power of attorney given pursuant to a scheme, as the scheme is itself given effect by statute (i.e. Part 26 of the Companies Act 2006) (see also *Re Premier Oil plc* [2020] CSOH 39). In the context of restructuring plans see *Re Virgin Atlantic Airways Ltd* [2020] EWHC 2376 (Ch).

[10] For discussion see e.g. *Scottish Lion Insurance Co Ltd* v. *Goodrich Corp* [2010] CSIH 6; 2010 SC 349 at [43] (cf. Lord Glennie at first instance, [2009] CSOH 127 at [55]). See also *Re Equitable Life Assurance Society* [2019] EWHC 3336 (Ch) at [39].

[11] See section 6.2.

which will be particularly important in rescue scenarios. This facility is not available in all jurisdictions. The fact that schemes can operate before insolvency is one of the reasons for a number of solvent but financially distressed foreign companies in recent years seeking to utilise the UK scheme jurisdiction. This issue is discussed in Chapter 7.

There are also disadvantages to using a creditor scheme, however. The procedural requirements of a scheme are onerous. The issue of class meetings can be complex and difficult.[12] Extensive and detailed explanatory statements must be produced by the company.[13] There is also the matter of two court hearings, and the close supervision of the process by the court. The counterbalance to the fact that the majority can bind the minority in a scheme is the fact that minority protection is provided through class meetings and via court supervision, particularly at the sanctioning stage. The role of the court at the sanctioning stage is not a mere rubber-stamping exercise.[14] Even where the majority approves the scheme, the court might refuse to sanction it in order to protect minority interests, for example where that majority has a special interest separate to that of the minority.[15] In general, the complexity of the scheme procedure, and the requirement for two court hearings, means that this period will be a minimum of six to eight weeks. Another limitation of schemes when used as stand-alone devices is that they allow for only a partial cramdown of dissenting creditors: schemes allow for the cramdown of the minority within a class, but the requirement for every class to consent before a scheme can be sanctioned means that a cross-class cramdown is not possible using a scheme alone. Practitioners have developed a mechanism for a de facto cross-class cramdown by combining schemes with administration,[16] and from 2020 English law has a de jure cross-class cramdown option in the Part 26A restructuring plan.[17] A further possible disadvantage that existed until 2020 was that a scheme involved no moratorium. Without a moratorium, in the period between the initial formulation of the scheme and the scheme becoming effective, each individual creditor is able to exercise all of the rights and remedies that it possesses against the

[12] See section 5.3.
[13] See section 2.2.2.
[14] For discussion see J. Payne, 'The role of the court in debt restructuring' (2018) *Cambridge Law Journal* 124.
[15] See section 2.4.3.
[16] For discussion see section 5.4.3.
[17] See section 5.8.

company unless a contractual standstill arrangement is entered into. The Corporate Insolvency and Governance Act 2020 now allows a moratorium to be added to a scheme, though it is not automatic.[18] Despite these disadvantages, the popularity of creditor schemes has increased steadily in recent years.

The remainder of this chapter will be structured as follows: after a discussion of the definition of 'creditor' for the purposes of a scheme (in section 5.2), and the division of creditors into classes (in section 5.3), the use of schemes for debt restructuring is introduced in section 5.4. In section 5.5 the use of a workout between the company and its creditors as an alternative restructuring mechanism is examined, and in section 5.6 the use of company voluntary arrangements (CVAs) as an alternative to schemes is considered. In section 5.7 the use of administration as an alternative to schemes is discussed. In section 5.8 the new restructuring plan is analysed and compared to a scheme of arrangement.

5.2 The definition of 'creditor' for the purpose of a scheme of arrangement

The term 'creditor' is not defined by statute for the purpose of a scheme of arrangement, and therefore the courts have developed the law on this issue on a case-by-case basis. They have tended to construe this term widely.[19] One of the recognised purposes of a scheme is to facilitate the financial rehabilitation of the company, and this is a strong policy reason to give the meaning of 'creditor' as wide a meaning as possible. However, as David Richards J recognised in *Re T & N Ltd (No. 2)*,[20] there may be dangers in defining the term too widely, since a scheme is a mechanism 'whereby an arrangement may be imposed on dissenting or nonparticipating members of the class and [therefore] such a power is not to be construed as extending so as to bind persons who cannot properly be described as "creditors"'.[21]

A creditor for the purpose of a scheme of arrangement is not the same as a creditor for other, potentially quite similar, purposes.[22] For instance, there is no alignment between the term 'creditor' for scheme purposes

[18] For discussion see section 5.4.4.

[19] *Re Alabama, New Orleans, Texas & Pacific Junction Railway Co* [1891] 1 Ch 213 at 236–7; *Re Midland Coal, Coke and Iron Co* [1895] 1 Ch 267 at 277; *Re R. L. Child & Co Pty Ltd* (1986) 10 ACLR 673 at 674.

[20] [2005] EWHC 2870 (Ch); [2006] 1 WLR 1728.

[21] Ibid. at [40].

[22] See e.g. the definition of 'creditor' for the purposes of CVAs, discussed at section 5.6.1.

and 'creditor' for the purposes of liquidation.[23] A creditor for the purposes of a scheme has been held to mean anyone who has a monetary claim against the company that, when payable, will constitute a debt.[24] The term 'creditor' therefore encompasses an actual creditor, that is, someone who is at present owed a debt by the company, but it also includes a prospective creditor, namely someone to whom a sum will become payable in the future, pursuant to a present obligation.[25] It has also been accepted that a person with a contingent claim against the company, that is, someone to whom a sum may become payable in the future, dependent upon the happening of a future event, qualifies as a creditor under a scheme of arrangement. The term 'creditor' in this context is therefore used 'in the widest sense, and . . . includes all persons having any pecuniary claims against the company'.[26]

One limitation, however, is that a scheme cannot bind a creditor who was not in existence at the time of the order convening the relevant meeting or meetings.[27] A second limitation is that only those creditors within the scheme are bound by it. As explained in Chapter 2, it is very common for the company to organise the scheme in such a way that some members or creditors are excluded from it.[28] These creditors will not be bound by the scheme and will retain their full rights.[29] This aspect of a scheme can be very valuable. In some restructuring schemes, it may be that the company deliberately wants to leave some creditors, such as the junior creditors or trade creditors, out of the scheme.

5.2.1 Contingent claims

It is clear that contingent creditors fall within the definition of 'creditor' for scheme purposes. However, the exact ambit of the concept of

[23] See *Re T & N Ltd (No. 2)* [2005] EWHC 2870 (Ch); [2006] 1 WLR 1728 at [36]–[37]. See also *Re R. L. Child & Co Pty Ltd* (1986) 4 ACLC 312 at 314.

[24] *Re Lehman Brothers International (Europe) (in administration)* [2009] EWCA Civ 1161; [2010] 1 BCLC 496 at [58].

[25] A good example of prospective claims allowed within the jurisdiction of a scheme is claims for future rentals under a lease: *Re Cancol Ltd* [1996] 1 All ER 37.

[26] *Re Midland Coal, Coke & Iron Co* [1895] 1 Ch 267 at 277 *per* Lindley LJ. The holders of share options are therefore regarded as creditors by virtue of their contingent claims against the company: *Re Compania de Electricidad de la Provincia de Buenos Aires Ltd* [1980] Ch 146.

[27] *Re B & S Distributors Pty Ltd* (1986) 5 NSWLR 492.

[28] See section 2.3.1.2.

[29] *Re Marconi Corp plc* [2003] EWHC 1083 (Ch) *per* Lindsay J at [18].

'contingent creditors' is not straightforward. It was discussed in *Re T & N Ltd (No. 2)*,[30] in which future claimants for damages in tort attributable to asbestosis were held to be creditors for the purpose of a scheme, on proof of exposure to asbestos, even though the judge held that they had no provable debt in the winding-up.[31] David Richards J regarded contingent liability for these purposes as being liability arising by reason of something done by the company (in this case the use or distribution of asbestos) that would *necessarily* arise if certain future events were to occur (in this case the onset of asbestos-related conditions in those exposed to asbestos by the company).[32]

In this context, a distinction can be drawn between someone who has already been exposed to asbestos and someone who has not been exposed to asbestos to date. The former can be regarded as a contingent creditor, on the basis that if they later develop asbestosis the company will be liable to pay damages. The latter cannot. In general, therefore, the court draws a distinction between those circumstances in which the company is *automatically* involved, by the operation of law, in the payment of the debt once the contingency occurs, and those in which the contingent liability is dependent upon the subsequent exercise of judicial discretion. In the latter situation it has been held that no contingent liability arises.[33]

In *Re T & N Ltd (No. 3)* the court grappled with some of the difficulties that arise when the court is faced with a situation where the company's negligence will cause loss to persons who are not as yet identifiable.[34] For example, where a person has been wrongfully exposed to asbestos by Company A and by another employer, but has not yet developed any disease, is that person a creditor of both employers? The court in *Re T & N Ltd (No.3)* held that they were, and that the other employer was also a creditor of Company A for scheme purposes, in respect of any contingent claim for contribution that might arise in the future. However, where only Company A had exposed the person to asbestos – a subsequent employer,

30 [2005] EWHC 2870 (Ch); [2006] 1 WLR 1728.

31 The court's decision in *T & N Ltd* that future asbestos claims were not provable debts for the purpose of winding up prompted the Insolvency Rules 1986 to be changed to provide that a liability in tort was a debt provable in a winding-up if either the cause of action had accrued at the date on which the company went into liquidation or all the elements necessary to establish the cause of action existed at that date except for actionable damage: Insolvency Rules 2016, r. 14.1(4) (previously Insolvency Rules 1986, r. 13.12(2)).

32 David Richards J considered the opinions of the House of Lords in *Winter (exors of Sutherland (decd))* v. *IRC* [1963] AC 235 on the nature of contingent liability.

33 E.g. *Glenister* v. *Rowe* [2000] Ch 76.

34 [2006] EWHC 1447 (Ch); [2007] 1 All ER 851.

Company B, had not yet done so – the court held that Company B was not a contingent creditor of Company A. Since nothing had been done by Company B that could result in a claim against it or a claim for contribution by it, the requirements for the creation of a contingent liability were missing.

The court employed similar reasoning in relation to the question of whether dependants with claims under the Fatal Accidents Act 1976 should be regarded as creditors for the purposes of a scheme. Dependants of an employee who had already died, without compromising his or her claim, had a right to make a claim under the Act, and were to be regarded as creditors for the purposes of the scheme, even if they did not appreciate that they had the benefit of such claims. Dependants of an employee who had already developed a relevant disease, but had not yet died, were potential claimants under the Act (their claims being contingent on the employee's death being caused by the disease, upon their continuing to be dependants at the time of death, and on the employee not having compromised the claim before death), and were still creditors for scheme purposes. Likewise, dependants of an employee who has been exposed to asbestos, but has not yet contracted the disease, were still creditors for scheme purposes (although subject to an additional contingency, namely the employee contracting the disease). However, those not currently dependants, but who might become so in the future, for example future spouses, or children born in the future, were not creditors for this purpose because that class of persons did not exist at the time the scheme was proposed. No scheme could therefore bind these future dependants.

5.2.2 Secured creditors

It is clear that schemes can include not only unsecured creditors but also secured creditors,[35] so that schemes can, and frequently do, involve the removal or modification of security. A scheme is therefore capable of affecting proprietary rights, but the extent to which it can do so is circumscribed.[36] The limits of this concept have been tested in two

[35] *Re Empire Mining Co* (1890) 44 Ch D 402, 409; *Re Alabama, New Orleans, Texas & Pacific Junction Railway Co* [1891] 1 Ch 213, 246; *Re Lehman Brothers International (Europe) (in administration)* [2009] EWCA Civ 1161; [2010] 1 BCLC 496 at [60] and [70]. This is in contrast to the position in relation to CVAs, discussed in section 5.6.

[36] Another example of the ability of schemes to affect proprietary rights is claims of the creditor against third parties, for example under guarantees, which may be compromised

ways in recent years: the first relates to whether a scheme can be used to amend the rights of beneficial owners, discussed in section 5.2.3; the second is whether schemes can be used to unilaterally impose a surrender of the company's leases on its landlords and is discussed here.

To understand this latter issue, the basis for the ability of schemes to compromise security rights needs to be set out. The justification for this approach rests on the fact that the security rights are dependent upon the debt owed by the company. As Patten LJ explained in *Re Lehman Brothers International (Europe) (in administration)*:[37]

> No one can dispute that a creditor with security for what is owed remains a creditor of the company. Their security exists and is only enforceable to the extent and for so long as the underlying indebtedness continues. . . . An arrangement under which that indebtedness is re-organised will therefore necessarily impact on any security held in respect of it and may involve the repatriation of the debtor's property free from the charge.

As Lord Neuberger explained it: 'the security is an incident of the debt; to put the point another way, it is parasitic on the debt'.[38] The security right is an integral part of the debtor–creditor relationship between the company and the creditor, and as a result a scheme can legitimately alter that security right in the same way that it can alter other aspects of the debtor–creditor relationship.

The boundaries of this issue arose for discussion in *Re Instant Cash Loans Ltd*,[39] which involved a scheme proposed by the company which purported to terminate the company's leases by way of an automatic 'surrender' to its landlords, subject only to a landlord's right to submit a pecuniary claim under the scheme for 'disclaimer damages' (i.e. damages calculated as if there had been a disclaimer of the lease by a liquidator). The judge found, following the decision of the Court of Appeal in *Re Lehman Brothers International (Europe) (in administration)*, that it is a fundamental principle of a scheme that it can only deal with rights between the company and a creditor 'as debtor and creditor'.[40] Such rights can be amended by a scheme, including, for example, the compromise of future rent payments.[41] Other rights, such as

within a scheme provided that the release of those claims is merely ancillary to the arrangement between the company and its own creditors: see section 2.1.1.

37 [2009] EWCA Civ 1161; [2010] 1 BCLC 496 at [60].

38 Ibid. at [82].

39 [2019] EWHC 2795 (Ch).

40 [2009] EWCA Civ 1161; [2010] 1 BCLC 496 at [65] *per* Patten LJ.

41 [2019] EWHC 2795 (Ch) at [15].

proprietary rights arising from a legal estate in land, including a lease, are outside the scheme jurisdiction as these are not rights arising between the parties as debtor and creditor. The judge, Zacaroli J, held that a lease cannot be terminated at the will of the tenant alone and that imposing a surrender of the leases was not necessary to ensure the effective compromise of a pecuniary liability; it was something additional imposed on the landlords and therefore outside the scope of the scheme jurisdiction.[42]

This suggests that scheme jurisdiction is focused on the modification or removal of rights that can properly be characterised as dealing with the rights of the company and its creditors inter se 'as debtor and creditor'. This is in accordance with the view that schemes are a means of enabling the company and its members/creditors to reach a compromise or arrangement about anything that they can properly agree between themselves. This is a broad view of scheme jurisdiction. Security rights fall within this definition and thus can be removed or modified by a scheme. Creditors' rights against third parties can also be regarded as part of the scheme as long as the 'release of such third party claims is merely ancillary to the arrangement between the company and its own creditors'.[43] However, it has limits. Rights which are not rights inter se the debtor and creditor, such as those in the *Instant Cash* case, are excluded,[44] as are third-party releases that are not ancillary to the creditor–debtor relationship.[45] It also appears that while schemes can be used for the modification or removal of the rights between creditors and debtors, they cannot be used to impose new obligations: 'in a creditors' scheme, it appears to me likely that the jurisdiction exists for the purpose of varying the rights of creditors in their capacity as such, and not imposing on such creditors new obligations'.[46]

5.2.3 *Beneficial owners*

The position of secured creditors may be contrasted with that of the beneficial owners of property held on trust by the company. This issue

[42] The scheme in *Re Instant Cash Loans Ltd* was ultimately approved, on condition that the offending provision was removed.

[43] *Re Lehman Brothers (Europe) International (in administration)* [2009] EWCA Civ 1161 at [65].

[44] In fact, Zacaroli J in *Re Instant Cash Loans Ltd* was of the view that both proprietary and contractual rights can potentially be excluded from scheme jurisdiction in this way: [2019] EWHC 2795 (Ch) at [22].

[45] See section 2.1.1.

[46] *Re Apcoa Parking Holdings GmbH* [2014] EWHC 3849 (Ch) at [164] *per* Hildyard J and see section 2.1.1.

was discussed in *Re Lehman Brothers International (Europe) (in administration)*.[47] In that case the administrators of a company proposed a scheme the effect of which was to modify the rights held by clients of the company. The clients held property rights under trusts of which the company was the trustee. One question for the court was whether the clients could be regarded as creditors for the purpose of the scheme. There was no dispute that these clients could be regarded as (unsecured) creditors, to the extent that they also held pecuniary claims against the company, for example in respect of claims against it for equitable compensation for breach of trust. The question was whether the court had jurisdiction to sanction a scheme in so far as it compromised or removed their rights over the trust property.

The Court of Appeal held that the concept of 'creditor' for these purposes is not limitless. It did not extend to those whose relationship is not that of a debtor/creditor at all. The court held that its jurisdiction under Part 26 of the Companies Act 2006 is circumscribed by the requirement that a scheme must be between a company and its creditors or members. A creditor for these purposes is someone who has a monetary claim *against the company* that, when payable, constitutes a debt. A proprietary claim to trust property is not a claim in respect of a debt or liability of the company. Therefore, the position of a beneficiary under a trust was held not to be analogous to the position of a secured creditor:

> In the case of a secured creditor, the security is an incident of the debt ... as section 895 enables a scheme which varies the debt, then it must follow that the variation must, as it were, be followed through to the security. No such argument can be mounted in relation to trust property held in the name of the company, which also happens to have a debt to the beneficiary, even if the debt arises out of the trustee–beneficiary relationship.[48]

The Court of Appeal in *Re Lehman Brothers International (Europe) (in administration)* was asked to consider another proposition: if a creditor of the company held some pecuniary claims against the company, and therefore could properly be regarded as a creditor in relation to those claims, then could it be regarded as a creditor under section 895 of the Companies Act 2006 for all purposes? If so, this would allow the scheme to extend to any property or interest of that person. This argument was dismissed by the Court of Appeal. Unless a person's claim renders them

[47] [2009] EWCA Civ 1161; [2010] 1 BCLC 496.

[48] Ibid. at [82] *per* Lord Neuberger, MR.

a creditor of the company, then the subject matter of that claim cannot be covered by a scheme of arrangement. The mere fact that a beneficiary happens also to be a creditor of a company does not entitle the company, or its liquidators or administrators, to include that property in a scheme when they would not otherwise be allowed to do so. In accordance with the discussion at section 5.2.2, the arrangement must be made with creditors in their capacity as creditors, and must concern their position as creditors.

5.2.4 *Bondholder schemes of arrangement*

The definition of a creditor for scheme purposes has proved particularly difficult to apply in bondholder schemes of arrangement.[49] Owing to the structure of most bond issues, the underlying bondholder, whilst holding the ultimate economic interest in the bond, may not be a 'creditor' of the issuing company for the purposes of voting on the proposed scheme.

The vast majority of bonds are now held through global custodian arrangements. In Europe, the global note is usually held by a depository on behalf of Euroclear and/or Clearstream, the two major ICSDs (International Central Securities Depositories) in Europe. The two ICSDs are therefore usually first-tier intermediaries, and the rights of the underlying bondholder (the ultimate account holder)[50] are derived from a credit to its securities account either with these ICSDs or more usually from another intermediary which itself holds a securities account with a higher-tier intermediary. In this scenario, the issuer has no direct relationship with the underlying bondholders and will generally not even be aware of their identities. The documentation may contain the right for underlying bondholders to require the issue of definitive certificates in certain, usually very limited, circumstances, for example where there has been an event of default under the terms of the bond, although it is rare for definitive certificates actually to be issued. This structure has various benefits, including enabling speedy and easy trading of bonds, and allows

[49] For further discussion of this issue in the context of the headcount test see section 2.3.3.2.2.2.

[50] For discussion of the chain of trusts and sub-trusts analysis see *Re Lehman Brothers International (Europe) (in Administration)* [2010] EWHC 2914 (Ch); *SL Claimants* v. *Tesco plc* [2019] EWHC 2858 (Ch). The ultimate account holder is the end investor at the end of the intermediated chain. This useful term was recently used by the judge in the case of *Madison Pacific Trust Ltd* v. *Shakoor Capital Ltd* [2020] EWHC 610 (Ch).

the underlying bondholders to keep their identity secret from the issuer, which is a feature of the system that is important to many investors.

The question arises of who, in this arrangement, is a 'creditor' for the purpose of considering and voting on a scheme. As discussed, the starting point for the courts is that a creditor consists of anyone who has a monetary claim against the company which, when payable, will constitute a debt.[51] The analysis of which party in a bond issue can take action to enforce a claim against the company for recovery of an amount owed to it, in its own name and for its own account, and thereby may be treated as a creditor, will depend ultimately on the terms of the relevant instruments. However, typically, the covenant to pay in the bond is expressed to be in favour of the 'holder' of the bonds. While the bond is in global note form, the holder will generally be the common depository for the ICSDs. It is this person who is prima facie the creditor in relation to the global note. Where the structure incorporates a separate trustee, the terms of the trust deed will usually contain a promise to pay given by the issuing company to the trustee, albeit that the promise to pay will be held on trust, and the trust deed will provide the trustee with the power to take enforcement action. In such circumstances, the trustee may also be considered to be the creditor in respect of the relevant bond because the power of the 'holders' to take proceedings against the issuer is typically delegated to the trustee (who can do so in its own name and for its own account), in all but exceptional circumstances.

Of course, if an underlying bondholder has been issued with definitive certificates, then it can be regarded as the 'holder' of the bonds and may therefore be regarded as a creditor. However, doubts have been raised as to whether such a person can be regarded as a creditor before that point. One possible way in which to regard the underlying bondholders as creditors is based on the notion that they are the beneficial owners of the debt obligation held in their name. Such an approach is difficult to sustain given the nature of the beneficiary's position, and the decision of the Court of Appeal in *Re Lehman Brothers International (Europe) (in administration)*[52] discussed in section 5.2.3. This argument is therefore not a good basis for treating the underlying bondholders as creditors for scheme purposes.

51 *Re Lehman Brothers International (Europe) (in administration)* [2009] EWCA Civ 1161; [2010] 1 BCLC 496 at [58].

52 [2009] EWCA Civ 1161; [2010] 1 BCLC 496.

Another, potentially more compelling, argument is to regard the underlying bondholders as contingent creditors. On this analysis, the right to require definitive certificates to be issued is sufficient to treat them as contingent creditors of the company, even before this right is triggered, and whether or not the right is ever triggered. This solution contains some potential weaknesses. It obviously depends on the documentation providing this right, and not all will do so.[53] Furthermore, it could be argued that unless and until this right has actually been exercised by the underlying bondholders, they should not be regarded as creditors of the company. The contingent creditor argument has not been fully tested before the courts as yet, but it seems potentially problematic. A contingent debt is one that may or may not fall due in the future. Claims that are certain to accrue are future claims.[54] A contingent liability is therefore an existing legal obligation whereby the company will be liable to pay *if* a certain event materialises, such as the employee contracting asbestosis, or a court or arbitrator subsequently determining that the company is liable to pay.[55] By contrast, in the bondholder scenario, the contingency relates not to whether the liability arises but to the identity of the person who may enforce the liability. So, the future event does not determine whether or not the company will pay, merely to whom the company will make payment. The bondholder scenario therefore does not fall within the definition of contingent creditor adopted for scheme purposes to date, and utilising this approach leads to the potentially problematic situation in which two different persons (the 'holder' of the bonds in a strict sense and the ultimate beneficial owner) are simultaneously regarded as a creditor in relation to the same debt.

Despite these concerns, in recent years this contingent creditor argument has become standard practice, in order to allow the ultimate account holder to vote in the scheme directly, without holding definitive notes.[56] Whilst this approach has the benefit of avoiding the problems arising from the headcount test, it is problematic from an analytical

[53] See e.g. the occupational pension scheme trusts in *Re Equitable Life Assurance Society* [2002] BCC 319.

[54] See e.g. *Re Liberty International plc* [2010] EWHC 1060 (Ch) at [15].

[55] See e.g. *Community Development Pty Ltd* v. *Engwirda Construction Company* (1969) 120 CLR 455; *Haine* v. *Day* [2008] EWCA Civ 626.

[56] See e.g. *Re Castle Holdco 4 Ltd* [2009] EWHC 1347 (Ch); *Re Gallery Capital SA and Gallery Media Group Ltd*, unreported, 21 April 2010; *Re Magyar Telecom BV* [2013] EWHC 3800 (Ch); *Re Zlomrex International Finance SA* [2013] EWHC 3866 (Ch); *Re New World Resources NV* [2014] EWHC 3143 (Ch); *Re Lecta Paper UK Ltd* [2019] EWHC

viewpoint. The removal of the headcount test, as advocated in section 2.3.3.2, would deal with this particular problem.[57] The Law Commission is consulting on this issue, and it is to be hoped that the headcount test will be abolished, removing the need for this contingent creditor argument.[58]

5.3 The division of creditors into classes

One of the procedural requirements for a scheme is that creditors meet in classes, and when a scheme involves a complex capital structure, a number of different class meetings may be required.[59] The starting point is the classic judgment of Bowen LJ in *Sovereign Life Assurance Co* v. *Dodd*, which states that a class 'must be confined to those persons whose rights are not so dissimilar as to make it impossible for them to consult together with a view to their common interest',[60] together with the decision of Chadwick LJ in *Re Hawk Insurance Co Ltd*.[61] The courts will consider both the rights that are to be released or varied under the proposed scheme and any new rights that the scheme proposes to provide to replace those removed or varied. As discussed in section 2.3.2, it is rights and not interests that are relevant in this context[62] (although those interests can, of course, be taken into account at the sanctioning stage by the court).[63] For the purposes of class composition, the relevant 'rights'

3615 (Ch); *Re NN2 Newco Ltd* [2019] EWHC 1917 (Ch); *Re New Look Financing plc* [2020] EWHC 2793 (Ch). In Singapore see *Re Swiber Holdings Ltd* [2018] SGHC 211.

57 See also J. Payne, 'Intermediation and bondholder schemes of arrangement' and R. Salter, 'Enforcing debt securities', both in L. Gullifer and J. Payne (eds.), *Intermediation and Beyond* (Hart, 2019).

58 Law Commission, *Intermediated Securities: Call for Evidence*, August 2019, 15–17. This view is supported by City of London Law Society, Response of the Joint Working Party of the City of London Law Society Company Law, Financial Law and Regulatory Law Committees to the Law Commission's Consultation on Intermediated Securities, 8 November 2019, 9. See also Law Commission, *Intermediated Securities: Who Owns Your Shares? Scoping Paper*, November 2020, ch. 4 esp. para. 4.56.

59 The approach of the English courts to creditor class meetings is similar to that adopted in other jurisdictions. In Australia, for example, see *First Pacific Advisors LLC* v. *Boart Longyear Ltd* (2017) 320 FLR 18; [2017] NSWCA 116; *Re Boart Longyear Ltd* (2017) 121 ACSR 328; [2017] NSWSC 567. In Cayman Islands see *Re Ocean Rig UDW Incorporated* 2017 (2) CILR 495.

60 [1892] 2 QB 573 at 583.

61 [2001] EWCA Civ 241; [2001] 2 BCLC 480, discussed in detail in section 2.3.2.

62 See e.g. *Re Noble Group Ltd* [2018] EWHC 2911 (Ch); *Re Stripes US Holdings Inc* [2018] EWHC 2912 (Ch).

63 See section 2.4.2.

are the rights of the legal owner of the relevant claim.[64] The courts are keen to avoid giving undue veto rights to minorities, and therefore take a practical, common-sense view of this issue since 'if one gets too picky about potential different classes, one could end up with virtually as many classes as there are members of a particular group'.[65] As David Richards J said in *Re Telewest Communications plc (No. 1)*,[66] class composition is a matter of judgment on the facts of each case, but 'a broad approach is taken and . . . differences may be material, certainly more than de minimis, without leading to separate classes'.[67]

This issue is often more important in the context of creditor schemes than member schemes, since creditors generally have a greater freedom to bargain for a range of rights that are distinct (potentially in relatively minor ways) from those of other creditors. The rights of members tend to be more uniform. A good example of the common-sense approach that the courts have adopted in relation to de minimis differences between creditor rights can be seen in the McCarthy & Stone plc scheme in which one potential class consisted of the senior term-loan holders, who were all secured lenders under term loans.[68] They each held guaranteed liabilities. They shared *pari passu* in all realisations and recoveries, by virtue of an intercreditor agreement. Under the proposed schemes, they were each to acquire the same rights proportionate to their lendings to the companies. However, there were minor differences in the rates of interest payable under the facilities. The judge viewed the interest rate differences as so small in the context of the outstanding indebtedness that the senior term-loan holders could consult together with a view to a consideration of their common interest.[69]

[64] See e.g. *Re Lehman Bros International (Europe) Ltd* [2018] EWHC 1980 (Ch). Consequently, the fact that the legal owner of the claim may be required to vote in accordance with the instructions of a third party (e.g. a beneficial owner or sub-participant) is not relevant to class composition: see *Re Abbey National Plc* [2004] EWHC 2776 (Ch). The involvement of such third parties may, however, be relevant in assessing the fairness of the scheme at the sanction hearing.

[65] *Re Anglo American Insurance Co Ltd* [2001] 1 BCLC 755, 764 *per* Neuberger J.

[66] [2004] BCC 342 at [37].

[67] See also Hildyard J in *Re Lehman Bros International (Europe) Ltd* [2018] EWHC 1980 (Ch) at [70] and *Re Codere Finance 2 (UK) Ltd* [2020] EWHC 2441 (Ch).

[68] McCarthy & Stone plc, scheme of arrangement (and pre-pack administration) (2009). See also the discussion at section 5.3.3.

[69] *Re McCarthy & Stone plc* [2009] EWHC 1116 (Ch). See also *Re Primacom Holdings GmbH* [2011] EWHC 3746 (Ch) and *Re Lecta Paper UK Ltd* [2019] EWHC 3615 (Ch). Note, however, that in these cases insolvency was used as the correct comparator; where

In order to determine the difference that the proposed scheme of arrangement would make to the rights of the claimants, it is necessary to determine the correct comparator.[70] If the company is insolvent at the time, the starting point will be the rights of those creditors on a winding-up. However, where the company is solvent, the rights of creditors on insolvency might not be an accurate comparator.[71] Matters may not always be straightforward, however, especially where the alternative to the scheme is unclear. In such circumstances the courts have adopted a pragmatic approach. In *Re Co-Operative Bank Plc*,[72] for example, Hildyard J stated that it was not necessary to be certain that an insolvent liquidation would be the outcome, absent the scheme; it was enough that the consideration by scheme creditors would be informed by the very real risk of insolvency. In *Re Stronghold Insurance Company Limited*,[73] in the face of the company's marginal solvency, the court struggled to ascertain the relevant comparator (solvent liquidation, insolvent liquidation or continued solvent run-off). Hildyard J ultimately looked at the position in the 'near to mid-term' and assessed the correct comparator as a continued solvent run-off, albeit with a risk of liquidation in the future.

The situation in relation to restructuring the debts of financially distressed companies may well be a little ambiguous. They may be cash-flow insolvent, but if they are economically viable, an argument could be made that the correct comparator is not the rights of creditors in a winding-up but rather the rights of creditors in a rescue scenario, which would involve a higher going-concern valuation for the company. From the court's point of view, it will be important to receive detailed evidence to support whichever comparator the company is putting forward.[74]

When defining classes at the convening stage, the focus of the court is on a comparison of the existing rights of the creditors which would be altered or extinguished by the scheme, and the new rights to which they would become entitled, bearing in mind the relevant comparator as described above. Consequently, it will generally be the case that creditors with different rights prior to the scheme, for example different levels of

a different comparator is used (e.g. a solvent run-off as in *Re British Aviation Insurance Co Ltd* [2005] EWHC 1621 (Ch); [2006] BCC 14) then the outcome may well be different.

70 See section 2.3.2.2.

71 See e.g. *Re British and Commonwealth Holdings Plc (No. 3)* [1992] 1 WLR 672.

72 [2013] EWHC 4072 (Ch) at [11]–[13].

73 *Re Stronghold Insurance Company Limited* [2018] EWHC 2909 (Ch).

74 See e.g. *Re Lecta Paper UK Ltd* [2019] EWHC 3615 (Ch) at [13].

seniority, will constitute different classes. So, for example, senior secured creditors might form one class, unsecured creditors another class and subordinated creditors a third class. The importance ascribed to differences in the nature of the rights held by creditors is likely to vary according to the seniority of the debt and the comparator chosen. In *Hawk Insurance*, where the comparator applied was liquidation, all of the unsecured creditors were treated as comprising the same class, despite differences in the nature of the rights held.[75]

A number of issues arise for discussion in this context, many of which are similar to those that arise in defining classes for the purpose of member schemes.[76]

5.3.1 *Lock-up agreements and the payment of fees*

Just as bidders might seek irrevocable undertakings from shareholders in the target in advance of a bid, lock-up agreements are sometimes entered into between creditors and the company in advance of the scheme meeting for which the creditor will generally be paid a fee, in order to provide some comfort for the company about the likely outcome of the meeting. This was not an issue that existed when the scheme legislation was first drafted, and the courts have needed to respond to the development of this area by companies and their advisors. This is an area which has received judicial attention in recent years, with judges demonstrating an increasing willingness to scrutinise lock-up arrangements, benefits and structures.[77] Snowden J in *Re Sunbird Business Services Ltd* noted: 'The widespread use of lock-up agreements in recent years is . . . not without difficulties. The payment of such fees has been accepted in a number of cases at first instance, but serious concerns remain.'[78]

The courts are becoming increasingly focused on two issues: whether payment of such fees could result in separate classes,[79] and the provision of timely, adequate and appropriate information to creditors. Further,

[75] A similar approach has been adopted in other jurisdictions; see e.g. *Re Kaisa Group Holdings Ltd* [2017] HKLRD 18 (Hong Kong); *First Pacific Advisors LLC* v. *Boart Longyear Ltd* [2017] NSWCA 116 (Australia). The courts have, however, counselled against following this approach in an inflexible manner: *Re Noble Group Ltd* [2018] EWHC 2911 (Ch) *per* Snowden J at [90].

[76] See section 3.5.

[77] See e.g. *Re Sunbird Business Services Ltd* [2020] EWHC 2493 (Ch); *Re Codere Finance 2 (UK) Ltd* [2020] EWHC 2441 (Ch).

[78] [2020] EWHC 2493 (Ch) at [115].

[79] For the equivalent discussion in the context of takeover schemes see section 3.5.2.4.

there should not be unequal information provision to different groups of creditors; there is a danger of mismatched and even inconsistent information provision to creditors, particularly where creditors bind themselves to a lock-up arrangement at different times, when different information is available.[80]

The mere fact that a lock-up agreement has been put in place will not of itself operate to fracture a class of creditors.[81] The courts will consider all of the circumstances surrounding that lock-up in determining whether it impacts on the issue of separate classes. In particular, the existence and nature of any consent fee paid under the lock-up agreement will be considered. In general, the courts have been prepared to take the view that 'the simple fact that a benefit was conferred in return for agreement to vote in favour of the scheme'[82] is not sufficient to require the relevant parties to be placed in a separate class. In reaching this conclusion, three factors are particularly relevant: whether the offer to enter into a lock-up agreement has been extended to all scheme creditors, the size of the payment, and whether the payment is likely to have impacted on the way that the creditors voted at the scheme meetings. In *Seat Pagine*, for example, David Richards J concluded that there was no requirement to constitute separate classes owing to the facts that the offer was extended to all scheme creditors, the level of the payment was relatively small (1 per cent) and there was no evidence that the payment would have a serious impact on the way a creditor voted.[83]

In practice, the second and third of these factors amount to much the same issue: was the size of the fee such that it is likely to impact on the way a creditor will vote? This question, together with whether the fee is offered to all creditors of a class, tends to be the focus for the courts.[84] As

[80] *Re Sunbird Business Services Ltd* [2020] EWHC 2493 (Ch) at [116]–[119]. The 'paucity of information' provided by the company to the creditors ahead of the creditor vote was a key reason for the refusal of the judge to sanction the scheme in this case.

[81] *Re Telewest Communications plc (No. 1)* [2004] EWHC 924 (Ch) at [53]. A similar approach is adopted in other jurisdictions, e.g. *Re Ocean Rig UDW Incorporated* 2017 (2) CILR 495 (Cayman Islands); *Re Winsway Enterprises Holdings Ltd* [2016] HKCFI 1915 (Hong Kong).

[82] *Re Seat Pagine Gialle SpA* [2012] EWHC 3686 (Ch) at [22].

[83] See also *Re DX Holdings Ltd* [2010] EWHC 1513 (Ch); *Re Primacom Holdings GmbH* [2011] EWHC 3746 (Ch); *Assénagon Asset Management SA* v. *Irish Bank Resolution Corporation Ltd* [2012] EWHC 2090 (Ch); *Re Lecta Paper UK Ltd* [2019] 3615 (Ch); *Re New Look Secured Issuer plc* [2019] EWHC 960 (Ch). See also *Re Winsway Enterprises Ltd* [2016] HKCFI 1915; *Re Kaisa Group Holdings Ltd* [2017] HKLRD 18; *Re Ocean Rig UDW Incorporated* 2017 (2) CILR 495.

[84] See e.g. *Re Stripes US Holdings Inc* [2018] EWHC 2912 (Ch); *Re Noble Group Ltd* [2018] EWHC 2911 (Ch).

between these two factors, the likely impact on the creditor vote is the more important. In *Primacom*, for example, Hildyard J regarded the fact that the fee was offered to all scheme creditors as relatively less important than the issue of whether the fee had a serious impact on the way in which creditors voted.[85] Snowden J in *Re Noble* seems to have taken a similar view:

> For my part, I think that in a case in which any form of fees are offered to some, but not all scheme creditors contingently on the scheme being sanctioned, the Court will inevitably have to form a view about the materiality of the fees when judging whether the rights of the creditors who will not be paid the fees are sufficiently dissimilar that they cannot consult together with a view to their common interest with those who will be paid the fees. Put simply, if the fees are immaterial to the decision, then the creditors can consult together: if they are material, then they probably cannot.[86]

Since the overriding question, so far as the amount of the fee is concerned, is whether it is likely to influence voting intentions, the proportion it bears to the face value of the scheme debt will often be of little importance.[87] The extent of any consent fee should be measured against what scheme creditors will 'receive' under the scheme. Of relevance is likely to be the proportion the fee bears to the value of the scheme consideration and the returns that creditors are likely to make if the scheme does not go ahead (for example in a liquidation, if that is the appropriate comparator).[88] Furthermore, where the fees are being offered in return for financial support or other financial accommodation or risk, as opposed to simply being offered in exchange for an agreement to support the restructuring, evidence as to whether the fee includes an element of bounty or is in line with market rates may also be relevant.[89] The timing of the offer may also be important.[90]

In *Re Codere Finance 2 (UK) Ltd*,[91] Falk J considered the relevance of the lock-up arrangements being conditional on the success of the scheme:

[85] *Re Primacom Holdings GmbH* [2011] EWHC 3746 (Ch) at [57].
[86] *Re Noble Group Ltd* [2018] EWHC 2911 (Ch) at [149].
[87] See e.g. *Re ColourOz Investment 2 LLC* [2020] EWHC 1864 (Ch).
[88] *Re Stripes US Holdings Inc* [2018] EWHC 2912 (Ch) at [19]; *Re Noble Group Ltd* [2018] EWHC 2911 (Ch) at [151]. It may also be relevant to consider the proportion the fee bears to the real (trading) value of the scheme debt.
[89] *Re Noble Group Ltd* [2018] EWHC 2911 (Ch) at [151].
[90] *Re Stripes US Holdings Inc* [2018] EWHC 2912 (Ch) at [20].
[91] [2020] EWHC 2441 (Ch).

> I have real doubt that the court should, in determining class composition, leave out of account rights conferred by lock-up agreements simply because they are not conditional on the scheme being implemented. This is particularly so where the parties to the agreement have framed the terms of the agreement in such a way as to confer those rights only in circumstances where it can reasonably be inferred that the parties considered that there is a strong likelihood of the scheme being implemented . . ..
>
> If any such rights could always be ignored, then it would be open to a body of creditors to negotiate clearly preferential rights in their favour but ensure that they are excluded from class composition considerations by making them technically not conditional on the scheme being implemented, even though as a commercial matter they are part of the same transaction and, in reality, are highly unlikely to be conferred unless the scheme proceeds.[92]

Even if the classes are not fractured as a result of the existence of lock-up arrangements, it is possible for the court to take account of this issue at the sanctioning stage.[93] So the court may consider at the sanctioning hearing whether the votes of those in receipt of consent fees are not representative of the class, on the basis that these voters are actuated by the consent fees to override the interests of those other persons participating in the meeting.[94]

The effect of the payment of fees on the question of creditor classes is, however, broader than simply those offered in return for a lock-up arrangement.[95] It is an increasingly common feature of restructuring practice for a group of larger or more active creditors of a company in financial difficulty to band together and to approach the debtor company to negotiate a restructuring.[96] This group may provide a focal point for negotiations between the company and creditors generally, and may also arrange interim financial support for the distressed company. It is common for such a group to demand and receive a variety of payments during the process of negotiation. As Snowden J noted in *Re Noble Group Ltd*:

> Any payments to a limited group of creditors in connection with a restructuring can have a potential impact both upon the class question

[92] Ibid. at [51]–[52].
[93] See section 2.4.
[94] See e.g. *Re Apcoa Parking Holdings GmbH* [2014] EWHC 3849 (Ch); *Re Lehman Brothers International (Europe) Ltd* [2018] EWHC 1980 (Ch).
[95] See e.g. *Re Noble Group Ltd* [2018] EWHC 2911 (Ch).
[96] See e.g. *Re NN2 Newco Ltd* [2019] EWHC 1917 (Ch).

> and upon the question at the sanction hearing of whether, to the extent that the recipients of such payments make up the majority voting in favour of the scheme, they are really representative of the interests of the wider class of creditors as a whole.[97]

Where several different kinds of fees are being offered in a restructuring, these fees need to be considered not only individually but also as a whole when determining their likely effect on the outcome of the voting intentions of the creditors. This is relevant both to the issue of the overall size of the fees, where the totality of the fees needs to be considered 'rather than simply dismissing each category of fees seriatim as de minimis',[98] and to the consideration of what, cumulatively, any particular creditor stands to gain from the scheme (or the wider restructuring) and the extent to which that is different from the benefits available to the general body of creditors.[99]

The courts have divided the discussion of fees into two broad categories, although variations are possible:[100] those that do not form part of the consideration paid under the scheme, and those do. The first category includes fees paid by the company to some creditors independently of a proposed scheme and its associated restructuring agreements and which are not dependent on the scheme taking effect. An example of this would be 'work fees' which are sometimes described as 'commercial fees' paid in return for the members of the ad hoc group committing their time and resources to negotiations with the company.[101] Fees in this category, which are not dependent on the scheme taking effect, do not need to be taken into account for class purposes. Key concerns for the courts appear to be whether the fees are proportionate, commercially justifiable and fully disclosed. Courts need to be alert to the attempted use of this category as a disguise for payments that more properly belong in

97 [2018] EWHC 2911 (Ch) at [111].
98 Ibid. at [128] *per* Snowden J.
99 Ibid. at [129].
100 See e.g. *Re NN2 Newco Ltd* [2019] EWHC 1917 (Ch) in which a lock-up fee was paid to members of an ad hoc group by a creditor of the company (rather than the company itself), conditional upon the scheme receiving sanction and being implemented (but not dependent upon how the particular member of the ad hoc group voted). This fee was held not to fracture the class on the basis that there was 'a commercial reward for detriment suffered by the ad hoc group that was not suffered by other scheme participants' (at [46]). Furthermore, it was not disproportionate, it was fully disclosed and, on an objective view, the fee was not material to a decision whether to support the scheme.
101 In *Re NN2 Newco Ltd* [2019] EWHC 1917 (Ch) the judge also noted the detriment suffered by the ad hoc group by becoming the recipients of 'insider' information such that they thereby disabled themselves from dealing with their holdings.

the next category. Courts will therefore wish to ensure that the payments are made for legitimate reasons, are genuinely independent of the scheme and restructuring, and do not amount to a disguised part of the consideration offered under the scheme and restructuring.

The second category contains fees that are part of the consideration paid under the scheme, in which case the analysis of whether those in receipt of the fees need to comprise a separate class follows similar lines to those considered in relation to the fees paid for lock-up agreements. Given that these fees tend to be offered only to a subset of creditors, the predominant concern is the likelihood that these fees will impact on voting intentions. The court will have to form a view about the materiality of the fees when judging whether the rights of creditors who were not paid the fees were sufficiently dissimilar to those who were paid the fees that they could not consult together with a view to their common interest. Thus, if the fees were immaterial to the decision of a creditor to support the scheme, the creditors could consult together; but if they were material, then they probably could not. In evaluating whether the fees were material to a creditor's decision, the court will take account of the same issues as discussed in relation to lock-up agreements. Again, these are issues that can be revisited at the sanctioning hearing if necessary. The court may therefore examine the numbers of those not in receipt of a fee who voted in favour of the scheme, as part of the decision whether to sanction the scheme.[102]

This is an area where the importance of adequate information for the court is particularly clear. The courts have increasingly shown themselves to be willing to challenge the 'bare assertions in the evidence'[103] provided to them and to require more information as necessary. This is vital in order for the courts to make a proper assessment of these issues.

5.3.2 *Creditors in more than one class*

The second issue, which also arises in relation to takeover schemes, is the position of persons that find themselves in more than one class.[104] Creditors with different interests, which might potentially conflict with the interests of the other members of the class, are allowed to attend and

[102] See e.g. *Re NN2 Newco Ltd* [2019] EWHC 2494 (Ch) [17]–[18].

[103] See *Re Indah Kiat International Finance Company BV* [2016] EWHC 246 (Ch) at [40], discussed at section 2.2.3.

[104] For the discussion in the takeover context see section 3.5.2.2. See e.g. *Re Heron International NV* [1994] 1 BCLC 667.

vote at the class meeting. Their separate interest will not give rise to a separate class and their presence will not invalidate the decision of the meeting.[105] Similarly, those that are both shareholders and creditors will not generally form a different class.[106] Again, however, the court can take account of their distinct interests at the sanctioning hearing, in determining whether it is appropriate to sanction the scheme.[107]

5.3.3 *Creditors who are treated differently under the scheme*

Even where the rights of a creditor are the same as other creditors before the scheme, different treatment within the scheme may require that creditor to be placed in a separate class. For example, in *Re Noble Group Ltd*,[108] one of the creditors, Deutsche Bank, was treated materially differently and more favourably than other creditors within the scheme. One part of Deutsche Bank's claim against the company, the 'DB Excluded Claim', would be released in return for the issue of senior notes that would be issued to Deutsche Bank alone. Consequently, Snowden J took the view that there were two linked arrangements under the scheme – one between the company and Deutsche Bank, and the other between the company and the remainder of the scheme creditors – and that it would be impossible for Deutsche Bank to have a discussion as to its common interest with the remaining scheme creditors regarding these arrangements. As a result, Deutsche Bank was placed in a separate class.

However, the differential impact of the scheme on creditors will not always give rise to separate classes.[109] In *Re Noble Group Ltd*,[110] for example, Snowden J considered the effect of a stated bar date and adjudication procedure on different creditors. The bar date and

[105] See e.g. *Re NEF Telecom Company BV* [2012] EWHC 2944 (Comm); *Re Stripes US Holdings Inc* [2018] EWHC 2912 (Ch); *Re Syncreon Group BV* [2019] EWHC 2068 (Ch); *Re New Look Secured Issuer plc* [2019] EWHC 960 (Ch); *Re Lehman Bros International (Europe) Ltd* [2018] EWHC 1980 (Ch); *Re ColourOz Investment 2 LLC* [2020] EWHC 1864 (Ch) at [88].

[106] See e.g. *Re Landmark Corporation Ltd* [1968] 1 NSWLR 759; *Re Metrovacesa SA* [2011] EWHC 1014 (Ch).

[107] *Re Alabama, New Orleans, Texas & Pacific Junction Railway Co* [1891] 1 Ch 213; *Re Lehman Bros International (Europe) Ltd* [2018] EWHC 1980 (Ch).

[108] For an example see *Re Noble Group Ltd* [2018] EWHC 2911 (Ch) at [92]–[94].

[109] This is also the approach adopted elsewhere, see e.g. *Re Kaisa Group Holdings Ltd* [2017] HKLRD 18.

[110] [2018] EWHC 2911 (Ch).

procedure were the same for all creditors that the company sought to place within a single class, but the nature of the creditors (and therefore the nature of their claims against the company) was quite different. Some were finance creditors, whose claims were unlikely to be the subject of any dispute, whereas the claims of other creditors arose in contract and tort and were strongly contested by the company. In this case, the appropriate comparator was taken to be a winding-up so that the claims of all creditors of the proposed class would all rank equally and be subject to the same procedure for proof of debts, no matter how they had arisen. Although there would be greater uncertainty of outcome for some of the creditors as a result of being required to undergo the process set out in the scheme to establish their claims, Snowden J accepted that this did not constitute a difference of existing rights against the company or rights conferred under the scheme. However, as he rightly noted, use of a different comparator would potentially change this outcome.[111]

Rather more difficult was the question of whether an offer to 'risk participate' via the payment of new money, which had been made to all creditors that the company sought to place in a single class, nevertheless impacted differentially on different kinds of creditors such that they should be placed in different classes. Whereas the finance creditors were already in a relationship with the company under which they had voluntarily extended credit to it, other creditors, particularly those whose claims against the company arose involuntarily, did not have financial accommodation as part of their core business and would be very unlikely to wish to take up the offer to risk participate. Consequently, it could be said that this latter group were being offered a 'separate deal' by the company.[112] Snowden J concluded that the reasons why some of the scheme creditors might be very reluctant or even unable to elect to risk participate ultimately related to their individual circumstances and commercial interests rather than their rights and were not therefore a reason to fracture the class. The difficulty with this approach is that the inability of certain creditors to participate may go beyond their interests (their willingness or appetite for accepting the offer to risk participate) and relate instead to the nature of the offer made to them; if the offer to them is effectively illusory, then it might be more appropriate to regard this as

[111] *Re Sovereign Marine & General Insurance Co Ltd* [2006] EWHC 1335 (Ch); *Re Stronghold Insurance Company Limited* [2018] EWHC 2909 (Ch).

[112] [2018] EWHC 2911 (Ch) at [101].

a difference in the rights that are being offered to the creditors such that the class should be fractured.

5.3.4 *Class meetings and 'empty creditors'*

The assumption behind the requirement that a majority of each class should approve a scheme is that the voting rights held by a creditor or member are coupled with an economic stake in the company, so that the member's right to vote is coupled to a right to receive dividends, and the creditor's right to vote is linked to the debt holders' contractual rights to receive interest and principal. However, this will not always be the case.[113] Members may hold a right to vote, but might have no economic exposure to the company (for example by hedging their risk) or, if they take a significant short position in the company's securities, might even result in a negative exposure to the company, so that the member might actually be better off if the company fails (this is termed 'empty voting'). Similarly, creditors might decouple their control rights from their economic exposure to the company, for example by buying credit derivatives (such creditors are termed 'empty creditors'). As a result, creditors that appear to have the same rights, and would therefore be placed in the same class for the purposes of considering and approving a scheme of arrangement, may nevertheless have different interests that might affect how they decide to vote in that class meeting. If a creditor has purchased enough credit derivatives to have a negative exposure to the company (i.e. that creditor will be better off if the company fails), the creditor could vote against the scheme in order to try to secure this outcome.

Judges can take account of different interests held by members or creditors of the same class at the sanctioning stage. This potentially works well where this difference in interest involves members or creditors using their position to vote through a scheme that is contrary to the interests of the class as a whole. Here, the position is different, however, and involves the members and/or creditors using their position to vote

[113] H. Hu and B. Black, 'The new vote buying: empty voting and hidden ownership' (2006) 79 *Southern California Law Review* 811–908; H. Hu and B. Black, 'Hedge funds, insiders and the decoupling of economic and voting ownership: empty voting and hidden (morphable) ownership' (2007) 13 *Journal of Corporate Finance* 343–67; H. Hu and B. Black, 'Equity and debt decoupling and empty voting II: importance and extensions' (2008) 126 *University of Pennsylvania Law Review* 625–739; H. Hu and B. Black, 'Debt, equity and hybrid decoupling: governance and systemic risk implications' (2008) 14 *European Financial Management* 663–709.

against a scheme. This is rather more difficult to tackle, since the court has no power to sanction a scheme that has not been approved by every class.[114] This issue arose for consideration in relation to member schemes in *Re Dee Valley Group plc*,[115] in which the English court was asked to consider the validity of splitting shareholdings in order to defeat the headcount test in a scheme designed to effect a takeover.[116] The board obtained a direction of the court to allow the chairman of the court-appointed meeting to ignore the transferred shares in circumstances where the split votes would have meant that the headcount test would not be satisfied and the scheme would thus fail. On the facts, the court held that the chairperson had sufficient evidence to conclude that the only explanation for the conduct of certain shareholders was that they were furthering a share manipulation strategy to defeat the scheme and it was therefore proper for him to reject those votes. This inventive approach has the merit of dealing with the problem of share splitting, but is unsatisfactory in a number of ways, not least because it creates a test that is likely to be difficult to apply on facts less stark than those in *Dee Valley*.[117] In relation to the issues raised in this section, disclosure of these kinds of scenario, where creditors decouple their voting interest from their economic exposure to the company, is not common, and therefore it might be very difficult for the company or other creditors to discover these interests in order to be able to raise these concerns with the court.

5.4 The use of schemes as a debt restructuring tool

Debt restructuring is a process that allows a company facing cash-flow problems and financial distress to reduce and renegotiate its delinquent debts, in order to improve or restore liquidity and rehabilitate it so that it can continue its operations, possibly with a view to selling the company or its business.[118] Rehabilitation of this kind will often be preferable to

114 This may be compared with the position in relation to Part 26A restructuring plans, discussed in section 5.8.

115 *Re Dee Valley Group plc* [2017] EWHC 184 (Ch).

116 Discussed further at section 2.3.3.2.2.1.

117 See section 2.3.3.2.2.1.

118 A sale of the business to a new owner in an auction process will not always be possible or desirable, however, especially in times of financial crisis, where markets are illiquid, leading to a loss of value if assets are sold at 'fire sale' prices or, worse, if sales can occur only on a break-up basis. See e.g. A. Shleifer and R. Vishny, 'Liquidation values and debt capacity: a market equilibrium approach' (1992) 42 *Journal of Finance* 1343. There may

liquidation and dissolution. This, of course, presupposes that the company is not economically distressed but merely financially distressed, that is, it is cash-flow insolvent but nevertheless economically viable: there is a business that is worth saving, either within the present company or in a new entity.[119] Where the company is economically distressed (so the net present worth of the business as a going concern is less than the total value of its assets, were they to be broken up and sold separately), liquidation may be the only sensible option.[120] A restructuring of the company's debts can be good for the company, allowing it to return to its business activities once liberated from its debt burden, but it can also be beneficial for creditors and other stakeholders in the company if it allows a company to continue and flourish rather than fail. It is not a coincidence that since the 2008 global financial crisis there has been a renewed focus worldwide on reforming the law in order to promote more effective restructuring options for distressed but viable companies, and the Covid-19 pandemic has added further impetus to these reform plans.

To take a simplified hypothetical example, a company, A Ltd, is financially distressed, with its economic performance below that forecast in its business plan. It has just two types of debt: senior debt and (contractually subordinated) junior debt.[121] The company is unable to meet forthcoming payments on its senior debt and cannot afford to pay the interest on its junior debt. The company is cash-flow positive at an operating level, i.e. there is a business worth saving, but the original business plan was too optimistic and the company has no chance of ever being able to repay all of its senior and junior debt. The creditors could wait for an event of default, then accelerate their debt and push the company into liquidation, but it will generally be preferable for the

also be other reasons why sales will not be possible, such as where the transfer of crucial assets to a new entity is not feasible. Outside these scenarios, sales can have some advantages over restructuring as they avoid the need for potentially costly bargaining between the company and its stakeholders.

119 For a discussion of the distinction between financial and economic distress see D. G. Baird, 'Bankruptcy's uncontested axioms' (1998) 108 *Yale Law Journal* 573.

120 See section 6.3 for a discussion of the use of schemes as an alternative to, or alongside, liquidation.

121 This subordination can be structural or contractual. It is now settled that a creditor can agree to subordinate its claims against a debtor to those of some or all of the other creditors of the debtor (*In re SSSL Realisations (2002) Ltd (in liquidation)* [2006] EWCA Civ 7; [2006] Ch 610), and that this can be done either expressly or impliedly (see e.g. *Cattles plc* v. *Welcome Financial Services Ltd* [2010] EWCA Civ 599; [2010] 2 BCLC 712).

company and its directors to keep the company, or at least the business, going if possible. It may also be preferable for creditors, at least those creditors judged to be still 'in the money' (i.e. those whose claim against the company is still deemed to have some value), to support some form of restructuring and reorganisation. Various forms of restructuring may be used to deal with these difficulties. The most common involve the postponement of imminent liabilities into the more distant future; the conversion of fixed liabilities for more fluid ones, for example a debt-for-equity swap; and debt write-downs whereby all creditors of a particular type agree a pro rata reduction in the value of their claims.

In order for a debt restructuring mechanism to be effective, there are a number of components that are likely to be valuable: (i) the ability to tackle the financial distress at an early stage; (ii) leaving the directors in control of the company; (iii) the ability to impose the restructuring on dissenting creditors; (iv) access to some form of stay while the restructuring is negotiated; and (v) access to financing while the restructuring is negotiated and then implemented.[122] The remainder of this section will assess the extent to which these components are satisfied in a scheme of arrangement.

5.4.1 *The ability to tackle financial distress at an early stage*

It will generally be advantageous to a company if its financial difficulties can be tackled at an early stage, as this will maximise the opportunity to avoid liquidation. Placing a debt restructuring mechanism in insolvency law, for example, and making insolvency a precondition for access to the mechanism, will reduce the capacity for early intervention.[123] Schemes of arrangement can be utilised whether the company is solvent or insolvent.[124] In common with contractual workouts, CVAs and restructuring plans,

[122] See J. Payne, 'Debt restructuring in English law: lessons from the US and the need for reform' (2014) *Law Quarterly Review* 282; J. Payne and J. Sarra, 'Tripping the light fantastic: a comparative analysis of the European Commission's proposals for new and interim financing of insolvent businesses' (2018) *International Insolvency Review* 178.

[123] In Australia, for example, schemes of arrangement (see s. 411 of the Australian Corporations Act 2001) may be contrasted with deeds of arrangement (see Part 5.3A of the Australian Corporations Act 2001). While companies must enter administration before they can make use of a deed of company arrangement, no such requirement exists for creditor schemes of arrangement, and creditor schemes are increasingly being used for high-value debt restructuring arrangements; see e.g. *Re BIS Finance Pty Ltd* [2017] NSWSC 1713.

[124] See e.g. *Scottish Lion Insurance Co Ltd* v. *Goodrich Corp* [2010] CSIH 6.

insolvency is not a precondition for schemes (and, unlike restructuring plans, there is no requirement of financial distress). Furthermore, by appearing in companies legislation (the Companies Act 2006) rather than insolvency legislation, it may be that a scheme of arrangement can avoid the stigma that can attach to an insolvency mechanism.

5.4.2 *Leaving the directors in control*

Having the directors remain in control of the company during the restructuring process can be valuable, at least where the company's financial distress is not a result of the directors' incompetence or wrongdoing. This is because the directors know the company and its creditors well and are thus best placed to negotiate the change in contractual arrangements. Furthermore, a fear of being sidelined by an external manager might dissuade directors from seeking a rescue option; leaving them in control can therefore operate as an incentive for the directors to tackle the company's difficulties via a restructuring. Schemes of arrangement do leave the directors in control; in common with contractual workouts, CVAs and restructuring plans, there is no displacement of directors. This is in contrast to the position with administration.

5.4.3 *Imposing the restructuring on dissenting creditors*

Creditors can, of course, agree to alter their contractual bargain with the company via a contractual workout. However, as discussed in section 5.5, it is easy for a contractual workout to be disrupted by the actions of one or more creditors, even, potentially, a single creditor holding a very small amount of the company's debt. This can be done either through the creditor refusing its consent, in order to extract additional value from the company (the exercise of hold-up rights), or by the creditor seeking to enforce its debt while the restructuring is being negotiated, and potentially petitioning for the company to be wound up if the debt remains unpaid. These forms of behaviour can allow individual creditors to delay or even prevent the successful agreement of a contractual workout. This may well be value destructive for the company concerned, and may have an effect on the availability and cost of capital for a company *ex ante*. Furthermore, a process of prolonged informal negotiation, while the debtor seeks to satisfy the requirements of all creditors, can be disadvantageous, and may be completely impractical if the debtor is facing an acute liquidity crisis.[125] The law can therefore intervene in order to promote an agreement between the parties. The two most obvious ways for the company to do this are by enabling the restructuring to be imposed on dissenting creditors, discussed in this section, and by imposing some form of moratorium, discussed at section 5.4.4. Of course, the introduction of these legal constraints on the ability of creditors to make use of their contractual rights raises concerns about the possibility of abuse and the law must therefore find ways to deal with these concerns.

Dissenting creditors can be bound by a restructuring in a number of different ways. For instance, the restructuring could be imposed on certain types of creditors (e.g. unsecured creditors) but not others (e.g. secured creditors); it could be imposed on the dissenting creditors of a particular class if the majority of that class consents; or it could be imposed on whole classes of dissenting creditors or shareholders in some circumstances.

A scheme of arrangement allows for a limited form of 'cramdown' of dissenting creditors. Any kind of shareholder and creditor can potentially be crammed down, including secured creditors, and the majority of a class within a scheme can bind the minority within that class. However, as discussed in Chapter 2, the court cannot sanction a scheme unless all of the classes have agreed to it.[126] This is a broader form of 'cramdown' than is available using a CVA or administration,[127] but it is less extensive than the full cross-class cramdown seen elsewhere, such as in US Chapter 11,[128] in the reformed Singaporean scheme of arrangement[129] or, now, in a Part 26A restructuring plan.[130] Under a cross-class cramdown, a restructuring can go ahead despite the dissent of one or more classes of dissenting members or creditors if certain conditions are fulfilled. The value of this can be appreciated if the hypothetical example of A Ltd set out above is considered. Assume that the company is deeply indebted, that the relevant comparator is liquidation and that the junior creditors form a single class. If a single junior creditor attempts to exercise their hold-up rights, then, providing the

[125] S. Chatterjee, U. S. Dhillon and G. G. Ramirez, 'Resolution of financial distress: debt restructurings' (1996) 25 *Financial Management* 5.

[126] Companies Act 2006, s. 899 as discussed at section 2.4.

[127] See sections 5.6.1 and 5.7.2.5.

[128] 11 USC § 1129(b), discussed further at section 5.8.1.1.

[129] Singapore Insolvency, Restructuring and Dissolution Act 2018, s. 70, discussed further at section 5.8.1.3.

[130] See section 5.8.

majority of the junior creditors are in favour, the scheme can go ahead. However, if the majority of the junior creditors resist the plan, then, under a scheme alone, the restructuring will fail. This will be particularly problematic where the value of the company breaks in the senior debt such that the junior creditors are out of the money.[131]

Practitioners have tackled this problem by developing the use of schemes twinned with administration, usually a pre-pack administration, in order to achieve a de facto cramdown of a whole class, such as the junior creditors in the above example. When a scheme is twinned with a pre-pack administration, the scheme is used to novate all or a substantial amount of the debt owed to senior creditors to a newco. Once the scheme has been sanctioned, all or part of the company's assets and business is sold to newco via a pre-pack administration sale, leaving the debt owed to junior creditors behind in the original company.[132]

This kind of restructuring was first proposed in the MyTravel Group plc restructuring in 2004.[133] The group had a huge and unsupportable level of debt. Attempts were made to reach a consensual arrangement between the company and its creditors, but these attempts failed: the bondholders objected to the allocation that they would receive in the proposed workout. Instead, the company proposed a scheme under which the senior debt would be restructured and the business and assets of MyTravel would be sold to a newco owned by the senior lenders, leaving the junior creditors behind in the old company with their claims intact, but essentially worth nothing, since all of the assets had been transferred to newco. The alternative was liquidation under which the bondholders would get nothing.

Crucially, the bondholders were not party to this scheme. It is an important and valuable aspect of schemes that companies do not need

[131] See e.g. *Re MyTravel Group plc* [2004] EWCA Civ 1734.

[132] In some circumstances the use of this structure may depend on the terms of any intercreditor agreement. This will be particularly relevant where the junior creditors have the benefit of security and guarantees. The senior creditors will need to be able to bypass the junior creditors and dispose of the main operating companies free from junior borrowing and guarantee liabilities, and will look to the terms of the intercreditor agreement to provide them with these rights. Ideally, from the senior creditors' perspective, the intercreditor agreement will give them the ability to direct the security trustee on the enforcement of security and the release of existing guarantees, to allow the assets to be sold to a newco.

[133] [2004] EWHC 2741 (Ch); [2005] 1 WLR 2365; [2004] EWCA Civ 1734; [2005] 2 BCLC 123, CA.

to deal with all of their creditors in a scheme.[134] In particular, creditors can be excluded from a scheme where their rights are unaffected by the scheme.[135] In this way, schemes are distinct from the collective process that is observed in mechanisms such as UK administration, US Chapter 11 or Australian deed of company arrangements in which all creditors must be included.[136] It was argued in *MyTravel* that the bondholders' rights were not affected as their claims against oldco before and after the scheme were unchanged. The Court of Appeal agreed with this analysis and the bondholders could be excluded from the scheme on this basis, but the court also confirmed that the bondholders could attend the sanctioning hearing to challenge the scheme on fairness grounds: the bondholders argued that while the scheme might not technically alter their contractual rights against oldco, the transfer of the assets from oldco to newco did impact on their rights in practice.[137] At the sanctioning stage, the extent of the bondholders' remaining economic interest in the company would be relevant. Once sanctioned, this structure would allow a de facto cross-class cramdown to occur since the restructuring could go ahead against the wishes of the junior creditors (this being only a de facto cross-class cramdown because the junior creditors were not part of the scheme).

In the end, the MyTravel scheme progressed no further since the threat of this scheme was enough to encourage the bondholders to agree to the consensual restructuring. However, this structure has subsequently been adopted and utilised in other restructurings. The restructuring in *Re Bluebrook Ltd*[138] is a good example, and the junior creditors did take their concerns about the schemes in that case to the sanctioning hearing. Bluebrook Ltd and two of its indirect subsidiaries were balance-sheet insolvent. Rather than go into liquidation, three schemes of arrangement were devised between the companies and the senior lenders. The schemes gave effect to a restructuring arrangement whereby the business of the group was transferred to a new corporate structure via the use of a pre-pack administration, and the senior lenders effectively substituted their

134 The ability to exclude creditors also exists in relation to Part 26A restructuring plans: *Re Virgin Atlantic Airways Ltd* [2020] EWHC 2376 (Ch), discussed further at section 5.8.2.

135 See section 2.3.1.2.

136 For discussion see H. Eidenmueller, 'What is an insolvency proceeding?' (2018) 92 *American Bankruptcy Law Journal* 53.

137 [2004] EWCA Civ 1734.

138 *Re Bluebrook Ltd* [2009] EWHC 2114 (Ch); [2010] 1 BCLC 338.

debt for shares in the restructured group.[139] As in *MyTravel*, the junior creditors were left out of the schemes on the basis that their rights were unaffected. The transferor companies were released from the debt and the scheme companies were then placed into administration. This enabled the business of the company to continue, unburdened by the huge debt that had hung over Bluebrook and its subsidiaries. The sanctioning of this scheme was not uncontroversial, and in particular the mezzanine lenders, whose claims were subordinated to those of the senior lenders, challenged this reorganisation at the sanctioning hearing.

The approach adopted by the court at the sanctioning hearing is to ask whether those objecting to the scheme have any remaining economic interest in the company. Where creditors (or members) have no remaining interest in the company, the view of the court is that their complaints should have no weight. This approach is appropriate. In general, in English company law the focus is on the residual claimant at any given point in time. So, for example, directors are required to act to promote the success of the company 'for the benefit of its members as a whole'[140] when the company is solvent, but must take account of the creditors' interests when the company is insolvent, or verging on insolvency.[141] Where the company is insolvent, the shareholders have no economic interest left in the company and therefore should not be able to block a restructuring scheme, or be able to extract value from the senior creditors as a result of this blocking power. Similarly, where the subordinated creditors are out of the money, they should not have the ability to block the scheme.

This does raise a key issue, however, namely that of valuation, which is at the heart of minority protection in these cases. Where schemes of arrangement are used as a stand-alone mechanism, there are two protections for dissenting creditors: the fact that creditors meet in classes of those holding the same rights (and all classes must agree to the restructuring) and the oversight of the court to ensure, inter alia, that the classes are correctly constituted and the scheme is otherwise fair, as discussed in section 2.4. As long as this occurs, there should not be wealth transfers from dissenting to consenting creditors since all those within the same

[139] On the facts, things were slightly more complicated since the senior lenders left behind £12 million of debt in the scheme companies and these debts were not released.

[140] Companies Act 2006, s. 172(1).

[141] *West Mercia Safetywear Ltd* v. *Dodd* [1988] BCLC 250; *BTI 2014 LLC* v. *Sequana SA* [2019] EWCA Civ 112.

class will get the same deal. However, once it becomes possible for a restructuring to be imposed upon a whole class of dissenting creditors/members, the opportunity for wealth transfers from the assenting creditors to the dissenting creditors arises. A *Bluebrook*-type restructuring could be a means of ensuring the rescue of a company or group that will otherwise fail, but since the junior creditors are left behind in an oldco now stripped of assets and without the possibility of participating in the future growth of the business, it could also be seen as a means of transferring wealth from one constituency to another, for instance from the junior creditors to the senior creditors.

However, the issue of valuation is not one that has been dealt with very often in scheme cases;[142] the discussion of this issue in *Re Bluebrook* is a rare example, but it indicates some of the complexities involved. Broadly, the approach in the English courts has been to focus on the question of what would happen if the scheme were not sanctioned.[143] This is necessarily a more conservative approach than considering what each creditor would receive if the restructuring were to be successful.[144] In the *MyTravel* restructuring, for example, it was stated that if the scheme did not go ahead, the company would have gone into liquidation.[145] As a result, a liquidation valuation for the company, i.e. one in which the assets of the company were valued as they would be if disposed of in an insolvent liquidation, was felt to be appropriate.[146] By way of contrast, in *Bluebrook*, Mann J valued the company on a going-concern basis,[147] which will generally yield

[142] This may be compared with US Chapter 11, for example, which embeds the issue of valuation within the statutory provisions: 11 USC § 1129 and see K. O'Rourke, 'Valuation uncertainty in Chapter 11 reorganizations' (2005) *Columbia Law Review* 403.

[143] *Re Marconi Corp plc* [2003] EWHC 1083 (Ch).

[144] For discussion see S. Paterson, 'Debt restructuring and notions of fairness' (2017) 80(4) *Modern Law Review* 600.

[145] A liquidation methodology was also used in *Re Tea Corporation Ltd* [1904] 1 Ch 12 and *Re Telewest Communications plc (No. 1)* [2004] EWHC 924; [2004] BCC 342.

[146] For discussion of the valuation methodologies available in a distressed company scenario see M. Crystal and R. Mokal, 'The valuation of distressed companies – a conceptual framework' (2006) 3 *International Corporate Rescue* 63 (Part 1) and 123 (Part 2).

[147] The *Bluebrook* decision on this point should be treated with care, since Mann J limited his determination, merely stating that 'for the purposes of this case, and in order to assess the fairness of the schemes, a going-concern value is appropriate' ([2009] EWHC 2114 (Ch); [2010] 1 BCLC 338 at [40]). However, by analogy, the introduction of the Part 26A restructuring plan, with its assessment of whether members of the dissenting class will be worse off than they would be in the event of the relevant alternative (Companies Act 2006, s. 901G(3) discussed at section 5.8.2), may well support this approach in the future.

a higher value than a liquidation valuation.[148] In a situation in which the company is only financially distressed, the alternative to the scheme may well be some other form of restructuring or rescue rather than liquidation, in which case a going-concern valuation will be more appropriate than a liquidation valuation.[149] The going-concern approach was therefore the correct approach to adopt in *Bluebrook*, and should similarly be used in the future where the restructuring involves an economically viable entity.[150] The choice of valuation mechanism has a role in protecting dissenting creditors since the liquidation comparator provides less protection for junior creditors concerned about wealth transfers than a going-concern valuation. Senior creditors thus have an incentive to press for a liquidation valuation which will reduce the potential for junior creditors to be judged to have an ongoing economic interest in the business and will make it more likely that the restructuring can go ahead without their consent. Arguing that liquidation is the only alternative also has the effect of holding a gun to the judge's head and puts significant pressure on the judge to sanction the scheme. Courts needs to be prepared to resist this pressure and determine whether this rhetoric is really justified, in order to protect the interests of the junior creditors.[151]

Once this matter is resolved, a further issue arises in relation to valuation that can have an important effect on the court's ability to protect minorities, namely how a going-concern valuation is to be determined. One option is a market price valuation of the business. This is arguably the most accurate measure of a company's worth at a given time. The benefit of this option is that it can be established through a properly conducted sales process and thus avoids the subjectivity inherent in the other major option, namely market valuation opinions provided by expert valuers. Such market valuation opinions often lead to costly and lengthy valuation fights with each party hiring their own valuer to provide an opinion that supports their position. This is also messy and

[148] See Crystal and Mokal, 'The valuation of distressed companies', note 146 above; J. Westbrook, 'The control of wealth in bankruptcy' (2004) 82(4) *Texas Law Review* 795, 811.

[149] See e.g. Westbrook, 'The control of wealth in bankruptcy', note 148 above and the 'relevant alternative' test introduced in relation to Part 26A restructuring plans in s. 901G(3) of the Companies Act 2006, discussed at section 5.8.2.

[150] Crystal and Mokal, 'The valuation of distressed companies', note 146 above, at 126, who argue that a going-concern value should also have been adopted in *MyTravel*.

[151] There is some evidence that the English courts are starting to do this: *Re Van Gansewinkel Groep BV & Ors* [2015] EWHC 2151 (Ch) at [24].

difficult for the courts to mediate, unlike a market testing process which provides a clear benchmark for the court. The market valuation approach has many advantages, but it also has disadvantages. It may be difficult to establish a proper market exercise, particularly if the market is depressed at the time of the valuation, in which case it may be difficult to establish a genuine auction process. There is a danger that senior lenders may be able to take advantage of a temporary dip in market conditions, in order to cut out the junior creditors, as Mann J recognised in *Bluebrook.*[152]

In the event, this was not an issue in *Bluebrook*. The scheme companies and the senior lenders did three things to try to establish the value of the company: they commissioned a report from PricewaterhouseCoopers that valued the business on three different approaches;[153] they conducted a marketing process; and they extrapolated a value for the business based on a surveyor's valuation of a number of the group's sites.[154]All of these valuations fell well short of the £313 million of outstanding senior debt,[155] including where the market valuation stripped out the 'alpha factor' so that the valuation was not linked to current market conditions, suggesting that the junior members were resolutely out of the money. The judge was highly critical of the Monte Carlo simulation model analysis put forward by the mezzanine lenders, which he described as 'plainly a mechanical, and not judgmental, assessment'.[156]

152 *Re Bluebrook Ltd* [2009] EWHC 2114 (Ch); [2010] 1 BCLC 338 at [49].

153 The methodologies adopted in the PricewaterhouseCoopers report were: (i) the income approach, which valued the business on a discounted cash-flow basis; (ii) a market approach, which looked at comparable publicly traded companies; and (iii) a leveraged buy-out analysis, which looked at the debt capacity, to assess the level of equity investment that a private equity investor might be prepared to make.

154 It makes sense for the company and its advisors to conduct a thorough analysis of the situation in advance of the scheme, to support the valuation range being placed on the company and to protect the scheme against challenge by aggrieved junior creditors on the basis of valuation. In the WIND Hellas restructuring scheme in 2010, for example, which involved a scheme and a pre-pack administration, the company and its advisors conducted an extensive M&A bidding process prior to selecting a preferred bidder for the underlying business.

155 It was estimated that a purchaser would pay no more than £265 million for the business. Concurrently, an investment bank conducted a third-party sales process with a view to establishing whether a buyer for the group could be found. This process resulted in only one offer, which placed a value on the group of £150 million to £188 million. An exercise by property valuers valued the group's sites at £164 million on a swift-sale basis and £208 million on a full-market basis. The judge viewed the discounted-cash-flow analysis as the most reliable of these methodologies, with the other valuations obtained by the scheme companies providing a useful cross-check.

156 [2009] EWHC 2114 (Ch); [2010] 1 BCLC 338 at [45]. The Monte Carlo simulation involved the repeated calculation of the discounted-cash-flow valuation using a random

It is clear that the English courts are at an early stage in tackling these issues, certainly compared to the discussion of valuation in relation to US Chapter 11, for example. The introduction of the Part 26A restructuring plan will prompt the development of this topic.[157]

As a consequence of twinning schemes and administration, a de facto cramdown of whole classes can therefore be achieved. While a practical solution to the absence of a de jure cross-class cramdown option in English law, it has disadvantages. In particular, requiring these procedures to be combined can be unwieldy and the need to transfer the assets of oldco to newco has tax implications and can be costly. As discussed at section 5.8.1, this helps to explain the development of the Part 26A restructuring plan, which allows a cross-class cramdown to occur within a stand-alone mechanism.

5.4.4 *The availability of a moratorium*

5.4.4.1 The need for a moratorium

During the period in which a restructuring is being negotiated and implemented, there is the potential for one or more creditors to disrupt the restructuring either by exercising their rights to demand payment or by seeking to put the company into liquidation. One way to address this possibility is to put some form of stay in place. The need for creditors to be constrained from such action is well understood in the context of insolvency law, as a means of keeping the business and assets together so that they can be sold for the highest possible price.[158] In the same way, a stay can be beneficial as a means of providing a breathing space for the company within which to reach an arrangement with its creditors and to keep the business and assets together long enough for a reorganisation to be effected. At its simplest, this might merely prevent the creditor from asserting its debt claim against the company for the period of negotiation. It is likely to be more valuable, however, if the stay also prevents the initiation of insolvency proceedings and other legal process, given the

sampling of input and assumptions, followed by the aggregation of the results into a distribution of the probabilities of different valuation outcomes and resulting in a valuation range of between £210 million and £700 million.

157 See section 5.8.2.

158 See e.g. T. Jackson, 'Bankruptcy, non-bankruptcy entitlements, and the creditors' bargain' (1982) 91 *Yale Law Journal* 857; T. H. Jackson and R. E. Scott, 'On the nature of bankruptcy: an essay on bankruptcy sharing and the creditors' bargain' (1989) 75 *Virginia Law Review* 155.

impact of the commencement of such proceedings on the position of managers, on counterparties and on the company's goodwill. The stay could even be extended further, to include a constraint on the ability of the creditor to terminate its contract with the company in this period.[159]

Until 2020 no statutory moratorium existed that could be used in conjunction with an English scheme.[160] This potentially left companies undergoing a restructuring scheme exposed. The complex nature of the procedure for a scheme, involving two court hearings and requiring meetings of classes of creditors to be held, means that at least eight weeks are generally necessary between the formulation of the scheme and the eventual court order sanctioning it. In the absence of a statutory moratorium, three possibilities exist to deal with this gap. First, the creditors can agree to a contractual standstill arrangement, where they voluntarily commit to refrain from exercising their contractual rights in these ways. This can work well where small, homogenous groups of creditors are involved in the restructuring. Many restructuring schemes exclude the trade creditors and involve only the finance creditors, and this increases the chance of agreeing a standstill arrangement amongst this smaller group of creditors, many of whom are repeat-players. However, where numbers grow, and creditors become more heterogenous, such agreements become more difficult.[161] Changes in the credit market in recent years may have increased the challenges in this regard. Second, the scheme can be twinned with administration, which has had a statutory stay attached to it since its inception,[162] but this can have implications for the timing of the restructuring, since administration is an insolvency mechanism. Third, the court can be asked to exercise its discretion to grant a stay in order to protect a scheme of arrangement that is being put together, as occurred, for example, in *Sea Assets Ltd* v. *PT Garuda Indonesia*[163] and *Bluecrest Mercantile BV; FMS Wertmanagement AÖR* v. *Vietnam Shipbuilding Industry Group*.[164]

[159] For discussion see section 5.7.2.4.

[160] The meaning of 'moratorium' used here is the same as that utilised for administration in the Insolvency Act 1986 (Sch. B1, paras. 42–3), i.e. a statutory stay.

[161] See e.g. S. Paterson, 'Rethinking the role of corporate bankruptcy theory in the twenty-first century' (2016) 36(4) *Oxford Journal of Legal Studies* 697.

[162] See section 5.7.2.4.

[163] 27 June 2001, unreported, discussed in G. Moss, 'Scheme of arrangement: a recent example' (2003) 16(1) *Insolvency Intelligence* 6.

[164] [2013] EWHC 1146 (Comm) in which the judge agreed to a stay of proceedings under the Civil Procedure Rules, r. 3.1(2)(f) pending consideration of a proposed scheme of arrangement, on the basis that the scheme had a reasonable prospect of success.

Indeed, on some occasions the sole purpose of the scheme is to impose a moratorium against enforcement action by creditors in order to provide an opportunity for the negotiation of the restructuring to take place, and the courts have accepted that this is a valid use of a scheme.[165] These three possibilities continue to exist even following the introduction of the restructuring moratorium in 2020, and indeed there are reasons why companies may still wish to make use of them instead of the new moratorium.

The need for some form of stay while a restructuring is negotiated and put in place is a common problem. Many of the jurisdictions that have imported the English scheme lack an automatic statutory stay attached to the scheme; this includes Hong Kong,[166] India,[167] Bermuda,[168] the British Virgin Islands (BVI),[169] and the Cayman Islands.[170] However, this is an issue that is starting to be addressed. In some jurisdictions it is

[165] See e.g. *Re Metinvest BV* [2016] EWHC 79 (Ch); *Re DTEK Finance plc* [2016] EWHC 1083 (Ch). A similar approach has been followed in Australia: *Re BIS Finance Pty Ltd* [2017] NSWSC 1713 [24]–[27].

[166] For discussion of the position in Hong Kong, and the mechanisms for dealing with the lack of a statutory moratorium attached to schemes, see *Re Z-Obee Holdings Ltd* [2018] 1 HKLRD 165; *Re China Oil Gangran Energy Group Holdings Ltd* [2020] HKCFI 825. The Hong Kong government plans further legislative reform in this area: Hong Kong Financial Services and the Treasury Bureau, *Companies (Corporate Rescue) Bill Proposals* (June 2020).

[167] Indian Companies Act 2013 ss. 230–40 (this is a change from the pre-existing provisions in Indian Companies Act 1956, s. 391 which allowed the Tribunal broad power to grant a moratorium after an application for convening had been made). However, it appears possible to obtain a moratorium under s. 14(1)(a) of the Indian Insolvency and Bankruptcy Code 2016 by entering a resolution plan, or even by entering liquidation (see s. 33(5)).

[168] One of the ways in which this has been dealt with in Bermuda is by appointment of provisional liquidators for the explicit purpose of obtaining a stay in aid of schemes of arrangement: *Re Z-Obee Holdings Ltd* [2017] Bda LR 19; *Re Up Energy Development Group Ltd* [2016] Bda LR 94 (this is a mechanism that is not allowed in other jurisdictions; see e.g. Hong Kong, *Re Legend International Resorts Ltd* [2006] 2 HKLRD 192).

[169] In the BVI the court has accepted that the appointment of provisional liquidators can be used to obtain a stay in aid of a scheme of arrangement: *Re Constellation Overseas Ltd* (ECSC-BVI (Comm), 5 February 2019). In addition, the court in that case granted a stay under s. 174(1) of the BVI Insolvency Act 2003.

[170] The courts in the Cayman Islands have held that directors cannot present a winding-up petition to obtain the appointment of provisional liquidators in aid of a scheme of arrangement in the absence of shareholder approval (see *Re China Shanshui Cement Group Ltd*, 2015 (2) CILR 255). However, if the company can induce creditors to apply for a winding-up petition, it can then apply for provisional liquidators on its own: *Re CHC Group Ltd* (unreported, McMillan J, 24 January 2017, Cause No: FSD 5 of 2017). This is distinct from the position elsewhere, see e.g. Bermuda, note 168). There may be legislative change in the Cayman Islands to deal with the need for a moratorium for debt restructuring schemes: S. Kassam and L. Petith, 'The Cayman restructuring toolkit –

the courts that have stepped in to deal with this issue. In Canada, for example, the legislation introducing the Canadian scheme of arrangement (termed a plan of arrangement) contains no express statutory stay, but there are several cases in which the court has been prepared to imply a power to grant a stay order at the initial court hearing.[171] In other jurisdictions legislative changes have been introduced. For example, Singapore has had a limited moratorium in place for some time,[172] but this is not an automatic statutory stay and depends on an application to court requesting that a moratorium be put in place. The moratorium contains other limitations. First, the courts have interpreted the legislative provisions to mean that, while the moratorium can potentially be requested before the convening hearing, nevertheless the scheme proposals have to be sufficiently advanced to allow the court to assess the viability of the plan.[173] This leaves the debtor vulnerable to legal action during the process of putting together the scheme of arrangement. Second, these provisions do not provide a blanket moratorium against all actions against the debtor but simply allow the debtor company to obtain orders staying actual actions brought by creditors and not potential actions, so the debtor may have to keep returning to court as more actions are commenced against it. In 2017 Singapore introduced an enhanced moratorium as part of its broader restructuring reforms,[174] which can take effect even before the scheme is proposed[175] and restrains

exploring the flexible restructuring options on offer in the Cayman Islands' (2018) 15(6) *International Corporate Rescue* 353.

171 See e.g. *In the Matter of a Proposed Plan of Arrangement of Call-Net Inc*, 20 February 2002, No. 01-CL-4423 (Ontario Supreme Court); *In the Matter of a Proposed Plan of Arrangement of Tembec Arrangement Inc, Tembec Industries Inc and Tembec Enterprises Inc*, 24 January 2008, No. 08-CL-7367 (OSC); *In the Matter of a Proposed Arrangement by Abitbi Consolidated Inc*, 2009 QCCS 6444 (Quebec Supreme Court); *In the Matter of a Proposed Arrangement by Mega Brands*, 2010 QCCS 646 (interim order) and *In the Matter of a Proposed Arrangement by Mega Brands*, 2010 QCCS 1105 (final order) (QSC); *Re 4519922 Canada Inc*, 2015 ONSC 124 (CanLII) (2015) 22 CBR (6th) 44.

172 See Singapore Companies Act, s. 210(10) discussed in *Re Pacific Andes* [2018] 5 SLR 125. A similar provision exists in Malaysia: Malaysian Companies Act 2016, s. 368(2) (see previously Malaysian Companies Act 1965, s. 176(10)).

173 *Re Kuala Lumpur Industries Bhd* [1990] 2 MLJ 180; *Re Conchubar Aromatics* [2015] SGHC 322; *Re Pacific Andes* [2018] 5 SLR 125.

174 Singapore Companies (Amendment) Act 2017, introducing ss. 211A–211D Singapore Companies Act (and see now Singapore Insolvency, Restructuring and Dissolution Act 2018, ss. 64–6).

175 Singapore Insolvency, Restructuring and Dissolution Act 2018, s. 64(1). See Meng Seng Wee, 'The Singapore story of injecting US Chapter 11 into the Commonwealth scheme'

a wide variety of originating processes and enforcement actions.[176] Once an application for a moratorium is made, an initial automatic moratorium, which is as broad as that which the court may grant after hearing the application, comes into being for a period of thirty days or until the application is decided by the court.[177] The main substantive requirement for the court in order to apply for a moratorium is evidence of support from the company's creditors and an explanation of how such support will be important for the success of the proposed scheme.[178] Australia has no general moratorium attached to schemes, but in 2017 an automatic stay on enforcement of ipso facto clauses triggered by a company's entry into a scheme was introduced.[179]

The difficulties that can arise from the lack of a statutory moratorium attached to a scheme have been recognised in England for some time, including in the first edition of this book.[180] They were raised by the Cork Report in 1982,[181] and the Company Law Review also acknowledged that this was an issue requiring attention, but stated that, as an insolvency law issue, it fell outside the Review's terms of reference.[182] This issue was considered again in 2009–10 by the Insolvency Service in its consultation document on corporate rescue, which recommended the introduction of a restructuring moratorium,[183] although ultimately no change resulted

(2018) 15(3) *European Company and Financial Law Review* 553. For discussion of the operation of the moratorium see *Re IM Skaugen SE* [2019] 3 SLR 979. For discussion of the use of the moratorium in Singapore see Wai Yee Wan, C. Watters and G. McCormack, 'Schemes of arrangement in Singapore: empirical and comparative analyses' (2020) 94 *American Bankruptcy Law Journal* 463.

[176] Singapore Insolvency, Restructuring and Dissolution Act 2018, s. 64(1)(a)–(f). The moratorium is expressed to have extraterritorial in personam effect (see s. 64(5)(b). For discussion see *H & CS Holdings* v. *Glencore International AG* [2019] EWHC 1459 (Ch).

[177] Singapore Insolvency, Restructuring and Dissolution Act 2018, s. 64(8).

[178] Ibid., s. 64(4).

[179] See Australian Corporations Act 2001, s. 415D inserted by the Treasury Laws Amendment (2017 Enterprise Incentives No. 2) Act 2017, Sch. 1 Part 2. For further discussion see section 5.7.2.4.

[180] J. Payne, *Schemes of Arrangement: Theory, Structure and Operation* (Cambridge University Press, 2014), 5.7 and ch. 9.

[181] Report of the Insolvency Law Review Committee, *Insolvency Law and Practice* (Cmnd 8558, 1982) (Cork Committee), para. 406.

[182] Company Law Review, *Modern Company Law for a Competitive Economy – Final Report*, URN 01/943, 2001 (CLR, *Final Report*), para. 13.11.

[183] Insolvency Service, *Encouraging Company Rescue – A Consultation* (London: DTI, June 2009); Insolvency Service, *Encouraging Company Rescue – Summary of Responses* (London: DTI, November 2009) paras. 24–6; Insolvency Service, *Proposals for a Restructuring Moratorium – A Consultation* (London: DTI, July 2010).

from these proposals.[184] In May 2016, the Insolvency Service put forward a new set of proposals, which again included the introduction of a restructuring moratorium.[185] To understand the revival of these proposals just five years after they had been dropped, attention can be given to the increased political focus in the UK and elsewhere on rescuing companies in the intervening period, through indicators such as the World Bank's Doing Business figures.[186] Allied to this, and perhaps more pertinently, was the fact that, after a period of dominance for the UK as a restructuring centre, other jurisdictions started to introduce their own restructuring mechanisms with the potential to rival the UK debt restructuring regime,[187] one of the core elements of these being some form of statutory stay. Many of these regimes took their inspiration from the US Chapter 11 procedure, which does include such a stay.[188] Even where regimes have taken inspiration from the UK scheme of

[184] The Insolvency Service reported that the responses to its 2010 consultation paper did not support the need for urgent change: 'It is generally felt that the existing UK insolvency framework is coping and adapting well to the challenges that the current round of restructurings are posing, and the urgency of the case for introducing a new moratorium is not fully made out': Insolvency Service, *Proposals for a Restructuring Moratorium – Summary of Responses* (London: DTI, May 2011) 5. One explanation for this view is that creditors can agree a standstill arrangement amongst themselves. An alternative explanation is that the development of the distressed debt market in the UK in the last decade or so means that financial creditors who no longer wish to remain invested in a company can exit without needing to go through the process of enforcing their claim against the company.

[185] Insolvency Service, *A Review of the Corporate Insolvency Framework: A Consultation on Options for Reform*, May 2016 and see Insolvency Service, *Summary of Responses – A Review of the Corporate Insolvency Framework*, September 2016.

[186] These are produced annually; see e.g. World Bank Group, *Doing Business 2020: Comparing Business Regulation in 190 Economies.* For discussion on the background to the government proposals in 2018 see S. Frisby, 'Of rights and rescue: a curious confluence' (2020) *Journal of Corporate Law Studies* 39.

[187] Within Europe these changes were introduced at national level (see e.g. Spanish Law 38/2011 of October 2011 and Law 4/2014 of 7 March, discussed by I. Tirado, 'Scheming against schemes: a new framework to deal with business financial distress in Spain' (2018) *European Company and Financial Law Review* 516) and at EU level (see Directive (EU) 2019/1023 of the European Parliament and of the Council of 20 June 2019 on preventive restructuring frameworks, on discharge of debt and disqualifications, and on measures to increase the efficiency of procedures concerning restructuring, insolvency and discharge of debt, and amending Directive (EU) 2017/1132). Similar changes also took place beyond Europe; see e.g. Wai Yee Wan, Watters and McCormack, 'Schemes of arrangement in Singapore', note 175 above. For further discussion see J. Payne, 'Debt restructuring in the UK' (2018) *European Company and Financial Law Review* 449 and S. Paterson, 'Reflections on English law schemes of arrangement in distress and proposals for reform' (2018) 15 *European Company and Financial Law Review* 472.

[188] 11 USC § 362.

arrangement as well as US Chapter 11, as the EU Restructuring Directive does, they tend to include some form of moratorium. In the EU Restructuring Directive, for example, there is the concept of a stay of individual enforcement actions to support a restructuring, subject to the debtor meeting certain requirements. A stay can be implemented for four months in the first instance and extended to a maximum duration of twelve months, provided that the debtor can effectively demonstrate that 'relevant' progress has so far been made in negotiations on the restructuring plan, and that such extension will not unfairly prejudice the rights of affected parties or result in the liquidation of the debtor under national law.[189]

In the UK, in 2018 the government published a set of proposals for legislative change, which included the introduction of a restructuring moratorium.[190] These proposals sat on the shelf for eighteen months, but the Covid-19 pandemic and the financial distress it generated brought this issue back onto the legislative agenda. The Corporate Insolvency and Governance Act 2020 includes a number of significant responses to the corporate financial distress caused by the pandemic. In common with many other jurisdictions, the Act included some temporary measures aimed at easing the immediate financial difficulties created by the Covid-19 pandemic;[191] however, the Act also includes some significant permanent changes which are based on the 2018 government proposals. One of these is the introduction of a restructuring moratorium which largely follows the government's 2018 proposals. Another major change is the introduction of a restructuring plan, discussed at section 5.8.2.

5.4.4.2 The restructuring moratorium

The Corporate Insolvency and Governance Act 2020 introduces a restructuring moratorium[192] that is stand-alone and is not

[189] Directive 2019/1023 on preventive restructuring frameworks, on discharge of debt and disqualifications, and on measures to increase the efficiency of procedures concerning restructuring, insolvency and discharge of debt, and amending Directive (EU) 2017/1132, Arts. 6–7.

[190] See BEIS, *Insolvency and Corporate Governance: Government Response*, 26 August 2018.

[191] See e.g. Australian Coronavirus Economic Response Package Omnibus Act 2020; New Zealand Covid-19 Response (Further Management Measures) Legislation Act 2020; Singapore Covid-19 (Temporary Measures) Act 2020.

[192] Corporate Insolvency and Governance Act 2020 (CIGA), ss. 1–6 and Schs. 1–8, which introduces new provisions into the Insolvency Act 1986 (for Great Britain) and into the Insolvency (Northern Ireland) Order 1989 (for Northern Ireland).

a precursor to an insolvency process, although it can be used in that way.[193] The optional nature of this moratorium is beneficial, as some distressed companies may be wary of announcing moratorium protection because of the unwanted publicity this may draw to their financial position.[194] The restructuring moratorium commences when certain documents are filed at court by the company and can be used alongside various restructuring mechanisms including schemes, CVAs and restructuring plans. Consequently, it can be used with a scheme in certain circumstances, but it need not be, and, for the reasons discussed in this section, the uptake of combining schemes with a restructuring moratorium may be relatively limited.

The restructuring moratorium is debtor-in-possession and allows directors to continue to run a company, subject to the appointment of a licensed insolvency practitioner (the monitor) and certain other restrictions. The objective of the moratorium is to provide protection to the company from adverse creditor action for a short period whilst the directors attempt to restructure and rescue the business.

The directors of a company can obtain a moratorium by application to court for a court order. Where there is no outstanding winding-up petition against the company and the company is an English company, the moratorium can be commenced without a court application simply by filing relevant documents with the court.[195] The directors must file a statement that the company is or is likely to become unable to pay its debts and the proposed monitor needs to confirm that, in their view, it is likely that a moratorium for the company would result in the rescue of the company as a going concern.[196]

The effect of the restructuring moratorium is to impose both a constraint on the ability of creditors to assert their debt claims against the company and a constraint on initiating insolvency proceedings and other legal processes.[197] It is broadly similar to the moratorium in place in administration, although with some differences

[193] By contrast, the Singapore reforms target schemes of arrangement more specifically and the enhanced moratorium focuses on that mechanism; see Singapore Insolvency, Restructuring and Dissolution Act 2018, ss. 64–6.

[194] The enhanced moratorium introduced into the Singapore scheme regime in 2017 likewise does not arise automatically.

[195] Insolvency Act 1986, Part A1, Ch. 2, ss. A3–A4 (and for overseas companies see s. A5). During the Covid-19 period, some variations were introduced to the moratorium provisions; see CIGA, Schs. 4 and 8.

[196] Insolvency Act 1986, Part A1, Ch. 2, ss. A6 (and for overseas companies see s. A5).

[197] Ibid, Part A1, Ch. 4.

of detail.[198] A company subject to a moratorium will obtain the benefit of a payment holiday from certain pre-moratorium debts. Pre-moratorium debts are: (a) any debts or liabilities to which the company becomes subject before the moratorium comes into force; or (b) any debt or liability to which the company has become or may become subject during the moratorium by reason of any obligation incurred before the moratorium.[199] However, there are a number of pre-moratorium debts that are still required to be paid, including the monitor's remuneration and expenses, goods or services supplied during the moratorium, rent (for the moratorium period) and wages, salary and redundancy payments (not limited to those falling due during the moratorium).[200] These carved-out debts will reduce the benefit of the restructuring moratorium in practice. The other category of debts that must be paid in the moratorium period is moratorium debts, that is, any debt or other liability to which a company becomes subject during the moratorium other than by reason of an obligation incurred before the moratorium came into force, and any debt or other liability to which the company has become or may become subject after the end of the moratorium by reason of any obligation incurred in the moratorium. Any unpaid moratorium debts and some pre-moratorium debts without a payment holiday, described as 'priority pre-moratorium debts', then get super priority in an insolvency occurring within twelve weeks of the end of the moratorium.[201] There was discussion following the publication of the Corporate Insolvency and Governance Bill as to whether lenders would be able to use contractual rights to accelerate a loan during a moratorium. Acceleration of a bank loan would be likely to lead to the termination of the moratorium by the monitor given that the company would in almost all cases be unable to pay the accelerated liability. The accelerated debt would then acquire super-priority status in a subsequent insolvency or restructuring procedure. The relevant provisions were debated at length in the House of Lords and amendments were introduced to the Bill. As a result, it is clear under the Act that lenders can accelerate loans in the moratorium if they have the contractual right to do so, but that 'relevant accelerated debt' will not be a 'priority pre-moratorium debt' for the

[198] For discussion of the moratorium that arises on administration see section 5.7.2.4.
[199] Insolvency Act 1986, Part A1, Ch. 4, s. A18(3).
[200] Ibid.
[201] Insolvency Act 1986, s. 174A.

purposes of super priority in a subsequent insolvency or restructuring procedure.[202] This means that, for the moratorium to be fully effective, the company will need to have the support of its lenders, and possibly enter into some form of waiver or standstill agreement with them. This potentially limits the benefits and widespread use of the restructuring moratorium.

During the moratorium period, various actions of creditors are prevented. Unlike moratoria adopted elsewhere in recent years, which allow the stay on enforcement actions to be either general (affecting all creditors) or targeted towards individual creditors,[203] the UK restructuring moratorium can only affect all creditors. It does not have the option of excluding certain creditors, whether these are smaller creditors, those in financial difficulties themselves or other creditors on whom the burden of the moratorium might fall disproportionately.[204] The restructuring moratorium is thus relatively inflexible. During a moratorium, creditors cannot petition for the winding up of the company; no resolution for the winding up of the company may be passed by the shareholders other than if recommended by the directors; no application for administration may be made other than by the directors; no notice of intention to appoint an administrator by the holder of a qualifying floating charge can be lodged at court; and no administrative receiver may be appointed.[205] These restrictions do not bind the directors, however, so they remain able to take these steps. The Act also provides for the following restrictions on enforcement and legal proceedings against the company: no right of forfeiture can be exercised in relation to premises occupied by the company;[206] there can be no enforcement of security over the company's property, subject to specified exceptions;[207] no repossession of goods is permitted;[208] no 'legal process' can be issued or continued against the company or judgments enforced;[209] and no notice of the crystallisation of a floating charge may be given during the moratorium, nor can any other

202 See Insolvency Act 1986, s. 174A(3)(4).
203 See e.g. EU Restructuring Directive, (EU) 2019/1023, Art. 6(3).
204 Other jurisdictions operate a more flexible approach to this issue; see e.g. the Canadian approach described in J. Sarra, *Rescue! The Companies' Creditors Arrangement Act* (2nd ed., Thomson Reuters Canada Ltd, 2013).
205 Insolvency Act 1986, Part A1, Ch. 4, s. A20.
206 Ibid, Part A1, Ch. 4, s. A21(1)(a).
207 Ibid, Part A1, Ch. 4, s. A23 (and see s. A21(1)(c)).
208 Ibid, Part A1, Ch. 4, s. A21(1)(d).
209 Ibid, Part A1, Ch. 4, s. A21(1)(e). However, this does not apply to employment disputes.

event be permitted to occur that would have the same effect as such a notice.[210] The company may borrow and incur credit provided it discloses that there is a moratorium, and it may grant security over property provided that the monitor consents.[211]

A further constraint during the restructuring moratorium is a restriction on the ability of creditors to terminate their contracts with the company 'by reason of' (or 'ipso facto') insolvency. The provisions dealing with ipso facto clauses were introduced in the 2020 Act and are intended to deal with the difficulty that companies in distress can face whereby suppliers stop or threaten to stop supplying the company. Those suppliers may rely on the right to terminate the contract because of the insolvency, and may use this threat to require the payment of all arrears as the price for continued supply and/or to change the terms of the contract with the company, perhaps by increasing prices for the goods or services. The new provisions dealing with ipso facto clauses apply more generally following the introduction of the Act, not just to the restructuring moratorium, and are discussed in more detail at section 5.7.2.4.[212] It is notable that while the ipso facto provision applies in the event that a company enters a 'relevant insolvency procedure',[213] defined to include a moratorium, administration, a CVA, liquidation or

210 Ibid, Part A1, Ch. 4, s. A22. These restrictions can be overcome with the permission of the court, save that no application to court can be made for permission to enforce a pre-moratorium debt to which the payment holiday applies or to crystallise a floating charge. Unlike administration, there is no provision whereby the monitor can grant their consent to such proceedings during the moratorium.

211 Ibid, Part A1, Ch. 4, ss. A25, A26. There is some ambiguity as to whether new security granted by a company during a moratorium can be enforced. While the Act states that such security may be enforced if the monitor consented to the grant of the security, the relevant provision also refers back to the overall prohibition on enforcement of security. This seems to indicate that a new as well as existing security holder cannot enforce during the moratorium, but the drafting is unclear.

212 Similar changes have occurred elsewhere, see e.g. Australia, where an automatic stay on the enforcement of ipso facto clauses triggered by a company's entry into a scheme was introduced in 2017: see 415D Australian Corporations Act 2001, inserted by Sch. 1, Part 2 of the Treasury Laws Amendment (2017 Enterprise Incentives No. 2) Act 2017 (see also ss. 434J and 451E for other instances of the operation of this automatic stay). The automatic nature of this stay where certain creditor schemes take place is distinct from the UK position. For discussion see J. Harris and C. Symes, 'Be careful what you wish for! Evaluating the ipso facto reforms' (2019) 34 *Australian Journal of Corporate Law* 84; C. Byrne, 'Rescuing the rescue culture? Australian corporate restructuring after the safe harbour and ipso facto reforms' (2019) 27 *Insolvency Law Journal* 122.

213 Insolvency Act 1986, s. 233B(1).

a restructuring plan,[214] schemes of arrangement are not included in this list.

Clearly, a moratorium can be valuable from a company's perspective during the period that a restructuring is negotiated and put in place, but from the creditors' perspective a moratorium can pose a threat, as it may be misused by companies. Given that it involves a significant constraint on creditors' legal rights, it can be justified only where the imposition can be regarded as beneficial to the creditors as a whole, in order to rescue a viable but financially distressed business. One concern is that a moratorium can be used by directors to prop up a company which is not economically viable and is not capable of rescue, and that the moratorium simply prolongs the moment when the company's difficulties are dealt with, while the company continues to lose money in the meantime. Another is that directors of viable companies may utilise a restructuring to shake off liabilities which the company is capable of meeting. A number of protections are included in the Corporate Insolvency and Governance Act 2020 to deal with these concerns.

One relates to the length of the moratorium: the moratorium automatically ends twenty business days from the day after the moratorium comes into force.[215] This can be extended by a further twenty business days without creditor consent and can be extended for up to twelve months with the consent of creditors and/or a court order.[216] The moratorium will automatically be extended in some cases (such as where the company proposes a CVA) or brought to an end if the company enters into an insolvency process (e.g. upon the appointment of administrators or liquidators).[217] The initial period of twenty business days is a very short period of time for a company to negotiate and be ready to implement a substantive restructuring. Therefore, it seems likely that the majority of moratoria will be extended and last at least forty business days. Even this is short compared to the length of moratoria available elsewhere in the world. Singapore's restructuring regime, introduced in 2017, includes an automatic moratorium of 30 days, which is

[214] Ibid, s. 233B(2).

[215] Ibid, Part A1, Ch. 3, s. A9.

[216] Ibid, Part A1, Ch. 3, ss. A10–A13.

[217] Ibid, Part A1, Ch. 3, ss. A14–A16. In addition, the monitor is obliged to end the moratorium in certain circumstances, for example if the company fails to pay certain debts due during the moratorium (such as trade or finance creditors or wages) or the monitor determines that the moratorium is no longer likely to result in the rescue of the company as a going concern.

extendable;[218] the EU Restructuring Directive includes a moratorium with an initial 4-month period, extendable up to 12 months;[219] and US Chapter 11 involves a 120-day moratorium, which again may be extended in certain circumstances.[220] There is clearly a concern to protect creditors by not having an overly long moratorium, but this needs to be weighed against the value of the mechanism as a breathing space for companies within which to negotiate the restructuring. It remains to be seen whether the period provided in the 2020 Act will be valuable in this regard.

Further creditor protections are put in place via eligibility requirements. As a requirement of obtaining a moratorium, directors have to state that, in their view, the company is, or is likely to become, unable to pay its debts.[221] This may be regarded as being particularly targeted at the second concern raised above (that directors of viable companies may utilise a restructuring to shake off liabilities which the company is capable of meeting). This is balanced by the requirement that the proposed monitor state that, in its view, it is likely that a moratorium for the company would result in the rescue of the company as a going concern,[222] which is targeted at the first concern above, namely that directors may seek to use the moratorium to prop up unviable companies. In addition, the moratorium is not available to certain companies, such as banks, insurance companies and companies involved in certain financial market transactions.[223] This is sensible given that companies such as banks are subject to their own special resolution regimes. The list of excluded companies is broader than this, however. Notably, any company that is party to a capital market arrangement (involving debts of at least £10 m) is also excluded. These exclusions mean that many large corporates that are party to bond financing arrangements will not be able to benefit from a restructuring moratorium and will have to continue to find other ways to protect themselves during a restructuring, such as by negotiating a consensual standstill. A further form of protection is that no application can be made if the company has entered into a moratorium in the previous twelve months without an order

[218] Singapore Companies (Amendment) Act 2017 and see now Singapore Insolvency, Restructuring and Dissolution Act 2018, Part 5. For discussion of whether the Singapore moratorium will be recognised in Hong Kong see *Re CW Advanced Technologies Ltd* [2018] 3 HKLRD 552.

[219] Directive (EU) 2019/1023, Arts. 6(4), 6(7).

[220] 11 USC §§ 362, 1121.

[221] Insolvency Act 1986, Part A1, Ch. 3, ss. A6(1)(d).

[222] Ibid, Part A1, Ch. 3, ss. A6(1)(e).

[223] Ibid, Sch. ZA1.

of the court.[224] Again, the purpose behind this provision (to safeguard creditor interests) seems unarguable.

The Act therefore seeks to balance the benefit obtained by the company from a moratorium with protection of the creditors. The appointment of a monitor is also part of the creditor protection package. The monitor has a range of functions, including bringing the moratorium to an end by filing a notice at court if they think that the moratorium is no longer likely to result in the rescue of the company as a going concern; the objective of rescue has been achieved; they are unable to carry out their functions as the directors have not provided them with the relevant information; or the company is unable to pay moratorium debts which have fallen due or pre-moratorium debts for which the company does not have a payment holiday.[225] The Act also introduces a number of mechanisms whereby the actions of a monitor or company directors may be challenged[226] and a number of new offences are created, including the offence of fraud during or in anticipation of a moratorium.[227]

Although the provisions of the Corporate Insolvency and Governance Act 2020 are based on the government proposals of 2018, there are some important differences. For instance, the 2018 proposals were somewhat unclear as to just what 'rescue' meant in this context, specifically whether it was corporate or business rescue that was envisaged. The Act clarifies that it is corporate rescue that is intended (the monitor needs to take the view that a moratorium for the company will result in the rescue of *the company* as a going concern).[228] It is not clear how much work the monitor is expected to undertake to form the view that the moratorium is likely to result in the rescue of the company as a going concern. It is likely that the boundaries of this test will need to be established by the courts. The requirement that a rescue of the company, rather than the business, as a going concern is likely will mean that the moratorium cannot be used to stabilise a company's position in preparation for a sale of the business, whether through a pre-pack administration or otherwise.[229] This suggests

224 Ibid, Sch. ZA1, para. 1.

225 Ibid, Part A1, Ch. 5, s. A38(1).

226 Ibid, Part A1, Ch. 6.

227 Ibid, Part A1, Ch. 7.

228 The Insolvency Service's consultation in 2016 seemed to envisage rescue as meaning corporate rescue rather than business rescue; see Insolvency Service, *A Review of the Corporate Insolvency Framework*, note 185 above, para. 7.21.

229 Concerns were raised around both these points in the House of Lords debates on the legislation, with suggestions made that the moratorium should be available where it

that a moratorium is unsuitable for use where a scheme is twinned with a pre-pack administration, discussed at section 5.4.3.

In another change from the initial government proposals, the timing of the availability of the moratorium has shifted. The test in the Act is that the company is, or is likely to become, unable to pay its debts, i.e. is already insolvent on a cash-flow basis, or is likely to become so. In the 2018 proposals, one of the eligibility requirements was that the company be 'prospectively insolvent', that is, it would become insolvent if no action was taken, but companies that were already insolvent were excluded.[230] The government's proposal therefore contained a tricky test for directors, since directors would have to apply for the moratorium at the point at which insolvency was inevitable, but before it had occurred, which would be a potentially challenging call. Moving away from this test was sensible, but the inclusion of cash-flow insolvent companies in the 2020 Act brings its own challenges. From the creditors' point of view, the concern is likely to be that a moratorium will lead to potential abuse as directors delay the commencement of insolvency proceedings. Presumably, the short time frame of the moratorium and the need for rescue to be judged 'likely' by the monitor both at the start and throughout the moratorium are intended to alleviate these concerns. It might be said that a moratorium also potentially undermines the drive to get directors to tackle the company's problems in a timely fashion. As regards the part of the test that focuses on companies being 'likely' to become unable to pay their debts, much will depend on how this phrase is interpreted by the courts. Getting this wrong could lead to the exclusion of financially troubled companies which could benefit from a moratorium without there being any real prospect of abuse. While some schemes are used to deal with companies that are actually insolvent or on the brink of insolvency, many operate at an earlier stage in a company's financial difficulties and it may be that such schemes would not then make use of this restructuring moratorium. The aim of this restructuring moratorium is set out in the government's 2018 proposals: 'The introduction of a moratorium with a clearly defined and streamlined entry process should reduce the cost of restructuring and will be accessible to companies of any size. This will aid company rescue by giving companies time and space to consider available options when it is

could rather than would result in rescue, and where the business could be rescued but the company could not. Neither of these suggested changes was accepted.

[230] See BEIS, *Insolvency and Corporate Governance*, note 190 above, paras. 5.28–5.29.

most needed.'[231] It is clearly valuable to create a mechanism of this kind, and it may well be of value as a stand-alone device. A number of aspects of the moratorium mean that its value as an adjunct to a scheme is likely to be limited. These include the focus on corporate rescue, and the exclusion of large corporates from its ambit. It therefore seems likely that many companies concerned about creditors enforcing their debts or commencing proceedings during a restructuring scheme will need to continue to look to existing mechanisms to deal with these concerns, in particular standstill agreements and discretionary arrangements with the court. This may not be overly problematic. Even without a statutory moratorium, English schemes seem to have operated well, at least those in which sufficient finance creditors are prepared to continue to support the business. The existence of an active distressed debt trading market provides an alternative route for lenders who do not wish to support the proposed restructuring.[232] Of course, changes in the distressed debt market or in the willingness of the courts to exercise their discretion in this regard might mean that the deficiencies in the restructuring moratorium become more of a concern.

5.4.5 *The availability of rescue finance to fund the restructuring*

A further potential component of an effective restructuring regime is the existence of rescue finance, that is, finance designed both 'to keep the lights on' for a period in order to enable the debtor to negotiate with its creditors and to enable the restructuring agreed between the parties to be implemented. The availability of both of these forms of financing can be seen as a key aspect of effective corporate restructuring, allowing the continued operation of the business of the debtor or the preservation of the value of the assets of the estate.[233] Some jurisdictions have developed mechanisms to encourage such financing, including provisions whereby lenders who provide funds to the company during the restructuring process can obtain 'super priority' in certain circumstances.[234] This can

[231] Ibid., para. 5.13.

[232] For discussion see Paterson, 'Rethinking the role of corporate bankruptcy theory', note 161 above.

[233] Payne and Sarra, 'Tripping the light fantastic', note 122 above.

[234] See e.g. 11 USC § 364(d). For discussion see Payne and Sarra, 'Tripping the light fantastic', note 122 above. Other jurisdictions have introduced such provisions in recent years in order to emulate the US Chapter 11 package; see e.g. Singapore Companies (Amendment) Act 2017 introducing s. 211E into the Singapore Companies Act (Cap. 50), now Singapore Insolvency, Restructuring and Dissolution Act 2018, s. 67, applied in

increase the company's chance of survival by encouraging new or existing lenders to put money into struggling businesses. However, although no statutory provisions exist in the UK which specifically relate to this issue,[235] neither does English law actively prevent such financing. Options for super priority do exist,[236] although, in practice, market-based solutions have arisen to deal with this issue. New funding in administrations is typically provided by the existing floating charge holder, which has no need to vary its existing security, and any assets not covered by the floating charge will already be subject to fixed charges. The pressure for rescue financing is also reduced to some extent because pre-pack administrations often come with their own financing provisions in place. Further, it is possible for lenders to agree these matters amongst themselves, and existing lenders can contractually subordinate their claims to those new lenders if they choose to do so.[237] The need for legislative reform in this regard is therefore highly debatable, and indeed any reforms could disrupt the existing market solutions that have developed. Although the Insolvency Service put forward some tentative proposals for reform in this context,[238] the government rightly dropped any rescue finance proposals from its final recommendations in view of the responses to the consultation to this effect,[239] and no rescue finance provisions were included as part of the Corporate Insolvency and Governance Act 2020 reforms.

5.4.6 *Summary*

Schemes have been available as a mechanism for reorganising company debt for well over a century. However, the debates in the 1980s and 1990s

Re Attilan Group Ltd [2018] 3 SLR 898; [2017] SGHC 283. For discussion see A. Chia, M. P. Sandrasegara and S. Menon, 'Super-priority in rescue financing: lifeline or lasso?' (2017) 5 *Journal of International Banking and Financial Law* 286; P. J. Omar, 'Super-priority and the Singapore scheme: the Attilan case' (2018) 15 *International Corporate Rescue* 99.

235 It has been suggested that section 19(5) and Schedule B1 paragraph 99 of the Insolvency Act 1986 provide a potential route to post-petition financing: G. McCormack, 'Super-priority new financing and corporate rescue' [2007] *Journal of Business Law* 701–32; V. Finch, 'The dynamics of insolvency law: three models of reform' [2009] *Law and Financial Markets Review* 438–48, although this option has not been fully explored.

236 See e.g. Insolvency Act 1986, Sch. 1; Insolvency Rules 2016, r. 3.51.

237 *Re Maxwell Communications Corporation plc (No. 2)* [1994] 1 All ER 737.

238 Insolvency Service, *A Review of the Corporate Insolvency Framework*, note-185 above.

239 See Insolvency Service, *Summary of Responses: A Review of the Corporate Insolvency Framework*, note 185 above and BEIS, *Insolvency and Corporate Governance*, note 190 above.

over corporate rescue largely dismissed schemes of arrangement as a viable restructuring tool.[240] Over the last twenty years or so, the use of schemes in this regard has been increasingly recognised, particularly for large restructurings. There was a surge of such restructurings in the aftermath of the 2008 global financial crisis and the Covid-19 pandemic has also prompted an increase.

As discussed in sections 5.5, 5.6 and 5.7, the scheme jurisdiction has a number of significant advantages over contractual workouts, CVAs and administration, but also a number of disadvantages. Some of these disadvantages can be dealt with by twinning schemes with administration, particularly pre-pack administrations, but disadvantages remain. These issues, in part, prompted the introduction of the restructuring plan in 2020, which aims to create a valuable and powerful restructuring tool. These issues are explored in the final part of this chapter, where the use of schemes is compared and contrasted with that of the restructuring plan.

5.5 The use of a contractual workout to restructure a company's debt

As an alternative to the various English legislative mechanisms discussed in this chapter that may be used to restructure the debt of a financially distressed company, a simpler solution may be possible, namely the use of a contractual arrangement between the creditors and the company to facilitate the restructuring. In a situation where the company is financially distressed but the business is still fundamentally sound, it may be possible for a workout to be agreed, that is, for contractual arrangements between the company and its creditors to be put in place, without the need for formal proceedings or the involvement of the court.

240 Schemes were regarded as expensive and overly complex in 1982, and were not regarded as of practical importance as a debt restructuring tool, leading to the introduction of alternative devices to rescue failing companies, in the Insolvency Act 1986: see Cork Committee, *Insolvency Law and Practice*, note 181 above, ch. 7. Similar views continued to be held nineteen years later: see *Report of the Joint DTI/Treasury Review of Company Rescue and Business Reconstruction Mechanisms* (London: TSO, 2000) at para. 43. The Australian Law Reform Commission similarly regarded schemes as 'cumbersome, slow and costly' and introduced deed of company arrangements in 1993 as an alternative debt restructuring device: Australian Law Reform Commission, 'General insolvency inquiry', Report No. 45, 1988, Vol. 1 at 26. In Australia, schemes have increasingly been seen as valuable as a debt restructuring tool; see e.g. *Re BIS Finance Pty Ltd* [2017] NSWSC 1713; *First Pacific Advisors LLC* v. *Boart Longyear Ltd* [2017] NSWCA 116.

Restructuring agreements can take a variety of forms. For example, the creditors might agree to convert their debt into equity or into convertible debt, to extend the terms of their loans, to value and settle contingent claims, to waive part of their claims or even to forgo their claims entirely. However, this is not a closed list and a workout can potentially include any arrangements that the creditors can properly agree amongst themselves and with the company. One of the advantages of agreeing an informal workout is that the negative connotations associated with a formal insolvency process may be avoided.[241] However, there are two potential problems associated with workouts.

The first difficulty arises from the fact that all of the creditors bound by the agreement will need to agree to it. There is no possibility for the majority of creditors to bind the minority, unless this has been agreed as part of the contractual arrangements.[242] This can lead to various issues. Identifying all of the relevant parties and getting them to agree to the proposed arrangements might not be straightforward. Changes in the credit market in recent years mean that it is no longer the case that a single bank (or even a small consortium of banks) will be the major creditor for many companies. Instead, companies, particularly large companies, will obtain their financing via a number of different sources, which may include hedge funds, private equity groups, investment banks and distressed-debt investors. Companies might look to asset-backed lending, subordinated debt products and the debt capital market, as well as more traditional loans, for their financing. The debt market has also developed in that debts are frequently sold, so that, even during restructuring, the identity of the investors in the company's debt might be changing.

Quite apart from the number of creditors that may need to be involved in any potential agreement, it might also be difficult to identify all of

[241] For discussion of these difficulties see J. Armour, 'Should we redistribute in insolvency?' in J. Getzler and J. Payne (eds.), *Company Charges: Spectrum and Beyond* (Oxford University Press, 2006).

[242] See *Saltri III Ltd* v. *MD Mezzanine SA SICAR* [2012] EWHC 3025 (Comm); [2013] 2 BCLC 217 in which an intercreditor agreement between senior and mezzanine creditors was used to effect a restructuring that worked to the advantage of the senior creditors and the disadvantage of the mezzanine lenders. Attempts by the mezzanine lenders to challenge the actions of the security trustee acting under the intercreditor agreement were unsuccessful: although this agreement may not have been designed with the possibility of such a restructuring in mind, that did not mean that such a restructuring was not an option if, on the proper construction of the intercreditor agreement, it could be permitted.

them. This might be because of the complexity of the arrangements in place or because the debts are changing hands frequently. The various different types of creditor may also have different assumptions and methodologies, and have different motives as regards the distressed company. For example, some may be prepared to take a long-term view of the company's distress, whereas others will be more interested in possible short-term gain. More problematically, if a creditor has used credit default swaps or similar instruments to lay off the risk of the company defaulting, that lender might even prefer the company to default, in which case the lender would have no incentive to agree to a restructuring (and, indeed, a strong incentive not to do so).[243] Even where creditors appear to have a similar interest in restructuring the company, it may be that other agreements entered into by one or more of them means that their interests are heterogeneous rather than homogeneous. Obtaining agreement amongst such a diverse group of creditors, even once they have been identified, might not, therefore, be straightforward.[244]

Another difficulty that arises as a result of all of the creditors needing to agree to the workout is the possibility of hold-up. For example, where all creditors are being asked to take a haircut, so that the debt of the company is written down by an agreed percentage, the minority creditors might refuse their consent unless they receive better terms or payment in full. A more extreme version of this difficulty arises where some of the creditors are being particularly disadvantaged in the suggested arrangement, for example where the economic position of the company is such that the arrangement involves the holders of the junior debt being cut out of the picture altogether, as occurred in the IMO Car Wash scheme.[245]

For very large companies, with multi-bank lending arrangements, guidelines provided by 'the London Approach' might enable multi-bank support for the distressed company to be put in place. The London Approach is an entirely informal set of principles developed with a view to providing a framework for bank support for distressed companies.[246] A similar approach, but reflecting a more international

243 For a discussion of this phenomenon of 'debt decoupling' see H. Hu and B. Black, 'Equity and debt decoupling and empty voting II: importance and extensions' (2008) 156 *University of Pennsylvania Law Review* 625.

244 See S. C. Gilson, K. John and L. H. P. Lang, 'Troubled debt restructurings: an empirical study of private reorganisation of firms in default' (1990) 27 *Journal of Financial Economics* 323.

245 *Re Bluebrook Ltd* [2009] EWHC 2114 (Ch), discussed at section 5.4.3.

246 See British Bankers' Association, *Description of the London Approach* (London: 2004). For discussion see J. Armour and S. Deakin, 'Norms in private insolvency procedures:

setting, is to be found in the INSOL Principles.[247] The costs of these processes are high,[248] and therefore their use tends to be confined to very large-scale rescue attempts. Developments in the debt markets, including the introduction of new credit-providers such as hedge funds, and the increasing fragmentation of debt, described above, have all placed strains on these processes, which rely on a relatively small number of like-minded creditors operating in a cohesive, collegiate manner.[249]

Second, because these are just informal contractual arrangements, traditionally no moratorium has come into effect. If the creditors wanted to put something of this kind in place, the only option was to agree such an arrangement amongst themselves. Standstill agreements can be used as a contractual device to bind the major creditors of the company, including the bank, the bondholders' representatives and the major trade suppliers. In general, these agreements state the exposures of the participating creditors at the standstill date, provide that the creditors agree to co-operate with each other, and require them to refrain from actions designed to improve their position as regards the other participating creditors (often with specified exceptions for the senior debt). In return, the company agrees to refrain from acts that would prejudice the position of the participating creditors. In large, complex restructurings, these agreements can be difficult.

The difficulties of organising the restructuring of financially distressed companies led to the introduction of a restructuring moratorium in 2020.[250] This is designed to create a breathing space during which a restructuring can be negotiated and implemented outside any formal insolvency procedure. Such a moratorium is considered to have a range of benefits, including allowing informal contractual standstill arrangements to be more effective since the knowledge that a statutory moratorium can be obtained will reduce the incentives for participants to engage in tactical approaches or to seek advantages through the threat of delay.[251]

the "London Approach" to the resolution of financial distress' [2001] 1 *Journal of Corporate Law Studies* 21.

[247] INSOL International, *Statement of Principles for a Global Approach to Multi-Creditor Workouts* (2nd ed., April 2017). See K. Van Zwieten, *Goode on Principles of Corporate Insolvency Law* (5th ed., Sweet & Maxwell, 2018) 12-03.

[248] K. Wruck, 'Financial distress, reorganization and organizational efficiency' (1990) 27 *Journal of Financial Economics* 419.

[249] See Paterson, 'Rethinking the role of corporate bankruptcy theory', note 161 above.

[250] See section 5.4.4.2.

[251] See Insolvency Service, *A Review of the Corporate Insolvency Framework*, note 185 above, para. 7.9.

As a result, reaching a contractual solution is not impossible, but it is certainly not straightforward. Often, the challenges described here will prove too difficult, and the only option for the company will be to engage in a more formal restructuring option.[252]

5.6 The use of CVAs and the comparison with schemes

This section will contrast schemes with CVAs. Unlike the provisions governing schemes, which are found in companies legislation (Part 26 of the Companies Act 2006), the provisions governing CVAs are found in insolvency legislation (Insolvency Act 1986, sections 1–7B).

In contrast to schemes, which have been in existence for more than a century,[253] CVAs were introduced for the first time in the 1985–6 insolvency law reforms.[254] Until the Insolvency Act 1985, English insolvency law regarded liquidation as the cornerstone of corporate insolvency law. However, the end-point of liquidation is always the dissolution of the company, and concerns began to be raised about the role of liquidation (and thus the dissolution of companies) as the focal point of English insolvency law. The report of the Cork Committee in 1982 was particularly critical of this approach, and instead advocated the development of a rescue culture in England.[255] Both CVAs and administration were introduced with the aim of promoting such a culture.

In particular, the Cork Committee considered that the law under review was deficient in failing to provide that a company could enter into a binding arrangement with its creditors by a simple procedure that would allow it to reorganise its debts. The only options available to a company at that time were a workout or the scheme of arrangement procedure. In section 5.5 the disadvantages to a company of using a workout are considered, in particular the need to obtain the separate consent of every creditor. The Cork Committee also considered that a scheme of arrangement was inadequate for this purpose, being, in its view, too slow and cumbersome to be satisfactory. Debt reorganisation schemes, at that point, were relatively under-used and under-developed.

[252] A common outcome is the use of a scheme involving a subset of the creditors, usually the financial creditors, combined with a standstill arrangement negotiated between that subset of creditors; see sections 5.4.3 and 5.4.4.1.

[253] See section 1.1.

[254] Initially, CVAs appeared as Insolvency Act 1985, ss. 20–26, which were then consolidated as Insolvency Act 1986, Part 1.

[255] Cork Committee, *Insolvency Law and Practice*, note 181 above.

Sections 1–7 of the Insolvency Act 1986 were introduced in order to provide companies with a swifter and simpler mechanism for reorganising their debts. The purpose of introducing CVAs was therefore to provide a contractual mechanism through which a company could restructure its debts and liabilities, allowing it to continue trading for the benefit of the creditors as a whole.

CVAs are intended to facilitate compromises or variations of contractual rights or other obligations. The effect of the resulting compromise is that it binds all of those creditors that, in accordance with the rules, were entitled to vote at the meeting approving the arrangement or would have been so entitled if they had had notice of the meeting.[256] There are some limits to the scope of a CVA, namely that only pecuniary obligations between debtors and creditors can be modified. It was held in *Discovery (Northampton) Ltd* v. *Debenhams Retail Ltd*[257] that property rights cannot be altered by a CVA.

CVAs can be initiated either by the directors[258] or by the liquidator or administrator if the company is being wound up or is in administration.[259] The directors, or the insolvency practitioner, may propose a CVA for either a composition in satisfaction of the debtor's debts or a scheme of arrangement of its affairs.[260] Neither creditors nor members have the power to make a proposal under a CVA.[261] However, in common with schemes of arrangement, it is not necessary for the company to be insolvent or unable to pay its debts for this procedure to be used.[262]

256 Insolvency Act 1986, Part 1.

257 [2019] EWHC 2441 (Ch). In this case, the landlords argued that the right to forfeiture which the CVA sought to prevent could not be excluded, on the basis that this was a property right that could not be abrogated by the CVA (see Law of Property Act 1925, s. 1(2), which provides that a right of re-entry or forfeiture is a proprietary right). The court agreed with this contention, although on the facts the success of this argument did not cause the CVA to fail since the CVA had severance provisions, and therefore the provisions dealing with forfeiture restraint in the CVA could be excised, allowing the CVA to go forward. For further discussion see section 5.6.1. A similar approach is adopted in schemes of arrangement: *Re Instant Cash Loans Ltd* [2019] EWHC 2795 (Ch).

258 Insolvency Act 1986, s. 1(1).

259 Ibid., s. 1(3).

260 Ibid., s. 1(1). The law regarding what constitutes a composition or scheme of arrangement under a CVA is very similar to that applying in relation to schemes: *March Estates plc* v. *Gunmark Ltd* [1996] 2 BCLC 1, 5.

261 Cf. schemes of arrangement as discussed at section 2.2.1.

262 A company may commence a CVA in England only if it is registered in England and Wales or if its COMI is located in England: Insolvency Act 1986, s. 1. While the UK was a member of the EU and during the transition period which ended on 31 December 2020,

Where the directors initiate the CVA, they will appoint a nominee (generally an insolvency practitioner) to act in relation to it.[263] The directors initiate the CVA by sending a written notice of their proposal, together with a copy of the proposal, to the nominee.[264] The proposal will provide a short explanation of why, in the opinion of the directors, a CVA is desirable and why the company's creditors can be expected to agree with it.[265] The Insolvency Rules set out the contents of the proposal that is intended, when taken together with the report from the nominee, to put the members and creditors in a position to reach an informed decision on the proposal.[266] This proposal serves a similar purpose to the explanatory statement under a scheme.[267] At the same time, the directors deliver to the nominee a statement of the company's affairs.[268] Where the company is in liquidation or administration, the liquidator or administrator will invariably take on the role of nominee.

Where the nominee is not the liquidator or administrator, they must report to the court, within twenty-eight days of the notice of the proposal for a CVA, stating whether meetings of the company and creditors should be summoned to consider the proposal and, if so, the date, time and place for such meetings.[269] The nominee must be satisfied that the debtor company's true financial position is not materially different from the information given to creditors, that the proposal has a real prospect of being implemented and that there is no unavoidable manifest unfairness.[270]

a CVA was a form of insolvency proceeding covered by the EU Recast Insolvency Regulation and thus entitled to recognition throughout the European Union, unlike a scheme of arrangement (for discussion see section 7.3.1).

263 Insolvency Act 1986, s. 1(2). Generally, the directors will have approached the nominee before this stage and the nominee is usually involved in drawing up the proposal.

264 Ibid., s. 2(3). In the case of a proposal by an administrator or liquidator that is not the nominee, the same procedure must be followed.

265 Insolvency Rules (England and Wales) 2016 (SI 2016/1024) (Insolvency Rules 2016), r. 2.2(1).

266 Ibid., r. 2.3(1). Where the proposer of the CVA is the administrator or liquidator, the proposal should contain, in addition to those matters covered by r. 2.3(1), details of the preferential creditors and any other matters that the insolvency practitioner considers appropriate (see r. 2.3(3)).

267 For discussion of the explanatory statement see section 2.2.2.

268 Insolvency Rules 2016, rr. 2.3, 2.6. The nominee can ask for further information (r. 2.8) and must be given access to the company's accounts and records (r. 2.8(3)).

269 Insolvency Act 1986, s. 2(2).

270 *Re a Debtor (No. 140 of 1995)* [1996] 2 BCLC 429.

Where the nominee recommends that meetings be held, then, unless the court directs otherwise, the nominee summons the meetings as proposed.[271] The proposal needs to be approved by 75 per cent of the creditors voting in person or by proxy by reference to the value of their claims (i.e. a majority-by-value test only).[272] It also requires the approval of 50 per cent in value of the members present at a shareholders' meeting.[273] If approved, the CVA becomes binding on the company and all those creditors who (i) were entitled to vote at the creditors' meeting (whether they were represented at the meeting or not) or (ii) would have been entitled to do so had they had notice of the meeting.[274] The CVA then binds even those creditors that did not approve the proposal. The scheme is administered by a supervisor, usually the person who was the nominee.[275] A CVA is generally terminated either by satisfaction of debts or by the supervisor initiating an administration or liquidation.[276]

5.6.1 *Who is bound by a CVA?*

In a scheme of arrangement, all of the creditors (and members) within the ambit of the scheme will be bound, whether they voted in favour of the scheme or not, provided the requisite majorities are obtained in the

[271] Insolvency Act 1986, s. 3(1). The nominee must summon every creditor of the debtor of whose claim and address they are aware, whether or not the CVA proposal affects the rights of those debtors. This is in contrast to schemes that need only be approved by those whose rights are affected, and therefore only those members and/or creditors need to be given notice of the meetings. Where the nominee is the liquidator or administrator see s. 3(2).

[272] Insolvency Rules 2016, r. 15.34(3). Creditors may decide to approve a CVA through one of the qualifying decision procedures, rather than a meeting: Insolvency Act 1986, ss. 3, 5 as amended. For the position regarding the approval threshold for schemes see section 2.3.3.

[273] Insolvency Rules 2016, r. 2.36(1). Value is determined by the number of votes conferred on each member by the company's articles.

[274] Insolvency Act 1986, s. 5(1).

[275] Ibid., s. 7(2). If the nominee is the liquidator or administrator, a separate person may be appointed as a supervisor. For example, a liquidator might wish to do this where they consider that it would be advantageous for the business of the company to be carried on but they lack the necessary powers (see Insolvency Act 1986, Sch. 4, para. 5).

[276] For a discussion of the full range of possible outcomes see A. Walters and S. Frisby, 'Preliminary report to the Insolvency Service into outcomes in company voluntary arrangements' (2011) available at www.ssrn.com/abstract=1792402; P. Walton, C. Umfreville and L. Jacobs, *Company Voluntary Arrangements: Evaluating Success and Failure* (Report commissioned by R3, May 2018).

class meetings and the court sanctions the scheme. In a CVA, all of the shareholders of the company will be bound, whether they voted in favour or not and, in some circumstances, even where the members' meeting voted against the CVA.[277] However, the position in relation to creditors in a CVA requires more explanation.

The concept of a creditor for CVA purposes was considered in *Discovery (Northampton) Ltd* v. *Debenhams Retail Ltd*.[278] The term 'creditor' is not defined for the purposes of Part 1 of the Insolvency Act 1986, but section 5(2) of the Act explains that the CVA will bind every person who was entitled to vote in the procedure by which the CVA was approved. Entitlement to vote on a CVA is determined by the Insolvency Rules 2016. These provide that every 'creditor' who has notice is entitled to vote 'in respect of that creditor's debt'.[279] The concepts of 'creditor' and 'debt' are therefore intertwined. If entitled to vote, the creditor will be bound by a successful CVA even if it did not receive notice of the meeting,[280] or did receive notice but did not attend or vote, or did attend and voted against the CVA.

It was contended in the *Debenhams* case that landlords are not creditors in relation to future rent for the purposes of a CVA, and therefore these claims cannot be compromised under a CVA. It was argued that future rent is not a 'debt' within the meaning of section 5(2) of the Insolvency Act 1986. The judge held that 'creditor' must be given a wide meaning for this purpose. Although the term 'debt' is not defined in the context of CVAs, it is defined in relation to administration and liquidation.[281] Specifically, the Insolvency Rules in this context extend the meaning to 'any debt or liability to which the company may become subject after the relevant date by reason of any obligation incurred before that date'.[282] The judge therefore considered that a 'creditor' for CVA purposes 'includes someone towards whom the company has a present

[277] Insolvency Act 1986, s. 4A. For discussion see section 5.6.5.

[278] [2019] EWHC 2441 (Ch).

[279] Insolvency Rules 2016, r. 15.28(5).

[280] Insolvency Act 1986, s. 5(2) (this change was introduced by Insolvency Act 2000, s. 2, Sch. 2). However, in *Re Uniglaze 2 (East Anglia) Ltd* [2015] 12 WLUK 156, the judge held that this section cannot have been intended to cover a situation where creditors are consciously excluded from participation in a CVA by reason of not having been given notice; the aim of the subsection must be to cover errors in giving notice or something of a similar nature, not a decision not to give notice.

[281] Insolvency Rules 2016, r. 14.1(3).

[282] Ibid.

pecuniary liability which will in the future or may on a contingency become payable as a debt'.[283]

Consequently, while a creditor must have a 'debt', the meaning of debt for these purposes extends well beyond a debt strictly so-called. It includes pecuniary liabilities (obligations that may turn into debts strictly so-called) that might spring out of an existing legal relationship. This is in accordance with David Richards J in *Re T&N Ltd (No. 2)*[284] in which he stated that the holder of a contingent claim is a creditor for the purposes of the provisions governing both schemes of arrangement and CVAs and, further, that the claim need not be a provable debt.[285]

The judge in *Debenhams* held that future rent might not be a provable debt and, in a strict sense, might not be a debt at all, but it is at least a pecuniary liability to which the parties might become subject in the future by reason of an existing obligation. The liability might be characterised as a contingent claim, as a contingent claim subject to special treatment under the Insolvency Rules, or simply as a non-provable claim, but it is a debt within the extended meaning of that term that applied for this purpose and the landlord was therefore a creditor. As a matter of jurisdiction, therefore, future rent can be included in a CVA.[286]

The chairman of the creditors' meeting has discretion to admit or reject a creditors' claim, wholly or in part, for the purposes of entitlement to vote (and, therefore, for the purposes of participation in the CVA, since the two are so closely linked).[287] The chairman might reject such a claim where the creditor is subordinated and all of the available assets will be exhausted in meeting the claims of the ordinary creditors.[288] In a scheme, a similar effect can be achieved by the scheme being structured

283 [2019] EWHC 2441 (Ch) at [28]. See also *Burford Midland Properties Ltd* v. *Marley Extrusions Ltd* [1994] BCC 604.

284 [2005] EWHC 2870 (Ch) at [42].

285 See, further, *Re North Point Global Limited* [2020] EWHC 1648 (Ch).

286 This expansive view of the meaning of 'creditor' is similar therefore to that adopted for schemes of arrangement, discussed at section 5.2, especially section 5.2.1.

287 Insolvency Rules 2016, r. 15.33(2). The chairman's decision is subject to appeal to the court by any creditor or member of the company: r. 15.35.

288 *Re British and Commonwealth Holdings Plc (No. 3)* [1992] 1 WLR 672. The chairman might also decide to reject a claim where it is too uncertain or speculative to accept for voting, even as a contingent claim. Where a creditor's claim is for an unliquidated, unascertained amount, it used to be the case that if the chairman refused to place a minimum value on it, the creditor could not vote at all (see *Doorbar* v. *Alltime Securities Ltd (No. 2)* [1995] BCC 728; *Re Sweatfield Ltd* [1997] BCC 744). The chairman may now value such a claim at £1 for the purposes of voting (but not otherwise), allowing such a creditor to be brought within the CVA: Insolvency Rules 2016, r. 15.31(3).

in such a way as to leave unaltered the rights of the subordinated creditors. This was discussed in section 5.4.3 in relation to the example of the IMO Car Wash scheme.[289]

However, merely determining who has the right to vote does not provide the definitive answer as to which creditors will be bound by a CVA. For instance, secured creditors have the right to vote at the meeting (although their votes are not counted for the purposes of determining whether the necessary majority has been reached),[290] but it is clear that CVAs cannot bind secured creditors or preferential creditors without their consent.[291] This is in contrast to schemes of arrangement, which clearly do allow for such creditors to be bound if the requisite majorities are obtained, and the court sanctions the scheme. In practice, as discussed in section 2.3.2, secured creditors will generally be placed in a separate class, and may well be distinguished further (for example, fixed and floating charges, first and second charges in relation to the same property). It is not impossible for a secured creditor to be in a class of one, in which case they will have a veto right over the scheme. In such a situation, the distinction between the position of secured creditors in CVAs and in schemes diminishes significantly.

5.6.2 *Minority creditor protection*

Minority creditors receive different types of protection in schemes of arrangement and in CVAs. These will be examined in turn.

5.6.2.1 Minority protection in a debt restructuring scheme

In a scheme of arrangement, minority creditor protection is provided (i) by the fact that creditors meet in (fully informed) separate class meetings when deciding whether to approve the scheme; and (ii) by the court's oversight role, particularly in sanctioning the scheme. The issues around placing creditors into the correct classes are discussed at sections 2.3.2 and 5.3. The role of the court in sanctioning schemes is discussed at section 2.4. This is not a rubber-stamping exercise, and, even if all of the classes have approved the scheme, the court might nevertheless decide not to sanction, for example if it determines that the scheme is unfair to some other relevant constituency. So, for example, if a group of creditors

289 *Re Bluebrook Ltd* [2009] EWHC 2114 (Ch); [2010] 1 BCLC 338, and see section 5.4.3.

290 Insolvency Rules 2016, r. 15.31(4), but see also r. 15.31(5)(6).

291 Insolvency Act 1986, s. 4(3).

are left out of the scheme, as the junior creditors were from the IMO Car Wash scheme,[292] they might nevertheless appear before the court at the sanctioning stage to argue that the scheme is unfair to them and should not be sanctioned. The court will carefully assess the scheme and the challenge of such a group in these circumstances. However, where it determines that the group has no remaining economic interest in the company, the court has accepted that it can then sanction the scheme despite these protests.[293]

5.6.2.2 Minority protection in a CVA

By way of contrast, CVAs involve no sanction of the court and there are no separate class meetings. All of the creditors meet in a single meeting. It is notable that the Cork Report in 1982,[294] which led to the introduction of CVAs, commented on the difficulties associated with determining separate classes for the purpose of schemes of arrangement, and did not recommend that separate class meetings be required for CVAs.[295]

It is also worth noting that the majority requirements are different in a scheme and in a CVA. In a CVA, the creditors' decision needs to be taken by 75 per cent of creditors voting in person or by proxy, measured by reference to the value of their claims.[296] This contrasts with the decision on a scheme, which must be both 75 per cent in value and a majority in number.[297] The original purpose of the additional headcount test in a scheme was to provide a form of protection for small creditors, operating as 'a check on the ability of creditors with large claims to carry the day'.[298] If this is a valuable form of protection then the absence of the headcount test in relation to CVAs might be regarded as problematic. However, as discussed in Chapter 2, the majority-in-number requirement in relation to schemes is controversial and can cause significant difficulties. It is suggested in Chapter 2 that this

[292] See e.g. *Re Bluebrook Ltd* [2009] EWHC 2114 (Ch); [2010] 1 BCLC 338.

[293] See section 5.4.3.

[294] Cork Committee, *Insolvency Law and Practice*, note 181 above.

[295] Ibid., para. 400ff.

[296] In a proposed CVA, a decision is not made if more than half of the total value of the unconnected creditors vote against it (Insolvency Rules 2016, r. 15.34(4)). No such rule exists in relation to schemes.

[297] Companies Act 2006, s. 899(1), discussed in section 2.3.3.

[298] Company Law Review, Modern Company Law for a Competitive Economy: Completing the Structure, URN 00/1335, November 2000 (CLR, Completing the Structure) at para. 11.34.

requirement should be removed.[299] Therefore, the approach to this issue adopted in relation to CVAs is preferable.

There has been some discussion as to whether this 75 per cent limit should be reduced, in order to promote the use of CVAs.[300] Balanced against this is the fact that a lower threshold would allow creditors to be bound against their will by a simple majority, which might be problematic and, arguably, undesirable, and to date no proposals for change of this issue have been brought forward.[301]

The absence both of separate class meetings for creditors and of a formal court sanctioning stage leaves minority creditors potentially exposed to abuse. Other forms of creditor protection have therefore been built into the CVA procedure. One of these is the role of the nominee in a CVA (discussed in section 5.6.3), who can be seen as watching over the interests of different groups in CVAs in a similar fashion to the court in schemes. In addition, if officers of the company make any false representation or omit to do something for the purpose of obtaining the approval of the company's members or creditors for a CVA, they commit an offence.[302]

Another significant protection is the ability, under section 6 of the Insolvency Act 1986, for any person entitled to vote at a meeting of creditors or members, or a nominee liquidator or administrator, to apply to the court to challenge the CVA on the ground of unfair prejudice or material irregularity.[303] The concept of a material irregularity refers primarily to breaches of the rules at the meetings. So, for example, an incorrect decision by the chairman to exclude a vote at the meeting may be a material irregularity.[304] In addition, where information relevant to

299 See section 2.3.3.2.

300 Insolvency Service, *A Review of Company Rescue and Business Mechanisms, Interim Report* (London: DTI, 1999) at 11.

301 Insolvency Service, *A Review of Company Rescue and Business Reconstruction Mechanisms*, Report by the Review Group (London: DTI, 2000) at 36. The view was also put forward that reducing the percentage would not have a significant effect on acceptance levels.

302 Insolvency Act 1986, ss. 6A(4) and 7A (a person guilty of this offence is liable to a fine or imprisonment for up to six years, or both). See also Theft Act 1968, s. 19, which creates an offence where an officer of a company, with intent to deceive members or creditors of the company about its affairs, publishes or concurs in publishing a written statement which to their knowledge is or may be misleading, false or deceptive in a material particular.

303 Insolvency Act 1986, s. 6(1)(2).

304 *Re a Debtor (No. 222 of 1990), ex p The Bank of Ireland* [1992] BCLC 137. To be a material irregularity, the wrong decision must be such as to possibly affect the outcome of the meeting: *Re a Debtor (No. 259 of 1990)* [1992] 1 All ER 641.

the CVA is not properly disclosed in a proposal, or that information is deemed to be false and misleading in a material way, this might also constitute a material irregularity.[305] An irregularity under section 6(1)(b) of the Act will be considered material if (and only if), objectively assessed, there is a substantial chance that if the irregularity had not occurred it would have made a material difference to the way in which the creditors would have considered and assessed the terms of the CVA.[306]

The concept of unfair prejudice is less easy to pin down. It seems to require some differential treatment that prejudices the creditor, but it is clear that the mere fact that creditors have been accorded differential treatment does not necessarily prove the existence of unfair prejudice.[307] The courts have made use of two comparisons to help them to determine whether unfair prejudice exists. The first is a comparison with the realistically available alternative process to the CVA, so, for example, the position of the creditors on a winding-up where the CVA is presented as an alternative to winding up. This was referred to as the 'vertical comparison' by Etherton J in *Prudential Assurance Co Ltd* v. *PRG Powerhouse Ltd.*[308] In *Discovery (Northampton) Ltd* v. *Debenhams Retail Ltd*,[309] the judge stated that just because it could be demonstrated that the return to a creditor under the CVA is better than (or at least the same as) the result that would be achieved in the relevant alternative insolvency process (for example liquidation), this did not mean that the reduction in rent in that case was automatically fair.[310] In other words, just because the vertical comparator is satisfied, it does not mean that the terms of the CVA cannot be unfair. This is because 'the court will consider the "fairness" of the CVA in the round'.[311]

305 See e.g. *Re Gatnom Capital & Finance Ltd* [2010] EWHC 3353 (Ch).

306 See *Re Trident Fashions Plc (No. 2)* [2004] EWHC 293 (Ch) *per* Lewison J at [46] and *SISU Capital Fund Ltd* v. *Tucker (Costs)* [2005] EWHC 2321 (Ch) *per* Warren J at [80]–[81].

307 See *Prudential Assurance Co Ltd* v. *PRG Powerhouse Ltd* [2007] EWHC 1002 (Ch); [2007] BCC 500.

308 Ibid. at [75]. This was applied in *Mourant & Co Trustees Ltd* v. *Sixty UK Ltd (in administration)* [2010] EWHC 1890 (Ch); [2010] BCC 882 and *Re Portsmouth City FC Ltd* [2010] EWHC 2013 (Ch); [2011] BCC 149.

309 [2019] EWHC 2441 (Ch).

310 Ibid. at [72]–[76]. The judge held that the CVA did not create new obligations, it merely varied existing ones.

311 Ibid. at [75].

The second is a comparison of the treatment of creditors under the CVA inter se, referred to as the 'horizontal comparison' by Etherton J in *Prudential Assurance Co Ltd* v. *PRG Powerhouse Ltd*:[312]

> Horizontal comparison is with other creditors or classes of creditors. In that context, another helpful guide, in the case of a CVA, is comparison with the position if, instead of a CVA, there had been a formal scheme of arrangement under [the Companies Act], on which the different classes of creditors would have been required to meet and vote separately.

Lightman J in *Re Wimbledon Football Club* stated that unequal or differential treatment between creditors might not lead per se to unfair prejudice but nevertheless would require explanation.[313] Differential treatment may be required to ensure fairness or the continuation of the business. However, if one group of creditors use the provisions to deprive a creditor of rights while preserving their own, this is likely to amount to unfair prejudice. A good example of this kind of scenario arose in *Powerhouse*. The company was an electrical retailer that, with financial support from its parent company, had acquired a number of high street stores and superstores. The landlords had taken parent company guarantees and indemnities in respect of the company's obligations under the leases. The company got into financial difficulties and wished to close a number of stores and to enter into a CVA. The terms of this arrangement were that those who were creditors in respect of the premises to be closed would receive 28p in the pound funded by the parent, while the rights and obligations of other creditors would be unaffected. The CVA contained provisions designed to release all creditors' claims against the company relating to the closed premises, and to release the parent company's guarantees to the landlords of the closed premises. At a meeting, all of the creditors of the company voted, including those whose rights and obligations were not affected by the CVA, and the CVA was approved by the requisite statutory majority.

The landlords challenged the CVA as unfairly prejudicial under section 6 of the Insolvency Act 1986 and sought declarations that it was invalid or ineffective in so far as it purported to affect their rights. Etherton J confirmed that differential treatment alone does not necessarily establish unfair prejudice, and nor does the fact that a particular class

312 [2007] EWHC 1002 (Ch) at [75]. This was applied in *Mourant & Co Trustees Ltd* v. *Sixty UK Ltd (in administration)* [2010] EWHC 1890 (Ch); [2010] BCC 882 and *Re Portsmouth City FC Ltd* [2010] EWHC 2013 (Ch); [2011] BCC 149.

313 [2004] EWHC 1020 (Ch); [2005] 1 BCLC 66.

of creditors could have blocked a scheme under a scheme of arrangement.[314] However, in all the circumstances, this CVA was unfairly prejudicial to the landlords. The landlords were all to receive 28p in the pound, whether or not they had the benefit of guarantees, and nothing extra for the loss of the guarantees, which had real value. Further, all the creditors, other than the affected creditors, were to be paid in full. The landlords were the class of creditors that would suffer least, if at all, on an insolvent liquidation of the company, by virtue of the guarantees, but they were the class most prejudiced by the CVA, under which their claims against the company and the parent company, as surety, were to be compromised by payment of a dividend that placed no value on those guarantees. It seems clear, then, that where one group of creditors uses its votes to deprive another creditor or group of creditors of their rights against third parties, while preserving their own rights, the courts are likely to find that unfair prejudice exists.[315]

The concept of unfair prejudice was considered further by the court in *Discovery (Northampton) Ltd* v. *Debenhams Retail Ltd*.[316] Control of Debenhams had passed to its finance creditors under a pre-pack administration. The purpose of the CVA was to restructure the balance sheet and to deal with its store portfolio. Different types of landlords were treated differently under the CVA depending on how stores operating from the various locations were performing. The CVA was approved by 94.71 per cent of Debenhams' creditors, but certain landlords (unsurprisingly those with the biggest discount) challenged the CVA on various grounds, including that the CVA was unfairly prejudicial under section 6(1)(a).[317]

The landlords challenged the fact that the CVA involved a reduction in the rent due to them. They argued that they should receive full contractual rent for the leased premises[318] and that the CVA could not be used to compromise their claims. The judge disagreed, holding that CVAs were

[314] *Sisu Capital Fund Ltd* v. *Tucker* [2005] EWHC 2170 (Ch); [2006] BCC 463.

[315] See also *Re a Debtor (No. 101 of 1999)* [2001] 1 BCLC 54.

[316] [2019] EWHC 2441 (Ch).

[317] There was also a challenge based on the argument that there was a material irregularity under s. 6(1)(b). This was based on a claim that the CVA had failed adequately to disclose the existence of potential clawback claims and had therefore failed to comply with the contents requirements set out in the Insolvency Rules 2016, r. 2.3(1). This challenge failed.

[318] This was on the basis of the principle in *Re Lundy Granite Co (1870–71) LR 6 Ch App 462* that provides that a company in administration or liquidation which makes beneficial use of leased premises must pay the full contractual rent for them. However, the judge

introduced in order to provide a flexible tool for compromising contracts, and landlords are not an exception to this principle. That said, the judge stressed that the new rent which the landlords were required to accept under the CVA could not be lower than the market rent and the interference with the contractual terms must be 'the minimum extent necessary in the circumstances'.[319] Furthermore, the landlords argued that the CVA was unfair because they were treated less favourably than other unsecured creditors (such as suppliers) without any proper justification, i.e. the CVA was unfair on the basis of the horizontal comparison. The judge was satisfied by the justification for differential treatment provided by the company and stated that it was understandable that it was more essential for the company to pay its suppliers if it wanted to continue business than to pay its landlord. Again, the judge was influenced by the fact that the CVA did not seek to reduce the rent to be paid to the landlords below the market rate.

In *Gertner* v. *CFL Finance Limited*,[320] the court considered the issue of good faith in the context of an individual voluntary arrangement (IVA). The principles developed there are also likely to be valuable in the context of CVAs. The judge held that what was required was for approving creditors to act in the interests of the class of unsecured creditors and that, if there were factors operating on an approving creditor's judgement that caused that creditor to be differentiated from the class, that creditor's approval of the arrangement must be disregarded and the arrangement so approved set aside. However, it is for creditors, not the court, to determine whether a proposed arrangement should be acceded to or not. This good faith rule therefore focuses not so much on the merits of the proposal (which is a matter for the creditors) but on the question of whether the creditor is acting in accordance with the interests of the class, and is similar to the approach adopted by courts at the scheme sanctioning hearing.[321]

How does the minority protection provided by section 6 of the Insolvency Act 1986 compare with the minority protection offered in a scheme? There are some important differences. For instance, the onus is different in the two scenarios. In the case of a scheme, it is for the proponents of the scheme to satisfy the court that it should be sanctioned.

distinguished the scenario in CVAs on the basis that this process is intended to be more flexible.

319 *Discovery (Northampton) Ltd* v. *Debenhams Retail Ltd* [2019] EWHC 2441 (Ch) at [71].

320 [2020] EWHC 1241 (Ch).

321 See section 2.4.3.

In the case of a CVA, it is for the objectors to show unfair prejudice.[322] Where the court is satisfied as to the grounds of challenge, it may revoke or suspend the approvals given by the meeting(s) and/or direct the summoning of further meetings.[323]

However, in many ways, the difference between schemes and CVAs, as regards the level of minority protection on offer, may not be as significant as it first appears. It seems that on a section 6 challenge by creditors, the courts will take account of issues akin to those considered by the courts in schemes. Although there is no statutory requirement for separate class meetings, this is an issue to which the court will have regard when considering the issue of unfair prejudice. In light of *Powerhouse*, some companies have resorted to a practice of importing class votes into the CVA procedure, presumably with the intention of warding off unfair prejudice claims. For example, in the 2007 debt restructuring of Schefenacker plc, the CVA proposal was made conditional on the approval of the statutory majority at the creditors' meeting and also required the support of in excess of 75 per cent of the bondholders.

In practical terms, the approach of the court in considering a challenge under section 6 of the Insolvency Act 1986 seems very similar to the role of the court in relation to schemes of arrangement. As described in Chapter 2, the trend in the courts is to apply the test of separate classes in such a way as to reduce the number of classes, thereby reducing minority protection at the convening hearing, leaving these matters to be dealt with at the sanctioning hearing. The courts set out a number of tests that must be considered at the sanctioning stage. Broadly, the court is concerned to determine whether the statutory requirements are met (such as the requirements for the explanatory memorandum and for the scheme to be approved by the requisite majorities); whether, in approving the scheme, the majority fairly represented the class; whether an intelligent and honest person, a member of the class concerned and acting in respect of their own interest, might reasonably approve the scheme; and whether there is a blot on the scheme.[324]

This approach is not dissimilar to the court's concerns in the section 6 scenario, which are to consider whether there has been a material irregularity or unfair prejudice in a CVA. The closeness of the connection

[322] *Prudential Assurance Co Ltd* v. *PRG Powerhouse Ltd* [2007] EWHC 1002 (Ch); [2007] BCC 500.

[323] Insolvency Act 1986, s. 6(4).

[324] See section 2.4.

between schemes and CVAs was recognised by David Richards J in *Re T & N Ltd.*[325] Comparing schemes and CVAs in this context, he stated:

> I do not . . . consider that there is any difference in the substance of the underlying test of fairness which must be applied. It is deliberately a broad test to be applied on a case by case basis, and courts have struggled to do better than the approach adopted by the Court of Appeal in *Re Alabama, New Orleans, Texas & Pacific Junction Railway Co* [1891] Ch 213 and summarised in the often-cited passage from a leading textbook, *Buckley on the Companies Acts*:
>
> 'In exercising its power of sanction the court will see, first, that the provisions of the statute have been complied with, second that the class was fairly represented by those who attended the meeting and that the statutory majority are acting bona fide and are not coercing the minority in order to promote interests adverse to those of the class whom they purport to represent, and thirdly, that the arrangement is such as an intelligent and honest man, a member of the class concerned and acting in respect of his interest, might reasonably approve.
>
> The court does not sit merely to see that the majority are acting bona fide and thereupon to register the decision of the meeting, but, at the same time, the court will be slow to differ from the meeting, unless either the class has not been properly consulted, or the meeting has not considered the matter with a view to the interests of the class which it is empowered to bind, or some blot is found in the scheme.'[326]

Although this passage relates to schemes of arrangement, the judge clearly regarded it as an equally apt description of the court's analysis of CVAs, where a creditor is challenging the CVA under section 6 of the 1986 Act.

In one important sense, however, the company's position in relation to CVAs described here is more problematic than it is in schemes. The scope for a challenge to be brought under section 6 in relation to a CVA creates an ongoing risk for the company.[327] This stands in sharp contrast to the finality of a court-sanctioned scheme, which cannot be challenged except in very limited circumstances.[328] The challenge under section 6 can be brought within twenty-eight days of the date of the report to the court of the meetings or, if by someone without notice of the meetings,

[325] [2004] EWHC 2361 (Ch); [2005] 2 BCLC 488.

[326] Ibid. at [81].

[327] The risk for CVAs might be long-lasting. In *Williams* v. *Carraway Guildford (Nominee A) Ltd* [2019] EWHC 3073 (Ch) the judge refused to strike out on the basis that once a CVA has terminated, the court has no power to revoke it; the law on this point could only be settled after full argument.

[328] See section 2.5.

twenty-eight days from the first day on which they become aware of a problem.[329] Therefore, if there is an untraced creditor (which may be possible in a complex, multi-tiered debt structure in which ascertaining all of the creditors, particularly the contingent creditors, may be difficult), there is potential for the CVA to be challenged months, or even years, after it has been approved.

5.6.3 *The role of an insolvency practitioner*

Schemes of arrangement are in essence agreements between companies and their creditors (which are then sanctioned by the court and registered) and, as a result, there is no need to involve an insolvency practitioner in formulating and implementing a scheme. This allows the directors of the company to remain in control of it. By contrast, even where a CVA is proposed by the directors, an insolvency practitioner needs to be involved as nominee and then supervisor of the CVA. As discussed in section 5.6.2, the involvement of the nominee is an aspect of the minority protection that exists in a CVA, as part of the quid pro quo for reduced court intervention, as compared to schemes, and in some ways nominees in CVAs have a similar role to that of the court in schemes. However, the two are not identical. In particular, there may be differences in the extent of the role and the costs connected with these choices.

Legal regimes dealing with financially distressed companies and wishing to facilitate some form of restructuring or rescue of those companies face certain choices regarding the system to put in place. One of the significant choices they face is whether to allow and facilitate a restructuring by the existing management of the company (a debtor-in-possession strategy) or to sideline the existing management and facilitate a restructuring or rescue by a combination of an external manager or agent and the company's creditors.[330] Both CVAs and schemes of arrangement can be regarded as debtor-in-possession procedures.

[329] Insolvency Act 1986, s. 6(3).

[330] For a discussion of the merits of debtor-in-possession versus practitioner-in-possession processes see N. Martin, 'Common law bankruptcy systems: similarities and differences' (2003) 11 *American Bankruptcy Institute Law Review* 367; D. Hahn, 'Concentrated ownership and control of corporate reorganisations' (2004) 4 *Journal of Corporate Law Studies* 117; G. McCormack, 'Control and corporate rescue: an Anglo-American evaluation' (2007) 56 *International and Comparative Law Quarterly* 515.

In a scheme, it is quite clear that the company's management remain in control through the recommendation and implementation of a scheme. In a CVA, where the company is not in administration or liquidation, then the company's directors remain in control, despite the involvement of the insolvency practitioner as nominee and then supervisor of the CVA.[331] This contrasts with the formal collective insolvency procedures of administration and liquidation, both of which involve the directors losing their control over the future of the firm. Of course, where the company is already in administration or liquidation, then the administrator or liquidator will deal with the company's affairs and the CVA will not be a debtor-in-possession procedure.[332]

The fact that the directors can remain in control may be an advantage or a disadvantage depending on the quality of the directors in question, and the reasons for the company's financial difficulties. Where it was the poor management of the directors that led the company into difficulties, the fact that they remain in control might be problematic. It might be difficult to persuade existing creditors to support the proposed arrangement if they believe that the directors caused the difficulties in the first place, although information asymmetries (especially in widely held companies) might mean that it is difficult or impossible for creditors to determine whether it was the directors or simply bad luck that led the firm into financial difficulties. There might also be a concern that the management are planning to use the CVA as a device that will allow them to set up a phoenix company, transfer the business and its assets to that new company and leave the creditors empty-handed. A further concern might be that directors in such a scenario may prefer a CVA to other options because it provides less scrutiny of their conduct. Nominees and supervisors of CVAs are required to make a report to the Secretary of State only where it appears that a director of the company is guilty of an offence for which the director is criminally liable in connection with a moratorium or the CVA itself.[333] If no subsequent administration or liquidation then takes place, the directors (who may have been liable for wrongful trading,[334] for example) might escape scrutiny. This may make the CVA procedure simpler, quicker and more straightforward than schemes, but it clearly has some potential downsides too.

331 This is subject to any provision to the contrary in the CVA itself.

332 Similarly, where a scheme of arrangement is coupled with liquidation or administration, it can no longer be regarded as a debtor-in-possession procedure.

333 Insolvency Act 1986, s. 7A. Cf. Company Directors Disqualification Act 1986.

334 Insolvency Act 1986, s. 214.

However, leaving the directors in control might be very positive, particularly where the company is in difficulties that are not related to poor management. The directors know the company best and may be thought to be in the ideal position to attempt a rescue of the company. If the directors are in the best position to run the business, it may also be asked why the nominee should be the one to negotiate with the creditors in order to set up the CVA and obtain the creditors' consent to it. It could be argued that one of the roles of a nominee is to signal to the outside creditors (i.e. creditors without insider knowledge of the company and/or understanding of its functioning) that the procedure is supervised by an independent expert.[335] However, research suggests that the expertise of insolvency practitioners in operating CVAs may vary enormously.[336] On occasion, directors might be better placed and better suited to perform this role. Internally generated solutions, and the recommendation and implementation of these proposals by the directors rather than by external insolvency practitioners, might sometimes be preferable, particularly where the company's troubles are not caused by poor management, where the directors are able to appreciate the necessary steps for a turnaround or rescue strategy to be implemented, and where they have the necessary skills to implement such a strategy.

Finally, a mechanism that leaves directors in control of the company whilst it deals with its financial distress can act as an incentive for a timely resolution of financial problems, since directors are more prepared to make use of such a mechanism (and retain their roles) instead of hoping for the best and avoiding any type of restructuring, as might otherwise be the case.

5.6.4 *The role of the court*

In schemes of arrangement, there are two mandatory court hearings. These perform an important role in providing minority protection, including determining whether members and/or creditors should meet in separate classes and, crucially, whether the scheme should be sanctioned. However, this process adds cost and delay, and the cost might

[335] The role and presence of a nominee, seen in this light, could be seen as a reason why creditors are willing to pay the nominee's fees where they could reach the same conclusion in a private workout instead.

[336] J. Flood, R. Abbey, E. Skordaki and P. Aber, *The Professional Restructuring of Corporate Rescue: Company Voluntary Arrangements and the London Approach*, ACCA Research Report 45 (London: ACCA, 1995) at 17–18.

render schemes particularly unsuitable for small companies already in financial difficulty. In contrast, there is no automatic court involvement in a CVA, although the court might become involved where, for example, a creditor challenges the CVA under section 6 of the Insolvency Act 1986 on the basis of unfair prejudice or material irregularity. The impact of the reduced court involvement as regards cost and time are discussed in section 5.6.7.

One other point to note here is that there is a lot of legislative guidance on the procedure and content of CVAs, in Part I of the Insolvency Act 1986 and in the Insolvency Rules 2016. There is no secondary legislation in relation to schemes that is equivalent to these provisions. Instead, the court is given discretion to deal with these matters as and when they arise. This means that schemes are potentially much more flexible devices than CVAs, though the downside is that companies may be less clear about the provisions relating to schemes, particularly where novel situations arise.

5.6.5 The role of members

In a scheme, it is generally the case that approval need not be sought from any class of members or creditors that are unaffected by the composition, such as where they have no remaining interest in the assets of the company. Members may participate in debt restructuring schemes, but will not always do so. If the company is insolvent then members would not normally participate in the scheme process. Even if they object to the scheme at the sanctioning hearing, without an economic interest their objections are unlikely to hold weight as they will be unable to demonstrate that the scheme unfairly prejudices them.[337]

By contrast, member meetings are always required for CVAs, whether the company is solvent or insolvent. It may be asked why the members should be consulted at all in circumstances in which the company is insolvent, and the members therefore have no remaining economic interest in the company. However, the difference between schemes and CVAs on this point may be less significant than it appears. Following the recommendations of the Insolvency Service,[338] changes were made to the provisions of the Insolvency Act 1986 in 2000,[339] so that where there is

337 *Re Bluebrook Ltd* [2009] EWHC 2114 (Ch); [2010] 1 BCLC 338.

338 Insolvency Service, *Revised Proposals for a new Company Voluntary Arrangement Procedure: A Consultative Document* (London: DTI, April 1995) at 16.

339 See Insolvency Act 2000, s. 2, Sch. 2, Part I, paras. 1, 5.

a conflict between a creditors' meeting decision to approve the CVA and the decision of the members' meeting, the creditors' meeting decision prevails, subject to the shareholders' right to challenge the CVA by application to the court.[340] No guidance is provided on the circumstances in which the court will order the decision of the members' meeting to have effect rather than that of the creditors' meeting. However, unless the members can demonstrate a continuing economic interest in the company, it is difficult to see why a court would prefer their view as to its future direction over that of the creditors. Therefore, in this instance it is difficult to see why the consent of the members to the CVA needs to be sought at all.

5.6.6 *The availability of a moratorium*

Prior to 2020, there was no moratorium available to be used in conjunction with schemes of arrangement, and the only moratorium available for CVAs related to small companies.[341] These companies were very small indeed, a company being eligible if, in the year before filing for the moratorium, or the previous financial year, the company satisfied two or more of the following: it had a turnover of less than £6.5 million per annum, had fewer than fifty employees or had a balance sheet total that did not exceed £3.26 million.[342] Schemes and CVAs outside this narrow category therefore needed to adopt other strategies to gain the protection of a stay, including operating in tandem with an administration in order to gain the protection of a moratorium,[343] or negotiating standstill

[340] Insolvency Act 1986, s. 4A.

[341] Insolvency Act 1986, s. 1A and Sch. A1. The small company moratorium was not available when CVAs were first introduced; it was introduced only via the Insolvency Act 2000 (see, for discussion, Insolvency Service, *Company Voluntary Arrangements and Administrative Orders: A Consultative Document* (London: DTI, October 1993)).

[342] The protection available under this moratorium was analogous to that which takes effect on administration; see Insolvency Act 1986, Sch. A1 (repealed by CIGA, Sch. 3, para. 2).

[343] However, see *JCAM Commercial Real Estate Property XV Ltd* v. *Davis Haulage Ltd* [2017] EWCA Civ 267 in which the Court of Appeal held that a conditional proposal to appoint an administrator in the event that a planned CVA failed was insufficient and that a company or its directors must have a fixed or settled intention to appoint administrators following the filing of a notice of intention to appoint administrators. David Richards LJ took account of the legislative background to a CVA proposal and the fact that a company obtains the benefit of a moratorium in respect of a CVA only in limited circumstances, and considered that, should a person be entitled to file a notice of intention to appoint administrators in these circumstances, it would provide an indirect means of obtaining a moratorium where it is not otherwise directly available.

arrangements. Even CVAs involving companies within the eligible group rarely made use of a moratorium, however. For example, of the 552 CVAs commenced in 2013 involving companies in England and Wales, 514 were small or micro companies, but only 8 of these used the small company moratorium.[344]

Without a moratorium, it is difficult to prevent individual creditors from instituting enforcement actions against the company during the first stages of a CVA, when negotiations are taking place. However, arguments against a moratorium suggest that it is a device open to abuse by directors of companies that have no chance of turnaround, and that it simply prolongs the agony of financial distress, or, alternatively, that it might be used by perfectly viable companies as a means of avoiding their obligations. These competing tensions have been visible in the law reform debates in this area for the last thirty years. The introduction of the small company moratorium (but no wider moratorium) for CVAs seems to have been driven by some of these concerns. However, this distinction between small companies and larger companies in this context was never very justifiable and there have been a number of attempts to introduce a broader moratorium for companies undergoing CVAs.[345] These reform plans eventually came to fruition in a set of government reform proposals in 2018,[346] but it was not until the Covid-19 pandemic that these proposals were finally implemented. The

[344] See Walton, Umfreville and Jacobs, *Company Voluntary Arrangements*, note 276 above. This is consistent with earlier studies: G. Cook, N. Pandit, D. Milman and A. Griffiths, *Small Business Rescue: A Multi-method Empirical Study of Company Voluntary Arrangements* (London: ICAEW, 2003); Walters and Frisby, 'Preliminary report to the Insolvency Service', note 276 above. Cost and complexity may have been factors in this outcome. For companies to access the small company moratorium, nominees had to be prepared to state from the outset that the CVA had a reasonable prospect of being approved and implemented, and that the company was likely to have sufficient funds available during the moratorium to enable it to carry on business. In order to be in a position to make these statements, nominees were likely to have to engage in significant due diligence and consultations with the company's creditors and suppliers. This work involved time and expense, and it may have been more cost-effective (and certainly easier) for a small company to use liquidation to save some of the business rather than attempt to save the company. Another explanation is that the reasonably simple capital structures of these companies, having only a single secured lender and relatively few major creditors facilitated the negotiation of standstill arrangements between the creditors pending consideration of a CVA.

[345] See e.g. Insolvency Service, *Proposals for a Restructuring Moratorium – A Consultation* (London: DTI, July 2010); Insolvency Service, A *Review of the Corporate Insolvency Framework*, note 185 above.

[346] BEIS, *Insolvency and Corporate Governance*, note 190 above.

restructuring moratorium introduced by the Corporate Insolvency and Governance Act 2020, discussed at section 5.4.4.2, is a stand-alone mechanism but is available to be used alongside CVAs involving companies of all sizes. At the same time as introducing this restructuring moratorium, the 2020 Act repealed the small company CVA moratorium.[347] CVAs and schemes are now on the same footing in this regard.

One difference between CVAs and schemes relates to the prohibition on enforcement of so-called ipso facto clauses in contracts for the supply of goods or services.[348] This prohibition draws inspiration from US Chapter 11 proceedings and is designed to preserve a business's operational capabilities through a restructuring. The provision applies in the event that a company that is party to a contract for the supply of goods or services enters a 'relevant insolvency procedure', defined to include a moratorium, administration, a CVA, liquidation or a restructuring plan, but not a scheme of arrangement.[349] Accordingly, the company's suppliers cannot rely on termination provisions which might otherwise have been triggered by the CVA taking effect.

5.6.7 *Complexity and speed*

One of the reasons for the Cork Committee's recommendation that CVAs be introduced in the UK was to provide creditors with a quicker and less cumbersome mechanism for achieving a voluntary arrangement than existed in relation to schemes of arrangement.[350] CVAs have two distinct advantages over schemes in this regard. First, there is no need for court involvement (unless creditors object under section 6 of the Insolvency Act 1986) and therefore the two compulsory court hearings in relation to schemes can be avoided. Second, there is no requirement in relation to CVAs for the members or creditors to meet in separate classes. These two issues will be examined in turn; in practice, these changes might not always result in the time savings that were intended.

The absence of court involvement in a CVA has been compensated for in other ways, such as the involvement of a fully qualified insolvency practitioner to act as nominee/supervisor. The role of nominee is particularly important in assessing the prospects for success of the CVA and

347 CIGA, Sch. 3, para. 2.

348 See section 5.7.2.4 for further discussion.

349 See Insolvency Act 1986, s. 233B(2)(b)–(f).

350 Cork Committee, *Insolvency Law and Practice*, note 181 above, paras. 400–3.

filtering out non-viable proposals. However, much of the information on which the nominee will rely to form a judgement will be supplied by the directors of the company (although, of course, directors are personally liable if they deliberately make false representations to the nominee).[351] A party that feels aggrieved by the acts or omissions of the nominee can apply to the court under section 6 of the Insolvency Act 1986.[352] There will be a temptation for the nominee to take a defensive position by doing their own due diligence; indeed, it has been suggested that in some circumstances there may be a 'clear danger' for the nominee who simply relies on the information being supplied by directors.[353] The effect of this additional due diligence is that the procedure becomes more expensive and cumbersome. The requirement for the nominee to make certain statements in writing about whether the CVA has a reasonable prospect of being approved only exacerbates this issue. As a result, the CVA procedure may not be as speedy and cheap in practice as might have been hoped.

Second, there is no requirement for members and creditors to meet in classes in CVAs. By contrast, the requirement for separate class meetings is present in schemes.[354] Getting this wrong can lead to the scheme not being sanctioned by the court, and yet the determination of what constitutes a separate class for this purpose is not easy. This is an issue that occupies the courts at both the convening and sanctioning hearings. The differentiation between different creditors is also a concern in CVAs, however, and these differences can lead to lengthy negotiations between the parties, and to court hearings on occasion, to deal with these matters, as the decision in *Discovery (Northampton) Ltd* v. *Debenhams Retail Ltd*[355] demonstrates.

5.6.8 *The use of CVAs in practice*

The Cork Committee proposed the CVA procedure as a response, in part, to the perceived problems and disadvantages of schemes of arrangement as a mechanism for effecting a compromise or arrangement involving an

351 Insolvency Act 1986, ss. 6A(4) and 7A.

352 An aggrieved party is not entitled to pursue a private law remedy: *King* v. *Anthony* [1998] 2 BCLC 517.

353 Law Society Company Law Committee, *Comments on the Insolvency Bill* (London: March 2000) No. 396, at 5.

354 See sections 2.3.2 and 5.3.

355 [2019] EWHC 2441 (Ch) and see section 5.6.2.

insolvent company. CVAs have certain potential advantages as compared to schemes. They offer the potential for a simpler, less complex procedure since there is no mandatory court involvement, there is no need for creditors or members to meet in separate classes and the creditor vote requires only a 75 per cent majority in value, without the addition of the headcount test that appears in relation to schemes of arrangement. However, as discussed, some of these advantages are more apparent than real. There are also disadvantages, in particular that CVAs do not bind secured creditors without their consent.

The number of CVAs has remained at a low level since their introduction in 1986.[356] Recent research has thrown light on the uses to which CVAs are put. This finds that 65 per cent of CVAs are terminated without achieving their intended aims.[357] This research finds that there is often 'a significant gap between the expected level of dividends and the actual dividends'[358] and some CVAs return very little to creditors.[359]

The CVA procedure might be thought to be best suited to small companies, where the reduced cost and complexity of the CVA compared to other mechanisms (such as schemes) would be of greatest benefit, and the disadvantage that it does not bind secured creditors might matter less, since secured debt often plays a smaller role in the financing of small companies. Nevertheless, few small companies use CVAs. Perhaps a reason why the number of CVAs each year remains relatively small is that the costs of a CVA still render this an expensive option for small companies.

Larger companies do not make much use of CVAs either: only 7 per cent of companies entering a CVA were non-small companies in

[356] In 2005–6, two years after the introduction of the CVA moratorium, there were only 540 CVAs compared to 2,661 administrations and 565 receiverships: Insolvency Service, *Enterprise Act 2002 – Corporate Insolvency Provisions: Evaluation Report* (London: DTI, 2008) at 17. In 2017, there were 17,243 total company insolvencies in England and Wales of which only 292 were CVAs: Walton, Umfreville and Jacobs, *Company Voluntary Arrangements*, note 276 above.

[357] See Walton, Umfreville and Jacobs, *Company Voluntary Arrangements*, note 276 above, 12. This is consistent with earlier research by Walters and Frisby which found that more than half of CVAs saw the procedure terminated prematurely: Walters and Frisby, 'Preliminary report to the Insolvency Service', note 276 above, at 8.

[358] Walton, Umfreville and Jacobs, *Company Voluntary Arrangements*, note 276 above, at 3. This is again in line with the results found by Walters and Frisby: 'Preliminary report to the Insolvency Service', note 276 above, at 26.

[359] In particular, dividends to unsecured creditors were rare in CVAs which terminated within six quarters of commencement: Walton, Umfreville and Jacobs, *Company Voluntary Arrangements*, note 276 above, at 3. This is again consistent with Walters and Frisby's findings: 'Preliminary report to the Insolvency Service', note 276 above, at 24.

a recent survey, and of these a significant proportion first entered administration.[360] Other options will generally appear more attractive. Where the rights of secured creditors need to be compromised, CVAs will not be valuable. The Cork Committee acknowledged that there was an important role for schemes of arrangement in complex cases, where a large company is proposing a complicated scheme,[361] and this seems to have been borne out in practice. Nevertheless, there has been a growing trend for CVAs to be used by some large retail companies seeking to compromise their contractual arrangements with their landlords. Typically, a retail CVA will treat landlord claims differently depending on a store's financial performance and/or the strategic importance of the premises. So, for example, landlords of performing sites that are key to the future success of the business will be paid rent in full; underperforming sites (which could be commercially viable) will be paid a reduced rent and underperforming sites which are not viable will be closed. A CVA allows unsecured creditor claims to be compromised in a number of ways to best support the future success of the business. There is no 'one size fits all' approach, with retail CVAs becoming more sophisticated than might historically have been the case. *Discovery (Northampton) Ltd* v. *Debenhams Retail Ltd*[362] is an example of such a case, and indeed the outcome of that case provides a boost for companies seeking to use CVAs to enter into compromise arrangements with their landlords. There has been an increase in the number of CVAs being put forward by tenants since the Covid-19 pandemic began, particularly by tenants in the retail, hospitality and leisure sectors. These post-Covid-19 CVAs have differed from traditional CVAs in that they seek to also compromise the claims of other categories of unsecured creditors such as HMRC, employees and non-essential suppliers. It remains to be seen whether the restructuring moratorium introduced in 2020 will provide an additional benefit in such cases.

5.7 The use of administration as an alternative to a scheme as a debt restructuring device

One important question for this chapter is why schemes are being used as debt restructuring tools instead of the mechanisms that have been specifically created by legislation to deal with these issues. In section 5.6,

360 Walton, Umfreville and Jacobs, *Company Voluntary Arrangements*, note 276 above, at 3.

361 Cork Committee, *Insolvency Law and Practice*, note 181 above, para. 422.

362 [2019] EWHC 2441 (Ch).

schemes were compared to CVAs as a debt restructuring device. In this section we consider why a scheme might be used instead of administration. The use of schemes in combination with administration has already been discussed at section 5.4.3.

5.7.1 The development of administration in English law

Administration was introduced into English law only in 1985, following the report of the Cork Committee that assessed the existing situation in English insolvency law and called for the development of a rescue culture in England.[363] It was recognised that when a company is in serious financial difficulties it has, broadly, three options. The first is to go into immediate liquidation. Sometimes, indeed often, this will be the only option available to companies. However, it may be that the company has a viable business, in which case other options arise: it might seek to trade out of its difficulties or it may be that, with a little time, it can dispose of its assets or its business to better advantage than on an immediate winding-up. While liquidation serves the first of these options, it does not facilitate the second or third. Accordingly, following the recommendations of the Cork Committee, the administration procedure was implemented in the Insolvency Act 1985 and re-enacted in the Insolvency Act 1986. Another aspect of this rescue culture was the introduction of CVAs, discussed in section 5.6.

In essence, administration is a procedure by which an external manager, the administrator, is appointed to manage the company.[364] The administrator has the power to trade freely, and to dispose of the business or the assets of the company as a going concern. This contrasts with the position of the liquidator, whose primary role is to liquidate the company's remaining assets and who, therefore, has limited powers to carry on the business of the company, and can do so only to the extent necessary for the winding-up.[365] The approach and objectives of administration are also different from those of liquidation. The purpose of liquidation is to realise and distribute the assets of the company and for the company then to be dissolved. By contrast, administration is intended to promote the rescue of companies, even though, in practice, rescue is not always the outcome achieved.

[363] Cork Committee, *Insolvency Law and Practice*, note 181 above.

[364] See, now, Insolvency Act 1986, Part 2, Sch. B1 and Insolvency Rules 2016, Part 3.

[365] Insolvency Act 1986, Sch. 4, Part II, para. 5.

There were difficulties with the operation of the administration procedure as it was initially introduced.[366] First, administration could usually be blocked by the appointment of an administrative receiver. Second, the requirement to obtain a court order caused significant delay and often substantial expense, making administration orders difficult for small companies. Third, the administrator had no power to make distributions even to preferential creditors without a court order.[367] Finally, an administration order could not be made if the company was in liquidation.[368] As a result the administration procedure introduced in 1985 proved less beneficial to the creation of a rescue culture than had been hoped.

Further proposals for the reform of insolvency law were, therefore, put forward,[369] most notably in the Enterprise Act 2002.[370] This Act abolished administrative receivership, except in specific cases, and made significant changes to administration in order to tackle the perceived difficulties referred to above.[371] For example, the requirement to obtain a court order was removed.[372] Another important change was the introduction of flexibility regarding the entry into and exit from administration, making it possible to move from winding up to administration,[373] and from administration to dissolution. The administrator was also given power to make distributions to secured and preferential creditors and, with the permission of the court, to ordinary unsecured creditors.[374] The

366 See D. D. Prentice, F. Oditah and N. Segal, 'Administration: the Insolvency Act 1986, Part II' [1994] *Lloyd's Maritime and Commercial Law Quarterly* 487.

367 The extent of the court's power to make such an order was also unclear: *Re TXU UK Ltd (in administration)* [2002] EWHC 2784 (Ch); [2003] 2 BCLC 341; *Re UCT (UK) Ltd* [2001] 1 WLR 436; *Re Powerstore (Trading) Ltd* [1997] 1 WLR 1280; *Re WBSL Realisations 1992 Ltd* [1995] 2 BCLC 576.

368 Insolvency Act 1986, s. 8(4) (see now Insolvency Act 1986, Sch. B1, para. 8(1)).

369 DTI, *Productivity and Enterprise: Insolvency – A Second Chance* (Cm. 5234, London: HMSO, 2001).

370 Subsequent reforms have also impacted on the administration regime, including the Small Business, Enterprise and Employment Act 2015.

371 For discussion see K. Van Zwieten, *Goode on Principles of Corporate Insolvency Law* (5th ed., Sweet & Maxwell, 2018) paras. 11-05ff.

372 It is now open to the holder of a qualifying floating charge or to the company or the directors to appoint an administrator by filing a notice of appointment and other prescribed documents: Insolvency Act 1986, Sch. B1, paras. 14, 18, 22, 29(1).

373 A liquidator can apply for an administration order whether the company is in compulsory or voluntary liquidation, and the holder of a qualifying floating charge of a company in compulsory liquidation can apply for an administration order (ibid., Sch. B1, para. 37).

374 The introduction of the power to make a distribution to ordinary unsecured creditors with the permission of the court required a number of consequential changes, specifically

administration procedure that emerged from the Enterprise Act was much more muscular, and more likely to facilitate rescue or rehabilitation of a company as a result.[375]

The administrator can be appointed either by an application to court (by specified persons, including the company, the directors or one or more creditors)[376] or by an out-of-court process in which the company, the directors or a qualifying floating charge holder files a notice of appointment and other prescribed documents.[377] Although the details of the appointment process differ, once appointed the administrator's duties and powers are the same, whichever route is followed. Crucially, even where the administrator is appointed by, or on the nomination of, the chargee, the administrator must perform their functions in the interests of the company's creditors as a whole.[378]

One important effect of an administration order is a general moratorium on the enforcement of remedies, whether the administration is begun out of court or on an administration order.[379]

There is a single purpose to administration, albeit a multi-tiered one:

> The administrator of a company must perform his functions with the objective of –
>
> (a) rescuing the company as a going concern, or
> (b) achieving a better result for the company's creditors as a whole than would be likely if the company were wound up (without first being in administration), or
> (c) realising property in order to make a distribution to one or more secured or preferential creditors.[380]

A hierarchy is created for these objectives: administrators must perform their functions in accordance with (a) above, unless this is not reasonably practicable or the objective in (b) would achieve a better result for the company's creditors as a whole.[381] The objective in paragraph (c)

the application to administration of a number of provisions previously confined to winding up, such as the rules on set-off (see Insolvency Rules 2016, r. 14.24).

375 Nevertheless, liquidation retains a very important role today, as a self-standing mechanism; see e.g. Insolvency Service, Statistics Release, 30 July 2020, www.gov.uk/government/collections/company-insolvency-statistics-releases.

376 Insolvency Act 1986, Sch. B1, para. 12.

377 Ibid., Sch. B1, paras. 14, 18, 22, 29.

378 Ibid., Sch. B1, para. 3(2).

379 See section 5.7.2.4.

380 Insolvency Act 1986, Sch. B1, para. 3(1).

381 Ibid., Sch. B1, para. 3(3).

can be adopted only if it is not reasonably practicable to achieve (a) or (b) and the administrator does not unnecessarily harm the interests of the creditors as a whole.[382]

Importantly, therefore, administration is not an end in itself but should instead be regarded as a gateway to a variety of different exits for the company.[383] Although administration can be used as a rescue device, it is clear that this is only one of the possible outcomes for the company. One possible, and not uncommon, outcome of administration for the company, for example, is for it to be wound up. Another very common outcome of administration is the restoration of the business to a position where either it can be sold as a going concern or the assets can be sold more advantageously than in liquidation. One particular form of administration that has arisen recently is pre-pack administration. This last option is important for the purposes of this chapter because schemes are often twinned with pre-packs.[384]

The central feature of a pre-pack is that a company in financial difficulty reaches an agreement for the sale of its business or all of its assets prior to the administrator's appointment, and this is done in collaboration with the major creditors. The agreement is placed in escrow and the sale typically takes effect immediately after the administrator's appointment. The business may be sold to a third party, but more usually it is sold back to the existing management or existing senior lenders.[385]

382 Ibid., Sch. B1, para. 3(4).

383 In determining which of these objectives to pursue, after determining the necessary information about the company, the administrator will prepare a statement setting out proposals for achieving the purpose of administration. This statement is sent to the Registrar of Companies and to every member and creditor of whose address the administrator is aware (Insolvency Act 1986, Sch. B1, para. 49(4)) within a strict time frame (Sch. B1, para. 49(5)). These proposals are then considered and voted on at a creditors' meeting (Sch. B1, para. 51) where the creditors can approve them, or modify them, with the administrator's consent.

384 Singapore introduced a pre-pack scheme in its 2017 restructuring reforms. In theory, these reduce the administrative costs of undertaking a scheme by streamlining the process, including removing the formal meeting of creditors that is called by the court. The court, however, must be satisfied that, if a meeting is called, the requisite number of creditors would have approved the scheme; see e.g. *Tan* v. *TT International* (2018) SGCA 69.

385 See e.g. Insolvency Service, *Report on the First Six Months' Operation of Statement of Insolvency Practice 16* (20 July 2009), 22 (81 per cent of pre-pack sales reviewed were to parties connected to the insolvent company). See also P. Walton and C. Umfreville, *Pre-pack Empirical Research: Characteristic and Outcome Analysis of Pre-pack Administration*, April 2014; Insolvency Service, *Pre-pack Sales in Administration Report*, 8 October 2020.

Pre-pack administration is not a creation of law but a development of practice.

Pre-pack administrations are common, accounting for 29 per cent of the total number of administrations.[386] One key attraction of pre-packs is that they enable a very rapid sale and this is more likely to preserve value, goodwill and confidence than a slower and more protracted administration process.[387] Additionally, they may avoid adverse publicity, may involve reduced professional charges and may enable more rapid access to funds.[388] A pre-pack may also be combined with a scheme of arrangement to deal with 'out-of-the-money' creditors or shareholders that are opposed to the restructuring.[389] However, pre-packs have also attracted criticisms, largely because they are regarded as 'insufficiently transparent'.[390] Unsecured creditors may be presented with a done deal, only being informed of the pre-pack when the sale is complete. Pre-packs may therefore be biased towards the interests of secured creditors, particularly the holders of floating charges. Concerns exist about the business being sold off at an undervalue, particularly when the sale is not to a third party but to a party connected with the company:

> A pre-packaged business has not, by definition, been exposed to the competitive forces of the market, which may lead to the business being disposed of for a consideration less than would have been obtained had it been marketed for an appropriate period. Where a pre-pack is effected through administration, the rights of stakeholders to participate in the decision making process, as envisaged by the Insolvency Act 1986, are frustrated.[391]

386 See Insolvency Service, *Pre-pack Sales in Administration Report*, 8 October 2020. This is similar to previous figures; see e.g. *Graham Review into Pre-packaged Administration: Report to the Rt Hon Vince Cable MP*, June 2014, 6.

387 See e.g. Insolvency Service, *Pre-pack Sales in Administration Report*, note 385 above.

388 See Walton and Umfreville, *Pre-pack Empirical Research*, note 385 above; S. Frisby, *A Preliminary Analysis of Pre-packaged Administrations*, Report to the Association of Business Recovery Professionals, August 2007.

389 See section 5.4.3.

390 Frisby, *A Preliminary Analysis of Pre-packaged Administrations*, note 388 above. See also Insolvency Service, *Pre-pack Sales in Administration Report*, note 385 above.

391 S. Frisby, *A Preliminary Analysis of Pre-packaged Administrations*, note 388 above, 8. Cf. A. Polo, 'Secured creditor control in bankruptcy: costs and conflict' (2012), https://papers.ssrn.com/sol3/papers.cfm?abstract_id=2084881, who finds that unsecured creditor recoveries in pre-packs, even connected party pre-packs, were not lower than in alternative procedures.

As a result of these concerns, the Joint Insolvency Committee issued guidelines for pre-pack administrations.[392] These set out the standards expected of practitioners who are involved in a pre-pack, as advisors or administrators, and in particular focus on the need to disclose information to the creditors, with the objective being to give creditors sufficient information to understand why a pre-pack was chosen over the alternatives and to ascertain whether sufficient regard was given to their interests. These guidelines set out a number of voluntary measures, including the information that should be disclosed in a pre-pack sale[393] and that in connected party sales the administrator should include an opinion from one of a group of independent business persons comprising the 'pre-pack pool' regarding the terms of the sale,[394] and a viability statement from the connected party purchaser stating how the purchasing entity will survive for at least twelve months from the date of the proposed purchase.

The Insolvency Service assessed these provisions in 2020.[395] One question for this review was whether these voluntary measures had had the desired effect of increasing confidence and transparency in relation to connected person sales in particular and, if not, whether the government should utilise its power to legislate to restrict or prohibit connected

[392] Joint Insolvency Committee, 'Statement of Insolvency Practice 16: Pre-packaged Sales in Administrations (SIP 16)' (these guidelines were updated in May 2013, and in 2015, the latter changes following the recommendations of the *Graham Review*, note 386 above).

[393] The information to be disclosed includes the extent of the administrator's involvement prior to their appointment; the marketing activities conducted by the administrator of the company; the valuations obtained and the basis of valuation; the reasons why it is not possible to trade the business and offer it for sale as a going concern during the administration; and particulars of the sale transaction including the identity of the purchaser and any connection between them and the company.

[394] If the purchaser in a connected party purchase submits the terms of the proposed sale to the scrutiny of the pool, a member of the pool will (after scrutinising the terms) issue one of three opinions: (i) that there was nothing found to suggest that the grounds of the proposed sale are unreasonable; (ii) that evidence provided has been limited but otherwise nothing has been found to suggest that the grounds for the proposed sale are unreasonable; or (iii) that there is a lack of evidence to support a statement that the grounds for the proposed sale are reasonable. A sale can proceed whichever opinion is provided, but an administrator is required, in their SIP 16 statement, to indicate whether an opinion was sought from the pool; if so, and if the opinion is provided to the administrator, the opinion should be included with the SIP 16 statement. This mechanism was introduced as a result of the *Graham Review*, note 386 above. Relatively little use has been made of this mechanism to date: Pre-pack Pool, *Annual Review 2018*.

[395] Insolvency Service, *Pre-pack Sales in Administration Report*, note 385 above.

person sales in administration.[396] Overall, this review found that while there was some evidence of positive change arising from the voluntary measures (for example, it noted an increase in the number of businesses being marketed), the progress was somewhat disappointing, particularly regarding the low number of referrals to the pre-pack pool. The conclusion reached by the review was that in many circumstances a pre-pack sale will provide the best outcome for creditors following an insolvency; it did not, therefore, propose that the power to ban connected party sales in administration should be used. However, the review did recommend further regulation and the use of the power in paragraph 60A of Schedule B1 of the Insolvency Act 1986 to ensure that proposed pre-pack sales are subject to a measure of independent scrutiny. As a result, inter alia, an administrator will be unable to dispose of property of a company to a person connected with the company within the first eight weeks of the administration without either the approval of creditors or an independent written opinion.[397] Changes will also be introduced to the voluntary guidelines, including improving the quality of information provided to creditors.

5.7.2 *A comparison between schemes and administration as a debt restructuring device*

There are a number of important differences that arise between schemes and administration as debt restructuring devices.[398]

[396] A power exists for the Secretary of State to make regulations regarding the disposal, hire or sale of company property to connected parties: Insolvency Act 1986, Sch. B1, para. 60A(10) (this power expires in 2021: CIGA, ss. 8–9).

[397] Insolvency Service, *Pre-pack Sales in Administration Report*, note 385 above; Insolvency Service, *Proposed Draft Regulations to Require Scrutiny of Pre-pack Sales to Connected Parties*, 8 October 2020.

[398] Prior to the end of the Brexit transition period on 31 December 2020, a further difference related to the potential for schemes and administration to be recognised elsewhere in the EU. The main purposes of the Recast Insolvency Regulation (EU) 848/2015 are to impose rules governing the jurisdiction in which an insolvency proceeding in the EU can be opened and subsequently administered and to set rules for both the recognition in other Member States and the enforcement of those insolvency proceedings. 'Insolvency proceedings' are defined as collective proceedings that entail the partial or total divestment of a debtor and the appointment of a liquidator (Art.1(1)). The relevant proceedings are listed in Annex A of the Regulation. As regards the UK, administration and CVAs were on the list, but not schemes of arrangement. The position regarding schemes, including whether English schemes would be recognised elsewhere in the EU, was somewhat complicated (see section 7.3). The situation regarding CVAs and administration was straightforward in this regard, and if it was important to ensure that English

5.7.2.1 A scheme is not an insolvency procedure

One significant difference between schemes and administration is that while administration is an insolvency procedure, schemes are not. They appear, instead, in the Companies Act 2006 and are regarded as part of company law. This has a number of consequences.

First, the fact that a scheme is not a formal insolvency process may make its use more appealing to directors wishing to avoid any perceived insolvency-related stigma. There tends to be a more negative perception of insolvency, amongst directors of companies and their creditors, than attaches to companies utilising schemes, and this negative perception can have a substantive impact on the company's business. Once it becomes known that a company is insolvent, or is verging on insolvency, the value of its business and assets tends to fall sharply.

Second, the entry into liquidation and administration will generally trigger cross-default clauses or contractual provisions for acceleration of liability, termination of the contract or the cessation of intellectual property rights. These consequences apply on any contractually specified event of default. Although the entry into insolvency proceedings is invariably included in contracts as a trigger, the entry into a scheme does not tend to be included in the same way.

Third, because a scheme is not an insolvency procedure, the rules that would normally apply as a result of insolvency legislation do not apply. This may or may not be beneficial. Since schemes are not insolvency proceedings, there are no statutory powers of investigation, and no specific statutory provisions to attack preferences or undervalue transactions. Fraudulent conveyance provisions can, however, be applied before, during or after the scheme. Further, in many situations, preferences and undervalue transactions, especially with insiders or connected persons, can be attacked via corporate law provisions of statute and case law.

5.7.2.2 Early intervention

Where the application for an administrator is made by someone other than the holder of a qualifying floating charge, it will not succeed unless the company is, or is likely to become, unable to pay its debts within the meaning of section 123 of the Insolvency Act 1986. There is no such requirement for an out-of-court appointment by the holder of

proceedings were recognised elsewhere in the EU, this might have been one reason to choose a CVA or administration instead of a scheme.

a qualifying floating charge.[399] In practice, however, this option for early intervention is rarely exercised. Banks holding qualifying floating charges prefer not to make the appointment themselves, for reputational reasons, and more often leave the appointment to the company or its directors, only influencing the choice of the appointee. As a result, in practice, administration will generally operate only once a company is insolvent, or insolvency is imminent. If the company's business is not viable, this will make little difference, but where rescue is a possibility, intervention earlier than this point may well be beneficial. Early intervention can also be valuable where the desired outcome is to prepare the financially distressed company for a sale of either its business or its assets in favourable conditions. The fact that this can be done without any of the stigma of insolvency attached might also be beneficial.[400]

One advantage of schemes of arrangement, therefore, which is of particular relevance to rescue scenarios, is that schemes enable early attention to be paid to corporate difficulties because they can be formulated and approved without the requirement of impending insolvency.[401]

5.7.2.3 Debtor in possession

Unlike schemes, CVAs and restructuring plans, administration is not a debtor-in-possession proceeding. The approach adopted in administration has been to sideline the existing managers.[402] The assumption is that where the company becomes insolvent, this will often be owing to a failure of management, and that therefore this group should not be put in charge of a company's rescue. Instead, administration places the company in the hands of an external manager, the administrator, a qualified insolvency practitioner who works in close co-operation with a creditors' committee.[403] In administration, unlike a scheme, the

[399] As for an out-of-court appointment by the company or its directors, see Insolvency Act 1986, Sch. B1, para. 27(2)(a).

[400] A similar argument can be made in other jurisdictions, for example in relation to Australian schemes of arrangement as compared to the alternative creditor-restructuring device, the deed of company arrangement, which requires the company to enter administration first.

[401] See e.g. *Re Cape plc* [2006] EWHC 1316 (Ch); [2006] 3 All ER 1222. For discussion see J. Townsend, 'Schemes of arrangement and asbestos litigation: in Re Cape plc' (2007) *Modern Law Review* 837.

[402] It is possible for a 'light-touch' administration to be put in place whereby the administrator devolves much of the responsibility for the day-to-day running of the company on the existing management.

[403] This is in contrast to the position adopted by other regimes, notably that of the USA, which, under Ch. 11 of its Bankruptcy Code, utilises the debtor-in-possession structure,

proposals for achieving the purposes of the administration are prepared and submitted not by the directors but by the administrator, and only the creditors are involved in approving them.

In a scheme, the existing management generally stay in place. It is possible to provide for the scheme to be administered by someone other than the board, the 'scheme administrator', although this is not usual.[404] More usually, the directors remain in control of the company during the scheme. Outside the terms of the scheme, the directors continue to manage the company as they see fit, and, of course, the terms of the scheme will rarely cover the whole of the company's business as it is very common to exclude creditors from the ambit of the scheme. Neither the court nor an insolvency practitioner takes control or otherwise supervises the company's affairs. The company engaged in a scheme need not seek permission from the court to enter into related party transactions, to enter into transactions outside the ordinary course of business, to pay its advisors' fees or otherwise to take actions that might diminish the value of the company's business. This, of course, stands in sharp contrast to administration where the control of the company's assets passes to an insolvency official, under the supervision of the court.

The benefits of a debtor-in-possession regime have been discussed earlier in this chapter. In particular, such regimes can encourage directors to tackle a company's issues at an early stage, and directors are often best placed to negotiate the restructuring with the creditors, at least where the company's financial distress was not caused by the directors' wrongdoing.[405]

and see the EU Restructuring Directive (EU) 2019/1023, which also utilises a debtor-in-possession regime.

404 Such an arrangement might be used, for example, where there is some suggestion of negligence or misfeasance on the part of the directors. There is no statutory office of scheme administrator (unlike, for example, supervisors or nominees of CVAs) and therefore a scheme administrator, if appointed, would need to derive all of their powers from the terms of the scheme itself. Although an order of the court pursuant to Part 26 of the Companies Act 2006 is binding on the company and the relevant class or classes of creditors, it is not binding on a third party such as a scheme administrator: *Re Glendale Land Development (in liquidation)* (1982) 17 ACLC 171. As a result, a scheme administrator would have to consent to act as such, and agree to be bound by the terms of the scheme, provided it is approved by the creditors and by the court; see e.g. *Re Sessions Video Distributors Pty Ltd* (1983) 10 ACSR 421. Depending on the extent of the scheme administrator's powers, they may be considered a shadow director of the company and for this reason could seek a form of indemnity from the company.

405 See section 5.4.2.

5.7.2.4 The existence of an automatic moratorium

One significant difference between a scheme and administration is that administration has attached to it an automatic statutory stay. Even though the restructuring moratorium can now be used in conjunction with schemes, this does not arise automatically; it is for the parties to decide whether or not to utilise this moratorium in relation to a scheme and, as discussed in section 5.4.4.2, there are reasons to doubt that this will occur very often.[406]

The definition of moratorium for the purpose of administration is provided by the Insolvency Act 1986[407] and involves a stay on the enforcement of remedies and a stay on insolvency proceedings and other legal processes. So, during the moratorium, no administrative receiver may be appointed,[408] no resolution can be passed for winding up the company[409] and no winding-up order may be made.[410] No step can be taken to enforce security over the company's property except with the consent of the administrator or the permission of the court.[411] No steps may be taken to repossess goods in the company's possession under any hire-purchase agreement, except with the consent of the administrator or the permission of the court.[412] A landlord may not exercise a right of forfeiture by peaceable re-entry in relation to premises let to the company except with the administrator's consent or the court's permission.[413] Generally, no legal process may be instituted or continued against the company or the company's property except with the consent of the administrator or the permission of the court.[414]

The description of the moratorium attached to administration above has been in place since administration was introduced in 1985. However, the concept was broadened by the Corporate Insolvency and Governance

[406] See section 5.4.4.2. The restructuring moratorium is debtor-in-possession, in contrast to the moratorium that arises automatically on administration.

[407] Insolvency Act 1986, Sch. B1, paras. 42–3. Different definitions of moratorium can be adopted. Indeed, strictly, a moratorium may be regarded as a period in which debts are not due and payable. However, the definition in the Insolvency Act 1986 focuses on the concept of a statutory stay and this is the sense in which the term moratorium is used in this book.

[408] Ibid., Sch. B1, para. 43(6A).

[409] Ibid., Sch. B1, para. 42(1) and (2).

[410] Ibid., Sch. B1, para. 42(1)–(4). There are limited exceptions for winding up under ss. 124A, 124B or 367 Financial Services and Markets Act 2000.

[411] Ibid., Sch. B1, para. 43(2).

[412] Ibid., Sch. B1, para. 43(3).

[413] Ibid., Sch. B1, para. 43(4).

[414] Ibid., Sch. B1, para. 43(6).

Act 2020 to include a restriction on the ability of creditors to terminate their contracts with the company 'by reason of' insolvency.[415]

When a company goes into an insolvency process, such as administration, suppliers often stop or threaten to stop supplying the company, relying on the right to terminate the contract because of the insolvency. They may use the threat of termination to require the payment of all arrears as the price for continued supply and/or to change the terms, perhaps by increasing prices for the goods or services. This can make the ongoing trading of the business, or the sale of the business as a going concern, more challenging and potentially reduces the return to creditors. Prior to the 2020 Act the Insolvency Act 1986 prevented utilities and IT systems suppliers from terminating supply upon insolvency,[416] but the restrictions within the 2020 Act are much wider and apply to all suppliers of goods and services (with some exceptions). The 2020 Act therefore seeks to maximise the opportunities for the rescue of businesses reliant on the continuation of supply agreements. This change to the law mirrors approaches that have been adopted elsewhere.[417] The US Chapter 11 regime, for example, restricts the ability of creditors to terminate their contracts on the basis of insolvency[418] and the EU Restructuring Directive has introduced constraints on the operation of ipso facto clauses.[419] Singapore has also implemented a provision to restrict the rights of creditors to terminate on insolvency.[420]

The 2020 Act extends the UK's existing 'essential supplies' regime by introducing a broad constraint on the operation of ipso facto clauses into the Insolvency Act 1986. The constraint operates in the event that a company that is party to a contract for the supply of goods or services enters a 'relevant insolvency procedure',[421] defined as a moratorium, administration, administrative receivership, a CVA, liquidation,[422]

415 See CIGA, ss. 14–19 and Schs. 12–13.

416 See Insolvency Act 1986, s. 233 and the Insolvency (Protection of Essential Supplies) Order 2015 SI 2015 No. 989.

417 In Australia see Australian Corporations Act 2001, ss. 415D, 434J and 451E, inserted by Treasury Laws Amendment (2017 Enterprise Incentives No. 2) Act 2017.

418 11 USC § 365(e) and § 541(c). For discussion see *In re Lehman Bros. Holdings Inc*, 533 BR 476 (Bankr SDNY 2016).

419 EU Restructuring Directive (EU) 2019/1023, Arts. 7(4), 7(5).

420 See Singapore Insolvency, Restructuring and Dissolution Act 2018, s. 440. This is modelled on a similar regime in Canada: Canadian Bankruptcy and Insolvency Act 1985, s. 65.1 and Canadian Companies' Creditors Arrangement Act 1985, s. 34.

421 Insolvency Act 1986, s. 233B(1).

422 The inclusion of liquidation in this list is somewhat odd. Since its purpose is to aid the rescue of a company as a going concern or of its business, permitting such interference in

provisional liquidation or a restructuring plan.[423] The provision is thus extended to apply in the two new restructuring procedures, the restructuring moratorium and the restructuring plan.[424] Notably, the Act does not include a scheme of arrangement in this list notwithstanding that its close counterpart, the new restructuring plan, is included.[425]

The changes introduced by the 2020 Act have two main effects.[426] First, a supplier's contractual right to terminate on the grounds of insolvency is permanently switched off as from the date of the relevant insolvency procedure. The prohibition is on termination or 'any other thing'[427] by reason of insolvency, and so also prohibits amending payment terms, for example by increasing prices. Second, a supplier's contractual right to terminate on the grounds of any pre-insolvency events of default are temporarily suspended until the relevant insolvency procedure comes to an end (unless the company exits into a subsequent insolvency procedure).

The 2020 Act provides that the prohibition of termination on the basis of insolvency covers *all* contracts for the supply of goods and services other than contracts excluded from the operation of the section. The prohibition applies only to contracts for the supply of goods and services and is therefore narrower than its US Chapter 11 counterpart, which generally applies to all executory contracts (subject to carve-outs).[428] The categories of supplier and categories of contract which are excluded are set out in Schedule 4ZZA of the Insolvency Act 1986.[429] Excluded suppliers are predominantly suppliers of financial services such as banks and insurers. Excluded contracts largely relate to financial services.[430]

contractual rights is arguably not justified in a typical liquidation where the business ceases to trade almost immediately. It is notable that winding up is excluded from the list of relevant processes to which the ipso facto provisions attach in other jurisdictions; see e.g. Singapore Insolvency, Restructuring and Dissolution Act 2018, s. 440(6).

423 Insolvency Act 1986, s. 233B(2).

424 See sections 5.4.4.2 and 5.8.2.

425 Cf. the Australian ipso facto reforms, introduced in 2017, which specifically include schemes of arrangement: Australian Corporations Act 2001, s. 415D, as do the Singapore provisions: Singapore Insolvency, Restructuring and Dissolution Act 2018, s. 440(6).

426 See Insolvency Act 1986, s. 233B(3)(4).

427 Ibid, s. 233B(3)(b).

428 See 11 USC § 365(e). The regime in Singapore is also broader than the UK regime: Singapore Insolvency, Restructuring and Dissolution Act 2018, s. 440.

429 See CIGA, Sch. 12.

430 A short-term exclusion was also inserted into the Act to deal with small suppliers in the Covid period: CIGA, ss. 15, 19.

It is clear that this provision can be beneficial to companies in financial distress, but there is a balance to be struck between the benefits of company rescue and imposing restrictions on freedom of contract. A measure of creditor protection is built into the Act. There are three exceptions, whereby termination by a supplier on account of an insolvency event will be permitted: (i) with the consent of an office holder (i.e. an administrator or liquidator) or the company itself, if it is subject to debtor-in-possession proceedings, such as a restructuring plan or a CVA;[431] (ii) with the approval of the court, where continuation of the contract would cause the supplier hardship;[432] and (iii) if a post-insolvency event of default occurs giving rise to a new event of default, such as non-payment.[433] Notably, the ipso facto provision does not provide for circumstances in which an office holder does not want to continue taking supply of certain goods or services (unlike its Chapter 11 counterpart).[434] Under the UK ipso facto regime, suppliers contracted to supply goods or services will be under a statutory duty to continue performing their contractual obligations, regardless of the office holder's intentions or ability to pay for the goods or services.[435] As there is no requirement for the company to assume or reject contracts within set time periods, suppliers could be left with a period of uncertainty in which they cannot terminate.

5.7.2.5 Cramdown

A cramdown involves the imposition of a debt restructuring while there are still objections from one or more creditors. Schemes can enable a cramdown to occur, albeit only within a particular class and not across classes, unlike the cross-class cramdown that is observed in the

431 Insolvency Act 1986, s. 233B(5)(a)(b).

432 Ibid, s. 233B(5)(c). CIGA does not define 'hardship' and it will therefore be for the courts to establish this threshold, but it is likely to mean the possible insolvency of the supplier if it is forced to continue to supply.

433 Ibid, s. 233B(6). A similar hardship provision is to be found in Singapore (Singapore Insolvency, Restructuring and Dissolution Act 2018, s. 440(4)) and in Canada (for discussion see *Toronto-Dominion Bank* v. *Ty (Canada) Inc*, 42 CBR (4th) 142, 2003 CanLII 43355; A. Ho, 'The treatment of ipso facto clauses in Canada' (2015) 61(1) *McGill Law Journal* 139).

434 11 USC § 365.

435 By contrast, it appears to be well established in Canada that the statutory provisions grant a supplier the right to demand immediate cash payments for the supply of goods and to resist being compelled to supply goods on credit, regardless of the terms of the contract: *HSBC Canada* v. *Tri-Tec Industries Ltd*, 22 CBR (5th) 120, 2006 CarswellOnt 3174; Ho, 'The treatment of ipso facto clauses in Canada', note 433 above.

restructuring plan and in other jurisdictions, such as in US Chapter 11.[436] As long as the scheme is approved by a majority in number representing 75 per cent in value of the relevant meetings,[437] and then sanctioned by the court and registered,[438] all creditors within the scheme will be bound.[439] Once approved and sanctioned, a restructuring implemented by means of a scheme can bind both secured and unsecured creditors. The claims of secured creditors can therefore be compromised without their individual consent, as long as the majority of the class of creditors within which the secured creditors are placed vote in favour of the scheme, and the other requirements for the scheme are fulfilled.

By contrast, it is a fundamental principle of administration that the creditors cannot approve proposals that would affect the enforcement rights of the secured creditors. UK insolvency law has always demonstrated deference for the rights of secured creditors, and other holders of real rights, such as sellers under retention-of-title clauses. Prior to the introduction of administration in 1985, administrative receivership provided certain debenture holders with a powerful tool to enforce their security, and liquidation did not interfere with the remedies of secured creditors or other claimants with assets held by the company. Administration demonstrates a similar unwillingness to interfere with the rights of secured creditors.[440] So, for example, the courts are reluctant to refuse leave to secured creditors to enforce their security where this might cause them significant loss.[441] As a result, administration (in common with CVAs) cannot be used to cram down the rights of secured creditors. So, one benefit of schemes is that, in contrast to administration (and CVAs), they enable a cramdown (within a class) of all creditors, including secured creditors, to take place. As discussed at section 5.4.3, although a cramdown of a whole class of creditors (or members) was not possible using any single mechanism before the introduction of the restructuring plan in 2020,[442] practitioners developed a de facto cross-class

436 For further discussion see section 5.8.

437 Companies Act 2006, s. 899(1).

438 Ibid.

439 Ibid., s. 899(3)(a). In addition, the company is bound or, if the company is being wound up, the liquidator and contributories are bound: s. 899(3)(b).

440 There are some exceptions, of course, such as the moratorium on the enforcement of security interests produced by an administration, and the administrator's power to dispose of assets subject to a floating charge, with the chargee's priority attaching to the proceeds (Insolvency Act 1986, Sch. B1, para. 70).

441 Ibid., Sch. B1, para. 43.

442 See section 5.8.2.

cramdown by twinning schemes with administration (particularly pre-pack administration).

5.7.2.6 Minority creditor protection

The fact that a scheme allows the minority to be bound by a decision of the majority raises issues of minority creditor protection that do not arise in the same way in administration.

In administration, the administrator will prepare a statement setting out their proposals for achieving the purpose of administration and send this to every creditor and member of whose address they are aware.[443] These proposals will then be voted on by a creditors' meeting.[444] The proposals need to be approved by a majority (in value) of those present and voting, in person or by proxy.[445] Once passed, the proposals will bind all creditors.[446] However, these proposals cannot include any action that affects the rights of a secured creditor to enforce its security, or would result in a preferential debt of the company losing priority to non-preferential debts, or in one preferential creditor being paid a smaller proportion of its debt than another,[447] unless the affected creditor consents. The potential for minority oppression is therefore significantly reduced, compared to a scheme.

To counter the possibility of any minority oppression arising outside these groups (principally in relation to the unsecured creditors), administration relies on the role of the administrator as an external, independent, professionally qualified individual with a duty to perform their functions in the interests of the company's creditors as a whole.[448] It is the administrator who puts forward the proposals to the creditors' meeting and who must consent to any modifications.

443 Insolvency Act 1986, Sch. B1, para. 49(4).

444 Ibid., Sch. B1, para. 51. The creditors' meeting can approve the proposals or propose modifications to them, although any modification requires the administrator's consent: para. 53(1)(b).

445 Insolvency Rules 2016, r. 15.34(1). Persons connected with the company are excluded from the vote (r. 15.34(2)). Where a CVA is put forward as part of the proposals, the proposals then need to be passed by a higher percentage (three-quarters in value of the creditors present in person or by proxy) (r.15.31).

446 Where a CVA is involved, the arrangement binds only those who are entitled to vote at the meeting approving the arrangement or would have been so entitled if they had had notice of the meeting (Insolvency Act 1986, s. 5(2)(b)). See section 5.6.1 for further discussion.

447 Insolvency Act 1986, Sch. B1, para. 73(1).

448 Ibid., Sch. B1, para. 3(2).

If a member or creditor believes that the administrator has acted inappropriately or unfairly in relation to its claim, it has limited options. Since the administrator's duties are owed to the company, the primary claim regarding an administrator who has acted inappropriately is a claim by the company.[449] However, an individual member or creditor will have the ability to claim in some circumstances. In particular, paragraph 74 of Schedule B1 of the Insolvency Act 1986 provides that a member or creditor can apply to court claiming that the administrator is acting or has acted unfairly so as to harm the interests of the applicant, or is proposing to act in a way that would unfairly harm the interest of the applicant. In each case, the unfair harm might be suffered by the applicant alone, or in common with some or all of the other creditors or members. It is not necessary to demonstrate that the administrator has acted unlawfully or in breach of some legal duty. However, both elements of the claim need to be satisfied, namely that harm is suffered and that it is unfair.[450] Causing harm to one particular creditor will not necessarily be unfair, since the administrator is required to have regard to the interests of the creditors as a whole.[451] The administrator will need to ensure that their decisions are properly informed and take into account all relevant considerations.[452] If they do so, the court has demonstrated a reluctance to substitute its judgment for that of the administrator.

In relation to schemes, the possibility of minority oppression is much more real. A scheme will usually be developed by the directors of the company, and a scheme can bind all creditors, both secured and unsecured, within the ambit of the scheme. There is no figure akin to the administrator to oversee the process. Instead, the mechanisms put in place to seek to ensure that the minority are not oppressed in a scheme are (i) the requirement for creditors (and members) to meet in classes when determining whether to vote in favour of a scheme or not; and (ii) court oversight, including the requirement that the court sanction the scheme before it can become binding. As discussed in section 5.3, the requirement for separate classes in relation to debt restructuring schemes is not straightforward, yet it can provide useful protection for minorities. By contrast, administration has no requirement for class meetings. The

[449] Ibid., Sch. B1, para. 75.

[450] *Re Lehman Bros International (Europe) (in administration)* [2008] EWHC 2869 (Ch); [2009] BCC 632; *Re London & Westcountry Estates Ltd* [2014] Bus L R 441.

[451] *BLV Reality Organization Ltd* v. *Batten* [2009] EWHC 2994 (Ch); [2010] BPIR 277.

[452] See *Davey* v. *Money* [2018] EWHC 766 (Ch).

majority requirements are also different in a scheme and in a creditors' meeting to approve an administrator's proposals. In the latter, the creditors' decision needs to be taken by 50 per cent of creditors voting in person or by proxy by reference to the value of their claims. This is in contrast to the decision on a scheme, which must be both 75 per cent in value and a majority in number.[453] The sanctioning role of the court in a scheme, discussed at section 2.4, has no equivalent in administration.

5.7.2.7 Summary

Administration can be a useful tool for dealing with insolvent companies.[454] However, it has a number of limitations as a potential debt restructuring tool for financially distressed companies as compared to a scheme of arrangement. In particular, schemes can operate at an earlier stage, can be used to compromise the arrangements of secured and unsecured creditors without their consent in certain circumstances and are debtor-in-possession. One of the potential benefits of administration, namely the automatic statutory stay that attaches to it, has also been diminished by the introduction of the restructuring moratorium that can be used in conjunction with schemes. The contrast becomes starker when administration as a stand-alone device is compared to the use of a scheme twinned with administration as a debt restructuring tool which can provide the benefits of a de facto cross-class cramdown.

5.8 Restructuring plans

In 2020, an entirely new form of restructuring mechanism was introduced into English law: the restructuring plan.[455] Based to a large extent on the scheme of arrangement, the restructuring plan contains within it one significant change from that mechanism, namely the potential for a cross-class cramdown.

[453] Companies Act 2006, s. 899(1). As discussed in Chapter 2, the majority-in-number requirement in relation to schemes is controversial and can potentially cause significant difficulties, especially in relation to bondholders. It was therefore suggested that this requirement should be removed: section 2.3.3.2.

[454] Concerns have, however, been raised around a number of issues, including costs and the levels of recoveries to unsecured creditors; see S. Frisby, *Interim Report to the Insolvency Service on Returns to Creditors from Pre- and Post-Enterprise Act Insolvency Procedures*, July 2007; V. Finch and D. Milman, *Corporate Insolvency Law* (Cambridge University Press, 2017) 323 et seq.

[455] CIGA, s. 7 and Sch. 9, introducing a new Part 26A into the Companies Act 2006.

5.8.1 *The need for a cross-class cramdown*

The benefits of being able to impose a restructuring on dissenting creditors (a cramdown) have been discussed earlier in this chapter.[456] Cramdowns can be structured in various ways. For example, there can be cramdowns of certain kinds of creditors (e.g. the unsecured creditors) but not of others (e.g. the secured creditors), as happens in CVAs.[457] There can be cramdowns of all kinds of creditors (secured and unsecured) but only where each class of creditors consents, i.e. cramdown by the majority of the minority within a class, as occurs in schemes of arrangement. Or there can be cramdowns of whole classes of creditors and/or members (a cross-class cramdown). The broader the form of cramdown, the more valuable it will be to the company seeking to restructure itself and achieve a rescue, but the greater the potential for minority oppression. As discussed in section 5.4.3, prior to the Corporate Insolvency and Governance Act 2020 there was no stand-alone mechanism in UK law which allowed a cross-class cramdown to occur, although by twinning a scheme with administration it was possible to achieve a de facto cross-class cramdown. Cross-class cramdowns are a tool found in debt restructuring mechanisms elsewhere in the world.[458] One of the most notable is the cross-class cramdown found in US Chapter 11, but a number of other examples exist.

5.8.1.1 Cross-class cramdown in US Chapter 11

In the United States, a company experiencing financial difficulty (or its creditors) can file with the federal bankruptcy court under Chapter 11.[459]

456 See section 5.4.3.

457 See section 5.6.1.

458 See e.g. the Dutch scheme (Act on the Confirmation of Private Plans, *Wet homologatie onderhands akkoord*). Even in jurisdictions without a cross-class cramdown in place, such as Australia, the value of this mechanism is recognised: J. Harris, 'Class warfare in debt restructuring – does Australia need cross-class cramdown for creditors' schemes?' (2017) 36(1) *University of Queensland Law Journal* 73.

459 Under Chapter 11, debtors prepare a disclosure statement that describes their proposed reorganisation proposal and payment plan. The proposed plan is voted on by the various classes of creditors and shareholders and then submitted to the court for final approval. The plan will put a new capital structure in place for the company. Once accepted, the effect of the plan will therefore be to convert the old claims of creditors and/or shareholders into new claims against the reorganised firm. For discussion of the advantages and disadvantages of Chapter 11 see E. Warren, 'The untenable case for the repeal of Chapter 11' (1992) 102 *Yale Law Journal* 437 and M. Bradley and M. Rosenweig, 'The untenable case for Chapter 11' (1992) 101 *Yale Law Journal* 1043.

This is a self-contained, pragmatic, court-driven process that facilitates debt restructuring and is aimed at rescuing the company. The policy of Chapter 11 is to avoid the social costs of liquidation and to encourage reorganisation, which will allow the assets of the company to be preserved rather than sold as scrap. Chapter 11 therefore focuses on preserving reorganisation or going-concern value rather than liquidation value. Although there are many similarities between Chapter 11 and the use of schemes to effect a debt restructuring,[460] there are also a number of important differences, the existence of the cross-class cramdown in Chapter 11 being one of them.[461]

For Chapter 11 purposes, creditors and/or shareholders must be divided into classes in order to consider and approve the plan.[462] Chapter 11 requires each class to vote in favour by a majority in number and two-thirds in amount of those actually voting.[463] The debtor makes a distinction between those creditors and/or shareholders whose claims are impaired (i.e. those whose contractual rights are to be modified or who will be paid less than the full value of their claims under the plan) and those whose claims are not. This is because only creditors and/or

460 Both schemes and Chapter 11 are debtor-in-possession; in neither is there a requirement for insolvency before a company can begin the process; in both, the proceedings are almost always begun by a voluntary petition filed by the corporate debtor (in the USA see 11 USC § 301, although see also § 303); in both, detailed disclosure is required that will enable members/creditors to make an informed judgement about the proposed reorganisation (in the USA see 11 USC §§ 1121, 1125); and, in both, creditors and/or shareholders must be divided into classes in order to consider and approve the plan.

461 See Payne, 'Debt restructuring in English law', note 122 above; Paterson, 'Reflections on English law schemes in distress', note 187 above; S. Shandro, 'UK's Chapter 11 plan: schemes of arrangement' (2006) *American Bankruptcy Institute Journal* 30; D. Stevenson, 'Grab the fire extinguisher: comparing UK schemes of arrangement to US corporate bankruptcy after JEVIC' (2019) 68 *Cleveland State Law Review* 73; H. Eidenmueller, 'What is an insolvency proceeding?' (2018) 92 *American Bankruptcy Law Journal* 53. Although there is often a focus on the ways in which schemes are deficient compared to US Chapter 11, there are some benefits to the scheme regime. In *Re Syncreon Group BV* [2019] EWHC 2412 (Ch), for example, a scheme of arrangement was used rather than US Chapter 11 proceedings, which was noteworthy given that the group had operations across the USA. The reasons cited by the companies for this choice were the anticipated higher costs of Chapter 11, that the English scheme of arrangement avoids the taint (and potential termination triggers) of an insolvency or bankruptcy proceeding, and potential issues regarding recognition of US proceedings in other jurisdictions.

462 11 USC § 1123(a)(1). The classification of creditors and/or shareholders into classes is based on the premise that claims or interests may be placed in the same class only if they are 'substantially similar' to the rest of the class: § 1122.

463 Ibid., § 1126(c).

shareholders whose claims are 'impaired'[464] vote on the plan by ballot.[465] Creditors and/or shareholders who receive nothing in the plan do not get to vote either; it is presumed that they reject the plan.[466]

Once voting has taken place, the court will conduct a confirmation hearing to determine whether to confirm the plan.[467] Any party with an interest may file an objection to confirmation of a plan. However, even in the absence of objections, before confirmation can be granted the court must be satisfied that there has been compliance with all the requirements of section 1129 of the Bankruptcy Code. In addition to being satisfied that the plan is feasible,[468] the court will consider whether to confirm the plan in light of the votes cast in the class meetings. It is possible for the court to confirm a plan even though one or more classes of impaired creditors voted against it. Specifically, the court can confirm a plan that has not been approved by all impaired classes provided the plan 'does not discriminate unfairly, and is fair and equitable with respect to each class of claims or interests that is impaired under, and has not accepted, the plan'.[469] So long as at least *one* class of impaired creditors votes in favour of the plan, the cramdown rule may be used to confirm the plan.

However, Chapter 11 imposes a number of safeguards to protect minorities. Unsurprisingly, given the more extensive nature of the cramdown that may be obtained under Chapter 11, these protections go further than those adopted under the English scheme procedure. In particular, Chapter 11 requires that (i) the plan must meet the 'best interests of the creditors' test, i.e. the plan cannot give impaired classes less than they would receive in a liquidation;[470] (ii) the plan must treat

[464] The Bankruptcy Code defines a claim as: (1) a right to payment or (2) a right to an equitable remedy for a failure of performance if the breach gives rise to a right to payment: 11 USC § 101(5).

[465] 11 USC § 1126.

[466] That does not necessarily mean they will get nothing, though. Creditors and/or shareholders who vote against or reject the plan are usually entitled to recover what they would have recovered if the company had filed a Chapter 7 liquidation bankruptcy.

[467] 11 USC § 1128.

[468] The court will want to see that the debtor will be able to meet the obligations that the plan imposes on it, and that it will not leave Chapter 11 only to fail again: 11 USC § 1129(a)(11). Confirmation of a Chapter 11 plan therefore requires that there be cash to pay administrative expenses and priority claims, and that the cash payments be provided for in the plan. The court must also find that confirmation of the plan is not likely to be followed by liquidation (unless the plan is a liquidating plan) or the need for further financial reorganisation.

[469] 11 USC § 1129(b)(1).

[470] Ibid., § 1129(a)(7).

each member of each class fairly;[471] and (iii) the plan must be fair and equitable.[472] In addition, US law has supplemented the 'fair and equitable' requirement with the absolute priority rule, which has been described as 'bankruptcy's most important and famous rule' and 'the cornerstone of reorganization practice and theory',[473] although it has faced a growing level of scepticism from commentators in recent years.[474] The absolute priority rule has two elements. First, the plan of reorganisation must pay any non-consenting class in full before any junior class receives anything under the plan on account of its interest. Second, a senior class may not receive more than 100 per cent of its claim where a dissenting junior class will receive less than 100 per cent. Once the plan is confirmed, it binds all creditors and equity holders, and the debtor is required to make plan payments and is bound by the provisions of the plan of reorganisation. The confirmed plan creates new contractual rights, replacing or superseding pre-bankruptcy contracts.[475]

As discussed in section 5.4.3, where cross-class cramdowns can occur, the issue of valuation is central to concerns about creditor protection. The approach to valuation adopted in the USA has been termed the bargaining and litigation approach.[476] Each creditor class retains its own expert to value the business and the assets of the company using standard

[471] Ibid., § 1129(b).

[472] Ibid.

[473] Ibid., § 1129(b)(2)(B), and see *Czyzewski* v. *Jevic Holding Corp* 137 S. Ct. 973, 979 (2017).

[474] See e.g. D. G. Baird, 'Priority matters: absolute priority, relative priority, and the costs of bankruptcy' (2017) 165 *University of Pennsylvania Law Review* 765; E. J. Janger, 'The logic and limits of liens' (2015) 2015(2) *University of Illinois Law Review* 589; S. J. Lubben, 'The overstated absolute priority rule' (2016) 21 *Fordham Journal of Corporate & Financial Law* 581. See also American Bankruptcy Institute, *Commission to Study the Reform of Chapter 11*, 2012–2014: *Final Report and Recommendations* (2014).

[475] 11 USC § 1141(d)(1) generally provides that confirmation of a plan discharges a debtor from any debt that arose before the date of confirmation. There are, of course, exceptions, e.g. confirmation does not discharge the debtor if the plan is a liquidation plan, as opposed to one of reorganisation, unless the debtor is an individual.

[476] D. G. Baird and D. S. Bernstein, 'Absolute priority, valuation uncertainty, and the reorganization bargain' (2006) 115(8) *Yale Law Journal* 1930. An alternative method of dealing with this issue, the options approach, suggests that out-of-the-money creditors receive an option with a strike price equal to the debt ranking ahead of them and a defined exercise period, which could be traded in the market and which would assume a higher value if the business recovered rapidly after the debt restructuring (see e.g. L. Bebchuk, 'A new approach to corporate reorganizations' (1988) 101(4) *Harvard Law Review* 775). This approach has not been adopted and was not met with enthusiasm in the American Bankruptcy Institute review of Chapter 11: ABI, Commission to Study the Reform of Chapter 11, 2012–2014, note 474 above.

valuation methodology, of which the discounted cash-flow method is one of the most commonly used.[477] If the parties do not agree, there may be a valuation hearing before a judge. This structure provides opportunities for the junior creditors to put forward their own valuations, but it contains potential problems too.[478] The valuation process can be long and costly[479] and the valuations unpredictable given the level of subjectivity in the approach. Further, the out-of-the-money creditors may fear the valuation fight less than the senior creditors as they have less to lose. This may incentivise the senior creditors to give something to the junior classes to effectively buy out their ability to hold up the restructuring by forcing the matter into a contentious court hearing. The out-of-the-money creditors may thus capture returns to which they are not strictly entitled. Enabling the subordinated creditors to use blocking tactics to extract value from a situation in which they should receive none is not ideal. Of necessity, the process of valuation is an inexact science, fraught with uncertainties, particularly where it is seeking to assess the future value of the company following reorganisation, and this valuation uncertainty is often cited as a cause of the noted deviations from the absolute priority rule in Chapter 11 cases.[480]

US Chapter 11 and, in particular, the cross-class cramdown contained within it have been very influential in a number of debt restructuring

[477] For discussion see O'Rourke, 'Valuation uncertainty in Chapter 11 reorganizations', note 142 above. However, some disquiet has been expressed about the use of this methodology: M. Simkovic, 'The evolution of valuation in bankruptcy' (2017) 91 *American Bankruptcy Law Journal* 299.

[478] For discussion see Baird, 'Priority matters', note 474 above; S. Paterson, 'Bargaining in financial restructuring: market norms, legal rights and regulatory standards' (2014) 14(2) *Journal of Corporate Law Studies* 333.

[479] For example, according to Baird, in the reorganisation of Residential Capital (*In re Residential Capital LLC*, 501 BR 549, 624 (Bankr SDNY 2013)), more than $100 million was spent in a dispute over how much to value the claim of a single group of secured creditors: Baird, 'Priority matters', note 474 above, 807.

[480] L. LoPucki and W. Whitford, 'Bargaining over equity's share in the bankruptcy reorganization of large, publicly held companies' (1990) 139 *University of Pennsylvania Law Review* 125. Some commentators suggest that the problem is caused by valuation uncertainty, which leads senior claimants to bargain with shareholders and surrender value to them in order to shorten long and expensive arguments over valuation methodology: Baird and Bernstein, 'Absolute priority, valuation uncertainty and the reorganization bargain', note 476 above. Alternatively, it has been suggested that this may be a result of the deep commitment to the entrepreneurial ethic in the USA (J. L. Westbrook, 'A comparison of bankruptcy reorganization in the US, with administration procedure in the UK' (1990) *Insolvency Law and Practice* 86, at 88) or because Chapter 11 emphasises the rescue of the company over and above the rescue of the business.

reforms introduced in recent years, including the UK reforms discussed at section 5.8.2. Before discussing the UK reforms, however, it is useful to consider other recent debt restructuring reform proposals that have sought to introduce a cross-class cramdown option. Two examples are considered here, namely the cross-class cramdown proposals contained in the EU Restructuring Directive and those contained in the Singapore debt restructuring reforms in 2017. These examples demonstrate that there are different ways of introducing a cross-class cramdown and of seeking to ensure that creditors are appropriately protected.

5.8.1.2 Cross-class cramdown in the EU Restructuring Directive

The EU Restructuring Directive includes a cross-class cramdown option as part of its restructuring regime.[481] The Restructuring Directive seeks to introduce a minimum standard amongst EU Member States for preventive restructuring frameworks available to debtors in financial difficulty.[482] It includes debtors remaining in possession of their assets and day-to-day operation of their business, a stay of individual enforcement of actions, and constraints on ipso facto clauses, as well as the cross-class cramdown. The Directive imposes a deadline for implementation into national law of 2021, subject to a one-year extension. A number of Member States have already designed the restructuring mechanisms that will fulfil their obligation.[483] From the UK's perspective, having left the EU before the deadline for implementation, it is not required to implement this Directive into national law. The changes introduced into the UK by the Corporate Insolvency and Governance Act 2020 get the UK to a similar place in any case.[484]

[481] Directive (EU) 2019/1023. A 'cram-up' option also seems to be available, with the possibility of more junior classes of in-the-money creditors imposing a restructuring on a more senior class (although it is not possible for out-of-the-money creditors to impose a cram-up or cram-down on dissenting in-the-money creditors): Art. 11(1)(b)(ii)).

[482] For discussion see L. Stanghellini, R. Mokal, C. Paulus and I. Tirado (eds.), *Best Practices in European Restructuring* (Walters Kluwer, 2018).

[483] See e.g. German Corporate Stabilization and Restructuring Act (Unter nehmensstabilisierungs- und -restrukturierungsgesetz); Dutch Act on the Confirmation of Private Plans (Wet homologatie onderhands akkoord).

[484] See, in particular, the discussions at section 5.4.4.2 as regards the new restructuring moratorium, section 5.7.2.4 regarding the constraints on ipso facto clauses and section 5.8.2 regarding the cross-class cramdown.

Cross-class cramdown within the Directive allows a restructuring plan to be confirmed even if the plan has not been approved by each and every voting class.[485] It can be imposed on dissenting creditor classes and on equity-holders, although the Directive leaves to Member States the decision as to the ability of the restructuring plan to affect equity-holders.[486] There must be some judicial or administrative approval of a plan which affects the interests of dissenting parties. The Directive requires that the restructuring is approved by a majority of the voting classes of affected parties,[487] provided that at least one of those classes is a secured creditor class or is senior to the ordinary unsecured creditor class, or, failing that, by at least one[488] voting class of affected parties other than equity holders or any class which on a going-concern valuation would be out of the money.[489] This rule seeks to make sure that the plan is approved by at least one class of creditors that is 'in the money' but will require a valuation of the debtor's assets as a going concern, which is likely to give rise to expert disputes and to be expensive and time-consuming.

There are a number of requirements in place that have to be satisfied before any restructuring plan can be confirmed, including that where there are dissenting creditors, the restructuring plan satisfies the 'best interest of creditors' test.[490] This requires that a creditor would be better off in the plan than in a liquidation.[491] There is an additional requirement

485 Directive (EU) 2019/1023, Art. 11(1). It is a matter for national law to determine class divisions, but, under the Restructuring Directive, at the very minimum, classes should be divided between secured and unsecured creditors. The reservation of class criteria to national law permits Member States to regulate class rights and voting rights and to provide a legal framework for any contested claims (see Art. 9(4)).

486 Ibid., Art. 12.

487 The Directive provides that Member States shall lay down the majorities required for the adoption of a restructuring plan and that those majorities shall not be higher than 75 per cent of the amount of claims or interests in each class or, where applicable, of the number of affected parties in each class: ibid., Art. 9(6).

488 It is open to Member States to increase this figure: ibid.

489 Ibid., Art. 11(1)(b).

490 Ibid., Art. 10(2)(d).

491 Ibid., recital 52: 'Satisfying the "best-interest-of-creditors" test should be considered to mean that no dissenting creditor is worse off under a restructuring plan than it would be either in the case of liquidation, whether piecemeal liquidation or sale of the business as a going concern, or in the event of the next-best alternative scenario if the restructuring plan were not to be confirmed. Member States should be able to choose one of those thresholds when implementing the best-interest-of-creditors test in national law.' It has been suggested that the 'next-best-alternative' test should be interpreted to mean the returns that would be achieved in the realistic alternative: R. Mokal and I. Tirado, 'Has Newton had his day? relativity and realism in European restructuring' (2018) *European Restructuring* 20.

for a cross-class cramdown to be approved, namely satisfaction of a fairness test. The fairness test is composed of three sub-tests: (i) the 'priority rule', which may be the 'absolute priority rule'[492] modelled on US Chapter 11 or, alternatively, the Directive allows Member States to adopt the 'relative priority rule' whereby dissenting voting classes of affected creditors must simply be treated at least as favourably as any other class of the same rank and more favourably than any junior class, with the preferred position apparently being the relative priority rule;[493] (ii) a requirement that no class of affected parties can, under the restructuring plan, receive or keep more than the full amount of its claims or interests;[494] and (iii) the 'no unfair discrimination principle' that dissenting voting classes of affected creditors shall be treated at least as favourably as any other class of the same rank.[495] Although the 'best interests of the creditors' test requires a liquidation valuation model, the fairness test requires the higher restructuring value to be satisfied. The Directive provides for disagreements over valuations, which seem likely to arise, but provides little guidance as to how these might be resolved.[496]

There are a number of important differences between the US Chapter 11 cross-class cramdown and its equivalent in the EU Directive. The most obvious is the default option for Member States to adopt the less rigid relative priority rule as an alternative to the absolute priority rule found in US Chapter 11.[497] Proponents of the relative priority rule state that it provides optionality for Member States and counters the disadvantages of the absolute priority rule. However, a number of concerns have been raised regarding the relative priority rule.[498] One concern is that it creates legal uncertainty for both investors

492 Directive (EU) 2019/1023, Art. 11(2)(a).

493 Ibid., Art. 11(1)(c) (with the absolute priority rule in Art. 11(2)(a) being a derogation from this position).

494 Ibid., Art. 11(1)(d).

495 Ibid., Art. 11(1)(c).

496 Ibid., Art. 14.

497 There has been some discussion of the introduction of a relative priority rule in the USA (see e.g. Baird, 'Priority matters', note 474 above) but this is not identical to the relative priority rule as introduced in the EU Restructuring Directive; see e.g. R. de Weijs, A. Jonkers and M. Malakotipour, 'The imminent distortion of European insolvency law: how the European Union erodes the basic fabric of private law by allowing "relative priority"' (2019) Amsterdam Law School Research Paper No. 2019-10.

498 For discussion of the advantages and disadvantages of the rule see T. Richter and A. Thery, INSOL Europe: Guidance Note on the Implementation of Preventive Restructuring Frameworks under EU Directive 2019/1023: Claims, Classes, Voting, Confirmation and the Cross-Class Cram-Down, April 2020, 35–6; de Weijs, Jonkers

and judges over the exact amount of incremental value that constitutes better treatment of the senior class over the junior class in order to satisfy the 'more favourably' requirement. Legal uncertainty may also be generated by the fact that this rule is generally less well understood than the tried and tested absolute priority rule. Critics of the relative priority rule suggest that it is unclear how the test should be applied. For example, comparing the position of creditors and shareholders may be difficult given that the position of the shareholders, as residual claimants, cannot be measured by a pay out percentage; assessing whether creditors have been treated 'more favourably' than shareholders therefore will not be straightforward. Furthermore, it is suggested that looking only at the pay-out percentages may not be the best way to compare the financial position of the respective classes in a restructuring, and that the relative priority rule may allow for transfers or redistributions of value between classes.[499]

A significant feature of the Directive is the level of optionality it allows for Member States; the Directive contains more than seventy regulatory options.[500] This will reduce harmonisation of restructuring regimes across Member States (one of the aims of the Directive) and create potential incentives for forum shopping.

5.8.1.3 Cross-class cramdown in Singapore schemes of arrangement

Singapore implemented significant reforms to its debt restructuring regime in 2017, including the introduction of a cross-class cramdown option.[501] Prior to the 2017 reforms, Singapore's schemes of arrangement were largely identical to English schemes of arrangement, on which they

and Malakotipour, 'The imminent distortion of European insolvency law', note 497 above. Cf. S. Madaus, 'Leaving the shadows of US bankruptcy law: a proposal to divide the realms of insolvency and restructuring law' (2018) 19 *European Business Organization Law Review* 615; Mokal and Tirado, 'Has Newton had his day?', note 491 above.

499 De Weijs et al. suggest that there is a danger that the relative priority rule subsidises shareholders at the expense of creditors and could lead to further over-leveraging of companies and instability in the economy: de Weijs, Jonkers and Malakotipour, 'The imminent distortion of European insolvency law', note 497 above.

500 H. Eidenmueller, 'The rise and fall of regulatory competition in corporate insolvency law in the European Union' (2019) 20 *European Business Organization Law Review* 547.

501 See Singapore Companies (Amendment) Act 2017, introducing s. 211H into the Singapore Companies Act (Cap. 50), now contained in the Singapore Insolvency, Restructuring and Dissolution Act 2018, s. 70. For discussion see Wai Yee Wan, Watters and McCormack, 'Schemes of arrangement in Singapore', note 175 above.

were based, although there were some differences of practice: for instance, twinning a scheme with the Singaporean equivalent of administration (judicial management) was rare,[502] and, in contrast to UK debt restructuring schemes which tend to be confined to the finance creditors, Singaporean schemes have also included individual investors, trade creditors and employees.[503] The introduction of a cross-class cramdown into the Singapore scheme of arrangement was part of a broader package of reforms, including the introduction of rescue finance and a restructuring moratorium, that borrowed heavily from US Chapter 11.[504]

Following these reforms, the Singapore court can allow a cramdown of one or more classes of dissenting creditors[505] if certain conditions are fulfilled. First, at least one class of creditors intended to be bound by the scheme must have consented to it by a majority in number and 75 per cent by value.[506] The Singapore provisions therefore retain the traditional scheme approval levels, rather than adopt the US Chapter 11 approval level of two-thirds when determining whether a given class is deemed to have accepted the terms of the restructuring. Second, the scheme is also approved by creditors comprising a majority in number representing at least 75 per cent of the value of those present and voting at the meetings of scheme creditors as a whole, i.e. there must be a sufficient majority of all the creditors whose debts the company would like to restructure that approve the restructuring, ignoring for this purpose the fact that they have been put into different classes to vote on the restructuring.[507] This requirement is not a feature of US Chapter 11 and makes the Singaporean cross-class cramdown harder to accomplish than its US equivalent; potentially, this requirement means that a cramdown can reliably be used only where the dissenting creditors comprise a relatively small part of the capital structure (regardless of whether they can be demonstrated to be receiving a significantly better

502 For an example see *Chew Eu Hock Construction* v. *CPF Board* [2003] SGHC 199.

503 For further discussion of the differences in the use of debt restructuring schemes in the UK and Singapore see Wai Yee Wan, Watters and McCormack, 'Schemes of arrangement in Singapore', note 175 above.

504 See Meng Seng Wee, 'The Singapore story', note 175 above.

505 The cramdown does not extend to shareholders.

506 Singapore Insolvency, Restructuring and Dissolution Act 2018, s. 70(1). The Singaporean cross-class cramdown provisions retain the headcount test, despite the fact that reforms introduced in Singapore in 2014 provide the court with discretion to waive the majority-in-number requirement: s. 210(3AB) Singapore Companies Act.

507 Singapore Insolvency, Restructuring and Dissolution Act 2018, s. 70(3)(a)(b). For discussion see Meng Seng Wee, 'The Singapore story', note 175 above, 572.

recovery than in liquidation). Third, the court must be satisfied that the scheme does not discriminate unfairly between two or more classes of creditors and is 'fair and equitable' in respect of each dissenting class.[508]

The meaning of 'fair and equitable' in this context has two components. The first is a version of the US Chapter 11 'best interests of the creditors' test and requires that

> no creditor in the dissenting class receives, under the terms of the compromise or arrangement, an amount that is lower than what the creditor is estimated by the Court to receive in the most likely scenario if the compromise or arrangement does not become binding on the company and all classes of creditors meant to be bound by the compromise or arrangement.[509]

The second component is a version of the absolute priority rule. In contrast to the US Chapter 11 rule, the Singaporean provisions apply to secured and unsecured creditors, but not to equity interests. As in Chapter 11, the absolute priority rule within the Singapore provisions requires that if a restructuring does not pay a particular class in full, no class junior to it may retain or receive anything on account of its old interest unless the senior class consents.[510]

It is recognised that valuation disputes often lie at the centre of the absolute priority rule, which can make the process time-consuming and costly. In an attempt to provide some assistance to the Singaporean courts, who do not have substantial experience in dealing with valuation in this context, the court is given a new power to appoint 'any person of suitable knowledge, qualification or experience to assist the Court in estimating the amount that a creditor is expected to receive in the most

[508] Singapore Insolvency, Restructuring and Dissolution Act 2018, s. 70(3)(c).

[509] Ibid., s. 70(4)(a).

[510] Ibid., s. 70(4)(b). If the creditors in the dissenting class are secured, they must receive deferred cash payments totalling the amount secured (and security preserved until such time) and be given a charge over the proceeds of their secured asset or be entitled to realise the 'indubitable equivalent' of the security. If the creditors in the dissenting class are unsecured, either they must be paid out in full or the scheme must not provide for any creditor or shareholder subordinate to the dissenting creditor to receive or retain any property. Under the terms of the absolute priority rule as initially introduced by the Singapore Companies (Amendment) Act 2017, to cram down a class of unsecured creditors required that the shares of existing shareholders be divested. However, since there was no procedure to compulsorily divest shareholders of their shares as part of a scheme of arrangement, the cramdown mechanism was dependent on the voluntary divestment of shares by shareholders in order to cram down unsecured creditors. This requirement was removed in the Singapore Insolvency, Restructuring and Dissolution Act, s. 70(4)(b)(ii)(B).

likely scenario if the compromise or arrangement does not become binding'.[511] Concerns around valuation mechanisms in the Singapore regime remain, however.[512]

5.8.1.4 The move towards a cross-class cramdown in the UK

The de facto cross-class cramdown created by twinning schemes with administration is a powerful tool that has been used by both English and foreign companies in recent years and is one of the factors that has led to England being a centre for debt restructuring. However, it has downsides, not least the need to utilise two mechanisms (a scheme and administration) and the need to transfer the assets to a newco, raising tax issues as well as potential problems if intercreditor agreements make such transfers difficult or costly. As a result, there have been increasing calls for English law to contain a cross-class cramdown available when using a scheme alone, including in the first edition of this book.[513] The reform of debt restructuring mechanisms in other jurisdictions, including the introduction of cross-class cramdowns also created pressure for English law to be reformed in order for it to retain its position as a premier debt restructuring regime. This led to reform proposals by the Insolvency Service in 2016, which included a cross-class cramdown,[514] and in 2018 by the government, which again included a cross-class cramdown option.[515] These proposals were shelved for two years, but the Covid-19 crisis provided an incentive to the government to dust them off and introduce them rapidly. The cross-class cramdown implemented in 2020 via the restructuring plan is not identical to either the Insolvency Service's proposals or the government's proposals in 2018. It is discussed in detail next.

5.8.2 *The UK restructuring plan*

The restructuring plan, introduced by the Corporate Insolvency and Governance Act 2020,[516] is modelled closely on the existing scheme

[511] Ibid., s. 70(5).
[512] See e.g. G. McCormack and Wai Yee Wan, 'Transplanting Chapter 11 of the US Bankruptcy Code into Singapore's restructuring and insolvency laws: opportunities and challenges' (2019) 19(1) *Journal of Corporate Law Studies* 69.
[513] See Payne, *Schemes of Arrangement*, note 180 above, 5.7 and ch. 9.
[514] Insolvency Service, *A Review of the Corporate Insolvency Framework*, note 185 above.
[515] BEIS, *Insolvency and Corporate Governance*, note 190 above.
[516] CIGA, s. 7 and Sch. 9, introducing a new Part 26A into Companies Act 2006.

regime (which remains available), but is intended to provide a company encountering financial difficulties with a more powerful restructuring tool than the existing scheme of arrangement process, in particular by including the option for a cross-class cramdown.[517]

A restructuring plan is an 'arrangement' or 'compromise' between the company and its creditors and/or shareholders or classes thereof,[518] and may be proposed by companies or their creditors or shareholders.[519] The restructuring plan is located in the Companies Act 2006 alongside schemes; it is a corporate restructuring process and is largely similar to other debtor-in-possession processes.

As in a scheme, it requires voting of creditors and shareholders in 'classes', although, in a helpful departure from the scheme procedure, the approval requirement is 75 per cent by value of that class voting in favour,[520] without the addition of the headcount test required for a scheme.[521] As with schemes of arrangement, it is possible to exclude creditors from the plan if those creditors' claims will be paid in full, i.e. where they are unaffected by the plan.[522] In the first restructuring plan to go to court, *Re Virgin Atlantic Airways Ltd*,[523] Snowden J expressed his

517 See e.g. the Explanatory Notes prepared by BEIS to accompany CIGA, paras. 15–16 and the Practice Statement (Companies: Schemes of Arrangement under Part 26 and Part 26A of the Companies Act 2006), 26 June 2020 which applies to both schemes and restructuring plans. The close relationship between the two mechanisms was recognised by Snowden J in *Re Virgin Atlantic Airways Ltd* [2020] EWHC 2376 (Ch) at [38].

518 Companies Act 2006, s. 901A(3)(a).

519 Ibid., s. 901C(1)(2). It seems most likely that it will be companies that propose a plan. The use by creditors is likely to be limited given the significant resourcing requirements that typically need debtor input to put together a realistic and credible restructuring plan (see section 2.2.1 for discussion of this issue in the context of schemes, which is likely to apply equally to restructuring plans). In addition, a plan can be proposed by a liquidator if the company is being wound up, or by an administrator if the company is in administration.

520 Ibid., s. 901F(1). There is a lower voting threshold for a Dutch scheme (*Wet homologatie onderhands akkoord*), which is two-thirds in value of claims of members of each class which are present and vote at the relevant class meeting.

521 See section 2.3.3.2. It is also notable that the requirement that more than half of the value of unconnected creditors vote in favour, which was included in the government's 2018 proposals, para. 5.155, does not appear in the Act.

522 *Sea Assets* v. *PT Garuda Indonesia*, 27 June 2001, unreported, discussed at sections 2.3.1.2 and 5.4.3. See *Re Virgin Atlantic Airways Ltd* [2020] EWHC 2376 (Ch). The court will take account of the reasons for the exclusion of those creditors at the sanctioning stage and will want to be satisfied that the exclusion was for 'respectable commercial reasons' (at [67]).

523 [2020] EWHC 2376 (Ch).

view that the ability for a company to propose a compromise or arrangement with some, but not all, of its groups of creditors was one of the most flexible and valuable features of the scheme jurisdiction under Part 26 and he saw no reason why the same approach could not be taken under a Part 26A restructuring plan. However, the judge noted that it should be fully explained to plan creditors if there were creditors ranking *pari passu* who would be more favourably treated, i.e. by being left uncompromised.

That said, every creditor or shareholder whose rights are affected by the plan must be permitted to vote.[524] In contrast to a scheme, the Act provides that an application can be made to exclude classes of creditors/shareholders from voting where the court is satisfied that 'none of the members of that class has a genuine economic interest in the company'.[525] The Act does not provide guidance on what constitutes a 'genuine economic interest' and who, therefore, should be denied a vote. This will need to be developed by the courts, which will presumably build on the case law that has already been developed in this regard in scheme cases such as *Re Bluebrook Ltd.*[526] It does mean that valuation issues will be at the centre of the operation of these provisions.[527]

In common with schemes, two court hearings are required: the first to order the required meetings of creditors/members 'in such manner as the court directs'[528] and the second to sanction the restructuring plan.[529] There is a requirement to provide information to creditors/members, and disclosure obligations are placed on directors that closely mirror the requirements in a scheme of arrangement.[530]

The closeness of restructuring plans to schemes of arrangement in procedural terms is emphasised by the Practice Statement, which sets out a number of issues regarding how schemes (and now restructuring plans) will operate. Originally published in 2002 and focused solely on schemes, this Practice Statement was replaced by a revised version on 26 June 2020,

[524] Companies Act 2006, s. 901C(3).
[525] Ibid., s. 901C(4).
[526] [2009] EWHC 2114(Ch) discussed at section 5.4.3.
[527] One other group is excluded from participation in a plan, namely creditors in respect of moratorium or pre-moratorium debts without a payment holiday under a restructuring moratorium which has ended less than twelve weeks before an application is made to the court to propose a restructuring plan (see section 5.4.4.2): Companies Act 2006, s. 901H.
[528] Companies Act 2006, s. 901C(1).
[529] Ibid., s. 901F(1).
[530] Ibid., ss. 901D and E. For discussion of the disclosure obligations in a scheme see section 2.2.2.

which expands the ambit to include restructuring plans.[531] By combining guidance applicable to compromises and arrangements under Part 26 and Part 26A of the Companies Act 2006, the 2020 Practice Statement reinforces the idea that these two mechanisms will follow largely similar processes (to the extent possible). The Practice Statement focuses on a number of issues, including the way in which classes of creditors/members will be considered by the court, requirements around disclosure, and details of how courts should deal with applications under Part 26 and Part 26A, particularly at the convening hearing.[532] For instance, the Statement explains that all applications under section 901C (to convene a meeting or meetings of creditors and/or members in relation to a restructuring plan) and all applications under section 901F (to sanction a restructuring plan) will be listed before a High Court judge, and the same judge should, if possible, hear both applications. The Practice Statement provides helpful guidance on some issues, but is notably silent on a number of other important matters such as valuation and the evidence that a company will need to put forward to support the view that a class does not have a 'genuine economic interest' and therefore should be denied a vote. These matters will therefore need to be developed by the courts.

The closeness of these procedural aspects of schemes and restructuring plans is beneficial to restructuring plans as it allows them to piggy-back on existing scheme case law.[533] Judicial decisions in relation to early restructuring plans confirm this approach. So, for example, the meaning of 'compromise' and 'arrangement' appears to be the same in restructuring plans as that developed in relation to schemes.[534] The courts have also applied the same test for determining class constitution in restructuring plans as in schemes, i.e. creditors/members should vote in the class where their rights are not so dissimilar to others in the class as to make it

[531] Practice Statement (Companies: Schemes of Arrangement under Part 26 and Part 26A of the Companies Act 2006), 26 June 2020.

[532] For an example of the application of these provisions in practice see e.g. *Re Virgin Atlantic Airways Ltd* [2020] EWHC 2191 (Ch); *Re Pizzaexpress Financing 2 Plc* [2020] EWHC 2873 (Ch).

[533] This approach is anticipated in the Explanatory Notes accompanying CIGA: 'While there are some differences between the new Part 26A and [the] existing Part 26 (for example the ability to bind dissenting classes of creditors and members), the overall commonality between the two Parts is expected to enable the courts to draw on the existing body of Part 26 case law where appropriate' (at para. 16).

[534] *Re Virgin Atlantic Airways Ltd* [2020] EWHC 2191 (Ch). For discussion of the meaning of these terms for scheme purposes see section 2.1.1.

impossible for them to consult together with a view to their common interest.[535] In *Re Virgin Atlantic Airways Ltd*,[536] Trower J considered that the principal differences between the two processes were: (i) that each affected creditor has an entitlement to participate in a meeting unless the court determines that none of the members of its class has a genuine economic interest in the company; (ii) that there is no numerosity requirement in the vote at a class meeting; and (iii) that there is provision for a cross-class cramdown. Although the judge did not engage in lengthy reasoning, given the lack of adversarial argument on the point, he held that none of these differences between restructuring plans and schemes of arrangement should be reflected in a different approach to class composition and, indeed, he noted that a common approach was preferable given the many procedural similarities between the two mechanisms.

The approach to class constitution should therefore be broadly the same, even having regard to the fact that the possibility of cross-class cramdown under a plan raises the possibility that, in some circumstances, a company may have an incentive to adopt a different approach to classes than occurs under a scheme, for example by increasing the number of classes or adopting a broader classification of creditors than previously permissible using a scheme. The court has confirmed that its role in relation to the convening hearing in a restructuring plan is the same as that in a scheme, i.e. it is not the court's role to consider the merits or fairness of the proposed plan at that stage.[537] Similarly, at the sanctioning hearing of the *Virgin Atlantic* restructuring plan, Snowden J followed the same approach as at a sanctioning hearing for a scheme, noting, however, that since all of the classes of creditors had sanctioned the scheme in that case, he was 'in a similar position to that which would have arisen had the Restructuring Plan been proposed as a scheme of arrangement under Part 26'.[538] The facts of the Virgin Atlantic plan were somewhat unusual in that three of the four classes had agreed unanimously in advance to be bound by the proposal. This raised the question of whether cross-class cramdown is available in circumstances where the assenting class consists solely of locked-up creditors, although subsequent cases have allowed a cross-class cramdown in these circumstances.[539]

535 *Re Virgin Atlantic Airways Ltd* [2020] EWHC 2191 (Ch). For discussion of the way in which class constitution is dealt with in schemes see section 2.3.2.

536 [2020] EWHC 2191 (Ch).

537 See *Re Pizzaexpress Financing 2 Plc* [2020] EWHC 2873 (Ch) at [23].

538 *Re Virgin Atlantic Airways Ltd* [2020] EWHC 2376 (Ch) at [46].

539 Ibid. at [50]. See *Re DeepOcean 1 UK Ltd* [2021] EWHC 138 (Ch).

The restructuring plan procedure applies in relation to any company liable to be wound up under the Insolvency Act 1986, which therefore includes foreign companies,[540] with a similar eligibility test to that which applies for a scheme of arrangement.[541] However, in contrast to a scheme of arrangement, in order to be eligible for the restructuring plan, the company must also satisfy two further hurdles. First, it must have encountered, or be likely to encounter, financial difficulties that are affecting, or will or may affect, its ability to carry on business as a going concern.[542] The company need not be insolvent to propose a plan. Second, the purpose of the compromise or arrangement proposed must be to eliminate, reduce, prevent or mitigate the effects of any of the company's financial difficulties.[543] The court has held that the requisite purpose of the compromise or arrangement is phrased broadly and is intended to be expansively construed.[544] It is also clear that these two conditions are part of the list of 'threshold' matters which fall to be dealt with at the convening hearing of a restructuring plan.[545]

This requirement of financial distress is not present in schemes, which can be utilised whatever the state of the company's finances, including when the company is entirely solvent without any hint of financial difficulties. Since the concept of 'financial difficulty' is very broad, potentially much broader than the insolvency concept of inability to pay debts, this is an issue on which courts will need to develop detailed guidance. In *Re Virgin Atlantic Airways Ltd*,[546] the court had little difficulty in finding that the company had encountered severe financial difficulties affecting its ability to carry on business as a going concern, given the near-

[540] Ibid., s. 901A(4). Certain 'regulated financial entities' may be restricted in their use of a restructuring plan. Entities that are regulated by the Prudential Regulation Authority will require its consent before applying to the court to initiate the plan process and regulations may be made under the Act excluding certain financial services entities that are authorised under the Financial Services and Markets Act 2000 and certain other companies or creditors from making use of a plan.

[541] See section 7.2. For an example of this test in operation in relation to a restructuring plan see e.g. *Re Virgin Atlantic Airways Ltd* [2020] EWHC 2191 (Ch), in which the court was content to adopt the same practice in relation to the Recast Judgments Regulation as that adopted in schemes of arrangement (discussed in section 7.3.2).

[542] Companies Act 2006, s. 901A(2).

[543] Ibid., s. 901A(3)(b).

[544] *Re Virgin Atlantic Airways Ltd* [2020] EWHC 2191 (Ch). On the facts the court was readily satisfied that the purpose of the plan put forward was to mitigate and, if possible, eliminate the company's financial difficulties.

[545] Ibid.

[546] [2020] EWHC 2191 (Ch).

shutdown of the global passenger aviation industry in the Covid-19 pandemic. At the convening hearing on 4 August 2020, evidence showed that, absent the proposed recapitalisation deal, the group's cash flow would drop to a critical level in the week commencing 21 September 2020; the company's directors considered that administration proceedings would be inevitable by mid-September; and returns to the company's unsecured creditors in administration would be substantially less than under the plan. However, in less stark scenarios this may be a more difficult issue to resolve, although the courts are likely to want to adopt a broad interpretation of this requirement.

Crucially, the restructuring plan allows for the cramdown of whole classes of creditors and shareholders. The intention underpinning the Act is that shareholder equity can be transferred, diluted or extinguished as part of a court-approved restructuring plan. This aligns the restructuring plan with Chapter 11 but stands in contrast to cross-class cramdowns elsewhere in the world (such as Singapore) which are confined to creditor classes. It is therefore possible for the restructuring plan to include provisions for shareholders that will involve a reduction in their equity interest in the company and which, provided that these provisions involve more than just a confiscation of their interest and so still represent a 'compromise' of their rights, will be capable of being imposed on them under the cross-class cramdown procedure. It is notable that amongst the amendments to the Companies Act 2006 that the 2020 Act makes to facilitate the implementation of restructuring plans, there is included a disapplication of pre-emption rights.[547] These powers are likely to be welcomed by those seeking to rescue financially distressed companies. However, prior to the 2020 Act, such rights had often given shareholders a right of consent over equity issued as part of a debt-for-equity swap. It now appears possible to remove that consent right as part of a restructuring plan, which has the potential to change the dynamics of negotiations between shareholders and lenders in complex debt restructurings.

Two conditions are provided in the 2020 Act for a cross-class cramdown to occur.[548] The first is that the court must be satisfied that, if the compromise or arrangement were to be sanctioned, none of the members

[547] CIGA, Sch. 7, Part 2, and see in particular the inserted s. 566A Companies Act 2006.

[548] The Secretary of State may, by regulations, add to these conditions or remove or vary any of these conditions: Companies Act 2006, s. 901G(6).

of the dissenting class would be any worse off than they would be in the event of the relevant alternative.[549] The 'relevant alternative' for these purposes is 'whatever the court considers would be most likely to occur in relation to the company if the compromise or arrangement were not sanctioned under section 901F'.[550] The second is that the compromise or arrangement has been accepted at a class meeting of at least one class of creditors/members who would receive a payment, or have a genuine economic interest in the company, in the event of the relevant alternative.[551] In addition, the Explanatory Notes accompanying the 2020 Act provide that the court has discretion to decline to sanction a plan if it is not 'just and equitable',[552] although, in common with many of the key terms included in Part 26A, no guidance is provided for the courts as to how they should interpret this term in the context of a cross-class cramdown. It seems likely to lead to courts drawing on their existing experience in sanctioning schemes.[553]

Prior to the 2020 Act, it was expected that the restructuring plan would include a version of the 'absolute priority rule', i.e. it would require that the claims of a dissenting class of creditors be satisfied in full before a more junior class receives any distribution.[554] That protection exists in US Chapter 11 to protect senior creditors' rights against compromise by junior classes of creditors and/or shareholders, and has been introduced in restructurings elsewhere in the world that have borrowed from the US Chapter 11 regimes, such as Singapore. In the event, the 2020 Act implements neither the absolute priority rule nor a relative priority rule such as that put in place in the EU Restructuring Directive. Instead, the Act replaces these forms of creditor protection with a requirement that creditors be no worse off than in the most likely alternative if the restructuring plan is not sanctioned. This is a form of protection that is familiar to English courts. It avoids some of the difficulties with applying the absolute priority rule that have been experienced in the USA.[555] The

[549] Ibid., s. 901G(3).

[550] Ibid., s. 901G(4).

[551] Ibid., s. 901G(5).

[552] BEIS, Explanatory Notes accompanying CIGA, para. 190.

[553] See the discussion in section 2.4.

[554] See BEIS, *Insolvency and Corporate Governance*, note 190 above, para. 5.164.

[555] Indeed, concerns about some of the unfortunate consequences of this rule led the government, in its 2018 proposals, to suggest that the absolute priority rule could be dispensed with in some circumstances, so that the court could confirm a restructuring plan even if it did comply with the absolute priority rule where that non-compliance was necessary to achieve the aims of the restructuring and was just and equitable in the

relative priority rule has been applauded by a number of academics as being a helpful move away from the strictures of the absolute priority rule,[556] but it has its critics.[557] As regards the relative priority rule contained in the EU Restructuring Directive, concerns have been raised about the fact that this is a new rule, untested in practice, which might sit oddly within a regime otherwise heavily dependent on the US regime.[558] There are some benefits to the test adopted for the UK cross-class cramdown. The focus of the UK regime is on the right central question: how should the restructuring surplus be allocated? The parties must be guaranteed at least what they would receive in the absence of the plan. The role of the plan is therefore to distribute the value created by the parties accepting changes to their rights by way of the plan. This is preferable to the situation under the US absolute priority rule, and it also has some advantages over the relative priority rule within the EU Directive. Further, it is not wholly new in that it builds on the approach adopted by the English courts in cases such as *Re Bluebrook*. That said, the UK approach depends heavily on the court developing this approach in the context of cross-class cramdown in the absence of much, if any, legislative guidance, as discussed further below.

One other issue that has been raised in this context is the question of whether the senior creditors are sufficiently protected by the restructuring plan model. In particular, the possibility raised by the structure of the restructuring plan introduced by the 2020 Act is that of a 'cram-up', i.e. a situation in which one or more classes of junior creditors and/or members approving the restructuring plan imposes a restructuring on one or more dissenting senior classes of creditors.[559] This is possible in

circumstances: ibid. In the event, however, the absolute priority rule was dropped completely.

556 R. K. Rasmussen and D. G. Baird, 'Chapter 11 at Twilight' (2003–4) 56 *Stanford Law Review* 673, 691–3; Baird, 'Priority matters', note 474 above, 785, 791; B. Wessels, S. Madaus and G.-J. Boon, *Rescue of Business in Insolvency Law* (Instrument of the European Law Institute, 2017) para. 686; and Madaus, 'Leaving the shadows of US bankruptcy law', note 498 above.

557 See e.g. de Weijs, Jonkers and Malakotipour, 'The imminent distortion of European insolvency law', note 497 above. One concern raised by these authors is the fact that, despite the similarity in terminology, the EU Directive version of the relative priority rule is distinct from that advocated by US academics arguing for a US relative priority rule.

558 Ibid.

559 In the Dutch scheme, a cram-up is not possible where the distribution of value under the plan deviates from the ranking that would have applied in a bankruptcy, unless there are reasonable grounds for such deviation, and the interests of the higher-ranking creditors are not prejudiced by it. However, the court can deny a request for confirmation on this

theory if the court is satisfied that no dissenting class(es) would be worse off than in the relevant alternative and the class(es) approving the plan would, in the relevant alternative, receive a payment or have a genuine economic interest in the company, as the court will then have jurisdiction to sanction the plan. However, there are various practical difficulties in achieving a cram-up of senior creditors, including that they often control the security enforcement process and could simply enforce security if they did not agree to the terms of the plan. Proving that a more senior class will be no worse off may also be challenging in practice.

A number of features of the restructuring plan are not articulated in Part 26A of the Companies Act 2006 and will need to be developed by the courts. At the time of writing, two restructuring plans have been sanctioned by the courts, relating to Virgin Atlantic Airways and Pizza Express, but in neither case was a cross-class cramdown necessary as, by the time of the court hearings, all classes of creditors had agreed to the plans. As a result, these issues still remain to be developed by the courts. One is the meaning of 'relevant alternative' and whether a creditor is 'worse off' under the restructuring plan than in that scenario. These issues are likely to be disputed amongst competing creditor classes. In terms of assessing the 'relevant alternative', this is something with which the courts have some experience in schemes cases, given that a key aspect of determining class composition is the appropriate comparator test.[560] This would seem to be a sensible starting point for this analysis. There has also been some discussion of this issue in the context of de facto cross-class cramdown scenarios, such as *Re Bluebrook Ltd*.[561] The courts will need to be prepared to question the view put before them by the company in some instances. The company, in alignment with its senior creditors, has an incentive to press for a liquidation valuation, thus reducing the possibility that junior creditors will be judged to have a remaining economic interest in the business; use of a liquidation comparator will provide less protection for junior creditors concerned about wealth transfers as compared to a going-concern valuation, which acknowledges that there are likely to be alternatives to the scheme other than liquidation in many cases, and should generally lead to a higher valuation of the company or

basis only if the request is from a creditor in a class that rejected the plan, and the creditor itself also voted against the plan.

560 See section 2.3.2.2.

561 [2009] EWHC 2114 (Ch) discussed at section 5.4.3.

group.[562] Where the assets have a higher value if kept together as a functioning unit than if sold off piecemeal, a going-concern valuation will more accurately reflect the reality of the situation.[563] There is some evidence that the English courts are prepared to question the view presented by the company in some circumstances in schemes,[564] and this will need to be developed further in restructuring plans.

Valuation evidence as to whether a creditor is 'worse off' in the relevant alternative will become crucial, and the approach to valuation will require development by the courts, as little reference to this issue is included in Part 26A of the Companies Act 2006 (unlike the position in US Chapter 11). The UK approach to valuation in the context of debt restructuring is still in its infancy. It has not been at the forefront of many of the de facto cross-class cramdown cases, *Re Bluebrook* being an exception in this regard. The courts have to date adopted a counterfactual approach: would the creditors be worse off in the proposed restructuring than they would be if the restructuring did not go ahead? This requires a determination of what the alternative would be, which might be liquidation (hence leading to a liquidation valuation)[565] but might be a going-concern sale of the company's business and assets (hence a going-concern valuation).[566] This is in keeping with the approach set out in the Act, which requires the courts to determine the relevant alternative and to ensure that creditors are not worse off under the proposed restructuring.[567] This is in contrast to the bargaining and litigation approach to valuation adopted in US Chapter 11, described in section 5.8.1.1, which involves each creditor class putting forward its own valuation, using standard valuation methodology (most commonly discounted cash flow) with the possibility of a court hearing to determine valuation if agreement cannot be reached. Although the US Chapter 11 approach is often held up as a gold standard in debt restructuring, the context within which Chapter 11

[562] See M. Crystal and R. Mokal, 'The valuation of distressed companies – a conceptual framework' (2006) 3 *International Corporate Rescue* 63 (Part 1) and 123 (Part 2); Westbrook, 'The control of wealth in bankruptcy', note 148 above.

[563] For this reason, the 'relevant alternative' test introduced in CIGA is preferable to the test initially proposed by the Insolvency Service which took liquidation valuation as its starting point (see Insolvency Service, Consultation Paper, May 2016, para. 9.20).

[564] *Re Van Gansewinkel Groep BV & Ors* [2015] EWHC 2151 (Ch).

[565] See e.g. *Re MyTravel Group plc* [2004] EWCA Civ 1734.

[566] See e.g. *Re Bluebrook Ltd* [2009] EWHC 2114 (Ch).

[567] Companies Act 2006, s. 901G(3).

operates is rather different from English debt restructuring.[568] The structured bargaining process between the various classes in Chapter 11 to obtain the necessary majorities for a plan of reorganisation can be costly in time and money.[569] It is also unfortunate that, in practice, the operation of Chapter 11 appears to allow subordinated creditors and shareholders to receive recoveries even where they are out of the money. For these reasons, the UK counterfactual approach is to be preferred.

Even once this is determined, however, difficult issues remain to be settled, on which Part 26A offers no guidance. As discussed above, in many cases the 'relevant alternative' may be a sale as a going concern rather than liquidation, but determination of the going-concern valuation is by no means straightforward. One option is a market price valuation of the business. The benefit of this option is that it can be established through a properly conducted sales process and thus avoids the subjectivity inherent in the other major option, namely market valuation opinions provided by expert valuers. Such market valuation opinions often lead to costly and lengthy valuation fights with each party hiring their own valuer to provide an opinion that supports their position. This is also messy and difficult for the courts to mediate, unlike a market testing process which provides a clear benchmark for the court. The market valuation approach has many advantages, but it comes with one significant problem from the point of view of junior creditors, namely that if the market is depressed at the time of the valuation, it may be difficult to establish a genuine auction process. There is a danger that senior lenders may be able to take advantage of a temporary dip in market conditions, in order to cut out the junior creditors, as Mann J recognised in *Bluebrook*.[570] This is therefore something to which courts will need to be alert.

Valuation within the restructuring plan presents a challenge for the English court. Prior to the introduction of the 2020 Act, the issue of valuation arose only where schemes were twinned with administration,

568 N. Segal, 'Schemes of arrangement and junior creditors – does the US approach to valuations provide the answer?' (2007) *Insolvency Intelligence* 49.

569 See e.g. G. Moss, 'Chapter 11 – an English lawyer's critique' (1998) *Insolvency Intelligence* 17.

570 *Re Bluebrook Ltd* [2009] EWHC 2114 (Ch), at [49]. In the event, this was not an issue in that case, as all of the valuations that Mann J looked at fell well short of the senior debt, including where the market valuation stripped out the 'alpha factor' so that the valuation was not linked to current market conditions.

in which case the court regarded the issue of valuation as being predominantly a matter for the administrator. Under a restructuring plan, however, there is no need for an administrator to be involved, and the issue of valuation will be one that the court will have to take into account when determining whether to sanction a restructuring plan involving a cross-class cramdown, even where the plan is uncontested. The courts will therefore need to have robust mechanisms in place to assess this. It is notable that the Singapore reforms include the ability for the court to appoint an expert to assist it in these matters.[571] No similar power is included in Part 26A of the Companies Act 2006. While the ability of the court to appoint an independent expert appears initially attractive, there are a number of difficulties with this option, in particular whether a court-appointed valuer will understand the purpose of the restructuring sufficiently and be able to represent the views of all parties and whether such a regime involves the judge delegating part of their discretion to this appointee. Ultimately, there may be no avoiding the need for judges to choose between the values that the opposing parties offer to the court, and the courts will need to develop the tools to achieve this in a way that provides a fair and balanced process which is nevertheless relatively swift, so that the restructuring is not slowed down, or derailed completely, by lengthy and contentious valuation arguments.

The 2020 Act's reforms also include a prohibition on enforcement of so-called ipso facto clauses in contracts for the supply of goods or services.[572] This draws inspiration from US Chapter 11 proceedings and is designed to preserve a business's operational capabilities through a restructuring. The rules restrict such action in relation to the restructuring plan procedure (as well as existing UK insolvency proceedings and the new stand-alone restructuring moratorium). Accordingly, the company's suppliers cannot rely on termination provisions which might otherwise have been triggered by the making of the convening order in respect of its restructuring plan, and debts arising as a result of acceleration of a loan or an early termination clause in a financial services contract can be compromised without the relevant creditor's agreement within a restructuring plan. It is notable, however, that the ipso facto provisions do not extend to schemes of arrangement, despite the closeness of the two procedures.[573] This is presumably owing to concerns that

571 See section 5.8.1.3.

572 See CIGA, ss. 14–15 and Schs. 12–13, discussed at section 5.7.2.4.

573 See Insolvency Act 1986, s. 233B(2).

schemes can operate at a much earlier point in time than restructuring plans, although in that case the provisions could have restricted the prohibition on the enforcement of ipso facto provisions in schemes to situations equivalent to the financial conditions for a restructuring plan. In the Australian ipso facto provisions, for example, which do include schemes, the legislation restricts the provisions to circumstances in which the scheme is being used 'for the purpose of the body avoiding being wound up in insolvency'.[574]

There is no automatic moratorium under the plan. A new stand-alone restructuring moratorium is introduced by the 2020 Act, but both eligibility and the nature of the protection granted are limited.[575] It is also worth noting that if a restructuring plan is proposed within twelve weeks following a restructuring moratorium process, any 'moratorium' debts and pre-moratorium debts that do not have a payment holiday may not be compromised without consent. This includes finance debts (except for those accelerated during the moratorium itself). This may make a restructuring plan preceded by a restructuring moratorium unworkable unless the finance creditors are willing to consent.

The restructuring plan is a potentially valuable tool for companies both in England and elsewhere. Similar to schemes, a restructuring plan that compromises English law debt is likely to be widely recognised in other jurisdictions following the Brexit transition period. This recognition is likely to be based either on private international law or on other cross-border frameworks.[576] Notwithstanding the introduction of far-reaching insolvency and restructuring reforms in other jurisdictions, it seems likely that, given the experience of the English courts with schemes to date, the restructuring plan will prove popular for companies looking to promote and successfully implement a restructuring proposal.

Schemes remain in existence following the introduction of restructuring plans. The option of restructuring via a scheme twinned with administration also remains; this is not prohibited as a means of avoiding the restructuring plan procedure. Restructuring plans may offer a useful

[574] Australian Corporations Act 2001, s. 415D(5) inserted by Treasury Laws Amendment (2017 Enterprise Incentives No. 2) Act 2017.

[575] See section 5.4.4.2. Proposing a restructuring plan is likely to trigger an event of default under most Loan Market Association-style loan agreements, and it remains to be seen whether the moratorium will be effective in preventing the exercise of remedies by such creditors.

[576] For discussion of this issue in the context of schemes see section 7.4 and see also *Re Gategroup Guarantee Ltd* [2021] EWHC 304 (Ch).

alternative to both schemes and schemes twinned with administration. The restructuring plan enables a restructuring of both out-of-the-money debt and equity to be implemented within the existing corporate structure without the need for a sale of the business through a pre-pack administration. Intercreditor agreements are highly negotiated documents in leveraged financings, particularly around releases, and the restructuring plan may provide alternative routes through intercreditor complications of this nature. The changes introduced by the 2020 Act bring the UK's toolkit for dealing with restructuring and insolvencies much closer to the US Chapter 11 framework. However, it remains to be seen how useful restructuring plans will be for financially distressed companies looking to restructure. As with schemes of arrangement, the procedural requirements for restructuring plans, including the need for two court hearings, and the costs that come with them are likely to mean that plans are most valuable for large companies. Much will depend on the extent to which a restructuring plan can fundamentally alter the rights of out-of-the-money dissenting creditors and shareholders to their detriment while still meeting the conditions for cross-class cramdown and pass the court's 'fair and reasonable' test.

In the first edition of this book, it was proposed that some of the advantageous aspects of US Chapter 11 should be borrowed and added to the English scheme in order to bolster its benefits as a debt restructuring tool.[577] In particular, it was suggested that those utilising schemes of arrangement should have access to a moratorium (which included constraints on ipso facto clauses) and a cross-class cramdown, the most valuable of these changes being the latter. The Corporate Insolvency and Governance Act 2020 has introduced all of these aspects into UK law, although, to access the ipso facto provisions and the cross-class cramdown, companies will have to utilise the restructuring plan rather than the scheme of arrangement. This is perhaps not a significant problem given how closely the plan is modelled on a scheme of arrangement, albeit the plan can be used in a more restrictive set of circumstances (in particular, the company must have encountered, or be likely to encounter, financial difficulties that are affecting, or will or may affect, its ability to carry on business as a going concern). The problems of valuation highlighted in the first edition remain a concern. There is a useful focus on the court's assessing the 'relevant alternative' rather than simply relying on

[577] See J. Payne, *Schemes of Arrangement*, note 180 above, at 5.7.2 and ch. 9; Payne, 'Debt restructuring in English law', note 122 above.

a liquidation valuation, but the difficulties of valuing the company on a going-concern basis, discussed above, and the potential for difficult and protracted litigation over valuation issues remain a concern.

5.9 Summary

This chapter has examined the most common form of creditor scheme, namely one designed to restructure the debt of a financially distressed company. After considering the definition of 'creditor' for scheme purposes, and the division of creditors into classes, the central section of this chapter considered the use of schemes to restructure debt, and the advantages and disadvantages of schemes for this purpose as compared to the main alternatives: contractual workouts, CVAs, administration and restructuring plans.

The point was made earlier in this chapter that the key components of an effective debt restructuring regime in the UK are for it to be able to operate at an early stage (pre-insolvency), be imposed on dissenting creditors, have the option of utilising some form of moratorium and leave the directors in control. In other regimes, some form of rescue finance might also need to be imposed or facilitated by legal intervention, but not in the UK for the reasons discussed in this chapter. Such a regime has potential benefits for the company, but the inroads in creditors' rights that the second and third of these features bring with them need to be balanced by creditor protection to ensure that minority rights are not abused in the process. Until the Corporate Insolvency and Governance Act 2020, it was schemes of arrangement that provided the broadest opportunity for a financially distressed company to restructure itself, particularly when twinned with administration since that involves a debtor-in-possession procedure which enables a de facto cross-class cramdown to occur. The resulting potential for minority oppression is deal with by a mixture of splitting the creditors/shareholders into classes and court oversight. In 2020 a potentially more powerful tool arrived – the restructuring plan – which allows a de jure cross-class cramdown. Both schemes and restructuring plans can now be combined with a restructuring moratorium. However, with this more powerful mechanism comes a greater possibility of minority oppression, with the courts having a potentially more difficult role in relation to valuation than previously. The exact parameters of the restructuring plan remain unclear. It has the potential to be a very valuable restructuring tool for both English and foreign companies, but much will depend on how it is developed by the courts.

6

Creditor schemes of arrangement: other examples

6.1 Introduction

In Chapter 5 some general issues regarding creditor schemes were discussed, including some of the reasons why creditor schemes may be attractive to companies in section 5.1, the definition of 'creditor' for scheme purposes in section 5.2, and the division of creditors into classes in section 5.3. One of the most common uses of creditor schemes in recent years, restructuring the debts of a financially distressed company, was explored in detail. However, creditor schemes can also be used in other contexts, including when the company is entirely solvent, and when the company is insolvent and liquidation is the only option remaining.[1] This chapter therefore examines some of the other uses that can be made of creditor schemes, in order to demonstrate the flexibility and value of schemes in this context. As discussed, schemes can potentially be used for any compromise or arrangement that the company and its shareholders and creditors could properly agree amongst themselves.[2] Therefore the examples below do not form a closed list but are simply illustrative of some of the uses to which schemes have been put in the creditor context.[3]

[1] The breadth of creditor schemes, discussed in this chapter, stands in contrast to Part 26A restructuring plans, discussed at in section 5.8.2, which operate in a narrower range of circumstances, namely where the company has encountered, or is likely to encounter, financial difficulties that are affecting, or will or may affect, its ability to carry on business as a going concern, and the purpose of the compromise or arrangement proposed is to eliminate, reduce, prevent or mitigate the effects of any of the company's financial difficulties: Companies Act 2006, s. 901A(2)(3).

[2] See Chapter 1 and section 2.1.1.

[3] See e.g. *Re Premier Oil plc* [2020] CSOH 39, which involved the novel use of a creditor scheme to implement an acquisition.

6.2 Settling outstanding or future claims within the insurance industry

One important use of schemes, which has been developed by insurance companies, is to settle the future claims of creditors. As discussed in section 5.2, for scheme purposes the term 'creditor' has been defined very broadly by the courts. In particular, the courts have determined that contingent creditors can be brought within the definition, and therefore can be bound by schemes of arrangement.

Schemes can be particularly helpful to insurance companies wanting to deal with contingent claims known as incurred but not yet reported (IBNR) obligations. This is particularly important for insurance offered in relation to issues such as asbestosis, where exposure to the harm occurs during the period covered by the policy but the personal injury resulting from that exposure might manifest itself only years, or even decades, later.[4]

This kind of scheme can be used where a company is in liquidation, as it can be a way of introducing a long-stop date into the submission of claims, in order to allow the liquidator to more quickly complete the process of assessing the claims against the company that must be paid, and thereby bring the liquidation to a conclusion.[5] These schemes are sometimes called cut-off schemes since they require scheme creditors to submit both their claim and their evidence for the claim to the scheme adjudicator by a specified date. Claims submitted after the specified date are excluded from distributions under the scheme, or will be dealt with in a manner specified by the scheme. In some instances the period prior to the cut-off date may be quite short. In *Re Pan Atlantic Insurance Co Ltd*,[6] for example, a cut-off date two months after the launch of the scheme was accepted by the court, although in that case the company had been in liquidation for seven years, and had not written any new business for twelve years.[7] The court will not sanction a scheme unless the terms are fair, and a significant element of this will be whether the scheme creditors have been given sufficient notice of the scheme.[8] It is common for schemes of this kind to provide a mechanism for a quick resolution of

[4] See e.g. *Re Stronghold Insurance Company Limited* [2018] EWHC 2909 (Ch).
[5] For a fuller discussion of the use of schemes in liquidation, see section 6.3.
[6] [2003] EWHC 1696 (Ch); [2003] 2 BCLC 678.
[7] Cf. e.g. *Re British Aviation Insurance Co Ltd* [2005] EWHC 1621 (Ch) in which a one-year cut-off period was felt to be more appropriate.
[8] Ibid.

such claims, and these mechanisms are often stated to be final and binding, with no right of appeal. In *Re Pan Atlantic Insurance Co Ltd* Lloyd J considered whether such a provision contravened Article 6 of the European Convention on Human Rights and concluded that it did not.[9]

Insurance companies might also wish to deal with the claims of contingent creditors while still solvent, by way of a solvent run-off, meaning that the company ceases to provide that type of coverage but continues to remain bound by existing contractual commitments under the policies it has already issued. As long as claims continue to be presented, and the company remains solvent, the claims will continue to be met in full. Run-off of insurance policies of this kind can take a long time to administer because claims may keep being presented for many years. Of course, the company could offer to commute its obligations to its policyholders, exchanging early payout for cancellation of the insurer's future obligation to pay claims as they arise in the ordinary course of business. Commutations are frequently based on actuarial calculations of the present value of future claims, determined in accordance with historical claims experience. An insured may be willing to accept a commutation of its policy rights if the amount of the early payout is sufficient. However, the insurer can compel the policyholder to enter into a commutation only if that insurer is in a formal, statutory winding-up or liquidation procedure. A policyholder with IBNR claims might refuse to commute its policy because of the extraordinary difficulty it would face in reaching agreement with the issuer about the value of its claim.

The use of solvent schemes to effect a compromise or arrangement with creditors was doubted by Lord Glennie in *Scottish Lion Insurance Co Ltd* v. *Goodrich Corp.*[10] Whilst accepting that section 899 of the Companies Act 2006 applies to solvent as well as insolvent companies, he said:

> . . . [T]he common thread is that the scheme is put forward in a situation where, as counsel for the respondents submitted, there is a problem requiring a solution; that it is in the interests of the creditors (or classes of creditors) as a body that a solution should be found and implemented; and that, to this end, the creditors must act as one and, in identifying the appropriate solution, must agree to be governed by the wishes of the majority, because if they did not then their failure to agree would ruin it for all. That is the situation in which, in my opinion, the principle of

[9] [2003] EWHC 1696 (Ch); [2003] 2 BCLC 678.
[10] [2009] CSOH 127; 2010 SLT 100.

> creditor democracy applies. But I do not see why it need apply in all cases where a scheme of arrangement is proposed. A solvent scheme is an instance of a case where, subject to other considerations, creditor democracy should not carry the day.[11]

On appeal, Lord Glennie's decision was overturned by a unanimous ruling of the Inner House of the Scottish Court of Session, which held that there is nothing in statute to suggest that applications for sanction of a solvent scheme are in principle to be dealt with differently from those where the company is insolvent or on the verge of insolvency. The Inner House held that insofar as Lord Glennie had imposed a precondition in the case of a solvent scheme that there was 'a problem requiring a solution', he was wrong to do so. The fact that there was no such 'problem' was merely one factor amongst many which would need to be considered at the sanction stage.[12] The appeal court held that it is in the very nature of the Companies Act that contractual rights of policyholders may be varied or extinguished, providing of course that the statutory majorities are properly obtained and the requisite test for the granting of sanction is satisfied. The reasonableness of the payment under the scheme in exchange for the variation of these contractual rights should form part of the court's discretionary evaluation of the scheme. The use of schemes to effect a compromise or arrangement between creditors of a solvent company, including a solvent run-off of this kind, is now well accepted.[13] To expedite the run-off process, a number of solvent UK insurance companies have used schemes of arrangement in order to reach agreement with their policyholders as to the amounts that need to be paid on any policies.[14] Utilising a scheme allows them to terminate their long-standing contractual commitments to their policyholders without entering into a formal insolvency or liquidation proceeding and without having to enter into formal commutation with each policyholder. In a run-off scheme, interim payments are made to creditors with liquidated and established claims against the

[11] Ibid. at [55].

[12] [2010] CSIH 6; 2010 SC 349. The courts are also concerned with those that do not engage in the proposed scheme, particularly if the numbers are large. The court may wish to consider whether there is a risk that some plan holders will be unwittingly bound: *Re Royal London Mutual Insurance Society Ltd* [2018] EWHC 3803 (Ch). Relevant considerations are likely to be the benefits that non-participating plan holders will obtain from the scheme and the extent to which the company has sought to engage with that group.

[13] See e.g. *Re Royal London Mutual Insurance Society Ltd* [2018] EWHC 3803 (Ch); *Re Dowa Insurance Co (Europe) Ltd* [2016] EWHC 1447 (Ch).

[14] E.g. *British Aviation Insurance Co Ltd* [2005] EWHC 1621 (Ch).

debtor, and reserves are then set aside for creditors whose claims are unliquidated or contingent. These latter claims are then paid when they become established, or liquidated, sums.[15] As long as the majority of each class agrees to the scheme, and the scheme is sanctioned, all of the affected policyholders will be bound. The effect of such a scheme is to enable the company to achieve finality in relation to these claims. These schemes can allow wholly solvent companies to manage their IBNR liabilities. Further benefits to the company from using a scheme to effect a run-off are that it enables a release of capital to the shareholders that had previously been held against the possibility of future claims, and it can allow the company to move forwards into a new area of operation. Use of a scheme also removes the parties' right of appeal to the court, whereas in a liquidation proof process a delay can occur by reason of an appeal to the court.[16]

There are some potential disadvantages to such schemes, not least the fact that the claims are estimated, and therefore some policyholders or creditors will receive less, and some more, than they would have received had the scheme not been implemented. The problems of estimation are obviously far more acute for IBNR claims than for claims that have already matured. In solvent run-off schemes, those with matured claims will receive the same amount inside as outside the scheme. However, those with IBNR claims will be in a different position inside and outside the scheme. Outside the scheme, their policies guarantee a fixed payout upon a certain contingency materialising. Inside the scheme, there will be an estimation of the contingency materialising in order to determine a fixed payout, which might or might not exceed the original sum guaranteed by their policies. Also problematic is the fact that, in order to achieve finality, a scheme may introduce a cut-off date by which point creditors must submit their claims. Any creditor failing to submit a claim by this date may not receive payment under the scheme. Issues of creditor protection will therefore be important, especially for those with IBNR claims, who are particularly in need of protection since they are the ones most affected by the scheme.

As discussed in Chapter 2, the main forms of minority protection in place in schemes of arrangement are, first, the fact that members and/or creditors meet in separate classes to vote on whether to approve the scheme and, second, the court's discretion to take into account various

[15] See e.g. the schemes involving T & N Ltd in 2006 and Cape plc in 2006.

[16] See *Re Stronghold Insurance Company Limited* [2018] EWHC 2909 (Ch).

factors when determining whether to sanction the scheme. The ability of creditors to meet in separate classes could potentially provide important protection to those with IBNR claims in a solvent run-off of an insurance company. The current position as regards the separate class meetings is set out in *Re Hawk Insurance Co Ltd.*[17] Chadwick LJ recognised the need to find a way to protect the minority without making fine-grained distinctions that would give minorities strong veto rights. Rather than the question being about whether the rights of members and creditors are sufficiently different as to warrant forming a class,[18] the question set by Chadwick LJ in *Hawk Insurance* is whether they are sufficiently similar as not to so warrant. In order to ascertain this issue, the court will need to compare the rights of the creditors outside the scheme with their rights within the scheme. In *Hawk Insurance*, Chadwick LJ took the view that in some instances those with actual claims and those with contingent claims could form a single class. However, *Hawk Insurance* involved an insolvent company and the correct comparator was therefore taken to be the position of those creditors on winding up.

In *Re British Aviation Insurance Co Ltd (BAIC)*,[19] Lewison J held that, contrary to the decision in *Hawk Insurance*, contingent creditors (those with IBNR claims in that instance) should be treated as being in a class separate from those with liquidated but unsettled claims or notified outstanding claims. The rationale for this was that in *BAIC*, unlike the position in *Hawk Insurance*, the alternative to the proposed scheme was for BAIC to continue to run off its business on a solvent basis.[20] As such, a solvent run-off, rather than an insolvent winding-up, was the appropriate comparator for the scheme. It was stated in that case:

> In a solvent run-off, policyholders with unsettled paid claims will be entitled to have their claims paid in full. They will have exactly the same right under the scheme. The risk against which they insured has materialised and the extent of the liability has been quantified; and all they have to

[17] [2001] EWCA Civ 241; [2002] BCC 300, discussed in section 2.3.2.

[18] See e.g. *Sovereign Life Assurance Co* v. *Dodd* [1892] 2 QB 573.

[19] [2005] EWHC 1621 (Ch).

[20] Where the alternative to the scheme is solvent liquidation, rather than a solvent run-off, the result as regards the need for separate classes might be different. See e.g. *Re La Mutuelles du Mans Assurances IARD*; *Re Scottish Eagle Insurance Co Ltd* [2005] EWHC 1599 (Ch); [2006] BCC 11 in which the court sanctioned two solvent schemes that did not put IBNR claimants in a separate class. The court distinguished *BAIC* on the grounds that solvent liquidation was a realistic alternative (in the case of the Scottish Eagle scheme) and that the insurance business in *BAIC* was very different from the nature of the claims in question.

> do is to collect the insurance proceeds. They incur no further risk. So the scheme does not disadvantage them in any way. For them the so-called compromise is not much of a compromise if it is a compromise at all. Policyholders with outstanding losses are in a slightly different position. There is no need to estimate the probability of a claim arising; that is already known. Their right in a solvent run-off is to wait until the quantum of the claim had been determined; and then to claim indemnity from the insurers. Under the scheme they will have to accept an estimate of that quantum instead; but they will not have to accept any estimate of the likelihood of a claim being made at all. This removes one of the greatest of the uncertainties from the process of estimation. There is some risk that an estimate will prove to be inaccurate; but it is a small one.
>
> So far as policyholders with IBNR claims are concerned, their right in a solvent run-off is to wait and see whether a claim materialises, and if it does, to have a full indemnity against the claim. They have already paid their premiums for the insurance cover, so they are at risk of no further expenditure in relation to a valid claim. Under the scheme they will receive cash up front. It may be an amount that is greater than or smaller than the liabilities that eventually materialise, but it will not be the same. The risk of inadequate resources to meet such liabilities is retransferred from the insurers to them. So the scheme may well disadvantage them.[21]

As a result, Lewison J concluded that creditors with IBNR claims did not share a common interest with creditors with settled claims and notified outstanding claims. Since the creditors' meetings consisted of a single meeting, the court could not sanction the scheme. Therefore, protection did exist for the minority in this instance. Since *BAIC*, it has become the norm for schemes in which the relevant comparator is a solvent run-off to treat those with IBNR claims as being in a separate class.[22]

Hildyard J in *Re Stronghold Insurance Company Limited*[23] accepted that the view put forward by Lewison J in *BAIC* (that, where solvent run-off is the appropriate comparator, those with IBNR claims should be placed in a separate class) is not a general rule and is subject to exceptions in particular factual situations.[24] Nevertheless, he concluded that

21 Ibid. at [89]–[90].

22 E.g. *Re DAP Holding NV* [2005] EWHC 2092 (Ch); [2006] BCC 48 cf. *Re Mercantile & General Reinsurance Company*, Scottish Court of Session, unreported, 1 September 2005; *Re La Mutuelles du Mans Assurances IARD*; *Re Scottish Eagle Insurance Co Ltd* [2005] EWHC 1599 (Ch); [2006] BCC 11.

23 [2018] EWHC 2909 (Ch).

24 For discussion see *Re Sovereign Marine & General Insurance Co Ltd* [2006] EWHC 1335 (Ch) at [113] *per* Warren J, and see *Re Dowa Insurance Co (Europe) Ltd* [2016] EWHC 1447 (Ch).

> the irreducible inherent uncertainties in the estimation of IBNR claims, where solvent run-off is still the most likely alternative and comparator, and the indications from objectors as to their concerns of being deprived of coverage in return for an estimation of value which may prove deficient, remain such that the proper course is to require a separate class meeting for policyholders with IBNR claims.[25]

It seems that the starting point for solvent creditor schemes is therefore that those with IBNR claims should be placed in a separate class.[26] This is a good example of how the appropriate comparator test, set out in section 2.3.2.2, can operate in practice to provide minority protection to creditors. On the facts of *Stronghold*, Hildyard J held that, although the company had assumed that the appropriate comparator was liquidation, it was, instead, continued solvency, and that those with IBNR claims should form a separate class. He did, however, state that this was 'a case nearing the cusp'.[27]

Other class issues can arise in these solvent run-off cases. In *Stronghold*, for example, Hildyard J considered whether there should be a further separate class for scheme creditors with rights requiring the company to provide third-party security to protect them in the event of insolvency. In the event, the judge rejected this argument on the basis that any difference in rights would not be such as to prevent policyholders being able to discuss the proposals with a view to their common interest.[28]

6.3 Schemes and liquidation

As discussed in Chapter 5, schemes can be used either alongside or instead of administration, in order to restructure the debts of a financially distressed company with a view to rescuing the company or its business.[29] However, in some circumstances, the rehabilitation and rescue of the company or its business is not possible. This will be the case, for example, where the company is not merely financially distressed but economically distressed, that is, the net present worth of the business as

[25] [2018] EWHC 2909 (Ch) at [103].

[26] A similar approach to this issue has been adopted in the Scottish courts: *Scottish Lion Insurance Co Ltd* v. *Goodrich Corporation* [2011] CSIH 18; 2011 SC 534.

[27] [2018] EWHC 2909 (Ch) at [100]. The judge considered, and rejected, the option of letting the matter proceed with a single meeting at the company's own risk, as Lindsay J did in *Re NRG Victory Reinsurance Ltd* [2006] EWHC 679 (Ch).

[28] Ibid. at [113].

[29] See sections 5.4.3 and 5.7.

a going concern is less than the total value of its assets. In such circumstances the company is no longer economically viable and the only real option is to break it up and sell the pieces.

The mechanism provided by insolvency law to dissolve a company is liquidation. The concept of liquidation has existed in English law for far longer than that of administration.[30] Liquidation is a collective insolvency process that leads to the end of a company's existence. This can be carried out by a liquidator, whose principal role is to collect in and realise the assets, ascertain claims, investigate the causes of failure and, after covering the expenses of liquidation, distribute the net proceeds by way of dividend to creditors in the order of priority laid down by the Insolvency Act 1986 and the Insolvency Rules 2016.[31] Once this has occurred, the company is dissolved pursuant to the provisions of the Companies Act 2006.[32] There are two main methods of winding up an insolvent company under the Insolvency Act 1986: a creditors' voluntary winding-up and a compulsory winding-up.[33] Alternatively, a company can enter administration and exit via liquidation.[34]

The liquidator's primary concern is the disposal of the business, through either the sale of the business as a going concern or the sale of individual assets on a break-up basis. The liquidator has power to sell any

[30] In 1844 Parliament enacted the Joint Stock Companies Act, which provided for the incorporation of a company as a distinct legal entity, and the Joint Stock Companies Winding-Up Act, which enabled a company to be made bankrupt in the same way as an individual. The Joint Stock Companies Winding-Up Acts 1848 and 1849 conferred general winding-up jurisdiction on the Court of Chancery. See generally K. Van Zwieten, *Goode on Principles of Corporate Insolvency Law* (5th ed., London: Sweet & Maxwell, 2018), para. 1-10. For a discussion of administration see section 5.7, especially 5.7.1.

[31] See generally Van Zwieten, ibid., chs. 5–8.

[32] Companies Act 2006, Part 31.

[33] A creditors' voluntary winding-up is initiated by members and is a mechanism whereby they put the company into a voluntary winding-up by reason of insolvency (Insolvency Act 1986, s. 84(1)(b)). A compulsory winding-up is a winding-up by order of the court made upon a winding-up petition being presented, in the case of insolvency, by the company, the directors or one or more creditors (s. 124). Most petitions are presented by creditors.

[34] This could be via a creditors' voluntary winding-up as an exit from administration by registration of an administrator's notice (Insolvency Act 1986, Sch. B1, para. 83(6)(b)) or via a compulsory winding-up as an exit from an administration by court order (Sch. B1, para. 79(4)(d)). There is some evidence that administration is being used, to some extent, as a liquidation substitute: S. Frisby, *Report to the Insolvency Service: Insolvency Outcomes* (London: Insolvency Service, June 2006) at 74ff.; A. Katz and M. Mumford, 'Study of administration cases', A Report to the Insolvency Service (London: DTI, 2006) at 22ff.

of the company's property,[35] but can only carry on the company's business so far as this is necessary for its beneficial winding-up.[36]

A liquidator may be appointed by a number of different persons, including the creditors, the company or the court.[37] On the making of the winding-up order, no action may be proceeded with or commenced against the company except by leave of the court,[38] and control of the assets passes to the liquidator. The winding-up order terminates the appointment and powers of the directors. The liquidator is an agent for the company, akin to the position of a director, with statutory duties that can be enforced by application to the court;[39] these duties are owed to the company and to the creditors as a class, and in general the liquidator owes no duties to individual creditors. The Insolvency Act 1986 seeks to maximise the distribution to creditors in other ways, by avoiding a number of transactions that might defeat creditors, such as late-executed floating charges,[40] transactions at undervalue,[41] preferences[42] and transactions defrauding creditors.[43]

One of the fundamental principles governing the distribution of assets on liquidation is that only assets beneficially owned by the company are distributable amongst the creditors. This therefore excludes property held by the company on trust, or subject to a security interest or under a conditional sale agreement.[44] As a result, the remedies of secured creditors and suppliers under reservations of title are unaffected by liquidation.

Creditor schemes can be used either as an alternative to liquidation[45] or within liquidation by a liquidator or administrator (as the case may be) in order to reach a particular compromise with creditors.

35 Insolvency Act 1986, Sch. 4, para. 6.
36 Ibid., Sch. 4, Pt. II, para. 5.
37 Ibid., s. 137.
38 Ibid., s. 130(2).
39 E.g. *Knowles* v. *Scott* [1891] 1 Ch 717.
40 Insolvency Act 1986, s. 245.
41 Ibid., s. 238.
42 Ibid., s. 239.
43 Ibid., s. 423.
44 For discussion see Van Zwieten, *Goode on Principles of Corporate Insolvency Law*, note above, ch. 6.
45 A scheme of arrangement can be used after a liquidation to effect a compromise with creditors in preference to one under s. 167 of the Insolvency Act 1986, where the assets are to be distributed otherwise than in accordance with the creditors' rights: *Re Trix Ltd* [1970] 1 WLR 1421; *Re BCCI SA (No. 3)* [1993] BCLC 1490; *Kempe* v. *Ambassador Insurance Co* [1998] 1 WLR 271 (Privy Council, Bermuda).

There are some advantages to using a scheme instead of a formal insolvency process. These were discussed in section 5.7.2 in the context of a comparison between schemes and administration. In summary, the advantages of a scheme are that (i) it is not an insolvency procedure; (ii) it allows for early intervention; (iii) it is a debtor-in-possession procedure; and (iv) it enables the cramdown of creditors within a class to take place. It can also be valuable that schemes do not need to include all of the creditors of a company (and it is usual to exclude certain creditors from a scheme) whereas liquidation is a collective process involving all of the creditors. Some of the advantages are less significant in the context of liquidation. For example, the advantage of early intervention is particularly significant where the rescue of the company or its business is on the cards, but will be less relevant at the point where the only option is liquidation. Similarly, whether a director or an insolvency practitioner takes on the task of disposing of the business and distributing the recoveries is likely to matter less: any specialist knowledge of the company that the directors may have is less likely to prove meaningful at this point. It is possible that avoiding the stigma of insolvency might be preferable for directors, and might help in the process of selling off the assets. The ability to cramdown might also have a beneficial effect, especially where there are outstanding contingent claims that need to be settled. One potentially beneficial aspect of liquidation is the automatic statutory stay that attaches to it, although the introduction of the restructuring moratorium in 2020 that can be attached to schemes (though it does not do so automatically) might reduce that potential advantage.[46]

It is relatively common for schemes to be used alongside liquidation. If a debtor is being wound up, the court will not be able to sanction a scheme unless the liquidator has approved it.[47] In *Re Hawk Insurance Co Ltd*, Arden J considered the interaction of the liquidator's powers under sections 165 and 167 and Schedule 4 of the Insolvency Act 1986 with schemes of arrangement.[48] She held that if the scheme does no more than is provided for under those provisions then those provisions should be used instead of the scheme. However, very often the purpose of adding a scheme to liquidation is to depart from the rules that would otherwise apply in liquidation.

[46] See section 5.4.4.2.

[47] *Re International Contract Co (Hankey's Case)* [1872] 26 LT 358.

[48] [2001] 2 BCLC 480.

For example, the *pari passu* principle provides that, in a winding-up, those assets of the company that are available for residual distribution shall be shared by unsecured creditors on a pro rata basis. However, it appears that where a scheme of arrangement is involved, this fundamental principle of insolvency law can be set aside.[49] Another example is provided by *Re Anglo American Insurance Co Ltd*.[50] In general, a liquidator is constrained to apply the mandatory set-off rules in accordance with rule 14.25 of the Insolvency Rules 2016.[51] However, in *Anglo American*, Neuberger J upheld a scheme that was binding on the liquidator but involved a departure from the mandatory set-off rules. Nevertheless, his view was that the court should rarely exercise its power in this way,[52] and it therefore appears that the court will scrutinise any departure carefully before sanctioning such a scheme.

Second, schemes can also add value as they can allow for more rapid identification of the company's assets and/or quantification of the scheme company's liabilities. A cut-off scheme operated by an insurance company, described in section 6.2, can provide a more flexible alternative to a formal liquidation of the scheme company. A distribution scheme of this kind can be particularly useful where the assets of various entities have become inextricably intermingled, or where (as is often the case with insurance companies) there are a significant number of contingent claims that are hard to quantify. In such circumstances, a liquidator would be faced with a number of difficult decisions, given the statutory framework that they must work within, potentially with the result that cash would have to be retained for several years until it became clear whether or not a contingency would arise. A scheme can be used to impose an alternative valuation and distribution mechanism, which could result in earlier payments to the company's creditors.

A third benefit of using a scheme is illustrated by *Re T & N Ltd (No. 3)*.[53] In that case the administrators of a company and its associated companies proposed to make a scheme of arrangement with those employees and former employees of the company and its associated companies, or their dependants, who had or might have claims for damages for personal injuries arising out of exposure to asbestos covered

[49] *Re BCCI SA (No. 3)* [1993] BCLC 1490 at 1510 *per* Dillon LJ. See also *Re Trix Ltd* [1970] 1 WLR 1421 *per* Plowman J.
[50] [2001] 1 BCLC 755.
[51] The equivalent provision for administration is Insolvency Rules 2016, r. 14.24.
[52] [2001] 1 BCLC 755 at 769.
[53] [2006] EWHC 1447 (Ch).

by employers' liability insurance. The insurers had denied liability for asbestos-related claims, and sought to avoid the policies. The administrators had brought proceedings against the insurers, and the proposed scheme of arrangement embodied a compromise of that litigation. In principle the scheme proposed that the scheme companies and actual or potential claimants would not assert claims against the insurers, and instead the insurers would establish a fund to be held on trust to pay a dividend on such claims as and when they were established. All rights of claimants would be assigned to the trustees. The scheme covered personal injury claims by employees and their dependants and contribution claims by other employers outside the group. The scheme in this case therefore involved the creditors of the company giving up their rights against a third party, the insurers. It was, nevertheless, held by the court to be an arrangement between the company and its creditors because the creditors' claims against the insurers were closely connected to their rights against the company.[54] The fact that the scheme here was held to be capable of extending to, and varying the rights of, the creditors against a third party means that this was not an arrangement that could have been facilitated by making use of any of the available insolvency procedures.

In terms of minority protection in this scenario, the creditors will of course meet in classes to approve the scheme. The correct comparator in this scenario is the position of the creditors on a winding-up.[55] The decision in *Re Hawk Insurance* provides a good illustration of the operation of this test in practice. The case involved the question of whether different types of unsecured creditor, some with vested claims and some with contingent claims, should be treated as being part of the same class for the purposes of voting on a proposed scheme. At first instance Arden J held that these creditors should be treated as comprising different classes.[56] Those with vested claims should be treated as being in the same class as other unsecured creditors, since they all had an accrued claim against the company for the full amount of which they have an immediate right to sue. By contrast, those with contingent claims had no such immediate right and the structure of the scheme was such that those

[54] This reasoning was approved in *Re Lehman Brothers International (Europe) (in administration)* [2009] EWCA Civ 1161, although the decision in *Re T & N Ltd (No. 3)* on this point was said to be 'near the outer limits of the scope of section 895' (at [83] *per* Lord Neuberger, MR). This is discussed further in section 2.1.1.

[55] *Re Hawk Insurance Co Ltd* [2001] EWCA Civ 241; [2001] 2 BCLC 480.

[56] [2001] 2 BCLC 480.

whose claims had not yet accrued would have those claims scaled down to proportions less than 100 per cent. Although these creditors would rank equally on insolvency (as they were all unsecured creditors), these differences, in Arden J's opinion, meant that they should not be treated as all one class for scheme purposes.

The Court of Appeal in *Hawk Insurance* disagreed with this approach. Chadwick LJ held that all of the unsecured creditors, including therefore those with contingent rights and those with vested rights, could meet as a single class for this purpose.[57] This was on the basis that the correct comparator, where the company is insolvent, is the rights of these creditors in a winding-up. As a result, some groups, such as secured creditors and preferred creditors, should meet separately since their rights on a winding-up are clearly different. Even within these categories it may be necessary to draw further distinctions. For example, within the category of secured creditors, further division will generally be required. A creditor with a claim protected by a fixed charge is far less vulnerable than one with security in a floating charge. Even creditors holding claims secured over the same property may have divergent interests. By contrast, all of the unsecured creditors in *Hawk Insurance* had the same rights on a winding-up, namely the right to submit their claims in the winding-up, and to have those claims accepted or rejected. The only difference would be that those with contingent claims held debts without a certain value, and therefore those debts would be subject to an estimate. However, in Chadwick LJ's view this did not mean that they should be treated as separate classes for scheme purposes. Those holding rights that are not being varied (e.g. the members) will not participate in the scheme at all because they have no remaining economic interest in the company.

As a consequence, in a scheme that is implemented in liquidation, the court is unlikely to sanction a scheme that leaves any person with rights that are being varied in a worse position than in liquidation.[58]

[57] Ibid. This broad approach to the analysis of classes for scheme purposes has subsequently been followed both by the English courts and more generally: see e.g. *Re Telewest Communications plc (No. 1)* [2004] EWHC 924 (Ch); [2004] EWCA Civ 728; *Re UDL Holdings Ltd* [2002] 1 HKC 172; *First Pacific Advisors LLC* v. *Boart Longyear Ltd* [2017] NSWCA 116; *Ocean Rig UDW Inc*, Cayman Islands Grand Court, 18 September 2017.

[58] See e.g. *Re T & N Ltd (No. 3)* [2006] EWHC 1447 (Ch).

6.4 Summary

This chapter, together with Chapter 5, has sought to illustrate some of the uses to which creditor schemes can be put. These examples are intended to demonstrate the flexibility that creditor-oriented schemes offer. Chapter 5 examined a particularly valuable and widespread form of scheme, namely one used to restructure the debts of a financially distressed company. However, as this is not the only way in which creditor schemes may be used, this chapter has explored some further uses of creditor schemes, although these are only examples and other uses are made of creditor schemes. In particular, the use of schemes to restructure solvent insurance companies has been common in recent years.

7

Cross-border issues

7.1 Introduction

This chapter will consider the extent to which foreign companies can make use of English schemes of arrangement. The English court's jurisdiction in this regard is ultimately a matter for the court at the sanction hearing, although, as discussed in Chapter 2, the practice has developed whereby matters of jurisdiction can be raised and considered at the convening hearing.[1]

Schemes of arrangement have proved popular as a restructuring tool for non-English companies. The advantages of English schemes of arrangement have been discussed in the previous chapters. Companies located in jurisdictions that lack a tool akin to the English scheme have sought to access the English court's jurisdiction to sanction a scheme. These issues have arisen in the context of creditor schemes.[2] It is now well established that financially distressed companies based elsewhere in the world can make use of the English scheme jurisdiction to restructure

[1] See e.g. *Re Van Gansewinkel Groep BV & Ors* [2015] EWHC 2151 (Ch). However, discussions of jurisdiction at the convening hearing do not bind the judge at the sanctioning hearing: *Re Apcoa Parking (UK) Ltd* [2014] EWHC 997 (Ch) at [15]–[17]. For discussion see section 2.2.3.

[2] For member schemes, the court will generally have jurisdiction to sanction a company under the Companies Act 2006 only if the company is incorporated under English law since issues relating to the share capital of a company are generally governed by the place of incorporation: see e.g. L. Collins (ed.), *Dicey, Morris and Collins on the Conflict of Laws* (15th ed., London: Sweet & Maxwell, 2018) at 1542–3. As a result the court will have jurisdiction to sanction a scheme under the Companies Act 2006 only if the company is incorporated in England or if the scheme complies with the Companies Act 2006 and the laws of the jurisdiction in which the company is incorporated.

their debts as long as certain requirements are fulfilled. This is discussed in sections 7.2 and 7.3.

Where schemes involve a cross-border element, an important consideration for the English court is the international effectiveness of the scheme. This might mean the scheme being recognised in the overseas jurisdiction where the company is registered, or where it has business operations, where its assets are situated, or where its creditors are located. If a creditors' scheme is not legally effective in a foreign jurisdiction, a creditor could pursue its contractual claim in those courts and undermine the scheme by improving its position compared to that of the other creditors under the scheme. Or that creditor could initiate separate restructuring or insolvency proceedings in that jurisdiction, which might then conflict with the English scheme. These points are well understood by the English courts,[3] and therefore an important aspect of whether English judges will sanction a scheme is whether the scheme will be legally effective in the relevant foreign jurisdictions. This issue is discussed in section 7.4.

Both the existence of and the basis for the English court's jurisdiction in this regard have become an issue for debate. In particular, it has been suggested that the use of schemes to restructure the debts of financially distressed companies enables forum shopping to take place. The idea of forum shopping often carries negative connotations and is associated with debtors seeking legal regimes that will favour the debtor at the expense of the creditors. In section 7.5 these concerns are assessed. It is argued that the approach of the English courts in this regard is pragmatic and defensible and that use of the English scheme jurisdiction can be regarded as an example of 'good' forum shopping.

7.2 Can foreign companies make use of the English scheme jurisdiction?

7.2.1 The meaning of 'a company' for scheme purposes

In assessing this issue, the starting point is the fact that, for the purposes of a scheme, section 895 of the Companies Act 2006 states that the arrangement has to be proposed between 'a company' and its creditors and/or members. The English court's jurisdiction to sanction a scheme therefore rests in part on the definition of 'a company' for scheme

[3] *Re Drax Holdings Ltd* [2003] EWHC 2743 (Ch); [2004] 1 WLR 1049 at [30] *per* Lawrence Collins J.

purposes. Only a scheme of a company within the meaning of section 895 of the Companies Act 2006 can be sanctioned by the English courts.[4]

For these purposes, 'a company' means 'any company liable to be wound up under the Insolvency Act 1986'.[5] The Insolvency Act 1986 grants power to the courts to wind up solvent and insolvent companies, and registered and unregistered companies.[6] It is well established that the term 'unregistered company' includes foreign companies.[7] The provisions of the Insolvency Act 1986 place no territorial restrictions on the English court's jurisdiction to wind up a solvent or insolvent foreign company. The statute simply provides that:

> The circumstances in which an unregistered company can be wound up are as follows –
>
> (a) if the company is dissolved, or has ceased to carry on business, or is carrying on business only for the purpose of winding up its affairs;
> (b) if the company is unable to pay its debts;
> (c) if the court is of opinion that it is just and equitable that the company should be wound up.[8]

On a strict analysis, if one of these conditions *must* be satisfied by the unregistered company, this could raise difficulties for solvent companies seeking to make use of a scheme. However, in such circumstances the courts have interpreted the question facing them to be not whether the company is liable to be wound up on the facts as they stand at present but whether the company is the sort of company that is capable of being wound up under the Insolvency Act 1986, should any of these conditions arise in the future.[9] As a result, it is not necessary to demonstrate that any of these conditions are *in fact* fulfilled in relation to a foreign company, only that they could be fulfilled in the future.

So, under domestic English law, the English court has jurisdiction, under the Insolvency Act 1986, to wind up a foreign company.

4 The definition of 'a company' for scheme purposes is also discussed in section 2.1.2.

5 Companies Act 2006, s. 895(2)(b).

6 Insolvency Act 1986, s. 221.

7 See e.g. *Banque des Marchands de Moscou (Koupetschesky)* v. *Kindersley* [1951] Ch 112. See also *Re Drax Holdings Ltd* [2003] EWHC 2743 (Ch); *Re Rodenstock GmbH* [2011] EWHC 1104 (Ch) at [21]–[23]; and *Re Van Gansewinkel Groep BV & Ors* [2015] EWHC 2151 (Ch) at [35]–[36].

8 Insolvency Act 1986, s. 221(5).

9 *Re Sovereign Marine & General Insurance Co Ltd* [2006] EWHC 1335 (Ch); [2007] 1 BCLC 228 at [33].

Potentially, therefore, a foreign company (solvent or insolvent) can make use of the English scheme jurisdiction. However, the English courts have not regarded these provisions as giving them carte blanche to wind up foreign companies without any further requirements, and have added their own conditions.

7.2.2 Additional conditions imposed by the court

The courts have imposed a number of conditions for the making of a winding-up order in relation to a foreign company. These conditions were first set down in the case of *Re Real Estate Development Co*[10] and later approved by the Court of Appeal in *Re Latreefers Inc.*[11] In *Re Real Estate*, Knox J stated that the additional requirements are:

> (1) that there must be a sufficient connection with England and Wales which may, but does not necessarily have to, consist of assets within the jurisdiction;
> (2) that there must be a reasonable possibility if a winding-up order is made, of benefit to those applying for the winding-up order; [and]
> (3) one or more persons interested in the distribution of assets of the company must be persons over whom the court can exercise a jurisdiction.[12]

The purpose of the second and third of these requirements is to ensure that winding-up orders are made only where some useful purpose will be served.[13] The purpose of the first is to ensure that the English court declines to exercise 'a prima facie exorbitant jurisdiction save where it [is] appropriate to do so'.[14] These requirements are intended to impose some conditions on the court's otherwise very broad jurisdiction under the Insolvency Act 1986.

The application of these three additional requirements to schemes of arrangement was unclear for some time. In particular, it was disputed whether these three conditions constituted strict limits on the court's jurisdiction or were simply principles to be taken into account by the court when exercising its discretion in determining whether to sanction a scheme of arrangement. This issue was considered by Lawrence Collins

10 [1991] BCLC 210.
11 [2001] BCC 174.
12 See *Re Real Estate Development Co* [1991] BCLC 210 at 217.
13 See e.g. *Re Rodenstock GmbH* [2011] EWHC 1104 (Ch); [2012] BCC 459 at [21].
14 Ibid. *per* Briggs J.

J in *Re Drax Holdings Ltd.*[15] The scheme in that case concerned companies incorporated in the Cayman Islands and Jersey. Collins J recognised that the second and third of these three conditions are less relevant for schemes, given that they envisage a winding-up that need not occur as part of the scheme. Crucially, he went on to hold that these three factors go to the discretion of the court to sanction the scheme, rather than being preconditions for the existence of its statutory jurisdiction.[16]

Therefore, as a starting point, English courts do have jurisdiction to sanction schemes involving foreign companies, although the court will not exercise its power unless sufficient connection with England is shown.[17] The court will also need to be satisfied that there is a reasonable prospect of the scheme being effective having regard, in particular, to its prospects for recognition in other relevant jurisdictions. The court will want to be sure that the scheme will achieve a 'substantial effect' in those jurisdictions and that the court would not be acting in vain in sanctioning the scheme.[18] So, for example, in *Re Noble* the factors taken into account by the court in this regard included that the vast majority of international creditors supported the scheme (so the likelihood of foreign challenge was slight), an identical scheme was being promoted in Bermuda, and Noble had sought recognition of the schemes in the USA. These two questions can be seen to be interrelated.[19]

What is considered to be a sufficient connection with England for this purpose has become more settled over time, although, of course, this is a fact-sensitive issue. One way for a sufficient connection to be established is if the company has substantial assets in England.[20] Another is where the relevant liabilities are governed by English law and subject to

[15] [2004] 1 WLR 1049.

[16] *Re Drax Holdings Ltd* [2003] EWHC 2743 (Ch); [2004] 1 WLR 1049. This analysis was confirmed in *Re Rodenstock GmbH* [2011] EWHC 1104 (Ch); [2012] BCC 459.

[17] *Rodenstock*, ibid. at [29]. The same approach has been adopted by the courts in Hong Kong (*LDK Solar Co Ltd* [2015] 1 HKLRD 458; *Re Winsway Enterprises Holdings Ltd* [2016] HKCFI 1915; *Kaisa Group Holdings Ltd* [2017] HKLRD 18) and Singapore (*Re TPC Korea* (2010) 2 SLR 617; *Re Pacific Andes Resources Development* (2016) SGHC 210), a position now put on a statutory footing: Singapore Insolvency, Restructuring and Dissolution Act 2018, s. 63 read with Companies Act (Singapore), s. 351). The proposed 'private' version of the Dutch Scheme of arrangement (*Wet homologatie onderhands akkoord*) envisages the use of that restructuring mechanism by foreign companies with a sufficient connection to the jurisdiction.

[18] *Re Noble Group Ltd* [2018] EWHC 2911 (Ch).

[19] *Re Magyar Telecom BV* [2013] EWHC 3800 (Ch) at [21]–[22], and see discussion at section 7.4.

[20] See e.g. *Re Drax Holdings Ltd* [2004] 1 WLR 1049.

English jurisdiction.[21] In *Re Primacom Holdings GmbH*,[22] for example, the scheme involved a financially distressed German company without a seat, its centre of main interests (COMI) or establishment in the UK, and with no creditors domiciled in England. Nevertheless, the fact that English law was the governing law for all creditor arrangements in that case meant that there was a 'sufficient connection',[23] and the scheme was sanctioned. Another recognised situation is where the relevant liabilities are governed by English law. In *Re Vietnam Shipbuilding Industry Groups*,[24] David Richards J held that the fact that the facility agreement in that case was governed by English law was sufficient to show that there was a connection between the scheme and the English jurisdiction and to make it a scheme that the court would be prepared to consider and, if thought fit, sanction. While, in the judge's opinion, the non-exclusive jurisdiction clause in that case also created a sufficient connection with the jurisdiction, the fact that the loan agreement was governed by English law was enough.[25]

Another category is where the liabilities are governed by foreign law but the COMI is in England, including in some instances where the COMI has been deliberately moved to England for the purposes of establishing scheme jurisdiction.[26] Where it is suggested that a company has changed its COMI for this purpose, the court will have regard to the question of whether the change has been made in a way which is 'ascertainable by third parties such as creditors, whether the change is based on substance and is not an illusion, and whether it has the necessary element of permanence'.[27] In the context of a scheme, whilst the English court will be astute to detect a COMI-shift performed for illegitimate or abusive reasons, it is well accepted that a company might legitimately seek the assistance of the court with the support of, and in order to achieve the best result for, its creditors.[28] In *Re Noble Group Ltd*,[29] Snowden J took account of a number

[21] See e.g. *Re Rodenstock GmbH* [2011] EWHC 1104 (Ch).
[22] [2012] EWHC 164 (Ch); [2013] BCC 201.
[23] See also *Re Seat Pagine Gialle SpA* [2012] EWHC 3686 (Ch) at [11] and *Re NEF Telecom Company BV* [2012] EWHC 2944 (Comm) at [41]; *Re Stripes US Holdings Inc* [2018] EWHC 2912 (Ch).
[24] [2013] EWHC 2476 (Ch).
[25] Ibid. at [8]–[9].
[26] *Re Magyar Telecom BV* [2013] EWHC 3800 (Ch).
[27] *Re Noble Group Ltd* [2018] EWHC 2911 (Ch) at [95] and see *Re Videology Ltd* [2018] EWHC 2186 (Ch).
[28] *Re Codere Finance (UK) Ltd* [2015] EWHC 3778 (Ch) at [18].
[29] [2018] EWHC 2911 (Ch).

of factors to demonstrate the sufficient connection with England including that the head office of the company had been located in London and all head office functions were carried out in London, the majority of board meetings were held in London, meetings of the audit committee, the risk committee and the corporate governance committee were also held in London and the London office was where the company's books and records were kept. The judge held that the factors linking the company to England were neither illusory nor temporary, and taken together with the overwhelming support from scheme creditors for the scheme, and subject to consideration of the effectiveness of the scheme, there was enough to establish a sufficient connection with England in that case.

At its heart, a creditor scheme of arrangement is a mechanism for compromising or restructuring liabilities and therefore, although characteristics of the debtor company (such as its COMI) may be a relevant consideration for this purpose, what is often central to the question of a 'sufficient connection' is the characteristics of the relevant liabilities themselves, such as the governing law that relates to them. There is something to be said for creditor choice here also. By agreeing to be bound by English law, the creditors are agreeing to be bound by all that that entails, including the possibility of a scheme of arrangement being used to bind the minority creditors in a restructuring agreed to by the majority and sanctioned by the court.

At times, the boundaries of the concept of 'sufficient connection' have been tested. In *Re Apcoa Parking Holdings GmbH*,[30] for example, the governing law of the finance documents in that case was not English law initially, but a clause in the finance documents allowed a change in the governing law by majority decision. This clause was utilised and the governing law was changed to English law. Minority creditors objected to this on the basis that the changing of the governing law was not carried out to accomplish any substantive commercial change in the economic relationship between the parties but purely to create a connection with England for the purpose of the proposed schemes. Although the judge accepted that the schemes in this case did 'test the boundaries of a jurisdiction which is by its nature potentially exorbitant',[31] he found that there was a sufficient connection with England and he did ultimately sanction the schemes. This is not altogether surprising. After all, there is no reason in principle why English law should have any less status or

[30] [2014] EWHC 3849 (Ch). See also *Re DTEK Finance plc* [2016] EWHC 3562 (Ch).
[31] [2014] EWHC 3849 (Ch) at [205].

effect as the governing law of liabilities where it results from a change of governing law as compared with the situation where it was the governing law from the outset. A focus on the relevant liabilities, leads to this outcome. However, in contrast to cases such as *Re Rodenstock GmbH*[32] in which the creditors had entered into contracts governed by English law, in *Apcoa* not all of the creditors had 'chosen' English law, although they had chosen to enter a contract which allowed a change of law by majority decision.[33] This creates the possibility of minority abuse and the courts clearly need to be alert to this issue. In *Apcoa*, the judge sanctioned the schemes on the basis that they were fair and had been approved at properly constituted class meetings. Moreover, the change of governing law was understood by all the scheme creditors and was intended to enable the schemes to be sanctioned. Presumably, one basis upon which the court might refuse to exercise its discretion to sanction a scheme is where it was not made clear to creditors who were asked to consent to the amendment to the governing law provision that the amendment was being sought for the purposes of then pursuing a scheme. Furthermore, the judge in *Apcoa* stated that he would be wary of accepting jurisdiction if the choice of law had been entirely alien to the parties' previous arrangements or if the change had no discernible rationale or 'even more generally, where in its discretion the court considers that, in the places in which the parties are, the extent of the alteration of rights between the parties for which sanction is sought would be considered a "step too far"'.[34]

In summary, therefore, for foreign companies, English courts have jurisdiction to sanction a scheme if a sufficient connection can be established and if it can be demonstrated that the scheme will be internationally effective, particularly in the debtor's seat of incorporation, where the debtor's key assets are located and where any creditors are likely to challenge the scheme. One of the ways to address this issue in practice is for the company to adduce the opinion of an expert on local law can state that there is a realistic prospect that the scheme will be held legally effective in that jurisdiction. This issue in large part relates to whether the scheme will be recognised in that jurisdiction; discussion of the factors

[32] [2011] EWHC 1104 (Ch).

[33] One response to the decision in *Apcoa* is for creditors to require unanimity for change in governing law clauses (and see e.g. the standard form leveraged finance facilities agreement produced by the Loan Market Association after *Apcoa* to do just this).

[34] [2014] EWHC 3849 (Ch) at [251].

taken into account when determining this matter are considered at section 7.4.

Until recently, schemes involving a subset of foreign companies had an additional set of issues to navigate. Prior to 31 December 2020 when the transition period following the UK's exit from the EU ended, the English court's ability to sanction schemes involving companies with creditors in EU states was potentially complicated by the existence of two EU Regulations, as discussed in section 7.3. After 31 December 2020, the concerns raised in section 7.3 drop away and the English court's ability to sanction such schemes is determined in the same way as all other schemes involving foreign companies, namely in relation to the requirement of a sufficient connection (discussed above) and international effectiveness (discussed in section 7.4). Nevertheless, the issues discussed in section 7.3 remain important, both in order to understand the English court's reasoning in this area and because they have potential implications for the issue of recognition.[35]

7.3 The effect of EU Regulations on the court's jurisdiction

Prior to the UK's exit from the EU, and the end of the transition period on 31 December 2020, the issue of the English court's jurisdiction to sanction schemes relating to foreign companies was complicated by EU legislation, in particular the Recast Insolvency Regulation[36] and the Recast Judgments Regulation.[37] These Regulations concern jurisdiction in proceedings brought within the EU, and the mutual recognition and enforcement of judgments of courts of the Member States.[38] The demarcation of these two Regulations is effectively that between solvency and insolvency: the Recast Judgments Regulation deals with the winding up of solvent companies and the Recast Insolvency Regulation deals with

[35] See section 7.4, in particular 7.4.2.

[36] Council Regulation (EC) 1346/2000 on Insolvency Proceedings recast by Regulation (EU) 848/2015 of the European Parliament and of the Council on Insolvency Proceedings and (EU) 2018/946 of 4 July 2018 which replaces Annex A (the Recast Insolvency Regulation).

[37] Council Regulation (EC) No. 44/2001 on Jurisdiction and the Recognition and Enforcement of Judgments in Civil and Commercial Matters recast by Regulation (EU) 1215/2012 of the European Parliament and of the Council on Jurisdiction and the Recognition and Enforcement of Judgments in Civil and Commercial Matters (the Recast Judgments Regulation).

[38] Specialist legislation has also been put in place to deal with insurance companies and credit institutions: see Directive 2009/138/EC and Directive 2001/24/EC. Discussion of these Directives falls outside the parameters of this book.

insolvent companies. The two Regulations are intended to dovetail with one another.[39] While the UK remained within the EU, or subject to EU legislation as a result of the transition arrangements, these Regulations potentially impacted on the English court's ability to sanction a scheme involving a company with creditors in other EU Member States.[40] This section sets out how the English courts dealt with the impact of these Regulations on schemes of arrangement.

7.3.1 The effect of the Recast Insolvency Regulation

The Recast Insolvency Regulation applies to

> public collective proceedings, including interim proceedings, which are based on laws relating to insolvency and in which, for the purpose of rescue, adjustment of debt, reorganisation or liquidation: (a) a debtor is totally or partially diverted of its assets and an insolvency practitioner is appointed; (b) the assets and affairs of a debtor are subject to control or supervision by a court; or (c) a temporary stay of individual enforcement proceedings is granted by a court or by operation of law, in order to allow for negotiations between the debtor and its creditors.[41]

The relevant insolvency proceedings are listed in Annex A of the Regulation.[42] As regards the UK, although a number of mechanisms were included in Annex A, including administration and CVAs,[43] schemes of arrangement were not. Consequently, schemes did not fall within the ambit of the Recast Insolvency Regulation.[44]

There was, however, a possible, unintended consequence of the Recast Insolvency Regulation for the English court's scheme jurisdiction. English domestic law deals with this issue by requiring that the company subject to the scheme must be 'liable to be wound up under the Insolvency Act 1986'. The question here is whether the Recast

[39] Case 133/78 *Gourdain* [1979] ECR 733.

[40] See the Civil Jurisdiction and Judgments (Amendment) (EU Exit) Regulations 2019 (SI 2019/479) (amended by SI 2020/1493 and SI 2020/1574) which, inter alia, revokes the Recast Judgments Regulation and its predecessors as they apply in the UK.

[41] Recast Insolvency Regulation, Art. 1(1).

[42] Ibid.

[43] For a discussion of the recognition of CVAs under the recast Insolvency Regulation see *Apperley Investments Ltd* v. *Monsoon Accessorise Ltd* [2020] IEHC 523.

[44] Note, however, that schemes combined with insolvency proceedings falling within the annexes (e.g. administration) would then come within the scope of the Insolvency Regulation.

Insolvency Regulation altered this requirement, given that for companies registered in EU Member States[45] this Regulation provides that the court has jurisdiction to wind up a company only if the company possesses an establishment in that Member State.

A strict interpretation of these provisions would suggest that, while the UK remained bound by EU law, this Regulation had direct effect and therefore if a company could not be wound up as a result of the application of this Regulation, then it was not liable to be wound up under the Insolvency Act 1986. On this analysis, the English courts would have no jurisdiction to wind up a company with a COMI in Germany, for example, under the Recast Insolvency Regulation and therefore that company would not be 'liable to be wound up' under the Insolvency Act 1986. Accordingly, it would not be 'a company' for the purposes of section 895 of the Companies Act 2006, and the English courts would have no jurisdiction to sanction a scheme involving such a company.

However, the English courts did not adopt this analysis, preferring a more purposive approach to this question.[46] Each time this point was before the English courts, the view was taken that this Regulation had no impact on the English court's scheme jurisdiction.[47] Two explanations were put forward to justify this conclusion. One view, suggested by the court in *Re DAP Holding NV*, was that a company's COMI is transient and subject to change, and therefore its COMI should not prejudice the court's winding-up jurisdiction.[48] The alternative view, accepted in *Rodenstock*,[49] was that this Regulation was simply never intended to limit the scheme jurisdiction of the English court at all. The crux of this argument rests on the fact that the provision now found in section 895 of the Companies Act 2006, namely that a company for scheme purposes is one 'liable to be wound up under the Insolvency Act 1986', was introduced into English legislation long before there were any European rules governing the allocation of jurisdiction.[50] On this analysis, there was no reason to suppose that the introduction of the Insolvency Regulation (or

[45] Note that Denmark decided not to opt into this Regulation and therefore is not a Member State for the purposes of this Regulation.

[46] For a criticism of this approach see L. C. Ho, 'Making and enforcing international schemes of arrangement' [2011] *Journal of International Banking Law and Regulation* 434 at 435–6.

[47] See e.g. *Re Noble Group Ltd* [2018] EWHC 3092 (Ch).

[48] [2005] EWHC 2092 (Ch); [2006] BCC 48.

[49] [2011] EWHC 1104 (Ch); [2012] BCC 459 at [63].

[50] *Re Sovereign Marine and General Insurance Co Ltd* [2006] EWHC 1335 (Ch); [2007] 1 BCLC 228 at [37].

indeed the Judgments Regulation) had any effect on these English domestic provisions.[51] Nothing on the face of the Regulation appeared directed at restricting the English court's jurisdiction in this regard; schemes of arrangement are not collective insolvency proceedings of the type dealt with by the Recast Insolvency Regulation and are not listed in Annex A to the Regulation. This analysis therefore adopted a domestic approach to determining the definition of 'company' for these purposes, so that, for example, the German-registered company in *Re Rodenstock GmbH*[52] was 'liable to be wound up' under the Insolvency Act 1986, even though the English court had no jurisdiction to wind it up as a result of the Regulation. The combination of these views[53] convinced the English court that the Recast Insolvency Regulation did not affect the English court's jurisdiction to convene scheme meetings or to sanction a scheme of arrangement.[54]

7.3.2 The effect of the Recast Judgments Regulation

The Recast Judgments Regulation provides a framework for the regulation of jurisdiction and the recognition of judgments in civil and commercial matters amongst EU Member States. The basic principle underlying Chapter II of the Regulation is that any person domiciled in an EU Member State must be sued in the courts of that Member State.[55] It was unclear whether and, if so, how this rule applied to schemes of arrangement. One of the main issues that arose in this context was

[51] Cf. Insolvency Act 1986, s. 221(4) which explicitly provides for the importing of rules of allocation of international jurisdiction into domestic law for voluntary winding-up.

[52] [2011] EWHC 1104 (Ch).

[53] In *Re Seat Pagine Gialle SpA* [2012] EWHC 3686 (Ch) David Richards J acknowledged that there were two quite different routes to the conclusion that, despite the effect of the Insolvency Regulation regarding the jurisdiction of the courts to wind up a foreign company, such a company could nevertheless still be regarded as a company liable to be wound up within the meaning of that expression in the Companies Act 2006 (i.e. that in *DAP* and that in *Rodenstock*). Nevertheless, because the outcome of the two routes was the same, and the judge agreed with that outcome, he was content to accept that the court had jurisdiction to sanction the scheme (involving an Italian company in that case) without having to choose between the two routes.

[54] See e.g. *Re Global Garden Products Italy SpA* [2016] EWHC 1884 (Ch) at [23]. See also *Re Van Gansewinkel Groep BV & Ors* [2015] EWHC 2151 (Ch) at [40]; *Re NN2 Newco Ltd* [2019] EWHC 1917 (Ch) at [32]; *Re Stripes US Holdings Inc* [2018] EWHC 3098 (Ch) at [53]; *Re Algeco Scotsman PIK SA* [2017] EWHC 2236 (Ch) at [45].

[55] Recast Judgments Regulation, Art. 4(1).

whether the Recast Judgments Regulation applied to schemes at all and, if it did, what impact it had on the English court's jurisdiction.[56]

The Recast Judgments Regulation applies to 'civil and commercial matters, whatever the nature of the court or tribunal',[57] while specifically excluding the following from its scope: 'bankruptcy, proceedings relating to the winding-up of insolvent companies or other legal persons, judicial arrangements, compositions and analogous proceedings'.[58] In some English cases, the view was taken that schemes of arrangement did not fall within the scope of the Judgments Regulation at all. In *DAP* this was argued on the basis that schemes could be regarded as 'judicial arrangements, compositions and analogous proceedings', and therefore outside the scope of the Regulation.[59] In *Primacom*, Hildyard J also took the view that the main jurisdictional provision in Chapter II (Article 4 of the Recast Judgments Regulation) could not apply to creditor schemes because it refers to a person being 'sued' in the Member State in which they are domiciled, and no one is sued in a conventional sense in scheme proceedings. Since schemes also fell outside the Insolvency Regulation, this approach pointed to a lacuna in the law such that schemes were outside both Regulations. Other English cases took the view that schemes fell within the phrase 'civil and commercial matters, whatever the nature of the court or tribunal' and were within the ambit of the Regulation. This view

[56] Another issue was similar to that discussed in relation to the Recast Insolvency Regulation in section 7.3.1, namely whether one of the unintended consequences of this Regulation was to impact adversely on the meaning of 'liable to be wound up' as the touchstone of the English court's scheme jurisdiction. Article 24(2) of the Recast Judgments Regulation encompasses proceedings that have as their object 'the dissolution of companies'. Although it is not free from doubt, the preferable view is that solvent liquidation does fall within this definition (see e.g. *Re Drax Holdings Ltd* [2003] EWHC 2743 (Ch) at [28]). Given that Article 24(2) therefore deprived the English court of jurisdiction to wind up any solvent company that had its seat in another Member State, the argument could be made that the Recast Judgments Regulation impacted restrictively on the meaning of 'liable to be wound up' for this purpose. Briggs J in *Re Rodenstock GmbH* [2011] EWHC 1104 (Ch) considered this argument, but concluded that it did not, on much the same grounds as in relation to the Insolvency Regulation, namely that the Judgments Regulation was never intended to have an impact on schemes. Support for this view can be found in the fact that solvent schemes did not exist in the original Brussels Convention countries, and therefore schemes were not provided for by the Judgments Regulation or its predecessors.

[57] Recast Judgments Regulation, Art. 1(1).

[58] Ibid., Art. 1(2)(b).

[59] *Re DAP Holding NV* [2005] EWHC 2092 (Ch); [2006] BCC 48.

maintained that the two Regulations must be interpreted so as to dovetail with one another, with no overlap and no lacuna.[60] Hence, since a scheme of arrangement was not within the Recast Insolvency Regulation,[61] it must fall within the Recast Judgments Regulation.[62]

Ultimately, the approach of the English court was to favour the view that the Recast Judgments Regulation encapsulated schemes, without, however, reaching any ultimate conclusion as to its applicability. Instead, judges sought to establish exemptions within the Recast Judgments Regulation that would allow for the exercise of the court's jurisdiction.[63] If jurisdiction could be found, it was then unnecessary to test the assumption that the Recast Judgments Regulation applied to schemes of arrangement.

Chapter II of the Recast Judgments Regulation contains a number of exceptions, the most important of which, for this purpose, are set out in Articles 8 and 25. Article 8 provides:

> A person domiciled in a Member State may . . . be sued . . . (1) where he is one of a number of defendants, in the courts for the place where any one of them is domiciled, provided the claims are so closely connected that it is expedient to hear and determine them together to avoid the risk of irreconcilable judgments resulting from separate proceedings . . . .

Article 8 was invoked in many scheme cases to establish that, where some of the scheme creditors were domiciled in the UK, the English court had jurisdiction to sanction a scheme affecting the rights of creditors domiciled elsewhere in the EU.[64] Since it was normally possible to identify at least a handful of UK-domiciled scheme creditors, this line of argument

[60] The view that there can be no gap between the Judgments Regulation and the Insolvency Regulation has been endorsed (albeit not in the context of a scheme case) by the ECJ in *Nickel & Goeldner Spedition GmbH* v. *Kintra UAB* (Case C-157/13) at [21] and in *Comité d'entreprise de Nortel Networks SA* v. *Rogeau; Rogeau* v. *Bloom* (Case C-649/13) at [26].

[61] See section 7.3.1.

[62] This argument was accepted in relation to schemes involving solvent companies by Briggs J in *Rodenstock* [2011] EWHC 1104 (Ch) at [47]–[51] but he left open the question in relation to schemes involving insolvent companies. In *Re Magyar Telecom BV* [2013] EWHC 3800 (Ch) at [28]–[29], David Richards J referred to *Rodenstock* and suggested that a scheme between an insolvent company and its creditors would fall within the Judgments Regulation, at least unless the company was subject to an insolvency proceeding falling within the Insolvency Regulation.

[63] See e.g. *Re Van Gansewinkel Groep BV & Ors* [2015] EWHC 2151 (Ch) at [45]; *Re NN2 Newco Ltd* [2019] EWHC 1917 (Ch) at [32].

[64] See e.g. *Re Global Garden Products Italy SpA* [2016] EWHC 1884 (Ch); *Re Stripes US Holdings Inc* [2018] EWHC 2912 (Ch); *Re Lecta Paper UK Ltd* [2019] EWHC 3615 (Ch).

proved to be a powerful tool in practice for locating an exemption to the Recast Judgments Regulation.

The question then arose as to how many UK-based creditors were needed to satisfy this requirement, and, specifically, whether the existence of a single UK-domiciled creditor (potentially holding a very low proportion of the total scheme liabilities) was capable of bringing a scheme within Article 8. In *Re Rodenstock GmbH*,[65] more than 50 per cent of the scheme creditors were domiciled in England and this provided some reassurance for Briggs J that he had jurisdiction to sanction the scheme. However, a number of cases indicated that Article 8 could be satisfied by a single scheme creditor domiciled in England.[66] On this analysis, Article 8 did not require the court to consider the number or value of UK-domiciled creditors, but the court did need to be satisfied that it was expedient for all relevant creditors to be bound by the scheme in order to 'avoid the risk of irreconcilable judgments resulting from separate proceedings'.[67]

The other principal exception to the application of the Recast Judgments Regulation that was utilised in scheme cases was Article 25(1), which provides:

> If the parties, regardless of their domicile, have agreed that a court or the courts of a Member State are to have jurisdiction to settle any disputes which have arisen or which may arise in connection with a particular legal relationship, that court or those courts shall have jurisdiction . . . Such jurisdiction shall be exclusive unless the parties have agreed otherwise.

Article 25 was typically invoked where the underlying contracts between the scheme company and its creditors contained an English jurisdiction clause. In such cases, it was argued that the English court had jurisdiction to sanction the scheme irrespective of where the scheme creditors were domiciled, because the scheme creditors had contractually submitted to the jurisdiction of the English court.

[65] [2011] EWHC 1104 (Ch).

[66] See e.g. *Re NEF Telecom Company BV* [2012] EWHC 2944 (Comm) at [43]; *Re Metinvest BV* [2016] EWHC 79 (Ch) at [32]; *Re DTEK Finance plc* [2016] EWHC 3562 (Ch) at [17]; *Re Lecta Paper UK Ltd* [2020] EWHC 382 (Ch) at [48]; *Re New Look Financing plc* [2020] EWHC 2793 (Ch) at [46]. This was in contrast to the view of Snowden J in *Re Global Garden Products Italy SpA* [2016] EWHC 1884 (Ch) at [28] that Article 8 jurisdiction was established 'on the basis that sufficient creditors by number and value are domiciled in the United Kingdom and that it is expedient to determine whether the scheme should bind the other scheme creditors in these proceedings in England'.

[67] Recast Judgments Regulation, Art. 8.

It was therefore clear that an exclusive jurisdiction clause in favour of the English court could, as a result of Article 25, confer jurisdiction on the English court to sanction the scheme. The English courts accepted that the wording of Article 25 meant that non-exclusive jurisdiction clauses had the same effect.[68] The courts also considered whether the same was true of asymmetric jurisdiction clauses. These are clauses which confer exclusive jurisdiction on the English court, but only for the benefit of the scheme creditors rather than the scheme company, and the scheme creditors are expressly permitted to commence proceedings against the scheme company in other jurisdictions. Doubt was cast on this possibility by Snowden J, obiter, in *Re Global Garden Products Italy SpA*,[69] but the weight of judicial opinion seemed to be in favour of asymmetric jurisdiction clauses falling within the ambit of Article 25.[70]

7.3.3 *Summary*

In recent years, schemes of arrangement have been used frequently to restructure the financial obligations of overseas companies that involve companies with creditors in EU Member States.[71] While the UK was subject to EU legislation, the two EU Regulations discussed in this section proved difficult for the English courts to apply in this context. The Recast Judgments Regulation was particularly problematic as its language is ill-suited to schemes of arrangement. The English courts adopted a pragmatic approach to applying these Regulations, and neither the Recast Insolvency Regulation nor the Recast Judgments Regulation prevented the English courts having jurisdiction to sanction a scheme involving companies with creditors in other EU Member States. The outcome of these cases was commercially attractive,[72] albeit that the outcome was achieved by the courts avoiding the difficult question of

[68] See e.g. *Re Vietnam Shipbuilding Industry Group* [2013] EWHC 2476 (Ch).

[69] [2016] EWHC 1884 (Ch) at [31].

[70] See e.g. *Re Vietnam Shipbuilding Industry Group* [2013] EWHC 2476 (Ch); *Re Hibu Group Ltd* [2016] EWHC 1921 (Ch). See also *Re NN2 Newco Ltd* [2019] EWHC 1917 (Ch), citing *Mauritius Commercial Bank Ltd* v. *Hestia Holdings Ltd* [2013] EWHC 1328; *Re Syncreon Group BV* [2019] EWHC 2412 (Ch).

[71] The success of the English scheme of arrangement jurisdiction prompted some EU Member States to introduce a domestic solution analogous to the English scheme procedure; see e.g. Spanish Law 38/2011 of 10 October and Law 4/2014 of 7 March. It was also one of the prompts behind the development of the EU Restructuring Directive (Directive (EU) 2019/1023).

[72] See section 7.5 for a discussion of forum shopping in this context.

whether jurisdiction to bind creditors domiciled in EU Member States needed to be established under the Recast Judgments Regulation.

With the UK's exit from the EU, following the end of the transition period, both of these Regulations have ceased to apply to the UK. Thus, these difficult questions drop away and for all foreign companies (including those with creditors based in the EU) the question of whether the English court has jurisdiction rests on demonstrating that there is a sufficient connection and that the scheme has a reasonable prospect of being effective. In this sense, the question of jurisdiction becomes more straightforward. However, the Recast Judgments Regulation ceasing to apply to the UK potentially impacts on the question of the recognition of schemes and thus their potential effectiveness.[73] Other routes therefore need to be found to assure the courts of the likely effectiveness of the scheme. In practice, the UK's exit from the EU may not change significantly the outcome of cases involving creditors in EU Member States, but it alters the hoops that have to be jumped through to reach that outcome.

7.4 Will schemes sanctioned by the English court be recognised and given legal effect elsewhere in the world?

In addition to determining that it has jurisdiction in the strict sense to entertain an application to sanction a scheme of arrangement, a court will also consider whether it is appropriate to exercise that discretion. For foreign companies, in addition to demonstrating a 'sufficient connection' to the jurisdiction, the court will need to be satisfied that there is a sufficient prospect of the scheme being recognised in other jurisdictions in which the company operates, owns assets or in which dissenting creditors might take action, such that the scheme will have some substantial effect and the court will not be acting in vain in sanctioning it.[74]

In *Rodenstock*, for example, Briggs J engaged in a careful consideration of whether the scheme would be recognised and given effect in Germany.[75] The opinions of two German law experts that a decision of the English court to sanction the scheme would be legally effective in Germany were taken into account by the court, as part of Briggs J's consideration of whether to exercise his discretion and sanction the

[73] See section 7.4.2.
[74] See e.g. *Re Global Garden Products Italy SpA* [2016] EWHC 1884 (Ch) at [34].
[75] *Re Rodenstock GmbH* [2011] EWHC 1104 (Ch); [2012] BCC 459 at [73]–[77].

scheme. The concepts of 'sufficient connection' and effectiveness are often closely related.[76] For example, where there are contractual documents governed by English law, this will satisfy the requirement of 'sufficient connection' and it should also be relatively easy to produce foreign-law evidence of an English scheme being effective abroad, since conflicts rules in other countries usually allow foreign-law contractual provisions to be modified by foreign-law proceedings (such as schemes).

If a scheme is not legally effective in the relevant foreign jurisdiction(s), a creditor could pursue its contractual claim in foreign courts and undermine the fairness of the scheme by improving its position relative to that of the other creditors of the company. Alternatively, without recognition of the scheme in another jurisdiction, a dissident creditor could seek to initiate a separate insolvency or restructuring process in another jurisdiction, which could conflict with the English scheme.[77]

This section therefore considers the various ways in which a scheme may be given recognition in foreign jurisdictions or, failing that, how this issue might otherwise be tackled.[78] As Snowden J confirmed in *Re Van Gansewinkel Groep BV & Ors*, the English court does not need certainty as to the position under foreign law, but it will wish to see some credible evidence to the effect that it will not be acting in vain in sanctioning the scheme.[79]

7.4.1 *Under private international law principles*

Domestic conflicts of laws rules in other jurisdictions usually provide rules for the discharge or variation of obligations. In English law, for example, the courts will recognise the discharge or release of a right or obligation governed by English law only if this is done in accordance with English law.[80] Foreign jurisdictions will often allow foreign-law contractual obligations to be modified by foreign-law proceedings such as schemes. As a result, in the case of contractual documents governed

[76] *Re Magyar Telecom BV* [2013] EWHC 3800 (Ch) at [21]–[22].

[77] See e.g. *Re Van Gansewinkel Groep BV & Ors* [2015] EWHC 2151 (Ch) at [71].

[78] Even if a foreign court does not formally recognise the scheme, it may recognise the impact of the scheme when hearing a creditor action based on a contract governed by English law, the terms of which have been modified by the scheme, i.e. the foreign court might provide de facto recognition of the scheme even if it will not provide de jure recognition: J. Windsor and P. Sidle, 'International recognition of schemes of arrangement' (2010) 9 *Journal of International Banking & Financial Law* 523.

[79] [2015] EWHC 2151 (Ch) at [71].

[80] *Gibbs & Sons* v. *La Société Industrielle et Commerciale des Métaux* (1890) 25 QBD 399.

by English law it is usually straightforward to produce foreign-law evidence of an English scheme being effective abroad.[81] However, recognition under private international law principles can be subject to local law issues and public policy considerations and therefore can introduce an additional element of uncertainty into the issue of recognition.

7.4.2 Under EU Regulations

There are three different EU Regulations that need to be considered in this regard: the Recast Insolvency Regulation,[82] the Recast Judgments Regulation[83] and the Rome I Regulation.[84] In relation to each Regulation, two issues need to be considered: can the Regulation be utilised as a means of recognising English schemes; and, if yes, what, if any, is the impact of the UK's exit from the EU?

As regards the Recast Insolvency Regulation, schemes of arrangement were not included in Annex A of this Regulation. Even before the UK's exit from the EU, this Regulation did not provide a mechanism for the automatic recognition of schemes in other EU Member States. Accordingly, even schemes involving insolvent companies could not be recognised and enforced via the Recast Insolvency Regulation unless they were firmly linked to one of the insolvency procedures recognised by that Regulation, such as administration. With the UK's exit from the EU and following the end of the transition period, the Recast Insolvency Regulation has ceased to have effect in the UK and even this possibility drops away.

Under the Recast Judgments Regulations, '[a] judgment given in a Member State shall be recognised in the other Member States without any special procedure being required'.[85] Prior to the end of the transition period following the UK's exit from the EU, there was an argument that the English court's sanctioning decision in a scheme was a judgment for this purpose and therefore should be automatically recognised and given

[81] See e.g. *Re NEF Telecom Company BV* [2012] EWHC 2944 (Comm) in which the court received an expert opinion that schemes would be recognised in the Netherlands under Dutch domestic private international law.
[82] Regulation (EU) 2015/848 (Recast Insolvency Regulation).
[83] Regulation (EU) No 1215/2012 (Recast Judgments Regulation).
[84] Regulation (EC) 593/2008 on the law applicable to contractual obligations.
[85] Recast Judgments Regulation, Art. 36(1).

effect to under the Judgments Regulation. However, as discussed in section 7.3.2, there has been some debate as to whether an English court decision sanctioning a scheme should be regarded as a judgment for the purpose of the Recast Judgments Regulation.[86] The English courts have not definitively resolved this issue. As a result, expert opinions provided to court regarding the likelihood of a scheme being recognised in other Member States generally listed the Recast Judgments Regulation as one potential basis for recognition, but also took account of others, such as recognition under private international law principles. Following the UK's exit from the EU and the end of the transition period, the Recast Judgments Regulation has ceased to have effect in the UK and recognition of an English court's sanctioning decision in the EU Member States is not possible on this basis. Given this, the UK has sought other means to ensure that judgments will be recognised elsewhere post-Brexit, in particular via the Lugano Convention on jurisdiction and the recognition and enforcement of judgments and via the 2005 Hague Convention on choice of court agreements,[87] discussed in sections 7.4.3 and 7.4.4.

The third potentially relevant EU Regulation is the Rome I Regulation.[88] This Regulation lays down the rules for determining the applicable laws of contractual obligations. Article 3(1) provides that a contract will be governed by the law chosen by the parties and Article 12 provides that the governing law of the contract should also govern 'the various ways of extinguishing obligations, and prescription and

[86] For example, the view adopted by the court in *Re DAP Holding NV* [2005] EWHC 2092 (Ch) was that sanctioning decisions in schemes fell outside this Regulation, whereas Briggs J in *Re Rodenstock GmbH* [2011] EWHC 1104 (Ch) took the view that judgments sanctioning such schemes were within the scope of the Judgments Regulation. Even adopting the latter view, a further potential difficulty was that the EU Member State in which recognition was sought would also have to come to the conclusion that the decision of the English court sanctioning a scheme was to be regarded as a judgment within the meaning of the Judgments Regulation. It was not at all clear that the courts in other Member States would necessarily take the same view as the English courts on this matter: see e.g. the German courts in *Equitable Life*, OLG Celle 8 U 46/09, 8 September 2009.

[87] A longer-term option might be the text of a new international convention concerning allocation of jurisdiction and the recognition and enforcement of judgments, namely the 2019 Hague Convention. The 2019 Convention is much broader in scope than the 2005 Hague Convention and is not limited to judgments arising from exclusive jurisdiction clauses. At this stage, however, widespread ratification of the 2019 Hague Convention is still a long way off.

[88] See the Law Applicable to Contractual Obligations and Non-contractual Obligations (Amendment etc.) (EU Exit) Regulations 2019 (SI 2019/834) (amended by SI 2020/1574).

limitation of actions' in relation to the contract.[89] To be applicable, schemes of arrangement have to fall within the scope of the Regulation. Certain matters are excluded from the ambit of the Regulation, including issues governed by the law of companies 'such as the creation, by registration or otherwise, legal capacity, internal organisation or winding-up of companies and other bodies corporate or unincorporated, and the personal liability of officers and members as such for the obligations of the company or body'.[90] The question arises whether schemes of arrangement fall within this exclusion. Schemes could be argued to fall within this exclusion on the basis that they are governed by company law, although this exclusion within the Regulation seems to be aimed predominantly at corporate governance issues and matters concerning the life and death of companies, rather than procedures to vary the contractual rights of the members and other stakeholders. Indeed, it could be argued that the sorts of schemes with which this chapter is concerned, namely creditor schemes aimed at restructuring the debt of the company, seem to be predominantly geared towards reorganising the contractual arrangements of the parties inter se, rather than affecting the company's share capital or the company per se. In various schemes, such as those in *Rodenstock* and *Primacom*,[91] academics from Germany provided expert opinions to the English courts to the effect that English law schemes were capable of being recognised and enforced in German law under Rome I. This evidence was significant for the exercise of jurisdiction by the English courts.[92] With the UK's exit from the EU and the ending of the transition period, the Rome I Regulation ceased to have direct effect in the UK, just like the other Regulations discussed in this section. However, with regard to the Rome I Regulation, the fact that this Regulation has ceased to have effect in the UK does not affect its application in remaining EU Member States. Unlike the Recast Judgments Regulation, which regulates recognition of judgments from Member States in other Member States' courts, Rome I contemplates that the expressed governing law of a contract (and that could be any governing law in theory, whether of an EU Member State or otherwise) is the right law to handle the extinguishment of rights under the contract.

[89] Ibid., Art. 12(1)(d).

[90] Ibid., Art. 1(2)(f).

[91] See *Re Rodenstock GmbH* [2011] EWHC 1104 (Ch); [2012] BCC 459; *Re Primacom Holdings GmbH* [2012] EWHC 164 (Ch); [2013] BCC 201. See also *Re Metrovacesa SA* [2011] EWHC 1014 (Ch) (in relation to Spanish law).

[92] See e.g. *Re Rodenstock GmbH* [2011] EWHC 1104 (Ch); [2012] BCC 459 at [76].

7.4.3 *Under the Lugano Convention*

On 8 April 2020 the UK submitted its application to accede to the 2007 Lugano Convention. The UK was previously a member of the Lugano Convention as a member of the EU but not in its own right.[93] The Lugano Convention governs jurisdiction and the enforcement of judgments between Member States and certain states that are members of the European Free Trade Association (EFTA). While not identical in effect to the Recast Judgments Regulation, the Lugano Convention may nevertheless provide a basis for the English courts to determine that a scheme would be given effect in those states that are party to the Convention. As with the Recast Judgments Regulation, the Lugano Convention does not apply to 'bankruptcy, proceedings related to the winding-up of insolvent companies or other legal persons, judicial arrangements, compositions and analogous proceedings'[94] and so similar questions may arise about whether some UK debt restructuring arrangements are covered by this Convention as have arisen in the context of the Recast Judgments Regulation.[95] In any case, the UK's accession to this Convention is not straightforward as it requires the unanimous agreement of the contracting parties, namely the EU, Denmark (as an independent state), Iceland, Norway and Switzerland. Whilst Switzerland, Iceland and Norway have expressed their support for the UK's application, for the UK to accede will also require agreement from the EU which, to date, has been unforthcoming.[96]

7.4.4 *Under the Hague Convention on choice of court agreements*

Another option for recognition rests on the 2005 Hague Convention. As with the Lugano Convention, the UK was previously a party to this

[93] In this regard see the Civil Jurisdiction and Judgments (Amendment) (EU Exit) Regulations 2019 (SI 2019/479) as amended).

[94] Lugano Convention, Art. 1(2)(b) and see Recast Judgments Regulation, Art. 1(2)(b).

[95] See section 7.3.2. See, in the context of UK restructuring plans, *Re Gategroup Guarantee Ltd* [2021] EWHC 304 (Ch).

[96] Lugano Convention, Art. 70. On 1 July 2021, a notification was issued of the EU's refusal to give its consent to the UK's accession to the Convention. An alternative route would be for the UK to become a member of EFTA under Article 56 of the EFTA Convention, 3 May 1960 (which requires permission from the EFTA Council), and accede to the Lugano Convention under a simplified procedure. Although the Lugano Convention accession question remains uncertain, on 13 October 2020 Norway and the UK announced the conclusion of a bilateral agreement to recognise and enforce rulings, to become effective from 1 January 2021 in the event that the UK fails to independently accede to the Lugano Convention.

Convention as a result of its membership of the EU. After leaving the EU, the UK needed to accede to this Convention in its own right, and on 28 September 2020 the UK deposited its instrument of accession to this Convention in order to ensure continuity in application of the Convention after the end of the Brexit transition period.[97] Unlike the Lugano Convention, the UK did not need the agreement of the EU to accede to this Convention. After the UK's accession, and where the Hague Convention applies, English judgments are enforceable within the EU, and in the other Hague Convention contracting states, currently Mexico, Montenegro and Singapore. However, there are a number of limitations to this Convention. The Hague Convention applies only where there is an exclusive jurisdiction clause which was entered into after the Convention came into force for the chosen state. The requirement of an exclusive jurisdiction clause is therefore more restrictive than that applied in relation to the Recast Judgments Regulation.[98] On the issue of timing, there is a division of opinion between the UK and the EU regarding when the Convention should be treated as having entered into force in the UK, with the UK taking the view that the Hague Convention should be treated as having been in force for the UK since 1 October 2015, when it came into force for the EU generally,[99] whereas the view of the European Commission is that the date should be from when the UK rejoined on 1 January 2021.[100] The former view is preferable, but this means that, at best, debtors proposing schemes relating to finance documents entered into before 1 October 2015 will not be able to benefit from the Hague Convention. The Hague Convention also excludes 'insolvency, composition and analogous matters',[101] potentially raising the question (similar to that which arises in relation to the Recast

[97] This is given the force of law in domestic law from 1 January 2021 by the Private International Law (Implementation of Agreements) Act 2020, which also amends the Civil Jurisdiction and Judgments (Hague Convention on Choice of Court Agreements 2005) (EU Exit) Regulations 2018 (SI 2018/1124).

[98] See section 7.3.2.

[99] Ministry of Justice, Cross-border civil and commercial legal cases: guidance for legal professionals from 1 January 2021, 30 September 2020. See also the Financial Markets Law Committee, *UK Withdrawal from the EU: The Recognition of Choice of Court Agreements under the 2005 Hague Convention*, October 2019.

[100] European Commission, Notice to Stakeholders: Withdrawal of the United Kingdom and EU Rules in the Field of Civil Justice and Private International Law, Brussels, 27 August 2020.

[101] Hague Convention on Choice of Court Agreements 2015, Art. 2(2).

Judgments Regulation and the Lugano Convention) as to the breadth of the application of this Convention.

7.4.5 *Under the UNCITRAL Model Law on Cross-Border Insolvency*

The UNCITRAL Model Law may assist in the recognition of English scheme decisions in jurisdictions where it has been implemented. The Model Law has been incorporated into national legislation by a large number of countries.[102] It is intended to promote harmonisation of certain key issues of cross-border insolvency, such as co-operation between courts in countries where the debtor's assets are located, and providing foreign creditors with access to local courts. Articles 15 to 21 of the Model Law set out the requirements to obtain recognition of a 'foreign proceeding'. Article 2 defines a 'foreign proceeding' as 'a collective judicial or administrative proceeding in a foreign State, including an interim proceeding, pursuant to a law relating to insolvency in which proceeding the assets and affairs of the debtor are subject to control or supervision by a foreign court, for the purpose of reorganization or liquidation'.

The Model Law provides recognition to foreign insolvency proceedings, but the degree of recognition depends on whether those proceedings are 'main' or 'non-main'. Foreign main proceedings are defined as proceedings taking place in the state in which the debtor has its COMI.[103] Foreign non-main proceedings are foreign proceedings, other than foreign main proceedings, taking place in a state in which the debtor has an 'establishment'.[104] This is similar, but not identical, to the approach adopted in the Recast Insolvency Regulation. For example, recognition of insolvency proceedings opened in another EU Member State is automatic under the Recast Insolvency Regulation, whereas under the Model Law it is dependent upon an application to court. In a similar way to the Recast Insolvency Regulation, it is the location of the debtor company's COMI, rather than the concept of 'sufficient connection', which dictates the opening of main proceedings under the Model Law and the resultant effects. Thus, if there is significant risk of extraterritorial creditor action, an overseas company is likely to seek to establish its COMI in England

[102] It was adopted in the UK as the Cross-Border Insolvency Regulations 2006, SI 1006/1030. Other countries that have adopted the Model Law include Australia, Canada, Colombia, Japan, Mexico, New Zealand, South Africa and the United States.

[103] UNCITRAL Model Law on Cross-Border Insolvency, Art. 2(b).

[104] Ibid., Art. 2(f).

before the commencement of the scheme process, to increase the likelihood of recognition overseas. A COMI in the jurisdiction can therefore be more valuable than a 'sufficient connection' with the jurisdiction for recognition purposes.

The Model Law provides a framework for the recognition of schemes of arrangement in those countries where it has been incorporated into national legislation. For example, the USA adopted the Model Law in 2005 and, as a result, based Chapter 15 of its Bankruptcy Code on the Model Law. This is discussed at section 7.4.6. The consequence of recognition under the Model Law is that a number of procedural issues involving the co-operation of the foreign court are facilitated, such as orders aimed at protecting and preserving assets in the foreign jurisdiction.[105]

7.4.6 Under Chapter 15 of the US Bankruptcy Code

Chapter 15 of the US Bankruptcy Code[106] allows any 'foreign representative' appointed in a 'foreign proceeding' who is authorised either to administer the financial restructuring, liquidation or reorganisation of a debtor's assets, or to act as a representative in a foreign proceeding,[107] to file a petition seeking recognition of the foreign proceeding in the United States.[108] The requirements for recognition are some type of documentation or certification from the foreign court confirming the existence of the foreign insolvency proceeding and the authority of the foreign representative to act. An order of the US Bankruptcy Court in Chapter 15 proceedings will bind any creditor subject to its jurisdiction and Chapter 15 recognition can therefore be a powerful tool.

These provisions were introduced in 2005, prompted by the adoption of the UNCITRAL Model Law on Cross-Border Insolvency. A foreign proceeding for this purpose is defined as 'a collective judicial or administrative proceeding in a foreign country, including an interim proceeding, under a law relating to insolvency or adjustment of debt in which proceeding the assets and affairs of the debtor are subject to control or supervision by a foreign court, for the purpose of reorganization or liquidation'.[109] Creditor schemes, including schemes involving solvent

[105] Ibid., Arts. 21, 25, 27.
[106] Introduced by the Bankruptcy Abuse Prevention and Consumer Protection Act 2005.
[107] 11 USC § 101(24).
[108] 11 USC § 1515.
[109] 11 USC § 101(23).

companies and covering US policyholders, have been successfully recognised in the USA for many years under the Chapter 15 procedure, and under its previous incarnation, section 304 of the US Bankruptcy Code.[110]

After notice and a hearing, a foreign proceeding is recognised automatically under section 1517, unless such recognition would be 'manifestly contrary to the public policy of the United States'.[111] Moreover, if the foreign proceeding qualifies as a 'foreign main proceeding', the subsequent recognition will have immediate and significant effects.[112] A foreign main proceeding refers to 'a foreign proceeding pending in the country where the debtor has the center of its main interests'.[113] Upon recognition of a foreign main proceeding, a number of provisions of the Code will apply with respect to the debtor and its property located in the USA, such as section 362, which provides for an 'automatic stay' of litigation and collection efforts.[114] Additionally, a foreign representative has the option of filing a full, voluntary Chapter 11 case.[115] Alternatively, a foreign proceeding can be classified as a 'foreign non-main proceeding', which is one pending in a country where the debtor has an 'establishment'.[116] The relief granted and the rights attached to such a proceeding are less than those for a foreign main proceeding: for

[110] For example, see *In re Board of Directors of Hopewell International Insurance Ltd*, 238 BR 25, 48–52 (Bankr SDNY 1999), aff'd 275 BR 699 (SDNY 2002); *In re Castle Holdco 4 Ltd*, Case No. 09-11761 (REG) (Bankr SDNY, 7 May 2009); *In re Avanti Communications Group PLC*, 582 BR 603 (Bankr SDNY 2018) and see J. D. Morton, 'Recognition of cross-border insolvency proceedings: an evaluation of solvent schemes of arrangement and Part VII transfers under U.S. Chapter 15' (2006) *Fordham International Law Journal* 1312 at 1352–4. Chapter 15 recognition has also been sought in relation to a restructuring plan under Part 26A of the Companies Act 2006: *Re Virgin Atlantic Airways Ltd* [2020] EWHC 2376 (Ch).

[111] 11 USC § 1506. For discussion see *In re Manley Toys Ltd*, 580 BR 632 (Bankr D NJ 2018).

[112] Relief under Chapter 15 is not limited to recognition or, in the case of a foreign main proceeding, the automatic application of certain sections of the Code to the debtor and its property in the United States. Upon recognition of either type of foreign proceeding, a court may grant 'any appropriate relief' under § 1521.

[113] 11 USC § 1502(4). While Chapter 15 does not define the 'center of its main interests', it contains the presumption that a debtor's registered office is the centre of a debtor's main interests: § 1516.

[114] 11 USC §§ 1520–21.

[115] Where a full Chapter 11 case is filed, the foreign representative is able to commence avoidance actions (e.g. actions for recovery of preferences and fraudulent transfers), something which is not within the powers of foreign representatives under Chapter 15.

[116] 11 USC § 1502(5). An establishment is defined as 'any place of operations where the debtor carries out a nontransitory economic activity': 11 USC § 1502(2).

example, a foreign representative of a non-main foreign proceeding is limited to filing an involuntary Chapter 11 case.

A good example of the use of Chapter 15 to recognise and give effect to schemes sanctioned in England is the scheme in *Re La Mutuelles du Mans Assurances IARD*.[117] Another example is the scheme in *Re Syncreon Group BV*[118] in which an English scheme was used to restructure debt issued by a US-based global enterprise, followed by recognition of the scheme in the USA under Chapter 15, and also in Canada, where the scheme was granted recognition under Part IV of the Companies' Creditors Arrangement Act (Canada). In recognising English schemes, the US courts have also given effect to third-party releases which are common in relation to English schemes[119] but are controversial in the USA.[120] As discussed in section 7.4.5, in relation to the Model Law, it is notable that it is the concept of 'center of main interests' rather than 'sufficient connection' that is at the core of the Chapter 15 recognition process.

7.4.7 *Under the concept of universalism*

The concept of universalism envisages that an insolvency proceeding opened in one jurisdiction should encompass all assets on a worldwide basis.[121] It may be contrasted with the idea of territoriality in which an insolvency proceeding opened in a jurisdiction is confined to the assets within the jurisdiction in question. Between the two is the concept of modified universalism, which accepts the central premise of universalism (that assets should be collected and distributed on a worldwide basis) but reserves to local courts certain issues, such as discretion to protect the interests of local creditors. In recent years, there has been a trend in favour of the concept of modified universalism. The UNCITRAL Model Law on Cross-Border Insolvency is an example of modified universalism at work, as is the

117 [2005] EWHC 1599 (Ch); [2006] BCC 11.

118 [2019] EWHC 2412 (Ch).

119 See section 2.1.1.

120 *In re Avanti Communications Group PLC*, 582 BR 603 (Bankr SDNY 2018).

121 See e.g. J. Westbrook, 'A global solution to multinational default' (2000) 98 *Michigan Law Review* 2276; cf. e.g. F. Tung, 'Is international bankruptcy possible?' (2001) 23 *Michigan Journal of International Law* 31; L. M. LoPucki, 'The case for cooperative territoriality in international bankruptcy' (1999–2000) 98 *Michigan Law Review* 2216; G. McCormack, 'Universalism in insolvency proceedings and the common law' (2012) 32(2) *Oxford Journal of Legal Studies* 325.

EU Recast Insolvency Regulation.[122] However, a question arises as to whether, if neither of these provisions operates in relation to a particular jurisdiction, a common law concept of modified universalism might nevertheless mean that schemes may be enforced in other jurisdictions.

A broad approach to this issue was adopted by the Privy Council in the *Cambridge Gas* case.[123] This case marks a watershed in the common law approach to international comity in cross-border insolvency. This approach suggests that there should be a single insolvency proceeding, either domestic or foreign, and that therefore a foreign insolvency representative must be extended recognition and assistance by the court. The principle of modified universalism developed in *Cambridge Gas* was subsequently applied as a means of recognising schemes. In *Re Contel Corp Ltd*, for example, the Supreme Court of Bermuda utilised the principles developed in *Cambridge Gas* to recognise a Singapore court order sanctioning a scheme of arrangement.[124] The scheme in this instance was between a company incorporated in Bermuda and its creditors in Singapore. The Bermuda court ordered that the scheme be recognised and granted full force and effect.[125]

However, two cases have subsequently cast doubt on the decision in *Cambridge Gas*: *Rubin* v. *Eurofinance SA*[126] and *Singularis Holdings Ltd*

122 As regards the UK, the modified universalist approach was endorsed by Lord Hoffmann in *Re HIH Casualty and General Insurance Ltd* [2008] UKHL 21; [2008] 1 WLR 852 at [30]. See also *Beluga Chartering GmbH* v. *Beluga Projects (Singapore) Pte Ltd* [2014] 2 SLR 815.

123 *Cambridge Gas Transport Corporation* v. *Official Committee of Unsecured Creditors of Navigator Holdings plc* [2006] UKPC 26; [2007] 1 AC 508. See also the UK decision of the House of Lords in *Re HIH Casualty and General Insurance Ltd* [2008] UKHL 21; [2008] 1 WLR 852.

124 [2011] SC (Bda) 14 Com.

125 In reaching this decision, the court took notice of the similarity between the scheme procedures in the two jurisdictions. For example, it seemed to be influenced by the fact that the requisite majority for approval of the scheme would have been the same under Bermudan and Singaporean law. Moreover, the court was influenced by the fact that the type of scheme in this case (a debt–equity swap) was common in Bermuda and was often approved by the Bermuda court. The court also noted that the scheme involved a high level of creditor participation. The fact that the court took account of all of these factors suggests that if circumstances had been different (for example if the scheme had been of a type not often seen in Bermuda or if creditor participation had been low) then it is possible that the court might not have granted recognition of the scheme. A difficulty might also have arisen had the governing law of the company's debts been a different jurisdiction, i.e. not Singapore or Bermuda, since a question might then have arisen as to whether the company's liabilities had been properly discharged.

126 [2012] UKSC 46; [2013] 1 AC 236.

v. *PricewaterhouseCoopers*.[127] In *Rubin*, the majority in the Supreme Court took the view that *Cambridge Gas* had been wrongly decided. In *Singularis*, the Privy Council was obliged to address the apparent conflict between *Cambridge Gas* and *Rubin* and give guidance as to whether the principle of modified universalism, as articulated by Lord Hoffmann in *Cambridge Gas*, was correct. In *Singularis*, although their Lordships recognised that the principle of modified universalism exists, they stated that the principle is much more limited in scope than is articulated in *Cambridge Gas*. In particular, modified universalism in insolvency proceedings does not mean that the domestic court has a common law power to assist the foreign court by doing whatever it could have done in a domestic insolvency. This is because the principle of modified universalism is subject to local law and local public policy and the domestic court can only ever act within the limits of its own statutory and common law powers. To this extent, *Cambridge Gas* is overruled. The use of the principle of modified universalism to recognise schemes therefore appears to have been constrained, although a number of decisions post-*Singularis* suggest that some form of recognition may still be possible.[128]

7.4.8 Under parallel schemes of arrangement

Where the assets are held in jurisdictions that have a restructuring regime akin to that of the English scheme of arrangement, parallel schemes of arrangement may be put forward in those jurisdictions in order to ensure that the creditors in those jurisdictions are bound. A large number of Commonwealth countries have scheme of arrangement provisions akin to those in England. Examples include Australia, New Zealand, Hong Kong, Singapore, Bermuda and the Cayman Islands. The use of parallel schemes of arrangement (where available) to bind creditors in those jurisdictions is a well-recognised technique. For example, in *Re Drax Holdings Ltd*,[129] parallel schemes were put forward in England, Jersey and the Cayman Islands.

[127] [2014] UKPC 36.

[128] See e.g. *Re Energy XXI Ltd* [2016] Bda LR 90; *Re Seadrill Ltd* [2018] Bda LR 39; and see P. Omar, 'Judicial cooperation in the post-Singularis world' (2018) 15 *International Corporate Rescue* 22. In the Cayman Islands see *Re China Agrotech Holdings Ltd* (2017) 2 CILR 526 in which the decision in *Singularis* was applied, but much the same outcome was achieved via the promotion of a parallel Cayman Islands scheme.

[129] [2003] EWHC 2743 (Ch); [2004] 1 WLR 1049.

7.5 Cross-border schemes and forum shopping

This chapter has discussed the ability of foreign companies to make use of the English scheme of arrangement in order to restructure their debts. This raises the question of whether this use of the English scheme of arrangement is being used to facilitate forum shopping, namely the practice of litigants having their legal case heard in the court thought most likely to provide a favourable judgment. These difficulties have been felt particularly acutely in the EU context as one of the stated aims of the Recast Insolvency Regulation is to avoid forum shopping,[130] although the concern is a more general one. Some of the schemes discussed in this chapter involve a relatively slight connection to England prior to the restructuring. In *Re Codere Finance (UK) Ltd*, for example, Nugee J noted:

> [W]hat strikes me as, on the face of it, slightly novel, so far as I am aware, is that this is a group of companies with a Spanish holding company and operating companies trading in Europe and Latin America with no apparent connection with the UK before the restructuring took place, apart from a fact which I regard as of not great significance in this context, which is that an intercreditor agreement was governed by English law. The notes which are sought to be restructured are obligations of a Luxembourg company. They are obligations governed by New York law, and it is clear from the evidence that the connection with the UK has been brought about deliberately by the acquisition of the scheme company as a UK company, the UK company then accepting liability as a co-obligor under the New York governed notes, and then the UK company seeking a restructuring, which will have the effect, it is suggested, of not only restructuring the UK company's liabilities, but also the Luxembourg company's liabilities and the guarantee liabilities of other companies within the group.
>
> That seems to me, at first blush, to be quite an extreme form of forum shopping, in which the restructuring is brought in the UK purely by incorporating a company to take on very large liabilities.[131]

However, it has increasingly been recognised that not all forum shopping is bad.[132] One particular concern that the avoidance of forum shopping is intended to address is uncertainty for the creditors, i.e. not knowing

[130] Recast Insolvency Regulation, recital 5.

[131] [2015] EWHC 3206 (Ch) at [7]–[8].

[132] See e.g. Opinion of A-G Colomer in Case C–339/07 *Seagon* v. *Deko Marty Belgium NV* [2009] ECR I–1767, fn. 49. See also Opinion of A-G Colomer in Case C–1/04 *Staubitz-Schreiber* [2006] ECR I–701 paras. 71–7 (6 September 2005) in which he distinguished good and bad forum shopping, good forum shopping consisting in ensuring that the

which law will be applied where the debtor becomes insolvent or, as here, restructures its debts to avoid liquidation. Creditors might be concerned that the foreign insolvency regime is unfamiliar, and potentially less attractive to them than the one that they had assumed would apply when they entered into the contractual relationship with the company. However, in the cases where companies have been able to make use of the English scheme jurisdiction, one of the most common ways in which 'sufficient connection' is shown is that the governing law for the creditor agreements is English law. It is difficult to see how creditors could be surprised if the contract (and their relationship with the company) is then subsequently amended using an English law restructuring mechanism. Furthermore, in these instances, the companies have generally sought to make use of the English scheme because a similar pre-insolvency restructuring device was unavailable in the jurisdiction in which they were incorporated, and there was no equivalent means to restructure the debts in that jurisdiction. Where companies seek to make use of another regime in order to facilitate a rescue and rehabilitation of the company that would not have been possible (or would have been more costly or more difficult) under its local regime, and where that other regime is in fact the law governing the contracts between creditors and the company, it is difficult to see that creditors are being maltreated.[133] On the contrary, this seems to be an excellent example of 'good' forum shopping.[134]

At the sanctioning hearing of *Re Codere Finance (UK) Ltd*, Newey J accepted these points:

> In a sense, of course, what . . . is sought to be achieved in the present case is forum shopping. Debtors are seeking to give the English court jurisdiction so that they can take advantage of the scheme jurisdiction available here and which is not widely available, if available at all, elsewhere. Plainly forum shopping can be undesirable. That can potentially be so, for example, where a debtor seeks to move his COMI with a view to taking advantage of a more favourable bankruptcy regime and so escaping his debts. In cases such as the present, however, what is being attempted is to achieve a position where

COMI is located in the best place to reorganise the company for the benefit of the creditors and other stakeholders.

133 Indeed, forum shopping is frequently instigated or supported by some or all of the creditors: W.-G. Ringe, 'Forum shopping under the EU Insolvency Regulation' (2008) 9 *European Business Organization Law Review* 579, 604.

134 See e.g. Opinion of A-G Colomer in Case C–1/04 *Staubitz-Schreiber* [2006] ECR I–701 paras 71–7 (6 September 2005); Opinion of A-G Colomer in Case C–339/07 *Seagon* v. *Deko Marty Belgium NV* [2009] ECR I–1767.

> resort can be had to the law of a particular jurisdiction, not in order to evade debts but rather with a view to achieving the best possible outcome for creditors. If in those circumstances it is appropriate to speak of forum shopping at all, it must be on the basis that there can sometimes be good forum shopping.[135]

Similarly, in *Re Noble Group Limited*,[136] Snowden J stated that, whilst the English court will be astute to detect a COMI-shift performed for illegitimate and abusive reasons, it is possible that a company might legitimately seek the assistance of the court with the support of, and in order to achieve the best result for, its creditors.

7.6 Summary

For foreign companies wishing to restructure their debt, an English scheme of arrangement can sometimes be more valuable than the domestic alternatives, and in recent years the English courts have become a popular destination for foreign companies seeking to make use of the English scheme jurisdiction.

It is clear that English courts have jurisdiction to sanction the scheme of a foreign company so long as that company has a 'sufficient connection' with England, and the court is satisfied that there is a reasonable prospect of the scheme being effective, having regard, in particular, to its recognition in other relevant jurisdictions. Both requirements have been discussed in this chapter. EU Regulations, particularly the Recast Insolvency Regulation and the Recast Judgments Regulation, have created some additional difficulties for the courts in relation to schemes involving creditors based in EU Member States. However, in the wake of the UK's exit from the EU, the direct effect of these Regulations has dropped away, simplifying the question of the court's jurisdiction, though potentially adding an additional element of uncertainty to the issue of recognition. The use of English schemes by overseas companies does not seem likely to reduce any time soon. It is argued here that cross-border schemes give rise to no significant concerns about forum shopping, and indeed can be regarded as an example of 'good' forum shopping, particularly where the English scheme allows a rescue and rehabilitation of the company to occur that would not have been possible under domestic law, to the advantage of the company's creditors.

135 [2015] EWHC 3778 (Ch) at [18].
136 [2018] EWHC 3092 (Ch).

8

Conclusion

Schemes of arrangement are an important and powerful tool which can be used to facilitate a wide variety of arrangements and compromises between a company and its members and/or creditors. Often a scheme can be more useful than the alternative mechanisms available to the company, such as the use of takeover schemes as an alternative to a takeover offer,[1] and the use of solvent run-off schemes by insurance companies as an alternative to the company offering to commute its obligations to its policyholders.[2] It is also common for schemes to be used in combination with the alternatives on offer, in order to capture and maximise the benefits of both options, as when schemes are combined with pre-pack administration.[3] In some instances, however, no alternative mechanisms exist for the company and schemes are therefore crucial in allowing companies to achieve reorganisations that would not otherwise be possible, such as where schemes are used to redomicile a corporate group.[4] As this book has sought to demonstrate, the uses to which schemes can be put are many and varied and continue to expand.[5]

Although they have been around for more than a century,[6] schemes have undergone something of a renaissance over the last twenty years or so. The pace of change has not slowed since the first edition of this book; indeed, legislative changes and judicial developments to scheme procedure and jurisdiction have been significant in this period. Some of these changes have responded to political and economic developments. The

[1] See Chapter 3 (and for the advantages and disadvantages of schemes compared to takeover offers see section 3.3.2).

[2] See section 6.2. Another example involves schemes used as an alternative to liquidation: section 6.3.

[3] See section 5.4.3. Another example is the use of holdco schemes in combination with an issue of dividends to effect the demerger of a company: section 4.3.2.

[4] See section 4.2.

[5] See e.g. *Re Premier Oil plc* [2020] CSOH 39 for a novel use of a creditor scheme to implement an acquisition.

[6] See section 1.2.

most significant legislative changes in this area since the first edition have been introduced as a result of the Corporate Insolvency and Governance Act 2020 and have responded to the need for stronger debt restructuring mechanisms to deal with financial distress. This has resulted in the introduction of a number of measures, including a restructuring moratorium and a 'super scheme' in the form of the new Part 26A restructuring plan. These proposals were formulated in the aftermath of the 2008 global financial crisis, but it took the additional prompt of the financial distress caused by the Covid-19 pandemic to get them onto the statute book. It cannot be ignored that regulatory competition also had a part to play in these reforms, as other jurisdictions developed their debt restructuring regimes, and concerns about factors such as the World Bank's Doing Business figures were also relevant. Other political and economic changes, in particular the effect of the UK's exit from the EU, have yet to play out in full and the use of the English scheme jurisdiction by foreign companies, particularly as regards the issue of recognition, will continue to evolve in coming years.[7]

The popularity and the perceived value of schemes have also driven change in the period since the last edition. The other main legislative change in this period, the Companies Act 2006 (Amendment of Part 17) Regulations 2015,[8] responded to the popularity of cancellation schemes as a means of effecting a change of control of a company as an alternative to a takeover offer. One of the reasons for their use was the stamp duty saving involved compared to a takeover offer or a transfer scheme. This legislative change sought to close the loophole. In doing so, however, it has created a new difficulty for the courts, namely the need to delineate precisely the boundary between cancellation schemes for the purpose of effecting a change of control (that are not allowed) and other forms of cancellation scheme that are still possible, a process that has not been straightforward.[9] The value of schemes as flexible mechanisms for reorganising companies has also prompted companies and their advisors to innovate in the uses made of schemes, and to push at the boundaries to existing scheme jurisdiction, requiring the courts to tackle a wide range of substantive and procedural issues in recent years.

The success of the English scheme owes a great deal to the role adopted by the English courts in this regard. Schemes are fundamentally a tool for

[7] See section 7.4.

[8] SI 472/2015.

[9] See section 4.2.2.2.

enabling courts to facilitate reorganisations between companies and their creditors and members inter se. The courts have recognised that their role is not to intervene in the substance of this reorganisation. Crucially, the role for the court at the sanctioning stage is not to judge the commercial merits of the scheme.[10] The court's role is, however, vital in setting the parameters of the scheme jurisdiction and ensuring that the appropriate balance between the majority and the minority is maintained. As is well settled, the court's role is not a mere rubber-stamping of the decision of the parties, and the effect of schemes is ultimately derived from the statutory provisions rather than the agreement of the parties. The last few years have seen the English court developing its role in this regard. In relation to the parameters of scheme jurisdiction, judges have had to interpret the term 'compromise or arrangement' in order to determine whether proprietary rights can be varied by way of a scheme[11] or whether they can be used to impose new obligations on the creditors or members.[12] It is clear from these decisions that the core of the scheme jurisdiction is the ability to vary or extinguish the rights and obligations that exist between the company and its members that can properly be regarded as rights held qua creditor or qua shareholder. Beyond these constraints, however, the courts have adopted a flexible and purposive approach to scheme jurisdiction, as may be seen from the decision in *Re Jelf Group plc*,[13] in which the court accepted that transfer schemes are an 'arrangement' between the company and its members even though the company barely participates in the scheme at all.[14]

As regards the need to balance the interests of the majority and the minority, the courts have developed this in recent years in a number of ways. The remit of the court's role at the convening hearing has increased. This is beneficial in that jurisdictional issues can be addressed at an early stage in situations where the court has no jurisdiction and

[10] See section 2.4.3.
[11] See sections 5.2.2 and 5.2.3.
[12] See section 2.1.1.
[13] [2015] EWHC 3857 (Ch) and see discussions at sections 2.1.1 and 3.1.
[14] There are many other examples of the commercially sensible approach of the courts included in this volume. See e.g. the decision in *Re Dee Valley Group plc* [2017] EWHC 184 (Ch) on split voting discussed at section 2.3.3.2.2.1. See also the approach adopted by the courts when applying the Recast Judgments Regulation prior to 31 December 2020 (when the Brexit transition period came to an end) to schemes involving companies with creditors based in other EU Member States, discussed at section 7.3.2.

would unquestionably refuse to sanction the scheme, thereby avoiding wasted time and resources where a problem exists.[15] The court has also shown an increased willingness to ensure that full and accurate disclosure is made to creditors and members, and to question 'bare assertions' from companies about class composition or other matters.[16] The courts have similarly emphasised the need to ensure that adequate time is given so that the parties have the opportunity to consider and respond to the proposals being put forward in the scheme.[17] Recent cases have demonstrated the court's willingness to challenge the company's use of lock-up and consent fee arrangements.[18] A further example of this more proactive role is the court's willingness to press companies on the correct comparator to be applied in scheme cases, that is what would be the outcome if the scheme were not to go ahead? This is important for determining the correct classes to vote on a scheme,[19] and can be relevant to issues of valuation.[20] This is particularly important in creditor schemes as arguing for a liquidation measure rather than a going-concern measure can be a way for the company and/or its senior creditors to advantage themselves at the expense of more junior classes.[21] The courts have been prepared to test the assertions of the company in this regard.[22] The courts have therefore shown themselves willing to take a proactive role in ensuring that the minority is protected, a role that is likely to become even more important now that de jure cross-class cramdowns are possible under the Part 26A restructuring plans.

There are a number of criticisms levelled at schemes regarding the uses to which they are put. The three main ones are considered in this book and, in each case, it is argued that the concerns are unfounded.

[15] Examples include the cross-jurisdictional issues discussed in Chapter 7, and the issues arising in relation to cancellation schemes as a result of the Companies Act 2006 (Amendment of Part 17) Regulations 2015, discussed at section 4.2.2.2. For a discussion of the court's role at the convening hearing see section 2.2.3.

[16] See *Re Indah Kiat International Finance Company BV* [2016] EWHC 246 (Ch) at [40] *per* Snowden J. Another example of the court's demand for additional information is in relation to lock-up agreements in creditor schemes; see e.g. *Re Noble Group Ltd* [2018] EWHC 2911 (Ch), discussed at section 5.3.1.

[17] See section 2.2.3.3.

[18] See *Re Sunbird Business Services Ltd* [2020] EWHC 2493 (Ch); *Re Codere Finance 2 (UK) Ltd* [2020] EWHC 2441 (Ch).

[19] See section 2.3.2.

[20] See section 5.4.3.

[21] Ibid.

[22] E.g. *Re Van Gansewinkel Groep BV & Ors* [2015] EWHC 2151 (Ch) at [24].

The first relates to the use of schemes to effect a takeover. The argument is sometimes made that the use of schemes to effect a change of control should be constrained or limited in some way, either because such use allows bidders to bypass the usual rules put in place to protect minorities in takeovers or because it allows bidders to obtain a company more cheaply or more easily (because of the lower approval threshold) than would be the case in a takeover offer, to the disadvantage of minorities.[23] Some overseas jurisdictions that have imported the English scheme have addressed these concerns in their legislation by constraining the use of takeover schemes in some way.[24] In Chapter 3 it is argued that these concerns are misplaced and that this example should not be followed in relation to English schemes. The Takeover Code covers takeover schemes as well as takeover offers: bidders do not bypass takeover regulation by using a scheme. Although the minority protection offered in a scheme is different from, and lesser than, that provided in an offer, this difference is explicable and justifiable when the different function and purpose of schemes (as compared to takeover offers) are taken into account.[25] In addition, there seems to be little support for the view that schemes have a dampening effect on the market for corporate control, or that they do not maximise shareholder value for the target shareholders, when compared to traditional offers, although this is an area in which further empirical work would be valuable.[26] The current approach of both the English courts and the UK Takeover Panel, that is, neutrality as to whether a takeover proceeds by way of a scheme or an offer, is the correct one.

The second relates to the use of schemes combined with pre-pack administration to restructure debt. Specifically, it is suggested that such schemes can operate in a manner that is unfair to junior creditors. In a restructuring such as that in *Re Bluebrook Ltd*,[27] the effect of twinning a pre-pack administration with a scheme is that the junior creditors get left behind while the business of the group is transferred to a new corporate structure and the senior lenders effectively substitute their debt for shares in the restructured group. The junior creditors are therefore left out of the restructuring and have only their claims against the old company (which has no remaining assets). However, in Chapter 5

[23] For discussion see section 3.7.
[24] Ibid.
[25] See section 3.6.3.2.
[26] See section 3.7.4.
[27] [2009] EWHC 2114 (Ch). For discussion see section 5.4.3.

it is argued that this is fair *if*, at the time of the restructuring, the junior creditors have no remaining economic interest in the company, i.e. the value 'breaks' in the senior debt. Of course, this then raises the issue of valuation. While this is an issue that has not been well developed by the English courts to date, the changes introduced by the Corporate Insolvency and Governance Act 2020, in particular the cross-class cram-down in Part 26A of the Companies Act 2006, will undoubtedly prompt the development of this area.[28]

The third potential concern relates to cross-border schemes and forum shopping. It is sometimes suggested that the use of English schemes to restructure the debts of foreign companies amounts to forum shopping, and should not be allowed. While the UK remained a member of the EU, this argument arose particularly in the context of companies with creditors based in other EU Member States making use of the English scheme to restructure their debts, in view of the fact that one of the stated aims of the Recast Insolvency Regulation is to avoid forum shopping.[29] The use of English schemes was felt to be particularly problematic since some companies made use of this mechanism to restructure their debts even without moving their seat or COMI to England.[30] However, there is a growing recognition of the distinction between 'good' and 'bad' forum shopping, with the Recast Insolvency Regulation, for example, being interpreted as seeking to prevent fraudulent forum shopping rather than all instances of forum shopping.[31] The use of schemes in this context should generally be regarded as a clear example of 'good' forum shopping.[32] In cases such as *Re Rodenstock GmbH*,[33] the English scheme allowed a rescue and rehabilitation of the company to occur that would not have been possible under domestic law, to the advantage of the company's creditors. In addition, where the governing law for the creditor agreements is English law, it is difficult to argue that the creditors could not have anticipated the use of an English law mechanism to restructure their debts.

This book has not sought to suggest that schemes are perfect and that no change or reform is needed. The uses to which schemes can be put continue to evolve, as do the procedures and processes attached to them,

[28] See section 5.8.2.
[29] See Recast Insolvency Regulation (EU) 848/2015, recital 5, and section 7.5.
[30] See section 7.3.
[31] See section 7.5.
[32] Ibid.
[33] [2011] EWHC 1104 (Ch); [2012] BCC 459.

the economic environment facing companies and the alternative reorganisation mechanisms that are available. The courts have been innovative in developing scheme jurisdiction, and they have made a significant contribution in fashioning schemes into the valuable tool that we see today. However, further legislative change is needed to capitalise fully on the benefit that schemes have to offer.

In the first edition of this book, four legislative changes were proposed in relation to schemes: (i) abolition of the headcount test; (ii) introduction of a cross-class cramdown; (iii) introduction of a statutory stay; and (iv) discretion for courts to be able to sanction schemes even where there is some technical defect regarding compliance with the statutory procedures, such as in relation to the composition of classes, if the court believes that, despite these defects, the scheme is nevertheless fair and that it would otherwise have been approved.[34]

There has been no legislative change in relation to points (i) and (iv) in the intervening period, and therefore these points remain to be addressed.[35] Indeed, the arguments in favour of abolishing the headcount test have grown stronger since the first edition. In particular, the decision in *Re Dee Valley Group plc*[36] has clearly demonstrated the difficulties of share splitting as an abusive form of behaviour arising from the need to comply with the headcount test. The fact that the Part 26A restructuring plan was introduced without the headcount test, despite its otherwise very close procedural similarities to schemes,[37] suggests that the difficulties of the headcount test are now understood. This approval requirement needs to be removed and it is hoped that a recent Law Commission initiative in this regard will bear fruit.[38]

In relation to points (ii) and (iii) there has been legislative change in the intervening period, as a result of the Corporate Insolvency and Governance Act 2020. As regards issue (ii), a cross-class cramdown has been introduced, not as an adjunct to a scheme (as was recommended in the first edition) but instead as part of a new debt restructuring

[34] See J. Payne, *Schemes of Arrangement: Theory, Structure and Operation* (Cambridge University Press, 2014), 386–9.

[35] In relation to point (iv) see section 2.4.2. This proposal was initially put forward by the Company Law Review (CLR, *Modern Company Law for a Competitive Economy: Final Report*, URN 01/942, July 2001, para. 13.7), but it was not taken forward by the government.

[36] [2017] EWHC 184 (Ch), discussed at section 2.3.3.2.2.

[37] See section 5.8.2.

[38] Law Commission, *Call for Evidence: Intermediated Securities*, August 2019, paras. 2.24–2.30; Law Commission, *Intermediated Securities: Who Owns Your Shares?* Scoping Paper, November 2020, para. 4.56.

mechanism, the restructuring plan. However, as discussed in section 5.8.2, the restructuring plan is procedurally very similar to a scheme, so that much of the case law regarding schemes can be applied to restructuring plans. Restructuring plans are effectively schemes with a cross-class cramdown, albeit that they operate in a more limited set of circumstances, namely when the company has encountered, or is likely to encounter, financial difficulties that are affecting, or will or may affect, its ability to carry on business as a going concern.[39] This is a potentially very valuable tool for companies, as an alternative to utilising a scheme combined with a pre-pack administration to achieve a de facto cross-class cramdown.[40] This new mechanism is still in its infancy and much will depend on the interpretation of the provisions by the courts, and in particular the ability of the courts to balance the interests of the majority and minority in a cross-class cramdown scenario. The legislation does not include either an absolute or a relative priority rule, the legislation instead providing that, for a cross-class cramdown to occur, the courts must be satisfied that none of the members of a dissenting class are worse off than they would be in the event of the 'relevant alternative' and that the compromise or arrangement must have been accepted at the class meeting of at least one class of creditors/members who would receive a payment or have a genuine economic interest in the company, in the event of the genuine alternative.[41] Valuation evidence as to whether a creditor is 'worse off' in the relevant alternative will become crucial, and the approach to valuation will require development by the courts since little reference to this issue is included in Part 26A of the Companies Act 2006 (unlike the position in US Chapter 11). Valuation has not been a significant aspect of the court's role in debt restructuring cases to date[42] and where it has arisen, it has been in the context of schemes twinned with administration where the administrator has therefore had the predominant role in dealing with issues of valuation. These issues of valuation will need to be developed to ensure that they are clear, transparent, fair to all parties and not too time-consuming.

As regards issue (iii), the Corporate Insolvency and Governance Act 2020 has introduced a restructuring moratorium. This is a stand-alone device that is not a precursor to any insolvency process, although it can be used in this way. As a result, it does not automatically attach to a scheme,

[39] Companies Act 2006, s. 901A(2), discussed in section 5.8.2.
[40] See sections 5.4.3 and 5.8.1.
[41] Companies Act 2006, s. 901G(3)–(5).
[42] A notable exception is *Re Bluebrook Ltd* [2009] EWHC 2114 (Ch).

but it can be attached in certain circumstances. This mechanism can therefore potentially address the difficulties that the parties face when negotiating a debt restructuring scheme, in that the company will be unprotected from creditor enforcement procedures in the period before the scheme is sanctioned. The effect of the restructuring moratorium is to impose a constraint both on the ability of creditors to assert their debt claims against the company and on initiating insolvency proceedings and other legal processes, so that it is broadly similar to the moratorium in place in administration, although with some differences of detail.[43] As discussed in section 5.4.4.2, there are a number of features of the restructuring moratorium that limit its potential usefulness for companies, and mean that its value as an adjunct to a scheme may be potentially rather limited. This includes the very short length of the moratorium: even though the initial twenty-day period can be extended by a further twenty days without creditor consent,[44] forty days is still not very long to negotiate and implement a complex restructuring. There is also the fact that lenders can accelerate their loans in the moratorium if they have the contractual right to do so (albeit that the accelerated debt will not be a 'priority pre-moratorium debt'), meaning that, to be fully effective, the company will need the support of its lenders, and possibly some form of standstill arrangement. Excluded from the moratorium are various companies, including those that are party to a capital market arrangement (involving debts of at least £10 m), so that many large corporates that are party to bond financing arrangements will not be able to benefit from the moratorium. The 2020 Act also makes it clear that the rescue envisaged is a corporate rescue rather than a business rescue, making the mechanism unsuitable for use where a scheme is twinned with pre-pack administration. As a result, the restructuring moratorium is unlikely to be particularly beneficial to schemes, and companies are likely to continue to rely on the alternative mechanisms that grew up in the absence of a moratorium, namely contractual standstill arrangements and the willingness of the courts to exercise their discretion to provide relief to companies in this situation.[45] At present, this does not seem problematic as these alternative devices appear to work reasonably well, at least where sufficient finance creditors are prepared to continue to support the business. The existence of an active distressed debt trading market

43 See section 5.4.4.2.

44 Insolvency Act 1986, Part A1, Ch. 3, ss. A9–A13.

45 See e.g. *Sea Assets Ltd* v. *PT Garuda Indonesia*, 27 June 2001, unreported, discussed at section 5.4.4.1.

provides an alternative route for lenders who do not wish to support the proposed restructuring. Changes in the distressed debt market or in the willingness of the courts to exercise their discretion in this regard might mean that the deficiencies in the restructuring moratorium become more of a concern in the future, in which case the provisions introduced by the 2020 Act may need to be revisited.

It would be beneficial to rethink the applicability to schemes of the ipso facto provision introduced by the Corporate Insolvency and Governance Act 2020. In the first edition it was argued that something akin to the ipso facto regime that exists in the United States would be valuable in relation to schemes, that is in a debt restructuring scheme, suppliers and customers should be prevented from exercising contractual termination rights on entering into a scheme. The 2020 Act extends the UK's existing 'essential supplies' regime by introducing a broad constraint on the use of ipso facto clauses into the Insolvency Act 1986. The constraint applies in the event that a company that is party to a contract for the supply of goods or services enters a 'relevant insolvency procedure',[46] defined as including, inter alia, a moratorium, administration, a CVA, liquidation or a restructuring plan.[47] Notably, the Act does not include a scheme of arrangement in this list notwithstanding that its close counterpart, the restructuring plan, is included.[48] This is presumably owing to concerns that schemes can operate at a much earlier point in time than restructuring plans, although a way to deal with this would be to restrict prohibition on the enforcement of ipso facto provisions in schemes to situations equivalent to the financial conditions for a restructuring plan. In the Australian ipso facto provisions, for example, which do include schemes, the legislation restricts the provisions to circumstances in which the scheme is being used 'for the purpose of the body avoiding being wound up in insolvency'.[49]

A further challenge for the future arises as a result of Brexit and relates to the recognition of schemes involving foreign companies. In particular,

[46] Insolvency Act 1986, s. 233B(1).

[47] Ibid, s. 233B(2).

[48] Cf. the Australian ipso facto reforms, introduced in 2017, which specifically include schemes of arrangement: Australian Corporations Act 2001, s. 415D, as do the Singapore provisions: Singapore Insolvency, Restructuring and Dissolution Act 2018, s. 440(6).

[49] Australian Corporations Act 2001, s. 415D(5) inserted by Treasury Laws Amendment (2017 Enterprise Incentives No. 2) Act 2017.

with the UK's exit from the EU, the possibility of the Recast Judgments Regulation being available as a basis for the recognition of an English court's sanctioning decision in EU Member States drops away.[50] Other mechanisms for recognition will be needed. This is not something which domestic UK legislation can fix, but some assistance may flow from the UK's accession to international conventions such as the Hague Convention on choice of court agreements. There are difficulties and limitations with this option, as discussed at section 7.4, and other mechanisms of recognition will need to evolve, particularly the use of private international law principles.

Schemes have become an extremely valuable corporate mechanism for restructuring both debt and equity. With these changes and developments, schemes should continue to operate as an indispensable corporate tool for the future.

[50] See section 7.4.2.

INDEX

For EU product safety concerns, contact us at Calle de José Abascal, 56–1°, 28003 Madrid, Spain or eugpsr@cambridge.org.

www.ingramcontent.com/pod-product-compliance
Lightning Source LLC
LaVergne TN
LVHW011658200926
848484LV00004B/991
* 9 7 8 1 1 0 8 8 3 5 3 2 9 *